SELF-CONCEPT

SELF-CONCEPT
Advances in Theory and Research

MERVIN D. LYNCH
Northeastern University

ARDYTH A. NOREM-HEBEISEN
University of Minnesota

KENNETH J. GERGEN
Swarthmore College

BALLINGER PUBLISHING COMPANY
Cambridge, Massachusetts
A Subsidiary of Harper & Row, Publishers, Inc.

International Standard Book Number: 0-88410-376-5

Library of Congress Catalog Card Number: 81-3538

Printed in the United States of America

Library of Congress Cataloging in Publication Data

Main entry under title:

Self-concept, advances in theory and research.

Papers of a symposium held Sept. 1978 in Boston and sponsored by Northeastern University and the University of Minnesota.
Bibliography: p.
Includes index.
1. Self-perception—Congresses. 2. Self-perception—Research—Congresses. I. Lynch, Mervin D., 1933-
II. Norem-Hebeisen, Ardyth A. II. Gergen, Kenneth J.
IV. Northeastern University. V. University of Minnesota (Minneapolis-St. Paul campus)
BF697.S426 155.2'01 81-3538
ISBN 0-88410-376-5 AACR2

DEDICATION

This volume is dedicated to the memory of Stanley Coopersmith who died of a heart attack in November, 1979. He contributed extensively to the research literature on self-concept and stimulated others to advance the state of knowledge in the area of self-concept.

CONTENTS

List of Figures xi

List of Tables xiii

Preface xvii

Acknowledgments xix

PART I: THEORETICAL ISSUES IN SELF-CONCEPT
—Kenneth J. Gergen 1

Chapter 1
Some Observations on Self-Concept Research and Theory—*Arthur W. Combs* 5

Chapter 2
Dimensions of the Dilemma
—*Robert E. Bills* 17

Chapter 3
The Unity Principle Versus the Reality and Pleasure Principles, *Or* The Tale of the Scorpion and the Frog
—*Seymour Epstein* 27

Chapter 4
The Boundaries of the Self: The Relationship of Authenticity in Self-Conception
—*Ralph H. Turner and Steven Gordon* 39

Chapter 5
The Functions and Foibles of Negotiating Self-Conception—*Kenneth J. Gergen* 59

Chapter 6
Reflective Process—*Stephen P. Spitzer* 75

Chapter 7
Self-Concepting: Another Aspect of Aptitude
—*Theresa J. Jordan and Philip R. Merrifield* 87

PART II: THE DEVELOPMENT OF SELF-CONCEPT
—*Kenneth J. Gergen* 97

Chapter 8
The Self as Social Knowledge
—*Michael Lewis and Jeanne Brooks-Gunn* 101

Chapter 9
Self-Concept Development in Childhood
—*Mervin D. Lynch* 119

Chapter 10
A Maximization Model of Self-Concept
—*Ardyth A. Norem-Hebeisen* 133

Chapter 11
The Spontaneous Self-Concept as Affected by Personal Distinctiveness
—*William J. McGuire and Claire V. McGuire* 147

Chapter 12
The Occupational Self: A Developmental Study
—*Morris Rosenberg and Florence Rosenberg* 173

Chapter 13
The Development of Self-Concept in Adolescence
—*Anne C. Petersen* 191

Chapter 14
The Development of the Self-Concept Through the Life Span—*Rene L'Ecuyer* 203

PART III: THE SELF IN APPLIED SETTINGS
—*Kenneth J. Gergen* 219

Chapter 15
Application of Causal Modeling Methods to the Validation of Self-Concept Interpretations of Test Scores
—*Richard J. Shavelson and Kenneth R. Stuart* 223

Chapter 16
Behavioral Academic Self-Esteem
—*Stanley Coopersmith and Ragnar Gilberts* 237

Chapter 17
The Significance of the Self-Concept in the Knowledge Society—*Bonnie L. Ballif* 251

Chapter 18
Issues Regarding Self-Concept Change
—*William H. Fitts* 261

Chapter 19
An Examination of the Nature of Change in Academic Self-Concept
—*Lorin W. Anderson* 273

Chapter 20
Comparison of Aggregate Self-Concepts for Populations with Different Reference Groups
—*Wilbur B. Brookover and Joseph Passalacqua* 283

Chapter 21
The Development of Self-Concept in the Elementary School: A Search for the Determinants—*Lawrence Dolan* 295

References 315

Name Index 345

Subject Index 351

About the Editors 361

About the Contributors 365

LIST OF FIGURES

11–1 Spontaneous Salience of Gender in One's Self-Concept as a Function of the Other Gender's Numerical Predominance in One's Household 167

13–1 Sex Difference in Self-Image 198

13–2 Cohort Differences in Self-Image from 1960s to 1970s 200

13–3 Urbanicity Differences in Self-Image 201

14–1 Constituents of Self-Concept: Internal Organization 207

15–1 Hypothesized Model of Causal Relationship Between Achievement and Self-Concept 228

15–2 An Alternative Causal Model of the Relationship Between Achievement and Self-Concept 229

15–3 Structural Equation Model of the Causal Relationship Between Achievement and Self-Concept 232

15–4 Structural Equation Model of the Causal Relationship Between Achievement and Self-Concept Utilizing Multiple Indicators 234

21–1 School by Grade Comparisons for the Three Self-Concept Measures 306

LIST OF TABLES

4-1	True and Spurious Self Anchorages	44
4-2	Correlation Between True Self and Spurious Self	45
4-3	Frequency of True Self-Spurious Self Combinations	46
4-4	Collapsed True Self-Spurious Self Combinations by Selected Variables	48
6-1	Proportion of Subjects Showing One or More Indicators of Reflection by Dichotomized Samples	78
6-2	Relationships Between Reflection and Criterion Variables	81
6-3	Subjects Showing One or More Indicators of Anxiety Divided According to the Distribution of Reflection Within Their Anxiety Statements	84
8-1	Developmental Sequence of Self-Recognition	113
11-1	Salience of Physical Characteristics (Percentage of Children Mentioning the Characteristic as Part of Their Spontaneous Self-Concept) as a Function of Its Distinctiveness Within the Child's School Group	156

11–2 Number of Discriminations on the Bases of Gender and Ethnicity for Each Individual in a Hypothetical Six-Person Group 161
12–1 Kind of Life Child Wishes to Lead as Adult, by Age 176
12–2 Job Wanted When Grown Up or Older, by Age 179
13–1 The Offer Self-Image Questionnaire (OSIQ) 194
16–1 BASE Item-Total Score Reliability Coefficients, Means, and Standard Deviations 240
16–2 BASE Norm Data Showing Means, Standard Deviations, *N*s, and Standard Errors of Measurement of Kindergarten Through Grade Eight Students 242
16–3 BASE Norm Data Showing Means, Standard Deviations, *N*s, and Standard Errors of Measurement for Preschool Students (Four-Year-Olds) 242
16–4 Factor Analysis of the BASE on Three Samples Showing Loadings, Percentage of Variance, and Total Variance Accounted for 244
16–5 Predictive Validity of BASE BASE–CTBS Achievement Correlations 246
16–6 Predictive Validity of BASE Total and Student Initiative Scores, BASE–CTBS Achievement Correlations (Spring 1977) 246
16–7 Means of BASE Total and Student Initiative Scores by Grade Level 247
16–8 Means and Standard Deviations of BASE Total and Student Initiative Scores by Grades (Spring 1977) 247
16–9 Differences Between Means of Pre- and Post–BASE Scores and *t*-Test for Four-Year-Old Preschool Children 248
16–10 Comparisons Between Teachers' Ratings of Students and Students' Self-Ratings on BASE Scores 249
16–11 Correlations Between Teachers' Ratings of Students and Students' Self-Rating on BASE Scores 250
17–1 Comparisons of Mean Scores of Motivated and Unmotivated Students on Total MOCOS and on the Self-Concept Subscale ($N = 381$) 254

17–2 Scores on Pictorial Self-Concept Scale, Structured Observations, Gumpgookies, and Motivation Rating Scale 259

17–3 Post-test Analysis of Variance for Conceptual Subscale Among Three Treatment Groups ($N = 70$) 260

19–1 The Academic Self-Concept Scale 275

19–2 Race and Sex Composition and Average School Marks of Samples Used in Study (by Grade Level) 276

19–3 Correlations of Academic Self-Concept Scores with School Marks and Teacher Ratings 277

19–4 Results of Varimax Rotation of Academic Self-Concept Scale (by Grade Level) 278

19–5 Means, Standard Deviations, and *F*-statistic for the Total Scale Scores (by Grade Level) 280

19–6 Means, Standard Deviations, and *F*-statistic for the Non-evaluative Subscale Scores (by Grade Level) 280

19–7 Mean, Standard Deviations, and *F*-statistic for the Evaluative Subscale Scores (by Grade Level) 280

20–1 Correlation Between Mean School Achievement and Mean Self-Concept of Academic Ability in Samples of Michigan Public Elementary Schools 287

20–2 Mean and Standard Deviations of Achievement and Self-Concepts of Academic Ability in Samples of Michigan Public Elementary Schools (Means of Schools Mean Unweighted) 288

20–3 Multiple Regression Analysis Showing Contribution of Percent White to Variance in Mean Self-Concept of Academic Ability, When Achievement and Socioeconomic Status Are Entered Prior to Percent White in a Representative State Sample and Two Subsamples of Michigan Elementary Schools 290

20–4 Means and Standard Deviations of Students' Perceived Evaluations and Expectations in Samples of Michigan Elementary Schools and the Zero Order Correlation Between Mean Perceived Evaluations and Expectations and Mean Self-Concept of Academic Ability in the Samples of Michigan Elementary Schools 291

21-1 Student and Parent Sample Sizes, Reading Achievement Percentiles, and Home Concern and Support Statistics 299

21-2 Intercorrelations of School, Home, and Achievement Variables 303

21-3 Correlation Between Explanatory Contexts and the Self-Concept Measures 305

21-4 Stepwise Regressions for Mutual Impact of Contextual Variables on the Self-Concept Measures 310

PREFACE

The past decade has witnessed a vital rekindling of interest in the character and function of self-concept in contemporary culture. This interest has also manifested itself throughout the social sciences, especially in psychology and sociology. To illustrate, at recent meetings of the Society for Experimental Social Psychology, the keynote symposium was on self-concept. The Social Science Research Council is in the process of putting together a conference on the development of self-concept in childhood, a conference that was stimulated in part by an international, interdisciplinary conference on self-concept development.

A volume of essays on self-concept research has recently been published in German by Klett–Cotta. In sociology, a recent resurgence of symbolic interactionist formulation has also renewed interest in self-concept. Recent publication of Zurcher's book, *The Mutable Self*, and L'Ecuyer's *The Self Concept* are both indicative of this renewal. Similarly, the results of a recent international conference bringing together the work of sociologists and developmental psychologists have just appeared in an Italian volume.

Interest in such matters has hardly been confined to the psychological and sociological spheres. Philosophers have taken a keen interest in such developments, as evidenced in Mischel's recent volume of edited essays, *The Self, Psychological and Philosophical Issues.* In effect, the topic of self-concept is a focal one in contemporary intellectual life.

The idea for a symposium for self-concept research emerged simultaneously from two independent teams of researchers. Stanley Coopersmith and I recommended in a report to the National Institute of Education that funding be provided for both self-concept research and a national symposium on self-concept. About the same time Ardyth A. Norem-Hebeisen and Kenneth Gergen applied to the National Institute on Drug Abuse for funding to sponsor a conference on self esteem. Norem-Hebeisen and I first met at the 1975 American Educational Research Association and began discussions toward implementation of a symposium at that time. By August 1976, at the American Psychological Association meeting in Chicago, plans for the symposium and this book were completed. Subsequent meetings between Norem-Hebeisen and me in Boston finalized plans for presenters, speakers, scheduling, and conference activities.

The symposium was held in Boston in September 1978 under the joint coordination of Norem-Hebeisen and myself. Twenty-six presenters and more than 120 persons attended. The materials emanating from that symposium comprise the major contents of this book. The symposium featured unique and broadly integrative presentations by the leading theorists and researchers in this domain, and allowed each one to discuss his or her most recent work before a reflective audience. Thus, this volume includes a variety of theoretical approaches as well as descriptions of recent advances in methodology and the application of self-concept research to such areas as education and life-span development.

This book is of special interest to social and developmental psychologists, sociologists, and education specialists. It should serve a vital need by furnishing a picture of the contemporary state-of-the-art, demonstrating the connections among the various disciplines, introducing new methodologies for study, sensitizing the reader to critical problems in self-concept theory, and providing the practitioner with major concepts and findings to use in the educational setting. The volume provides new and relevant material to the professional scholar, to graduate and undergraduate students in psychology, sociology, and education, and to practitioners within the school setting. It should be a necessary addition to university libraries.

Mervin D. Lynch

ACKNOWLEDGMENTS

The editors wish to thank all of the authors who participated in this symposium for their help and cooperation in timely submission of materials for the manuscript. The symposium was sponsored by both Northeastern University and the University of Minnesota. Our appreciation goes to Roland Goddu, former Dean, College of Education at Northeastern University, for providing sponsorship for the symposium, and to Harold Miner and his staff in the Bureau of Field Services at Northeastern University, particularly Linda Bird and Patricia Cawley Conners, for their help in advertising and managing the financial end of the symposium. At the University of Minnesota, Josephine Zimmar and Ruth Weiler provided early contact and negotiations with the conference presenters. Patricia Belcastro, Ibis Hanzel, and Maria Mesiti at Northeastern University provided help in typing and indexing of manuscripts. We also wish to acknowledge the contribution of Robert Bills whose speech is included in this book. His paper presentation as well as those of Marcee Smith, Ed Kifer, and Bruce Arneklev were not included because of space limitations.

I THEORETICAL ISSUES IN SELF-CONCEPT

Kenneth J. Gergen

During the formative stages of psychology the topic of self-knowledge was typically viewed as secondary. If the psychologist could but master the principles of psychological functioning, then one might derive from such principles whatever was necessary to know when the particular object of such processes was the self. With the advent of behaviorism in the 1920s little was done to enhance the understanding of self-knowledge. With the strong emphasis on observable stimuli and responses, psychological processes of any kind were rendered suspect.

Yet, within various intellectual eddies an active interest in processes of self-knowledge did begin to germinate. This interest was inspired in part by the psychoanalytic writings on ego, repression, and the mechanisms of defense; by symbolic interactionist treatises on the function of self-knowledge in the process of intersubjective communication; by role theorists concerned with the relationship between personal identity and the position of the individual in society; and by humanistic psychologists for whom the experience of self remained the ultimate safeguard against behaviorist barbarism. As radical behaviorism was gradually liberalized and increasing reliance was placed by theorists on hypothetical constructs, investigation of the self slowly became legitimized. By the 1950s research of self-esteem, for example, had become commonplace within the empirically oriented literature.

Yet, the liberalization of the behaviorist paradigm also set the stage for what was to become the cognitive revolution. Cognitive processes, having served as mere mechanisms mediating between stimulus and response, gradually took center stage. It was through cognition that stimuli took on their identity as stimuli; without cognition there could be no intelligent or intelligible behavior. With this general turn of events, inquiry into the self has come to enjoy a central role within social, developmental, and personality psychology. It has stimulated active interchange between psychologists and sociologists, psychoanalysts, clinicians, and practitioners in a variety of domains. Earlier compendia, such as those of Gordon and Gergen (1968), Hamachek (1965), and Stoodley (1962) have now been joined by a variety of challenging collections on diverse topics (see, for example, Filipp 1979; Giovannini 1979; Suls 1981; Wegner and Vallacher 1980). Wylie's massive attempt to integrate the results of empirical inquiry has been revised and expanded (Wylie 1974). Monographs by Laing (1961), McCall and Simmons (1966), Rosenberg (1979), Ziller (1973), and Zurcher (1977) have come to be central intellectual fare.

The present volume attempts to advance the dialogue among investigators in various sectors of psychology, and between psychologists and those in adjacent disciplines. The contributions have been divided into three major sections. The first deals primarily with more general theoretical issues as they have emerged from the past and continue into the present. The second section is devoted to issues in the development of self-concept; and the third, to the application of self theory and research.

In the present section the first chapter enables Arthur W. Combs to share observations on self-concept investigations garnered from his pioneering career in the domain. Combs' experience with the historical development of the field prompts him, on the one hand, to separate the more traditional psychology from the more essential study of phenomenology and, on the other, to challenge the phenomenologically oriented researcher to develop an enhanced clarity of theory and a vigor of method. Combs is optimistic about the possibility of drawing accurate inferences about self-concept and outlining the contours for in-depth inquiry into the processes underlying perceptual organization.

In Chapter 2, Robert E. Bills adds a series of insights also drawn from a long and distinguished career in the field. Bills uses his concern with perceptual organization to show that scientists themselves engage in such processes, and that because they do, multiple realities of human functioning are necessary and, though frustrating, ultimately desirable. Like Combs, Bills is also concerned with the development of useful methods. He contrasts Combs' inferential-based research with a technique-centered approach, and concludes with the hope that enhanced operational definition might bring needed unity into the field.

The first two chapters, reflecting concerns generated from history, serve as a prolegomenon for the remainder of the chapters in this section. The latter chapters each attempt to open new theoretical departures. Seymour Epstein (Chapter 3) marshals an impressive array of theoretical and empirical evidence to support his contention that one of the most basic needs of the individual is for unity or coherence in his or her conceptual system. Although echoing the beliefs of earlier theorists, the position gains a new cutting edge in Epstein's hands with its incorporation and extension of wide-ranging materials. Yet Epstein is not wholly a cognitivist or a phenomenologist. In the end he wishes to integrate the striving for unity with the individual's search for pleasure and reality.

While Epstein centers his discussion on what some view as the unified core of self-conception, Ralph H. Turner and Steven Gordon (Chapter 4) extend consideration to the periphery, to the individual's experience of spurious or inauthentic self. Unlike Epstein, Turner and Gordon do not search for inherent psychological tendencies to explain the phenomenal distinction between the true and the spurious. Rather, they see these diverging experiences as anchored in various experiences—with institutions, in social relationships, with success and failure, and with impulse expression and control. Interestingly, the authors suggest that feelings of inauthenticity relate to products of earlier socialization; it is the here-and-now in which feelings of authenticity are most often engendered.

Both the preceding chapters stand in sharp contrast to that of Kenneth J. Gergen (Chapter 5). While Epstein argues for a drive toward coherence, Gergen argues for the predominance of transient, inconsistent, and often fragmented concepts of self. While Turner and Gordon suggest that a stabilized, "true" view of self is the normal state toward which one strives, Gergen argues for shifting senses of true self; he believes that what is true is only found through successful social negotiation. For Gergen the individual's characteristics—both behavioral and phenomenological—are fundamentally products of social discourse.

With Stephen P. Spitzer's discussion of self-reflective processes (Chapter 6), the focus narrows. Spitzer is particularly interested in the condition of the individual thinking of himself or herself thinking. As he demonstrates, persons who are made to feel anxious confront a problem of self-identification, or those who ingest cannabis experience an enhanced state of self-reflection. Yet this state is used by the individual, maintains Spitzer, to reduce anxiety and to achieve a sense of identity. Such a mechanism might serve as a useful adjunct to the individual's attempt to reach unified coherence (as proposed by Epstein) or to determine what is indeed true or spurious about the self (relevant to the Turner and Gordon case).

Spitzer's emphasis on active thought processes is amplified in Theresa J. Jordan and Philip R. Merrifield's offering (Chapter 7). Rather than viewing self-conception as static structure, they argue for processes of memory, evaluation, transformation, and generation, all of which operate to increase adaptation to existing realities. The process of intervention, from this perspective, is one of helping the individual employ these cognitive processes more effectively in individualized circumstances.

In general, the chapters in this section usefully illustrate the broad array of concerns in current inquiry into the self. The overarching orientation is a cognitive one, and, as we shall see, this orientation pervades many other chapters in the book. Cognitive processes such as unification, reflection, memory, evaluation, transformation, and the like all play a part in current consideration of the self. The traditional emphasis on self-esteem and the dynamic underpinnings are therefore muted. Although the social inbeddedness of self-concept, a theme long central to the symbolic interactionist approach to self, also loses in the emphasis on cognitive process, it remains a critical focus both in the Turner and Gordon and the Gergen chapters. For the latter, indeed, all that is considered cognition must ultimately be viewed as a product of social construction.

1 SOME OBSERVATIONS ON SELF-CONCEPT RESEARCH AND THEORY

Arthur W. Combs

Recognition of the importance of self-concept as a dynamic in human behavior must certainly be regarded as one of the most fruitful contributions of humanistic psychology. Both in and out of the profession self-concept has become the subject of considerable research and applications to a wide variety of practical problems. Perhaps this book can help us understand with greater accuracy the parameters of self-concept, and its assets and liabilities. As my contribution to that end, I should like to comment on two matters—one, with respect to research on self-concept; the other, on some implications of self-concept theory for a new psychology.

SOME OBSERVATIONS ON SELF-CONCEPT RESEARCH

Self-Concept and Self-Report

Those writers who originally described self-concept saw it in phenomenological terms. They used self-concept to refer to the individual's personal experience of self. (See, for example, Allport 1955; James 1890; Lecky 1945; Maslow 1954; Mead 1934; Murphy 1947; Raimy 1943; Snygg and Combs 1949.) Self-concept is defined by such writers as an organization of meanings or perceptions comprising the person's experiential self. The concept is a necessary one for modern humanistic psychology. If we did not have it, we would have to invent it.

Unfortunately, the perceptual character of self-concept has not been clearly understood by many subsequent workers. Some, for example, have treated self-concept as object, as behavioral syndrome, or synonymous with self-image; and many have treated self-concept as though it were identical with self-report. This latter misconception has been especially devastating for the psychological literature. By now there must be several hundred studies, purportedly about self-concept, that turn out on closer examination to be, in fact, studies of self-report. I believe a great deal of this confusion arises from two factors: (a) the behavioral view of psychology in which most of us received our early training; and (b) the widespread belief that there are no scientifically respectable techniques available for exploring self-concept.

For several generations American psychology has been defined, almost exclusively, as the study of human and animal behavior. This definition restricts the study of persons to events that can be directly observed and described. As a consequence, events in the internal life of persons have largely been ignored or treated as unscientific or mystical. It is not surprising, then, that psychologists reared in that tradition should attempt to treat perceptual concepts like self-concept as behaviors, traits, or personality characteristics. Self-concept, however, is not a behavioral concept. It is a product of humanistic-phenomenological-experiential psychology designed to explore the internal life of persons.

Self-concept is not a behavior; it is a perceptual organization. The concept is a product of experiential-perceptual psychology that regards behavior only as symptom and personal meaning or perception as dynamic generators of behavior. Self-report in this frame of reference is a behavior representing what a person is willing, able, or can be seduced to say about self. Like any other behavior, it is, of course, affected by self-concept. It cannot, however, be accepted as identical with it. Too many other variables intervene between self-concept and self-report to modify or distort what a person is able or willing to say about self. A few of these variables may be: the willingness of the subject to cooperate, the subject's possession of adequate language to express his or her experiential self, social expectancies impinging upon the subject at the time he or she is asked for self-descriptions, the subject's own goals or purposes in the encounter, the relationship with the requester, and the subject's freedom from threat or coercion (Arbuckle 1958; Coller 1971; Combs and Courson 1963; Combs and Soper 1957; Gordon and Ward 1973; Packer 1964; Pineau 1958). These sources of inaccuracy are so great and so difficult to eliminate that I do not know of any self-report device that I would currently accept for serious research requiring assessment of self-concept.

THE USE OF INFERENCE FOR SELF-CONCEPT RESEARCH

Much more promising results are to be obtained, I believe, through the use of inferences about perception made by trained observers from observations of behavior, protocols, or personal documents. Unhappily, behavioral psychology generally attempts to restrict research to concrete, observable events in the fashion of physical science. Many of today's psychologists still carry this prejudice despite the fact that modern physical science freely employs inferential techniques in all manner of explorations. Scientists concerned with the future or with events not directly observable accept inferential techniques as a legitimate research process. A science that eschews the making of inferences, it seems to me, must be forever chained to the immediate and palpable. For perceptual-humanistic psychology concerned with the inner lives of individuals, the use of inference is an absolute necessity. This does not mean that humanistic research must be any less scientific. Science does not require a particular methodology; only that whatever processes are used in research be employed with care, discipline, and be subjected to appropriate tests of reliability. The use of inference in self-concept research can and should meet those criteria.

My colleagues and I originally approached the use of inferential techniques with the same trepidation as other psychologists. We have been surprised to find, however, that such procedures are far simpler than we had originally thought and are capable of providing highly reliable results. The technique is as follows: If it is true that behavior is a function of perception, it follows that it should be possible to infer from a sample of behavior the perceptions that produced it.

The first step in our procedure, therefore, is to acquire some sample of behavior likely to be expressive of the particular aspects of self we wish to explore. So, if we are interested in a teacher's self-concept, we might observe the teacher in his or her classroom; if we are interested in a politician's self-concept, we might structure an interview around the "problems in your job"; or if we are interested in the pastoral counselor's conceptions, we might construct hypothetical problems we would then ask him or her to solve. Samples of behavior we have used include interviews; direct observations of children, teachers, or students; play therapy; situational descriptions; critical incidents; autobiographies; or written statements from job applications.

From such materials raters are trained to make inferences about the subject's perceptions of self, others, purposes, goals, and general orientations. Ratings are usually made on some aspect of perception stated as a dichotomy and spread over a seven-point scale. A typical self-concept item, for example, might be "sees self as able or unable." The "able" end of the dichotomy might be described as, "The subject sees himself as having what is needed to deal with problems. He regards himself as able to make decisions and cope with events he confronts." At the "unable" end of the dichotomy would be, "The subject doubts his capacity to deal with problems. He is uncertain of his ability to make decisions or cope with events he confronts" (Combs 1969; Courson 1965).

Having established the dichotomies we wish to explore, perceptual raters are trained to a point where inter-rater agreements are 80 percent before participating in crucial phases of research. During the actual research process inter-rater agreements are periodically checked to assure agreement continues above the 80 percent level. These procedures have been applied in a number of studies exploring the perceptual organization of good and poor helpers in such professions as teaching (Brown 1970; Dedrick 1972; Dellow 1971; Doyle 1967; Gooding 1969; Koffman 1975; Picht 1969; Usher 1969; Vonk 1970), counseling (Combs and Soper 1967; Swanson 1976), pastoral care (Benton 1969), nurses (Dickman 1969), politicians (O'Roark 1975) and dormitory resident advisors (Jennings 1973).

Results of such research have been significant, far beyond our original hopes. In twelve studies reviewed by Wasicsko (1977), researchers explored sixty-five perceptual categories and obtained significant differences between good and poor practitioners in sixty-one. Exciting as these results have been, the point I wish to make here is not with the findings, but with the research techniques. These studies clearly demonstrate that perceptual variables, including self-concept, can be successfully explored by inferential techniques. What is more, the procedure turns out to be far less complicated than we had originally anticipated. Our experience, for example, has brought to light three facts that greatly simplify the use of inferential techniques.

1. Inferences about self-concept can be successfully made from remarkably small samples of behavior. We have been able to make self-concept inferences that significantly distinguish good teachers from poor ones, for instance, from classroom observations lasting as few as ten minutes, from critical incident protocols as short as a single page, even from a subject's statements written on applications for jobs or honors. Apparently the effect of self-concept on behavior is so pervasive that it can be picked up even from fairly small samples of behavior (Courson 1968).

2. The training of persons to make inferences about self-perceptions turns out to be a much simpler task than we anticipated. Originally, we had expected it would be necessary to subject raters to intensive training designed to orient them to thinking in perceptual terms, followed by repeated practice making inferences from behavioral samples, then comparing these with other observers in sessions extending over several weeks. Instead, we find that the process of learning to make perceptual inferences is comparatively simple, requiring a surprisingly short time for raters to reach acceptable levels of inference reliability (Wasicsko 1977; Wass and Combs 1974).

Most likely, making inferences is not difficult because it is something everyone already knows how to do implicitly. All of us are skillful at inferring what other people are thinking and feeling. Children are notoriously sensitive to how adults think and feel; it is a matter of survival for them. Even as adults we never outgrow this capacity, although we may use it more selectively with our wives, husbands, lovers, or bosses. Being aware of how people important in our lives are thinking and feeling is a skill we all rely upon for guiding daily behavior. Teaching people to empathize is, therefore, not a matter of teaching something entirely new. Instead, it is a question of helping people to do systematically and purposefully what they already do automatically with significant others in their lives.

3. A third factor affecting the making of perceptual inferences about self-concept observed in our research has to do with the global character of self-concept. According to perceptual theory, self-concept is a gestalt of many definitions of the self varying in significance or centrality in the economy of the individual. Various researchers, therefore, have attempted to study such aspects of self-concept as feelings of being loved, wanted, acceptable, able, autonomous, or self as scholar, as teacher, as husband or wife, or as black, white, and so forth, depending upon the particular goals of the researcher. One of the surprises from our research, then, is that self-concept can be treated in comparatively simple terms.

Intercorrelations of separate self-perceptions such as liked, wanted, acceptable, or able for a given person indicate considerable possible overlap and suggest that self-concept is a holistic, global gestalt. A factor analytic study by Combs and Soper (1963) confirms the global character of self-perceptions. This study explores the perceptual organizations of sixty children over a three-year period from kindergarten through second grade. The study makes inferences about thirty-nine perception categories of these children with respect to themselves, to adults, to other children, and to the subject matter of school. In factor analysis 70 percent of the total variance was included in a single factor described at this time as self-adequacy. This factor, by itself, included all but two of the thirty-nine items explored, and accounted for more of the total variance than all other factors in the analysis. These results suggest that the feeling of personal adequacy looms so large in the organization of the self-concept that it pervades the great majority of a person's interactions with the world. If this is true, it also greatly reduces the number of self-concept definitions needed for understanding a given personality or for the study of a person's interactions with the world.

SELF-CONCEPT CALLS FOR A NEW PSYCHOLOGY

Self-Concept and Perception

Self-concept as a perceptual phenomenon seems to call for nothing less than a new psychology. Many workers in the social sciences and the helping professions have found self-concept a useful construct for understanding human beings and for improving the human condition. Accepting this significance, however, involves the worker in much larger consequences, namely, the need for an entirely new perceptual-humanistic psychology. Employing self-concept as an isolated phenomenon is to draw it out of context. It is a basic principle in theory construction that events are true only in their own frame of reference. Transferring concepts directly from one frame of reference to another based upon different assumptions almost certainly introduces large measures of error or distortion. This runs the risk of providing only partial understanding of human personality and behavior or, worse still, of distorting understanding to the point that guidelines for action become inaccurate. The confusion of self-concept and self-report mentioned earlier is a case in point. Self-concept must be understood as one facet of a more comprehensive view of persons.

If self-concept is a perceptual organization, we must ask what other perceptions also affect behavior and personality. I am using the term perception here in a broader sense than its traditional use in behavioristic psychology. Most of us at this conference believe that adequate understanding of the nature of persons and behavior calls for some kind of humanistic-experiential psychology to supplement traditional approaches to our science. I believe that, too, and I am using the term perception here as a person's experience of events including self. Perception is synonymous with personal meaning.

People do not behave solely in terms of self-concept; self-concept is only one of a number of perceptual dimensions that determine behavior. Adequate understanding of persons must recognize and include the additional perceptual dimensions involved in the dynamics of personality and behavior. At this point we can discuss at least seven such variables. Elsewhere (Combs, Richards, and Richards 1976) I have suggested these variables as follows:

1. Perception is, in part, determined by the physical organism in which it occurs. The body provides the vehicle in which perception occurs, and its condition and function have important effects upon perceiving. Perception can also be affected by the acuity of sense organs, the health and vigor of the organism, even by the way the organism is perceived by others.

2. Perceptions are affected by the physical and social environments, past and present, in which the person has developed and currently is functioning. What is perceived is determined by opportunity.

3. Perception is influenced by time. Though perception seems almost instantaneous, it nevertheless occurs in time, and many perceptions are only possible as the end products of a series of previous ones—a time-consuming process. Other things being equal, we perceive more with longer exposure.

These three determinants—the physical organism, environment or opportunity, and time—have long been accepted as significant factors in the determination of behavior. They are also important variables in perceptual-humanistic psychology as determinants of perception and hence of behavior. The perceptual frame of reference, however, calls for understanding at least four additional factors, as explained in the next items.

4. Self-concept is both product and producer of perception. People learn who they are and what they are from experience. Once established, the perceptual organization of self, in turn, has selective effects upon further experience. Self-concept is thus a central dynamic in the phenomenal or perceptual field. Adequate usage requires that it be understood in its relationship to other aspects of perception.

5. Perception is determined by need. Perception, including perception of self, is no haphazard event. The process of perception is always directed toward fulfillment of personal need. Perceptual psychologists have called this need the maintenance and enhancement of self, personal adequacy, self-actualization, or self-fulfillment. By whatever name, the person's fundamental need exerts selective effects upon perception of events in the world, the self, and the relationship of those to each other.

6. Perception is further determined by goals, values, or techniques. These generalized perceptions about ends or means exert selective influences upon perception. Like self-concept, they are differentiated, as a consequence of experience and serve thereafter as guidelines for both the selection of goals and appropriate behaviors for achieving them. Understanding the self in action re-

quires understanding the organism's purposes or goals and the means which seem to him or her appropriate to achieve them.

7. The dynamics of perception do change. Finally, adequate understanding of perception demands some conception of how perceptions come into being and change. This is a vital matter for applied psychology, including education, therapy, counseling, and other professions seeking improvement in the human condition. Some of these dynamics, such as figure-ground relationships and principles of contrast, generalization, similarity, intensity, common fate, set, reinforcement, reward, and punishment, are derived from behavioral research. Others, such as effects of threat and challenge, expectancy, anchorage, identification, levels of awareness, and the effects of previous perceptions, are contributions of more recent perceptual-humanistic thinking.

THE NEED FOR A NEW PSYCHOLOGY

Traditional behavioristic psychology is an inadequate system for exploring such variables as self-concept, needs, goals, values, and the dynamics of perception change. Neither is it adequate to deal with humanistic concepts such as choice, will, self-actualization, expanding consciousness, or highly personal processes of human being and becoming. As a consequence, humanistic psychologists have been moved to seek more adequate concepts, assumptions, and frames of reference. I believe it is one thing to search for more adequate concepts. It is quite another matter to excuse ourselves from the need to be scientific.

As psychologists, we cannot ignore scientific requirements for care and discipline in practice and thinking. Furthermore, professional responsibility requires that what we do be supportable on some reasonable theoretical or research basis. To accomplish those ends seems to me to call for nothing less than an entirely new psychology capable of encompassing both time honored behavioral concepts and current experiential-perceptual-humanistic attempts to understand the phenomenological-internal aspects of being. Is it possible to construct such a psychology? I think it is.

Some workers in both theoretical and applied aspects of self-concept study have been so excited by the paradigm self-concept and its universal appearance as a factor in behavior that they have called for a new self psychology to deal with such matters. To this point I am not aware that anyone has successfully produced one, nor do I believe it is possible to construct a comprehensive self psychology. Self-concept is not a basic construct. It is an organization of more basic perceptions. As such, self-concept represents a construct of prime importance in more fundamental and comprehensive psychology of personal meaning or perception. By itself it is not enough.

CAN AN ADEQUATE PERCEPTUAL PSYCHOLOGY BE CONSTRUCTED?

If we begin with the fundamental assumption that behavior and personality are products of the perceptual field of the behavior, it is possible, thereafter, to construct a systematic psychology encompassing *both* humanistic and behavioral aspects of human being and becoming. Understanding behavior as symptom and perception as cause or dynamic can even help strictly behavioral psychologists solve some of their most pressing problems. Control of behavior, for example, can be immensely improved when the experimenter is aware of the personal meaning a stimulus has for the subject.

Examining events in perceptual terms can even provide new solutions to long-standing, unsolved problems. This was our experience in the helping professions studies mentioned earlier. For several generations experimenters have without success sought keys to good teaching in behavioral terms. We still are unable to isolate any teaching act, knowledge, method, or behavior that can be clearly established as characteristic of either good or bad teaching. Exploring the problem in perceptual terms, however, produced clear-cut distinctions between effective and ineffective teachers and the findings have already produced basic changes in thinking about teacher education, evaluation, and selection.

Can a perceptual psychology provide a frame of reference for such humanistic concerns as choice, self-actualization, self-determination, transcendence, authenticity, synergy, identification, and person centeredness? I have had no trouble with any of these matters approached in perceptual terms. They are all behavioral characteristics produced by a person's perceptions of self and the world. In such terms they make sense, and their dynamics and interrelationships become clear. Even more important, they fall into place in a disciplined theoretical gestalt that removes humanistic concepts for the criticism of vagueness, on the one hand, while providing a solid base for exploration consistent with scientific standards, on the other.

Persons interested in self-concept have already contributed many ideas and research which can readily be incorporated into a comprehensive perceptual psychology. In addition, a substantial literature has accumulated dealing with such perceptual matters as values, aspirations, prejudice, challenge and threat, likes and dislikes, need, motivation, and perceptual distortion, to name a few. In a recent book we collected a bibliography of more than 600 titles bearing upon perceptual aspects of human being and becoming, and that number is but a small percentage of what is available (Combs, Richards, and Richards 1976). Names like Allport, Ames, Cantril, Jourard, Kelley, Lecky, Murphy, Raimy, Rogers, Maslow, and Snygg come quickly to mind as having already contributed much toward a perceptual frame of reference. What we need now is a massive effort to bring these pieces together in a systematic theoretical framework.

I believe it can be done. In 1949 Donald Snygg and I made a stab at outlining a perceptual psychology in our book *Individual Behavior.* Beginning with the assumption that all behavior is a product of the perceptual field of the behaver, we sought to construct the framework for a comprehensive perceptual-phenomenological psychology. More recently, with Anne and Fred Richards, I have expanded the attempt under the title *Perceptual Psychology: A Humanistic Approach to the Study of Persons* (1976). The perceptual point of view has never been widely adopted among psychologists, but I remain convinced that as Don Snygg and I stated in 1949, "We believe this is, if not the truth, then something very like it" (Snygg and Combs 1949). I am not so naive as to suppose that my particular brand of perceptual psychology is anywhere near definitive. Since a theory is only an organization of the facts available at the time it is constructed, it is already dead when it can be stated, for new data and new insights are already at hand, requiring new and better theoretical positions.

We have to start somewhere, however, and those of us who have pursued the problems of human being and becoming in perceptual terms have found our explorations fruitful and exciting. We are also encouraged by the growing numbers of other workers, both in and out of psychology, who are finding it profitable to approach human problems in perceptual terms. We believe a comprehensive perceptual-experiential psychology can, indeed, provide a more adequate base, not only for exploring self-concept but for the humanist movement as well.

2 DIMENSIONS OF THE DILEMMA

Robert E. Bills

The first step in a rational solution to any problem is the recognition that a problem exists, and the second step is a clear definition of its elements. In this regard, well-defined problems are more easily solved than poorly defined or undefined ones. Self-concept falls into the latter category. Since it has been poorly defined, all problems pertaining to self-concept are difficult to solve. I will discuss five problems in defining it.

The first problem is to identify a point of view that may be adopted in defining reality. Haim Ginot pointed out that we can give children choices even if they don't like what is being presented. One of his favorite illustrations involved the child who did not like orange juice. Instead of saying, "Do you want some orange juice?" Haim would ask, "Do you want the large glass or the medium-sized glass?" Similarly, most of us have seen the cartoon of a rat talking to another rat and saying, "I have learned to control my psychologist. Whenever I want food, I merely press this bar and he gives it to me." Walt Disney's little dog Scamp makes the same point when he refers to certain people as "my humans."

It might be said that the child's belief that he has a choice is an illusion as is the rat's belief and Scamp's expression. But in this sense isn't everything an illusion? The world we know exists primarily by commonly accepted definitions. We accept these as representing the real world and then act in ways consistent with them. When the dog scratches on the door to be let out, one may believe the dog has been taught to do this and that the teacher is controlling the dog's behavior. From the dog's point of view, the dog is doing the controlling. The dog wants something and knows how to achieve its end. It is doubtful that dogs scratch on doors simply because they have been "taught" to do so. It is always with an end in view. What people do, at least from a perceptual point of view, is determined by and relevant to the nature of the world as they perceive it. When people believed the world was flat, they avoided the edges. Our beliefs determine how we perceive reality, and we behave in ways consistent with our beliefs. Much of what we believe is reality is the result of definition. Most people have seen the man in the moon. Or is it a man? In Spanish the word for moon is *luna*, the letter "a" showing that the moon is feminine. Do Mexicans see a man in the moon? No. They see a woman. Viewed from the earth, the moon changes its location continuously, and its lighted portion changes shape continuously. It is never in the same place at the same hour on two consecutive nights, and its shape changes from moment to moment. But viewed from the moon, the earth changes only in shape. There is a new earth, a first quarter earth, a full earth, and a last quarter earth. But any time a person stands in the same place on the moon, on the moon's side that faces the earth, the earth is always in the same place. If the person changes places, the earth is judged to have changed its position in relation to the moon. Thus, there are as many locations for the earth, as viewed from the moon, as there are places from which to view it.

Along similar lines, a person asked to count will probably say, "1, 2, 3, 4, 5, 6," and so on. People asked the sum of 12 plus 1 probably will say, "13." But methods of counting and adding are correct only under certain well defined circumstances. For example, on a 12-hour clock, 12 plus 1 equals 1. December is the twelfth month and again, 12 plus 1 is 1. In Europe and the military, 24 plus 1 equals 1.

When people count, they make many assumptions. They may assume that each unit is equal to every other unit; that there is a base 10, which is not always true, and every time the base 10 is reached, 1 is added to the number of times the base is passed; and that the system is infinite. Time is counted differently. The hours on clocks are equal intervals, but the system is finite and it has a base of 12.

Every time the base 12 is reached, counting begins again. Although all numbering systems call for equal intervals, measurements on different sizes of objects such as months, apples, and pears, may be conveniently overlooked when they are counted. Even though all hours are equal in length from an objective point of view, it is not true that from all points of view they are equal. Recall the *long* hours spent in school and the *short* hours spent fishing.

Now, this may all appear incongruous in the context of self-concept definition until it is realized how much trust each is placed in the universe being as people believe it to be. A favorite argument against daylight saving time in the Kentucky legislature during the early 1950s was the statement, "If God had wanted us to have daylight saving time, He would have made it that way."

So, here is one dimension of the problem of definition. The reality we cling to so dearly exists primarily by definition. Given a different set of definitions there is a different reality. This is what happened when a leap was made from mechanics into quantum physics. Euclid postulated that a straight line is the shortest distance between two points. Einstein started with the assumption that the shortest distance between two points is a curved line. Is Einstein correct and Euclid incorrect? No, both are correct. Given any set of logically consistent assumptions, mathematicians can construct a mathematics. Some of these mathematics can even be demonstrated to be logical counterparts of the way reality is presently defined. Who is to say that the others are not equally plausible given different beliefs about the nature of reality? Are behavioristic formulations valid and phenomonological formulations invalid? No. Each has some degree of validity within its own framework, and each is invalid within other frameworks.

Although we would like to think so, we do not live in a real world but one that is built with definitions to suit our own needs and ends. Once having defined the world so, it becomes the world of reality and, in turn, may serve as a deterrent to progress in defining a better world. Self-concept is a result of this type of definitional process. For an example of how definitions can affect reality, read the first two chapters of Isaac Asimov's book *The Tragedy of the Moon* (1973).

So, one problem in defining anything, including self-concept, is the matter of agreement. To the extent that their perceptions overlap, people can agree on a definition. But, where self-concept is concerned we do not all have overlapping perceptions, and thus do not agree with each other.

A second problem in self-concept definition is that the world that behavioral science has defined is one built primarily on a point of view external to the behaver. Early psychologists such as William James gave credence to a self, but later psychologists such as the introspectionists were unable to handle the concept. Still later, the behaviorists saw self-concept as unobservable, unmeasurable, and unnecessary in explaining human behavior.

One reason behaviorists have not found self-concept useful is their view of the purpose for psychology. Their purpose is the prediction and the control of behavior. The prediction and the control of behavior *seems* easier if the nature of the response we desire and the conditions we must observe to elicit the response are known. A consideration of the organism does not seem necessary in this paradigm. It does not appear necessary to ask, "Where is the behaver during behavior?" The relevant question to the behaviorist is, "How does A get B to respond as A desires?"

Psychologists who are interested in self-concept have not generally been concerned principally with prediction and control. Their concerns more often have been of a humanistic nature and give rise to questions such as, "What can A do to help B achieve self-realization?" or "What can A do to help B become his experience?" or "What can A do to help B develop greater congruence between the meanings of his experience for his organism and his present perceptions of those meanings?" or any number of similar questions.

Behaviorists see no value in assuming the existence of a self-concept. To them, it is an unnecessary construct and a deterrent to a truly scientific psychology dedicated to prediction and control. In at least one way, the behaviorists are correct. All people can ever deal with are concepts of reality and not with reality itself. What is called self-concept is a construct; it is not concrete reality. Instead, it came into existence as an explanatory concept. It has an "as if" quality. People behave as if they have a self-concept, just as people behave as if they have been stimulated or reinforced. But behaviorists are incorrect when they deny the usefulness of self-concept in understanding behavior, and they are incorrect when they insist that everyone must perceive as they do and deal with constructs such as "stimulus." "response," and "reinforcement" which they believe to be real.

Yes, stimulus, response, and reinforcement are constructs. They are constructs in the same way that self-concept is a construct, and they seek the same purpose: to explain. People respond *as if* they were stimulated or *as if* they have had previous reinforcement. The construct of reinforcement cannot be defined except through its consequences and these consequences differ from person to person; thus, what is reinforcing to one person is not necessarily reinforcing to another. Reinforcement can be defined neither through its antecedents nor by the behavior of the psychologist. As Wylie (1974) points out, behaviorists do not avoid the problems that confront self theorists. A stimulus is response-inferred in much the same manner that self-concept is response-inferred by some self-concept theorists.

Thus, a second problem in defining self-concept is this: What is seen as the purpose of self-concept? Is it to control human behavior or is it to free people to see the personal meanings of their own experiences? If it is the former, then there is little need for it; if it is the latter then a better definition is required so that researchers may work in concert with each other. Some self-concept investigators are interested in humanistic-type goals; others are more interested in prediction and control. Still others take a position between these extremes and argue that the achievement of humanistic goals requires prediction and control.

A third problem relates to the diversity of opinion surrounding definitions of self-concept. This diversity is readily seen in the plethora of tests appearing since the early 1950s that purport to measure it, and in the language used to talk about it. It is seen also in the diversity of definitions that stem from fields such as sociology and psychology.

Most psychological investigators of self-concept have pursued their own directions oblivious of the directions of others. Many people have constructed instruments purporting to measure self-concept. Although some of these measures agree to a small degree with each other, there is little reason to believe that they measure the same construct. For instance, there have been many variations and revisions of my self-concept measure, the Index of Adjustment and Values, each of the revisions presents a different type of self-concept. Some revisions represented a global self-concept; others were more specific types of self-concept such as self-concept as a student, self-concept as a friend, self-concept of ability, a real self, a perceived self, and so on, ad infinitum. Other revisions were made for the sake of revision and seemed to suggest that any changes made would be improvements on the original scale.

In contrast to those who have defined self-concept from constructed measurement devices, Combs and his co-workers (Combs, Richards, and Richards 1977) approached self-concept definition from the point of view that the self is not directly measurable by self-report—it can be known only by inference. It is held in this point of view that self-concept cannot be measured directly since asking people to observe their own perceptual field alters the field so much that the observations may be meaningless. The contrast of Combs's position with that of the test-inferred definitions of self-concept sharpens my point; there is marked disagreement existing among self theorists.

Is it possible to identify a common denominator for defining the self, and thereby make it possible for studies to lead toward a common understanding rather than to have them contradict each other or lead in diverse directions as present studies tend to do? If we can define the construct we have called self-concept in a manner acceptable to most of us, then we would add consistency to a field that needs it badly, and would make a fundamental contribution to a science of the self.

Another aspect of this third problem is conceptualization of self as an object or as an agent: Is self-concept perceived as a phenomenal or a nonphenomenal variable? Most self-concept theorists see self-concept as a perceived object and, thus, as phenomenal, whereas ego-theorists see self as an agent of action. It is probably important to recognize this difference of opinion.

A fourth problem relates to the sequencing of definition and measurement. Should research begin by defining self-concept, or by measuring it and then defining it in terms of the results obtained? In a way, most of the people who have proposed measures of self-concept have started with a methodology or a technique and have assumed that they are measuring self-concept. These people could be called the technique-centered group.

On the other hand, Combs and his co-workers start with a self-concept that they believe is not directly measurable, and they have sought to develop methods by which it can be inferred. This group could be called the inference-centered group.

In its work, the technique-centered group is left with the problem of construct validity, which may be an impossible one to solve starting where they do. To date, this group has been concerned most with concurrent validity—to what degree do its measures agree with each other? In general, the agreement has been low, which is not at all surprising in light of reliability problems and of the different constructs that are probably involved. Furthermore, many of the instruments make up a confusing set of items reflecting such diverse things as how we see ourselves, how we feel about ourselves, how friends, family, and other people see us or feel about us, and so on. Such items may measure self-concept, or they may measure other constructs such as self-regard or self-esteem, opinions of other people, and so forth.

The inference-centered group also has its unique problems. From this framework, any two observers approach a problem with different points of view, and the inferences they make about a third person are influenced by these points of view which often results in low inter-observer reliability and unknown validity. Furthermore, inferential techniques are cumbersome, costly to use, and so far cannot be used to study large groups of people.

As evidenced by the work of the majority of people in the field of self-concept, we have techniques and methodologies looking for constructs. Most of the work in the past twenty-five years has been of this type. Although the approach has yielded a large amount of useful empirical knowledge, it has not served to advance self-concept theory. In fact, there have been few refinements in self-concept theory during the past quarter century, and fewer yet that can be attributed to the approach I have called technique-centered.

Though not yet established, the approach of the inference-centered group may eventually prove more fruitful than its opposite. The approach has the advantage of being an open system; it starts with a well-defined construct, it has directionality, and it may solve another basic problem. Simply stated, the problem is this: It may never be possible to establish the construct validity of a technique or of a measure. The problem here is that the technique or the measure defines the construct and not the reverse.

The fifth and last problem is, "Can one use what is known about characteristics of definitions to arrive at a mutually acceptable definition of self-concept? Henry Cady (1967) had a similar problem when asked to develop a working definition of the term music education. Cady's first efforts at definition were rejected by the group members. He then consulted with philosophers, semanticists, and linguists before making a second effort. What he learned was that in regard to defining complex terms, people seem to differ more than they actually do because they have different styles for defining styles which do not appear to be useful in defining a term such as self-concept. The reason for this is that what is known about types or styles of definition is helpful in determining the characteristics of a definition, not in arriving at the definition.

What might be helpful in Cady's work are the techniques listed for defining terms. Such techniques involve: the use of synonyms and antonyms as means of description and differentiation; the use of ostensive definitions that describe instances of a term's presence or absence; componential definitions attempting to define a term by what it consists of; comparative definitions which seek to say what the term is and what it is not; and finally, operational definitions. In the case of self-concept, an operational definition of the construct would describe how the self-concept works, how it manifests itself, how it affects behavior, and might even point to the processes involved in its measurement.

Each of these definitional techniques would be helpful in further developing a definition of self-concept. Of these the least useful probably would be the use of synonyms and antonyms. The most useful would be a truly operational definition. Most of our present so-called operational definitions of self-concept are not really operational definitions. They follow the pattern that says, "Self-concept is defined in terms of what is measured by this test." An adequate operational definition would describe how self-concept works, how it manifests itself, how it affects behavior, and how it might be measured. It would operationalize the construct, a sharp contrast to the present approach of the technique-centered group that seems to be attempting to define the construct through the operations used for its measurement.

If Snygg and Combs's (1949) self-concept were operationalized as a definition, this would probably be a solution to the problem. To do this would involve accepting their construct, or a similar one, or modifying it until it became acceptable to a broader group. In this process, work such as Cady's would be helpful. Likewise, in operationalizing the finally agreed-on definition, the work of the technique-centered group should prove valuable. There have been many efforts to measure self-concept; certainly some of these techniques should prove valuable in an operational definition and especially if the techniques were modified in light of the accepted definition.

My position is somewhat between the two groups described. An operational definition would exclude neither group but would force the technique-centered group to improve its techniques and the inference-centered group to become more specific about the manifestations of self-concept. Until a common definition is agreed upon, self-concept researchers will each be like the Red Queen in *Alice's Adventures in Wonderland* (Carroll 1968) who insisted that when she used a word it meant exactly what she intended it to mean.

3 THE UNITY PRINCIPLE VERSUS THE REALITY AND PLEASURE PRINCIPLES, *OR* THE TALE OF THE SCORPION AND THE FROG

Seymour Epstein

According to many phenomenologists, the one most basic need of the individual is to maintain unity or coherence in the individual's conceptual system. From this viewpoint the existence of other needs is not denied but is relegated to a subordinate role, for it is assumed that their influence is determined by the overall conceptual system. What I wish to do in this presentation is to examine this viewpoint in some detail and to make clear that the idea is too good to be left to the exclusive possession of phenomenologists.

SOME VIEWS ON THE NATURE OF THE UNITY PRINCIPLE

According to Goldstein (1939), humans have a basic need to comprehend and organize the data of their experience. When the ability to organize experience into a coherent whole is threatened, as in the brain-injured soldiers observed by Goldstein, the individual attempts to simplify and restrict his or her environment so that it can be reduced to manageable proportions. When this cannot be accomplished, the catastrophic reaction occurs. The catastrophic reaction is a nightmare in which one is unable to make sense of experience and therefore is reduced to a state of helpless confusion. The anticipation of such a state is assumed by Goldstein to be a basic source of anxiety.

Lecky (1969) noted that the world would be chaotic and unmanageable if the individual did not impose order on it through the development of a unified conceptual system. He believed that people's concepts about themselves and the world are organized into a hierarchical, integrated system, in much the same way that a scientist's views are organized into an overall theory. The individual's conceptual system is equivalent to his or her personality. According to Lecky, you are essentially your conceptual system. The rest of you is merely skin and bones. What you make of them is more important than what they are, for if your conceptual system were to disorganize, you would no longer exist as a personality. Accordingly, individuals will go to any length to preserve their conceptual systems. The most basic need of all is to maintain the system's unity or coherence. Lecky (1969) expressed the matter as follows:

> We propose to apprehend all psychological phenomena as illustrations of the single principle of unity or self-consistency. We conceive the personality as an organizations of values which are felt to be consistent with one another. Behavior expresses the effort to maintain the integrity and unity of the organization. . . . All of an individual's values are organized into a single system, the preservation of whose integrity is essential [p. 109].

He further stated that "interpreting all behavior as motivated by the need for unity, we understand particular motives or tendencies simply as expressions of the main motive, pursuing different immediate goals as necessary to that end" (p. 109). One may ask, then, why people are not aware that they have an overriding need for consistency and coherence in the same way that they are aware that they are hungry or have needs for achievement or love? In other words, why is the principle of unity so often overlooked? Lecky's answer is as follows: "Since the general motive always appears in the form of a particular motive, . . . it is never directly accessible to introspection and cannot possibly become conscious except as a principle or logical abstraction" (p. 109).

According to Snygg and Combs (1949), the one primary need of the individual is "the preservation and enhancement of the phenomenal self" (p. 58). The phenomenal self is viewed as an extended self that includes everything referred to by the words "I," "me," and "mine." The phenomenal self is considered to be the nucleus of the phenomenal field, which comprises the individual's entire world of subjective experience. While preservation and enhancement might justifiably be considered as two different needs, ones that could even conflict with each other (Epstein 1980). Snygg and Combs regard them as one because they believe that enhancement serves to buttress the stability of the phenomenal self against *future* threats.

Rogers' views are similar to those of Snygg and Combs. Rogers (1951) states that the individual has one basic tendency, "to actualize, maintain, and enhance the experiencing organism." Again, these appear to be more than one need, but Rogers assures us that they describe different facets of a single process. In any event, it can be assumed that maintenance is central, for without it there would be nothing to actualize or enhance. Unlike Snygg and Combs, Rogers refers to maintenance *of the organism*, although elsewhere he also refers to maintenance of the phenomenal self. He regards an individual's self-concept, which is equivalent to the phenomenal self, to be the nucleus of the individual's conceptual system, and notes that in order to understand the organism as an "experiencing organism" it is necessary to understand the individual's self-concept.

In summary, all of the above theorists agree that there is essentially one basic need, which is to maintain the unity of the individual's conceptual system. Different theorists modify this by adding what they regard as different aspects of the overall need, but which others may regard as different needs, such as enhancement (Snygg and Combs, and Rogers) and self-actualization (Goldstein and Rogers), but all agree that maintenance is central. All other motives, both primary and derived, are regarded as subordinate, as they can only be experienced and expressed in a manner determined by the overall conceptual system. The above theorists all agree that when an individual's conceptual system is threatened by external events or by awareness of inner processes or thoughts that cannot be assimilated into the conceptual system, stress, which is subjectively experienced as anxiety, occurs in the system. The most basic source of anxiety is considered to be a threat to the integrity of the individual's conceptual system. Normally this results in constriction and defensiveness in an attempt to simplify the world of experience. Should defenses fail or be insufficient, catastrophic disorganization follows, which amounts to dissolution of the personality.

Let us contrast the above view, whose adherents are mainly humanists and phenomenologists, with the view of those who are more in the mainstream of psychology, such as psychoanalysts and learning theorists. According to these latter psychologists—who, for want of a better name I shall call "objectivists" to distinguish them from phenomenologists—the basic principles of human behavior are the reality principle and the pleasure principle. That is, objectivists believe that all behavior can be understood in terms of rewards and punishments received in a world of hard reality. They make no mention of the unity principle, which they must either regard as unimportant or as a subordinate principle that can be derived from the other principles. Motives as well as behavior are considered by objectivists to be subordinate to the pleasure and reality principles, as they are shaped by and exert their effects through the operation of these principles. Thus, biologically based motives such as sex, as well as acquired motives such as achievement, are assumed to develop or fail to develop along particular lines as the result of an individual's past history of reinforcement with respect to relevant behaviors. This view is essentially an economic one, for it assumes that the most basic reason for behavior is to maximize pleasure and minimize pain in a real objective world. Economists would, of course, express the same view by referring to maximizing profits and minimizing losses.

As compelling as the objectivist view is, it is insufficient in one very important respect: It ignores the equally compelling unity principle. Behavior is as much determined by the need to maintain coherence within an organized conceptual system as by the need to react in a manner that maximizes gains and minimizes losses in a real, external world. It is evident that people have sacrificed fortunes and life itself to support their conceptual systems. The unity principle is of such importance as to be ignored only at one's own peril, as illustrated in the following story of the scorpion and the frog.

One fine summer day, a scorpion came to the edge of a pond that he was unable to cross. He saw a frog swimming around, and asked the frog to take him across the pond. "Not on my life," said the frog. "I know your kind. It's a ruse to get me to come ashore so you can sting me. Besides, even if you didn't sting me, what would there be in it for me?" So you see, we have here a frog who is a good rational, realistic frog who avoids pain and seeks gain, and who assumes that scorpions operate by the same principle. The scorpion replied, "You don't have to come ashore. Just come near enough so I can jump on your back. I would not sting you, because, if I did, I would surely drown with you. Besides, if you ferry me across I will catch you many exotic insects." Having nothing to lose, and possibly something to gain, the frog consented. When they were half way across the pond, the scorpion stung the frog. In his dying breath, the frog asked, "Why, why, why?" to which the scorpion replied, "Because it is my nature." Of course, a more sophisticated scorpion would have said, "It is my self-concept." Or, if he had been a Kellian scorpion, "It is how I construe the world."

THE EXPLANATORY POWER OF THE UNITY PRINCIPLE

The principle that individuals are motivated to maintain a coherent, unified conceptual system has widespread explanatory power. It identifies a need in all higher order animals to establish an adequate representation of their environment so that they can cope with it with greater flexibility and efficiency than if their responses were instinctive reactions to discrete stimuli in the manner of bees and ants. As Kelly (1955), Lecky (1969), and Epstein (1973, 1976, 1980) have noted, we are no less dependent upon a coherent theory for directing our behavior in everyday life than a scientist is for directing his or her activities in a more limited realm. Only by organizing our concepts into an efficient system of higher and lower order generalizations from past experience with implications for future experience can we hope to adjust to the complex social world around us. In this respect, any theory is better than none, for at least a theory imposes an orderliness on experience, making life liveable, if not necessarily enjoyable. It follows that the unity principle must be as fundamental a determinant of human behavior as the pleasure and reality principles. Let us now examine some of the kinds of behavior that the unity principle can account for that cannot be readily explained by the other principles.

The Unity Principle in Animals

It is commonly considered that animals such as dogs operate by mechanistic principles, and that they do not have an organized conceptual system that influences their behavior. Although this is Pavlov's view, some of his experiments nevertheless support the existence of a unified conceptual system in dogs. In a famous experiment, one of his dogs was given food whenever it was shown an ellipse and not given food when it was shown a circle. Gradually the ellipse was made to approach the circle in appearance. No painful stimuli were employed, and there was nothing the dog had to do but eat the food when it appeared if it so wished. Yet, a remarkable phenomenon occurred when the animal could no longer discriminate the ellipse from the circle. Namely, the animal lost its ability to make all of the easy distinctions it had previously made, showed a widespread disruption of its other learned responses, and became a generally fearful and disorganized creature. The reaction lasted over a protracted period, despite the animal having been brought to a rest farm. Pavlov referred to the disorder as animal neurosis. It can better be described as animal psychosis, for it involves the shattering, or dissolution, of a conceptual system, which can be considered as the essence of schizophrenic disorganization (Epstein 1976, 1979). It is noteworthy that the cause of the breakdown was the inability to maintain the assimilation of an emotionally significant concept. Of course, in order to shatter the organization of a conceptual system, there must be an organization to begin with, so the experiment suggests that even dogs have rudimentary, integrated conceptual systems.

The Unity Principle and Normal Behavior

Elsewhere (Epstein 1973, 1976, 1979) I have considered the implications of the unity principle for schizophrenic disorganization. Here I would like to consider the implications of the unity principle for certain aspects of normal behavior. The operation of the unity principle in normal individuals has been well illustrated in laboratory studies by social psychologists who have observed the lengths to which people will go to reduce cognitive dissonance (e.g., Brehm and Cohen 1962; Festinger 1957). These studies have demonstrated that people will often behave against their own interests or in other ways that appear to be irrational in order to make their behavior appear consistent. In a series of studies that is of particular interest because it established relatively long-term effects, Rokeach (1973) demonstrated that when individuals are confronted with discrepancies in their values, they are motivated to resolve the discrepancies and, as a consequence, may undergo significant changes in attitudes and behavior. Vaughn (1977), in a study of what students learn and fail to learn in psychology classes, found that beliefs associated with important values are resistant to change, and that evidence contrary to past beliefs and values tends to be ignored or forgotten. Many students retained erroneous beliefs that they brought with them despite having been explicitly taught otherwise.

The view that individuals have a need to maintain the stability of their higher order constructs has much to tell us about everyday behavior. It is particularly revealing in indicating how people go about assimilating data in real life. Most people believe they form opinions by objectively assessing data, and inductively arrive at general conclusions. They are puzzled when other seemingly reasonable people who are exposed to the same facts come to opposite conclusions. Given people's need to maintain the stability of their higher order constructs, it follows that the higher order constructs will influence the search for and interpretation of data. Moreover, there will only be certain conclusions that can be accepted, given the need to protect the coherence of the conceptual system. Accordingly, data are often scanned to obtain general impressions of whether the information is consistent with a person's more general values and constructs. The scanning results in a generally favorable or unfavorable impression of the material according to whether it supports or refutes the person's values and basic concepts. The data are likely, then, to be selectively examined for examples that confirm the initial impression. The person will then argue, and believe, that the conclusion arrived at was established only after a careful and objective perusal of the data, for people tend not to question their basic postulates.

To present a concrete example of the above process, consider how journal articles must often be evaluated for publication, as revealed by the low rate of agreement among reviewers. The reviewer reads the article and is either favorably or unfavorably impressed with it, depending on how the conclusions relate to his or her own views. Having made a tentative judgment, the reviewer then carefully examines the article for evidence to support the judgment. Having found the evidence, and having ignored counter-evidence, the reviewer then writes a report based on the evidence that was noted, and considers the review to be objective and reasonable. The point is that this way of thinking is not restricted to reviewers of journals but is a highly general way of thinking, and it is adaptive in the sense that it helps people retain the stability of their higher order constructs, although it may be maladaptive in other ways. Effective adjustment obviously requires a balance between change and stability; between being able to change one's behavior and beliefs as a result of being exposed to new information, and being able to respond in a stable way as a result of having higher order generalizations that were derived from significant past experiences.

The Unity Principle and Psychoanalysis

There are several awkward concepts in psychoanalysis that can be attributed to a failure to consider the unity principle. I do not wish to imply that psychoanalysts completely ignore the unity principle, only that they do not give it the emphasis it deserves. As a case in point, let us consider how Freud might have explained the scorpion's behavior. In his original theory, when the pleasure principle reigned supreme, he would have resorted to tortuous psychodynamics, such as that the scorpion unconsciously identified the frog with his mother, for whom he had incestuous longings. This naturally produced terrible guilt feelings. The defense against love is hate. By killing her in symbolic form and himself in reality, both the hostility and the guilt were expressed. Thus, all the unconscious dynamics came to bear on a single act, and that is why it occurred. In his later theory, Freud would have had it easy, as all he would have had to do is attribute the scorpion's behavior to the death instinct. Let us examine this position further. It is to Freud's credit that he eventually realized that the pleasure and reality principles were not enough. They could not account for man's inhumanity to man as observed in the World War I, and they could not account for the terrifying repetitive dreams he observed in the traumatic neurosis. Freud realized that there must be some principle even more important than the pleasure principle. Unfortunately, since he did not think of the unity principle, he was forced to a bold but questionable resolution, namely, the postulation of a death instinct. Once this was done, he could account for repetitive and self-destructive behavior by attributing them to the "repetition compulsion," a component of the death instinct.

Freud noted that people often have a tendency to repeat the mistakes in their lives. A woman who has married the wrong husband swears she will never make the same mistake again, but somehow she does, despite her attempts to do everything possible to choose a different kind of man. As the Greeks noted a long time ago, people appear to be controlled by a daemonic fate that forces them to behave consistently in self-destructive ways. Freud noted that such self-destructive behavior cannot always be explained by unconscious gratification. He therefore formulated the concept of the death instinct. He argued that all energy runs down, that the life cycle endlessly repeats itself, that from dust we came and to dust we shall return. He concluded that the death instinct and the tendency to repeat must be part of a fundamental principal that cannot be further reduced. Such reasoning, of course, is completely analogical; it is more the stuff of poetry than of science. Contrast this with how the same phenomenon can be explained by the unity principle. The apparently perverse destiny that controls some people's lives can be attributed to the self-fulfilling hypotheses that people have about the nature of themselves and the world in which they live. Although their behavior may appear to be self-destructive, it is adaptive in the sense that it maintains a familiar view of the nature of the self and the world, and thereby maintains the unity of the individual's conceptual system. The more a concept has been derived from intense emotional experience, the more it is apt to become a broad postulate that plays a basic role in the structure of an individual's conceptual system. Accordingly, it is important for the individual to retain that postulate if the organization of the conceptual system is not to be endangered. It is for this reason that the individual seeks out and actively establishes conditions in reality that maintain negative as well as positive views about the self and the world.

Freud attributed the traumatic neurosis to intense stimulation that breached a presumed stimulus barrier that normally protects the brain from overstimulation. He noted that in addition to intensity of stimulation, surprise was a critical factor. He further observed that a physical wound afforded protection against the traumatic neurosis, and attributed this to displacement of cathexis from the trauma to the wound. He explained the anxiety in the traumatic neurosis as the result of a belated attempt to establish the anticipatory anxiety that, had it been present initially, would have prevented the surprise. Contrast this complicated and mechanistic explanation with one advanced by Lecky (1969). According to Lecky, the traumatic neurosis results from an assault on the unity of an individual's conceptual system by an experience of such intensity and significance that it cannot be ignored, and of such a nature that it cannot be assimilated into the individual's view of the world and his or her place in it. The repetition of the trauma in memory is nothing other than a continuous attempt to assimilate the unassimilable experience. Memories of the trauma keep occurring until either dissociation of the memory or its assimilation takes place.

One of the most important concepts in Freud's early as well as late theory is repression. While the empirical phenomenon of repression is well established, there are difficulties with Freud's explanation of it. According to Freud, a repressed impulse or thought has an energy of its own that presses for discharge. The force of the repressed impulse must be matched by an equal inhibitory force if the repression is to be retained. The individual thus has a reduced supply of energy available for other pursuits, and he or she experiences tension that cannot be dissipated through release. Through its indirect expression, the repressed impulse or thought produces symptoms and the pathology of everyday life, such as slips of the tongue. The idea of a force that is inhibited by another force and vents itself only indirectly is more appropriate for understanding steam boilers than human minds. Again, Freud's reasoning is by analogy. From what we know of human motives such as aggression, such motives do not consist of ready-made instinctive forces that accumulate energy until discharged. Rather, they are latent response dispositions that are activated by experiences. Even a person who is highly prone to anger does not experience anger under conditions that are wholly satisfactory to him or her. Such a person has a low threshold for being stimulated to anger when situations are interpreted in a certain manner, such as that he or she has been attacked, treated with inconsideration, or treated unjustly, and that the person who is responsible for this behavior deserves to be punished.

Let us now consider how repression can be explained from the perspective of the unity principle. We will begin with the assumption that there is a general tendency to assimilate experience into a unified conceptual system. Thoughts and memories that are too salient or significant to be ignored, but that cannot be assimilated without endangering the unity of the conceptual system, will tend to become dissociated. Given a tendency to assimilate all experience, dissociated thoughts and memories, because they cannot be assimilated, remain a potential source of stress. Should the dissociated thoughts or memories become more salient through appropriate stimulation, the dissociation will be difficult to maintain, and tension will be generated as the thoughts or memories can neither be ignored nor assimilated.

Expressed otherwise, when repression occurs, there is conflict between two tendencies, one to preserve the unity of the conceptual system by dissociating the material that cannot be assimilated, and the other to increase the unity and coherence of the conceptual system by assimilating the dissociated material. The forces and tensions that exist do not reside within the thoughts or repressed memories themselves, but are stresses associated with the assimilative process.

BEYOND THE UNITY PRINCIPLE

I have noted that a psychology emphasizing the pleasure and reality principles at the expense of the unity principle is necessarily incomplete. By the same token, a psychology that emphasizes the unity principle at the expense of the pleasure and reality principles is also incomplete. All three principles are important. The question may be raised as to whether the principles are equally important, or if one is more fundamental than the others. If the latter were true it should be observed that under stress, or in cases of pathology, the same fundamental principle would remain in operation after the others were no longer present; in other words, it would be the last to be surrendered. This is apparently not the case. If one examines different kinds of pathology, it is evident that any of the principles can be dominant. In depression, the individual retains contact with reality and coherence of the conceptual system, but ceases to function according to the pleasure principle. Expressed otherwise, the individual retains contact with reality and retains coherence of his or her conceptual system at the expense of feeling miserable. However, under mounting stress, depression may give way to disorganization, which can serve the pleasure principle, as disorganization destroys the conceptual system that structures self-hatred and misery, and thereby can prevent suicide. In delusions of grandeur, coherence of the conceptual system and the operation of the pleasure principle are retained, but contact with reality is sacrificed.

It is evident that what is needed is a theory incorporating all three principles into a unified system. Elsewhere (Epstein 1973, 1976, 1980), I have proposed such a theory that assumes that all individuals develop an implicit theory of reality for the purposes of assimilating the data of experience into a coherent conceptual system, of optimizing self-esteem, and of maximizing one's pleasure and pain balance over the course of a lifetime.

4 THE BOUNDARIES OF THE SELF
The Relationship of Authenticity in the Self-Conception

Ralph H. Turner
Steven Gordon[a]

The purpose of this discussion is to explore the relationship between what we call imprecisely but conveniently *true self* and *spurious self* experiences. We observed empirically that the relationship between these two experiences suggested a more complex structure than is implied by the simple idea of a unitary self-conception. By exploring this relationship, we hope to find clues to a view of self-conception that facilitates a refined understanding of the anchorages of self in the social structure.

SOCIAL CONSTRUCTION OF SELF AND SELF-BOUNDARIES

Our discussion will concern the self as a subjective construct in the individual's experience, rather than an objectively locatable entity or dynamism. We assume that individuals develop conceptions of themselves that have no metaphysically defensible referents and do not

a. The authors gratefully acknowledge support from the National Institute of Mental Health, grant USPHS MH 26243; research assistance from Shelley Garcia, Denise Heller Paz, Marilyn Sperbeck, and Barbara Shaw; and assistance in arranging for the administration of questionnaires in Australia and Britain by Robert Cushing, David Hickman, Robyn Hudson, Pamela Krist, Keith Macdonald, and Richard Volpata.

correspond precisely with any typical or modal behavioral characterization of the person.

The forerunner to this sociological view of self-conception was Thomas and Znaniecki's (1918) life organization, which Robert E. Park (1927), borrowing from William James, translated into the individual's conception of self. Manford Kuhn (1954; Khun and McPartland 1954; Spitzer, Couch, and Stratton 1970) operationalized self-conception with development of the Twenty Statements Test (TST) in which the subject is asked to write twenty answers to the question, "Who am I?" as if giving answers strictly to oneself. The assumption was that the most significant responses would locate the self by status and group membership in the larger social structure. A preponderance of such consensual identifications (and later, *B-mode* responses) was interpreted as signifying a secure and stable personal anchorage in society and as contributing to personal adjustment and stability.

The utility of this view of the relationship between person and society has come under increasing attack during the last two decades. The youth movements of the 1960s violently disavowed anchorage of the self in consensual social units, and loudly proclaimed the prevalence of social impediments to self-discovery. Less dramatic and more continuous, however, was a gradual shift in the kind of answers college students were giving to the TST, with *C-mode* or action replacing *B-mode* or social position as the most frequent form of response to the TST (Zurcher 1972, 1978).

If we approach the operational problem of identifying the self-conception and the intellectual problem of understanding the self-conception through the experiences from which it is inferred, we may be able to minimize preconceptions about its relation to social structure and escape a tendency toward reification. With this orientation in mind, we have employed two pairs of questions calling for extended open-ended responses. In questionnaire format, at the top of a full sheet of paper, the subject is asked:

> On some occasions my actions or feelings seem to express my true self much better than at other times. On these occasions the person that I really am shows clearly, I feel genuine and authentic, I feel that I know who I am.
>
> Try to recall one such occasion when your true self was expressed. Please describe the occasion and what you did or felt in detail.

Halfway down the sheet of paper is the second question:

> What was it about your actions or feelings on this occasion that made them an expression of your true self?

A second sheet of paper contains a pair of counterpart questions, similarly placed.

> On some other occasions my actions or feelings do not express my true self, and even misrepresent or betray the person that I really am. On these occasions I feel unreal and inauthentic; I sometimes wonder if I know who I really am. Afterwards I am likely to say something like: "I wasn't really myself when that happened."
>
> Try to recall one such occasion when your actions or feelings contradicted your true self. Please describe the occasion and what you did or felt in detail.

The clarification probe reads:

> What was it about your actions or feelings on this occasion that made them a contradiction of your real self?

Answers to each pair of questions are read and coded as a single answer, but the *true self* and *spurious self* questions are read and coded independently. The true self method is discussed more fully elsewhere (Turner and Schutte 1981). Our concern in this chapter is specifically with the relationship between answers to the true self and spurious self questions. Since we think of responses to these two questions as delimiting the self-conception, we speak of the *boundaries of the self.*

It would be simple to think about the self if true self and spurious self were exhaustive categories. But this is apparently not so. First, there are undoubtedly whole realms of activity that are largely irrelevant to the self. In the language of Sherif and Cantril (1947), there is no ego involvement. Matters would still be relatively simple if true self and spurious self constituted adjacent segments of a single dimension. But in most instances this is not so. When self-feeling revolves about some dimension of achievement, the feeling of true self does not arise at the same level of achievement at which one ceases to feel inauthentic, but at a considerably higher level. Thus there is a customary or normal self between the true self and the spurious self, a realm that is taken for granted, evoking neither type of feeling in active form. In asking about true self and inauthenticity experiences, then, one is establishing some of the boundaries of a customary self which may otherwise be taken for granted.

There are further indications that the true self and spurious self experiences may not always be organized along a single dimension. When this is so, the boundaries must be identified in qualitative as well as quantitative terms. And more significantly, the origin, dynamics, and functions of the two kinds of self-feeling may be different.

A full exploration of these questions would require the use of several different dimensions for classifying true and spurious self protocols. We have used two dimensions whose rationale is specifically relevant to a thesis advanced elsewhere (Turner 1976). The first dimension counterposes institution and impulse as anchorages for self-conception. For some people, feelings and actions that express ambition, self-control, morality, and altruism seem more real as expressions of their selves than impulsive and unpremeditated manifestations. These experiences are obviously rooted in the institutional structure. For other people such dispositions as ambition, rationally calculated behavior, and altruism seem artificial and externally imposed, constituting impediments to expression of the true self. The true self, for them, is marked by sheer unpremeditated spontaneity, as in the experience of impulse, undisciplined desire, and the wish to make intimate revelations to other people. We do not regard the latter as any less socially determined than what we call institutional anchorages, nor do we assume that institutionals would acknowledge the appropriateness of this designation for themselves. But the former kind of orientation anchors the self in the institutional structure, and the latter anchors it in self-conscious separation from the perceived institutional structure.

The second dimension is simply individual versus social orientation. The question is whether the relationship to other people is critical in identifying the experience as indicative of the self, or whether the relationship to other people is more or less irrelevant to the experience.

Combining the dimensions creates four types of self anchorages, each of which is designated for convenience by a single term. The self may be recognized in essentially individualistic achievement, including realization of ambitions, accomplishment, mastery of situations, self-control, and adhering to a standard of morality in the face of temptation when the emphasis is on the accomplishment rather than the social good that results. The social form of institutional anchorages is altruism, in which the self is realized through service to others, or self-sacrifice when service for others is implied. The individual form of impulse is called impulse release, and typically takes the form of just doing something on impulse, acting on desire without consideration for reason, custom, social expectation, or principle, or of experiencing a feeling or emotion when that experience is identified as a self-discovery. The social form of impulse involves being able to communicate inner feelings to someone else without concern for how those feelings would be interpreted or received. Although the term in its common meaning does not exactly represent the kind of experience involved, we have called this type of experience intimacy, since the central consideration is the elimination of interpersonal barriers to intimate expression.

Answers to the spurious self question can be coded in the same four categories, but we use names that express the negative pole in each case. Thus when lack of achievement creates a sense of inauthenticity, we identify the experience as failures. Selfishness is antithetical to altruism, plastic behavior (in the 1960s sense of being an imitation of the real thing) is opposite to impulse release, and insincerity opposes intimacy.

It has been proposed that there has been an historical shift away from self-anchorage in institution toward anchorage in impulse. The modal response of college students to this open-ended format is intimacy, more markedly so for women than men (Turner and Schutte 1981). When a closed-ended format is used ("The way to find out who you really are is to help someone who needs your assistance: strongly agree, agree, disagree, or strongly disagree") both college students and an adult sample endorse altruism most frequently. But the adult and college samples differ most strikingly in the relative endorsement of intimacy versus achievement, and in an overall difference with adults giving relatively more institution responses and students giving more impulse responses (Turner 1975).

We shall explore the differences and similarities between true self and spurious self anchorages, and then examine some hypothesized correlates of combined types of true self–spurious self anchorages. The data consist of 1,269 sets of responses that were codable for both true and spurious self, secured by comparable sampling procedures from students at University of California, Los Angeles (UCLA),

Australian National University (ANU), LaTrobe University in Melborne, Australia, and the University of Surrey in Guildford, England. Sampling procedures are described elsewhere (Turner 1975).

EMPIRICAL EVIDENCE ON TRUE AND SPURIOUS SELF

A decisive majority of true self anchorages are classified as impulse, while an even more decisive majority of spurious self anchorages are classified as institutional (Table 4-1). This difference turns up consistently in each of the four university samples, and applies to both men and women taken separately.

On the other dimension, there is a tendency of borderline significance for the true self to be more social than the spurious self, which is consistent for schools, but seems to be explained on the basis of a difference among females but not males. If there is a true tendency here, it must be viewed as trivial.

Coders were instructed to classify responses according to whether the respondents gave fairly clear indications that the behavior, feeling, situation, or response to which they referred was a common one or somewhat unusual. Most of the responses for both true and spurious self referred to experiences that were not everyday occurrences. That observation alone seems to indicate that there is another realm—the customary self—between the true self experience and the experience of inauthenticity. But there is also a significant and consistent though weak tendency for the true self experience to occur in a common situation more often than the spurious self experience.

Table 4–1. True and Spurious Self Anchorages.

Self Anchorage	*True Self*	*Spurious Self*	*Chi-Square*	*p*
Institution	39.5%	65.0%		
Impulse	60.5	35.0	164.80	$< .001$
Social	54.2	50.0		
Individual	45.8	50.0	4.27	$< .050$
Usual	21.7	15.8		
Not usual	78.3	84.2	15.40	$< .001$

The consistent difference in frequencies of institution and impulse anchorages for true and spurious self appears centrally important in understanding the relationship of self-conception to social structure. The experience of inauthenticity is more manifestly a matter how one fits into the institutional structure, while the experience of vital authenticity comes from transcending or escaping the manifest institutional structure. This apparent contradiction will be our central concern in this chapter.

Overall, the tendency is for each individual to give answers to the true and spurious self questions that fall into the same category (Table 4–2). We call these *pure type* combinations. Combinations that are similarly classified on one dimension but not on both are called *congruent types*. There may be a slight but unimportant tendency toward congruency on the institution–impulse dimension, but not on the social–individual axis. The first and third most frequent combinations, constituting nearly a quarter of all the subjects, juxtapose an impulse true self with an institutional criterion for inauthenticity (Table 4–3). The remainder of the five most popular combinations, which together make up half the responses, are pure types. Intimacy–insincerity ranks second, and the two institutional

Table 4–2. Correlation Between True Self and Spurious Self.

	Observed Frequency/Expected Frequency				
Type of True Self Experience	*Type of Spurious Self Experience*				
	Failure	*Selfishness*	*Plastic*	*Insincerity*	*Total*
Achievement	124/107	60/64	26/24	53/68	263
Altruism	82/97	101/58	13/22	42/61	238
Impulse release	130/130	67/77	35/29	86/82	318
Intimacy	181/183	80/109	43/42	146/116	450
Total	517	308	117	327	1,269

Note:
Coefficient of Contigency = .23
Chi-square = 68.480, 9 df, $p < .001$

All pure types	1.31
Institution-impulse congruent types	.95
Noncongruent types	.88
Social-individual congruent types	.86
Noncongruent types	.92

Table 4–3. Frequency of True Self–Spurious Self Combinations.

True Self–Spurious Self	*Frequency*	*Rank Order*	*Percent*	*Cumulative Percent*
Intimacy–Failure	181	1	14.3	14.3
Intimacy–Insincerity	146	2	11.5	25.8
Impulse release–Failure	130	3	10.2	36.0
Achievement–Failure	124	4	9.8	45.8
Altruism–Selfishness	101	5	8.0	53.8
Impulse release–Insincerity	86	6	6.8	60.6
Altruism–Failure	82	7	6.4	67.0
Intimacy–Selfishness	80	8	6.3	73.3
Impulse release–Selfishness	67	9	5.3	78.6
Achievement–Selfishness	60	10	4.7	83.3
Achievement–Insincerity	53	11	4.2	87.5
Intimacy–Plastic	43	12	3.4	90.9
Altruism–Insincerity	42	13	3.3	94.2
Impulse release–Plastic	35	14	2.8	97.0
Achievement–Plastic	26	15	2.0	99.0
Altruism–Plastic	13	16	1.0	100.0
Total	1,269		100.0	
Collapsed Combinations				
Pure and congruent institutional	367		28.9	
Pure and congruent impulse	310		24.4	
Institutional true self–Impulse spurious self	134		10.6	
Impulse true self–Institutional spurious self	458		36.1	
Total	1,269		100.0	

pure types rank fourth and fifth. At the opposite pole of frequency, the institutional true self–impulse spurious self combinations rank eleventh, thirteenth, fifteenth, and sixteenth. The various combinations of impulse true self with institutional spurious self make up over a third of all responses, while the institutional true self–impulse spurious self combinations account for only 11 percent of the cases.

It is also notable that when the spurious self anchorage is impulse, it is much more likely to be the social form (insincerity) than the individual form (plastic behavior). The four combinations involving the plastic behavior criterion for spuriousness rank twelfth, fourteenth, fifteenth, and sixteenth, while the counterpart true self anchorages of impulse release appear in third, sixth, ninth, and fourteenth positions. If the lower boundary of the self tends to be institutional, it tends to be social when not institutional.

Using the four collapsed sets of combination types, we have examined the relationships with several variables that should theoretically be correlated (Table 4-4). First, while women are usually found to be more conforming and accepting of the institutional system, their more salient identification of self seems to be with the realm of impulse. But there is no evidence that the relationships between true and spurious self anchorages are different for the sexes, since the sexual difference is greatest for the pure and congruent types, the males being more institutional.

Marital status, religious belief, and eminence aspiration were hypothesized to signify institutional anchorages. An apparent tendency for the married to answer more often in pure and congruent institutional terms falls just short of statistical significance. Students who answered the question, "Religiously do you consider yourself a believer or a nonbeliever?" by checking "believer" gave self-identification in one of the pure and congruent institutional combinations significantly more often than nonbelievers. Students were asked, "After you are established in your long-term career, when will you consider yourself successful enough to relax and stop trying very hard to get further ahead?" Those who answered this eminence aspiration question by checking answers from "never" to "when I have won the respect of my colleagues" significantly more often recorded self anchorages in the pure and congruent institutional categories than those who checked "as soon as I am secure in the occupation." While the combined types and these three variables are related as expected, the relationships do not single out distinctive functions for the upper and lower boundaries of the self. They tend rather to support an interpretation that the mixed types represent cases in which the self-conception is not simply and securely anchored in either institution or impulse.

A battery of four items was used to measure faith in institutions, including government, the economy, educational institutions, and organized religion. We hypothesized that the institutionally anchored should evaluate these established institutions more favorably than the impulse-anchored. A second battery of four items measured faith in people, including the belief that one can count on friends and peo-

Table 4–4. Collapsed True Self–Spurious Self Combinations by Selected Variables.

Selected Variables	*Pure and Congruent Institution*	*Pure and Congruent Impulse*	*Institution–Impulse*	*Impulse–Institution*
	Percent (Summed Horizontally)			
Men	37.5	18.2	10.8	33.5
Women	23.8	27.0	11.8	37.4
		Chi-square = 28.60, $p < .001$		
Married	37.7	19.7	13.1	29.5
Single	29.2	23.3	11.0	36.5
		Chi-square = 7.05, $p < .10$		
Believer	33.8	18.5	10.8	36.9
Nonbeliever	27.1	26.4	12.0	34.5
		Chi-square = 11.59, $p < .01$		
High eminence aspiration	32.1	19.9	11.9	36.1
Low eminence aspiration	28.4	31.5	8.6	31.5
		Chi-square = 12.12, $p < .01$		
High faith in institutions	35.6	19.0	10.0	35.4
Low faith in institutions	24.2	28.3	10.9	36.6
		Chi-square = 25.25, $p < .001$		
High faith in people	31.0	22.4	9.8	36.8
Low faith in people	26.4	26.9	11.5	35.2
		Chi-square = 4.50, N.S.		
High self-acceptance	32.0	22.3	12.5	33.2
Low self-acceptance	25.5	26.8	8.5	39.2
		Chi-square = 15.94, $p < .01$		
High self-search	27.2	24.8	9.8	38.2
Low self-search	31.0	24.0	11.5	33.5
		Chi-square = 4.38, N.S.		
Australian National Univ.	27.9	23.1	8.4	40.6
LaTrobe Univ. (Australia)	27.7	23.9	12.1	36.3
Surrey Univ. (England)	37.3	19.7	11.3	31.7
UCLA	23.4	31.3	10.6	34.7
		Chi-square = 25.52, $p < .01$		

ple generally for help in an emergency, and a positive estimate of folk wisdom. Endorsement of these items should be consistent with an impulse self anchorage, though a positive attitude toward institutions might also include a positive attitude toward people. Subjects expressing pure and congruent institutional self anchorages are significantly more favorable toward established social institutions. But faith in persons does not distinguish significantly between the self anchorages. These findings again do not clarify the distinctive functions of the true and spurious self thresholds.

Two other aspects of the self-conception were examined. An abbreviated version of the Berger (1952) self-acceptance inventory consisting of nine items was included in the questionnaire. The measure of self-acceptance was significantly associated with the self-anchorages. The highest rate of self-acceptance characterizes the relatively small group of mixed institutional true self–impulse spurious self types, with the pure and congruent institutionals only four percentage points lower. The pure and congruent impulse and mixed impulse true self–institutional spurious self types have almost the same lower rate of self-acceptance. The apparent conclusion from this association is that an institutional true self is associated with high self-acceptance and an impulse true self with low self-acceptance, while the anchorage of the spurious self is unrelated to self-acceptance. Here we have our first possible clue to different functions for the true and spurious self.

Subjects were also asked to agree or disagree on a five-point scale with two statements: "I often ask myself, who am I really?" and "My idea of myself is constantly changing." There was no observed relationship between these items and the self types.

Finally, there were significant differences among the four universities, some of which were consistent with common suppositions concerning national differences. The American university, UCLA, was highest on pure and congruent impulse anchorage, and the British university, Surrey, was highest on pure and congruent institutional anchorage. It is less obvious why the Australian National University should be highest on the impulse true self–institution spurious self combinations.

IMPRESSIONISTIC EXAMINATION OF COMBINATION TYPES

If we are to interpret the foregoing statistical findings and understand the relationship between true and spurious self anchorages, we must look more closely at the actual responses given by representatives of some of the combination types.

Intimacy-Failure

The most frequent combination type for women and the third most frequent for men is experience of the true self in intimacy and experience of spuriousness in failure. The accounts of authentic self-experience through intimacy have a familiar and almost stereotypic ring for readers familiar with the current rhetoric of self-disclosure. In these accounts the subjects discovered themselves in face-to-face interactive situations in which the customary barriers to uninhibited expression of feelings were absent or evaporated early in the interaction. The sense of authenticity did not arise from any sense of achievement or control in the situation, nor from well-conceived arguments or victory in social exchange, but from the exhilaration of communicating feelings freely. But in the most frequent combination (intimacy–failure) the lower self-boundary is not stated in terms of insincerity or restraints on self-disclosure. A tentative interpretation is that these subjects have been able to accommodate the customary restraints on free expression of feelings within the bounds of the customary self. The vital sense of inauthenticity comes from a different dimension of experience.

Careful reading of the protocols reveals a prevalent pattern. Few of these subjects refer to achievement in a task sense. The references are overwhelmingly to a loss of control, either of the situation or of self in the situation. In one instance the loss of personal control theme becomes salient in what might first sound like a simple case of insincerity. After reporting a typical true self experience in a reunion with old friends, one male subject reported the inauthenticity experience upon going out to dinner one evening with a "guy" who expressed views on a host of issues which contradicted the subject's, but to which the subject agreed.

> The odd thing about this occasion was that I had no reason at all to agree with this guy to keep him happy. He was not my elder, I didn't "need" anything from him, I was not overanxious to keep him as a friend, there was just no reason at all not to tell this guy he was full of shit. But I didn't! I began to think, Jesus! This guy is supporting everything that I thought I stood against—why didn't I tell him so? To this day I wonder why I didn't say anything. It scares me a little that I'm so weak-willed.

In another instance the problem of control centers about an inhibitory feeling of inferiority. A male subject describes the true self experience.

> Being with my old relatives in Sweden, I have no inhibitions. They don't judge me but take me for what I am. I don't feel I have to put myself on for them for fear of being rejected.

The subject feels inauthentic:

> Many times when I meet new people (mostly university students) of my own age. I feel inferior many times, sometimes physically, sometimes intellectually.

In one sense this appears contradictory to the locus of true self experience, since it is the lack of salient control by self or others that facilitates the sense of authenticity in the intimate relationship. But the contradiction is real only if we assume that the situation is constant. When the situation becomes so secure that the exercise and display of control are no longer necessary, the experience of authenticity is possible. But when the situation deteriorates to the point that the exercise of control is unsuccessful, the experience of inauthenticity occurs.

Others of these subjects have personal commitments that constitute the lower boundaries of the self. The honoring of these commitments does not produce the more intense true self experience, as it would for some institutionals. But their violation produces the sense of spuriousness. One female subject wrote in part:

> One occasion when I felt "genuine and authentic" was an argument or rather, a heated discussion with a close girl friend since eighth grade . . . instead of just passing over what she had done and not commenting on it (which is a habit of mine when talking to her sometimes), I voiced my disapproval and told what I thought of people that did that . . . I was able to tell off a good friend. . . .

> . . . The occasions when I felt my actions contradicted my true self were when I would go shopping or goof around when I had more important things such as schoolwork to do. . . . It's a feeling of "I know I should be studying but I don't want to miss out on any fun." My real self is much more concerned with school and grades but often times my actions do not reflect that attitude. . . .

These subjects, however they may address their own relationship to the institutional structure, find the true self in going beyond social order, rather than in repudiating it. The experience of inauthenticity rather than the experience of authenticity reveals the rootedness of the self in the institutional structure.

Impulse Release–Failure

An emphasis on freedom runs through many of the impulse release–failure protocols and links the authenticity and spuriousness experiences. But as we have already indicated, the exercise of freedom requires a situation under control. For example, a student who had formerly suffered numerous breakdowns experienced what might have been a disabling high, but discovered in the experience "new expectations or limitations of myself in regard to school and career. I felt anger and love with respect to my girlfriend." But on the other hand, the experience of inauthenticity was also associated with a "high," as follows:

> When I get high I become a playboy and inauthentic. Just recently when I was high I was pursuing several females in an inauthentic way. I felt unreal. I was actually depressed yet I was acting in a very gay and fun way coupled with hostility.

The experience of intense feeling is a precarious one that may lead to self-discovery or loss of control. But the personal commitment is to a kind of personal stability. When that stability is broken, the experience is one of unreality; when it is retained but enriched, the experience is one of authenticity.

Perhaps most often the crucial difference between true and spurious self experience is in the situation and the kind of impulses it evokes. One subject recalls a true self experience:

> It was after the fall quarter and my finals were done. I didn't have any classes to study for. I didn't have to go to track workouts. I could just be myself. . . . I was sort of carefree come-and-go when I wanted. I wasn't pressed by time. I could do just about anything I wanted at that time. Play football or basketball, go to parties, and make love to all the girls I wanted to.

But the same subject feels inauthentic when:

> I had got in a bitter debate with a young lady and she started attacking me with all kinds of nasty words. So I attacked her back but using worse language than she did. I hardly ever get upset to the point I let a girl force me to use the type of language I did, all the words were four-letter words. . . .

This man, like many of our subjects, finds his true self in a freeing situation. But the free expression of impulse when that impulse suggests loss of personal control is not experienced as the true self. The true self situation is perceived as removal of customary pressures, while the spurious self situation intensifies pressures.

Pure Types

Representatives of the pure type of intimacy–insincerity are like the first type in the sense of release and interpersonal closeness that marks the true self experience. But their experience of inauthenticity comes with the complementary situation in which they either passively fail to express their feelings in a situation in which they have strong feelings, or they actively dissimulate their feelings.

In most of these protocols there is a comprehensive contrast in the two group situations. The true self setting is a primary group, usually old friends, free of ritual and quite egalitarian. The inauthenticity setting is typically a more impersonal, transient group, often involving strangers and often highly ritualized or with a well-defined relationship of subordination to superordinates such as employers or parents. Compared with the two combined types, these subjects do not display a problem of self-control or situation control. Perhaps they are more socially competent so that the institutional preconditions to self-feeling are no longer salient. They are therefore sensitized to spuriousness at a lower point along the same dimension on which the true self experience takes place.

The fourth-ranking achievement–failure combination also exhibits a much simpler structure than the mixed types. Often the two accounts are counterpart stories involving, respectively, success and failure in two situations.

The fifth-ranking altruism combination is equally simple in most cases. The majority of instances involve helping or not helping at a personal level. Of all the types, the altruism–selfishness combination seems to equate the self dimension with value most completely. In some instances subjects rejected the idea that one could be more oneself on some occasions than others and explicitly offered realization or violation of a central life value as an alternative way of answering the question. In other instances there was unhesitating answer in terms of value. Some of the achievement–failure combinations are similarly equated with a life value, but one that is self-oriented rather than other-oriented. Many of the achievement–failure combinations, however, equate self with control more than with adherence to or attainment of particular values.

Institution–Impulse Combinations

In contrast to these most frequent combinations are the least frequent, combining an institution true self with an impulse spurious self. The most numerous of the institution–impulse combinations is achievement–insincerity. The true self is realized in the exhilarating experience of accomplishing a difficult task or exercising and maintaining self and interpersonal control in a challenging situation. In most of these cases the problem of insincerity appears to be related to the achievement motivation. The examples of inauthenticity seem to fall into two types. One context of inauthenticity is the involvement in groups representing incompatible values and lifestyles. The subject is unable to be honest and open either with the family or some other exponent of a more traditional lifestyle or with peers who represent a new or deviant lifestyle. The other type consists of instances in which the effort to master a situation exacts an unacceptable cost in personal misrepresentation and social distance.

The responses classified as achievement–plastic are quite similar, except that the violation of self lies in having acted against impulse rather than participating in an artificial interpersonal relationship. Most of the examples fall into the second type in which mastery, ambition, or sense of responsibility leads to self-alienation. In some of these instances the individual's sense of responsibility led to carrying more than one's fair share in a collaborative effort or sticking by a promise to a friend who never appreciated the sacrifice.

The altruistic–insincerity and altruistic–plastic combinations find the true self in some kind of service rendered for others and feel spurious in being pressured into representing themselves or acting in ways that misrepresent their real feelings. In some instances the true self and spurious self behavior is not greatly different, but the recipient is different. Service is performed for children and the needy, while concessions made to persons not obviously in special need are resented.

In understanding these institution–impulse combinations, it is helpful to remember that subjects with these self anchorages tend to register a high degree of self-acceptance. Indeed, the true self protocols exude this confidence in their own capabilities. The spurious self protocols convey the sense that they need not have compromised themselves in response to social pressure, except in those cases in which the problem is intimacy in a family that represents a traditional lifestyle.

SUMMARY AND INTERPRETATION

From the more objective portion of the foregoing analysis comes a series of findings concerning the relationship between true self and spurious self anchorages. There is a substantial tendency toward anchorage of true and spurious self experience in the same quadrant based on the two dimensions of institution–impulse and social–individual referents. But there is also a strong and consistent tendency for the true self to imply an impulse self anchorage and the spurious self experience to imply an institutional self anchorage. The anchorages for true and spurious self experiences relate similarly to what may be regarded as validating variables, such as sex, religious belief, marital status, and faith in social institutions. But in one suggestive finding, a measure of self-acceptance is related to the true self anchorage but not to the spurious self anchorages.

An impressionistic reading of selected protocols suggests several possible bases for the different anchorages of true self and spurious self experience. First is orientation to different interaction groups or audiences. The individual experiences a vital sense of authenticity in one group and has difficulty avoiding a sense of inauthenticity in another group. If we continue to work with the assumption that there is a trans-situational self-conception, the observation of different group settings helps to explain how potentially contradictory anchorages are managed through segregating experience, but not why there should be different self-anchorages.

The second basis for different self-anchorages may be that the spurious self experience relates to a *pre*condition rather than a sufficient condition for the sense of personal authenticity. The prevalent theme of loss of control in the accounts of inauthenticity, especially for those subjects who experience their true selves in impulse, suggests this observation. Achieving minimal self-control and control of a situation is not enough to evoke a vital self experience. But it is essential as a precondition to the kind of further experience that will evoke this sense. In a more general sense, there is always a minimal degree of conformity and personal coping with the institutional structure below which there can only be personal disorientation. Manford Kuhn (1954) made the correct assumption in hypothesizing self anchorage in the more or less consensual social order; he failed merely to recognize that the positive feeling of authenticity requires going beyond the level that merely avoids inauthenticity, with the result that other criteria often become relevant.

A third basis for different self anchorages is suggested by the observation that the inauthenticity experience often relates to products of an earlier period of socialization than does the authenticity experience. Frequently the institutionally anchored inauthenticity experience occurs with the family, while the impulse-anchored authenticity experience occurs with peers. If the individual had successfully transferred the locus and anchorage of self-feeling, abandoning the early for the late, there would be no feeling of inauthenticity in the settings related to early socialization—only indifference. But the effect of early socialization persists, not as a resource in attaining a sense of authenticity but as a potential source for inauthenticity feelings.

These three considerations are not mutually exclusive and can often be observed simultaneously in a single pair of protocols. Earlier socialization may have more to do with establishing the preconditions for coping with society and maintaining personal identity. The directions in which the vital sense of self is found may be established through later socialization, and the conditions for its realization more often found in more recent group settings.

There are some cases, however, that appear to contradict this pattern, especially the infrequent institution true self–impulse spurious self combinations. In these instances the spurious self experience more often seems to be a byproduct or "cost" of the attainment of the true self experience. Subjects who are driven by a quest for achievement or realization of a value discover themselves doing things they don't want to do and presenting a contrived front to their associates, which makes them feel inauthentic. An individual depends on at least two conditions in naming a particular experience as the occasion for some kind of self-feeling: whether that kind of experience evokes the self-feeling, and whether the experience is salient enough to be mentioned. It is reasonable to suppose that the subjects who combine institution-anchored true self experience with impulse-anchored spurious self experience simply encounter crucial failures in the institutional sphere much less often than they experience the sense of dissimulating and suppressing. The fact that they are characterized by relatively high levels of self-acceptance lends plausibility to this interpretation.

Our analysis has revolved around four ways in which the self-conception can be anchored. First, there are a large number of students whose self-conceptions are highly integrated into the institutional structure, to the extent that they have little sensitivity to any distinction between a normative self and a real self. Second, the largest number of students still encounter disorientation when minimal personal integration into the institutional structure fails, but reflect historical change in discovering the true self in experiences that seem to transcend the institutional sphere. A third and large group seem to have left the institutional anchorage behind altogether. In many cases we suspect it is because they have been sheltered from fundamental reality testing to such an extent that the preconditions to personal orientation in society have not been salient. The fourth and smallest group have adopted some segment of the institutional structure as anchorages for their true selves with such intensity that the salient experience of inauthenticity has become that of suppressing impulse and dissimulating in their relations with others.

5 THE FUNCTIONS AND FOIBLES OF NEGOTIATING SELF-CONCEPTION

Kenneth J. Gergen

This chapter will attempt to challenge several longstanding assumptions about the concept of self and to offer an alternative view of broad implication. In particular, questions will be raised with the view of self-concept as a cognitive structure that becomes progressively more stabilized, differentiated, and accurate as it is tested against aspects of the empirical world of self and environment. In contrast, the groundwork will be laid for viewing self-conception as a product of ongoing social interchange; its functions must be traced to the process of adaptation to the realm of intersubjectivity. The contours of these arguments and their implications will be more sharply delineated as the arguments progress.

Let us begin by considering the nature of self-experience and, particularly, experience of inner process. When people reflect on their experience during most interaction sequences, they would appear faced with what might be described as undifferentiated rousing. That is, they are aware of changes in momentary intensity—qualitative shifts across time—but states without clear boundary lines. People can often recall the particular images, sounds, or other sensations that entered experience from without, or fantasied actions, and perhaps even the fragments of an idea nearing expression. However, independent of input from the external world, or imagined actions in that world, a murky ambiguity seems to prevail with respect to the identity of ideas or feelings. It further appears that this rather undifferentiated murk may continue to prevail even when behavior is functionally successful. In other words, whether in the midst of an intense encounter with a friend, delivering a lecture, or trying to return a deep volley to the backhand, the person doesn't seem capable of identifying a clear set of feelings or thoughts that serve as obvious antecedents for his or her behavior.

Several lines of empirical research seem to support this contention. In their classic work on emotional recognition, Schachter and his colleagues have argued, for example, that there is little to differentiate among various emotional states on a purely physiological level (Schachter 1964; Schachter and Singer 1962). Rather, he argues, people more frequently experience generalized states of arousal; the way in which they define such arousal is largely influenced by the environmental context. In particular, people learn to label emotional states according to what is appropriate for a given circumstance. They may experience roughly the same form of arousal in the presence of children, a long-term friend, a long-revered teacher, or a lover. However, the manner in which they identify the arousal, whether it be parental affection, deep friendship, admiration, or romantic love, seems to depend primarily on the identity of the other. This line of thinking has been supported in a wide variety of studies on the identification of such emotional states as euphoria, anger, pain, and romantic love (see Berscheid and Walster 1974; Keoske and Keoske 1975; Nisbett and Schachter 1966; Valins 1966). Although there do appear to be limitations over this line of argument (Plutchik and Ax 1962; Marshall 1976; Maslach 1979), such research does illustrate that at a minimum, labelling of emotions is highly susceptible to contextual inputs. Emotional arousal alone does not lend itself to unequivocal identification.

Nisbett and his colleagues (Nisbett and Bellows 1977; Nisbett and Wilson 1977) have made a similar set of arguments with respect to cognitive processing. Research in the cognitive area generally indicates that although people are frequently aware of the results of their thinking, they do not seem to have significant access to the preceding line of mental events (Mandler 1975; Neisser 1967). As I sit writing this, for instance, I find the words arranging themselves in a sequence that, to my surprise, possess a reasonable orderliness. I do not know how the thoughts developed or collected themselves in this way.

Such processes of thought do not reach the state of conscious awareness; however, the products continue to spill themselves onto the page.

As research in this domain further demonstrates, when people are asked about their cognitions, they typically answer in terms of cultural rules pertaining to how they *should* be processing information (Nisbett and Bellows 1977). Thus, if people are shown a film under various levels of distracting noise they will say that their evaluations of the film have been influenced by the distracting noise even when there is no evidence for such effects. They do so, it is argued, because common knowledge suggests that they should be influenced. At the same time, because of the commonly accepted rules, people may discount the effects of their thinking processes when in fact they do make a difference (Nisbett and Wilson 1977). Factors such as the order in which evaluations are made may influence their positiveness. Yet, because cultural wisdom doesn't currently recognize this possibility, people may not judge that their mental processes have been biased in this way. Again, there may be limitations to this general line of argument (Smith and Miller 1978). It does appear, however, that the weight of the illustrative evidence lends strong support to Nisbett's contentions. We do not seem capable of looking inward and differentiating among or identifying with precision how we are thinking.

Much the same message lies buried in the spate of recent research on causal attribution. People might wish to think that they can look inward and identify when they make an autonomous decision to act. They want to believe that they can distinguish between instances in which they made a personal decision to act as opposed to being forced by circumstance. Surely, such distinctions abound in public discourse. People say that they do X because they thought about it and decided they wanted to do it, but that they were forced into doing Y out of threat. Yet, as research in this area demonstrates with compelling consistency, whether people view a given action as autonomously determined or situationally induced is highly malleable, and may be altered with relative ease. They may look back at the same behavior and reattribute its causal source depending on a variety of factors. For example, if an action ends successfully, they may come to believe that they have made an autonomous decision; if the outcome is poor, they will then perceive the same actions to have been forced by circumstance (Miller 1976; Streufert and Streufert 1969; Wiener and Kukla 1970). Further, people may reinterpret whether they have caused a given action depending on where they direct their attention in the sequence of events under review (Brickman, Ryan, and Wortman 1975; Taylor and Fiske 1975). As attention is turned to different aspects of the situation and to its antecedents, perception of causal locus for a given action may change dramatically. In effect, the causal source of a given action does not appear to be open to empirical assessment (Gergen and Gergen 1978).

Let us now turn more directly to the problem of self-conception. It has been traditionally maintained, both within the social sciences and society in general, that if the individual can but delve beneath the superficial overlay of everyday activity, he or she may locate a true and genuine basis for identity. If one can but look inward, examining carefully his or her feelings, thoughts, hopes, fears, motives, and so on, one can discover a true self, an experiential bedrock for identity. One may be able to determine whether, for example, fear or love of subject matter are truly motivating one's career aspirations; whether one is thinking clearly about one's relationships as opposed to rationalizing; whether one is setting one's course of action in an autonomous and forthright way as opposed to merely doing what others want. As can now be seen, to look inward for a clear and defining experience that may serve as an anchor for identity is not likely to yield success. Rather, in looking inward one primarily faces an obscure morass which may, with effort, yield up most any answer one faces (or fears). Inner experience of self is essentially constructed, and the form of this construction does not appear to be driven or determined by the experience itself.

DOES BEHAVIOR ANCHOR SELF-CONCEPTION?

If one cannot turn inward for a substantive basis for self-conception, what is to suffice for such purposes? What is to insulate self-conception against the whim of changing social current? On what firm basis can self-conception be reliably constructed? Perhaps the most obvious answer is contained in the existentialist emphasis on self-realization through behavioral commitment. As Nietzche once proclaimed, "Truth is for the individual as he himself produces it in action." This position seems eminently reasonable. Behavior is clearly and unambiguously apparent; we can all agree on whether it exists or not. Thus, for example, if one wishes to determine whether he or she is a good gymnast, one's gymnastic performance may be consulted. Does it succeed in landing one a position on the gymnastic team, or does it help to win team competitions? By the same token, one may know whether he or she is a thief by observing whether he or she has engaged in thievery, or may decide whether he or she is a warm and friendly person by observing whether he or she acts in a warm and friendly manner toward others. In more recent times this position has been adopted by Bem (1972) who has argued that the individual essentially determines what his attitudes are by making inferences from his own conduct. How do I know I am a lover of brown bread? asks Bem. By looking at what I do. If I find myself ravenously consuming brown bread, I can know that I like it.

Yet, when this line of argument is examined more carefully, important shortcomings are revealed. There are two major problems to be considered. The first is tied to what may be called the *enigma of cross-category translation*. This refers to the difficulty faced by the individual in translating an ongoing, shifting array of behavioral particulars into a temporally stable conceptual system. In effect, in the act of conceptualization the individual engages in the hazardous translation of process into structure. To illustrate, one might judge whether one was a good gymnast by consulting one's success in winning a gymnastic competition. However, winning a particular competition is but a single act in a broad stream of ever-changing events, while *being* a good gymnast implies a state of continuing identity. How can one be certain that the single passing event qualifies one for such trans-temporal classification? Similarly, does a single act of thievery merit the ascription that one is a thief? After all, the individual who steals on Thursday may have been wholly honest on all preceding days of the week. Is it proper to single out his probablistically peculiar actions of a Thursday as a basis for a classification that recognizes no temporal boundaries? Similarly, what proportion of comforting words must be spoken in a given period of time before one can properly view oneself as warm and friendly? Do one's moments of frowning or quiet withdrawal contribute simultaneously to the concept "cold and anti-social"? In effect, there are no clear ground rules for translating from events in motion to the stable world of self-conceptualization. Nor, given the essential differences in these modes, can the development of such rules be anticipated. An experiential world of process simply does not lends itself to translation into static terms. The ongoing stream of behavoral action is irreparably altered in the act of description.

The second major problem in attempting to base self-conception on overt behavior rests in the multiple and mutable rules for interpreting action. Just as in the case of emotions, behavioral acts do not come packaged with handy labels. One is essentially faced with continuous and ever-changing configurations of great complexity. It is hardly overstating the case to say that people never furnish each other with precisely the same patterns of action throughout an entire lifetime. Further, actions are not typically identified by their properties in themselves, but with respect to the underlying intention of the actor. An act of aggression cannot properly be classed as such unless one intends to aggress. As we have seen, the intentions themselves are not unequivocally identifiable. Thus, there may be considerable latitude available to the individual in terms of (a) what counts as a behavioral event, and (b) what concept or label is to be applied once the behavioral event is recognized. Different cultures at different points in history may recognize different sets of behavioral acts, and those acts may be subject to multiple conceptual or verbal labels.

To illustrate, in terms of the behavioral repertoire, in modern America people don't generally single out as having special significance the length and direction of gaze after performing a social toast. Such activity is not recognized as forming a meaningful pattern or behavioral event. In contrast, for a modern Dane, the length and direction of gaze form an extremely important component of the toasting ritual. Failing to perform the act properly may be viewed as highly discourteous. Similarly, cultures of the past did not recognize patterns of behavior that today we might call "cool," "straight" or "radical chic." In the case of multiple labels, we find that virtually any action is open to an immense number of competing and conflicting interpretations. Thus, for example, a single act of smiling may be viewed as a signal of affection, a means of avoiding intense relations, a plastic facade, a signal of class partisanship, or even an act of derision or aggression. The behavior remains precisely the same, but the interpretation is subject to dramatic variation depending on the viewpoint of the observer.

It is these sorts of variations in meaning and their social origins to which ethnomethodologists have devoted major attention (see Cicourel 1968; Garfinkel 1967). As one recent exploration demonstrates, there is considerable disagreement in the rules of the culture for determining gender. In general people think it is a simple matter to distinguish males from females; anyone who makes a mistake in such matters might be subject to derision. Yet, as Kessler and McKenna (1978) show, when more closely examined, considerable conflict is found in the rules of concept application. Children use different gender cues than do adults. Transsexuals use different rules than heterosexuals. Different criteria for gender are applied in the legal and medical professions. A person may define herself as a female, and be happily married under such a definition, only to find herself eliminated from competing in women's athletics on other grounds. It thus remains ambiguous as to who counts as male or female, and indeed, whether gender is not altogether a social construction.

As a result of the mutable and multiple rules of interpreting action, the placement of one's behavioral actions into any given concept or category is rendered problematic. One can observe one's own actions, but it remains highly ambiguous as to how one is to conceptualize them. Is an act of taking merchandise from a store without paying truly an act of thievery? It can also be viewed as an act of class warfare, a means of showing off to one's peers, a means of boosting one's self-esteem, an act of symbolic retaliation against power figures, and so on. The act itself gives us only the *excuse* for conceptualization; in itself it furnishes precious little grounds for deciding which concept applies.

It is perhaps for these reasons that the early research in which my colleagues and I were involved—namely, the investigation of situated self-conception—met with the success it did. As this research demonstrated, people were quite willing to alter their self-evaluation as others' evaluations of them changed in a situation (Gergen 1965). These changes were both publicly and privately expressed. Further, as one encountered others who were either highly desirable or undesirable in appearance, their own self-estimates changed (Morse and Gergen 1970). When a desirable person was encountered, self-evaluation plummeted; when an undesirable appeared, self-estimates were often boosted. And, self-evaluation changed as people concentrated on certain past experiences (Gergen and Taylor 1967) or commiserated with someone who was self-critical (Gergen and Wishnov 1965). In all these cases, people were found to be highly malleable with respect to self-conception. They would readily and willingly reconstruct their perceptions of self across time and situation (Gergen 1977).

To summarize the argument thus far, it is found that neither an examination of one's internal experience nor of one's external behavior furnishes objective grounds for self-conceptualization. The manner in which one conceptually constructs one's emotions, thoughts, and decisions is open to a broad range of exogenous influences. There appears to be precious little of sufficient clarity or palpability concerning the experience of mental or emotional life to furnish a reliable self-definition. Further, there appears little salvation in falling back on overt observable acts for a substantive basis for self-conception. Not only is it unclear how persons are to move from the level of continuous behavioral process to the static level of concepts but the rules for determining what counts as a behavioral act and how it is to be understood are also multiple and ever-changing. The conceptual construction of behavior is open to continued social negotiation.

IMPLICATIONS OF A GROUNDLESS SELF-CONCEPTION

If this major line of argument seems compelling, one should be prepared to accept several unsettling implications. First, there may be no means of satisfactorily substantiating any given concept of self. As demonstrated, the individual cannot alone identify with any merited confidence the nature of personal characteristics, motives, thoughts, or attributes. If one cannot trust oneself in this endeavor, then how can any other single person be trusted? There is logically no single person (including close friends, therapists, etc.) who can be trusted for an empirically valid account of character. And, if persons lack trust in any single individual, there is little reason to place trust in broad social consensus. From the present standpoint, consensus is not sufficient to establish "what is the case": it serves primarily as an indicator of agreeable or disagreeable interpretation. In terms of its reliance on objective evidence, such interpretation may be considered little more than folk mythology. In effect, one's identifying characteristics are not a given but a mythological creation, whether the source resides in the individual alone or in the social milieu.

A second implication of the preceding argument is that the process of self-conceptualization is highly circumscribed. Such conceptions may not figure prominently in the individual's attempt to function adequately in most settings. Why does this follow? If the relationship between concepts and overt behavior is as ambiguous as the present arguments indicate, then the individual's attempt at conceptual analysis of the situation (including his or her potential actions in that situation), is not likely to yield unambiguous guidelines for action. If the rules connecting concepts and behavior are both multiple and mutable, then there is little way in which the individual can know what concepts apply to a situation and what behavior should follow from any given conceptual analysis. Thus, for example, if the individual reaches the conclusion that he or she is a moral person or wishes to become a moral person, it is simply not clear how the concept may be realized in any concrete instance. What actions fall within the category of morality? For example, many people find that eating meat is simply a common activity that raises no particular moral challenge. For other persons, the same activity may be considered highly immoral. Thus the contemplated action is both moral or immoral depending on the perspective or set of interpretive rules one selects on the occasion. In effect, conceptual conclusions do not in themselves dictate behavioral actions. Outside the demands for normative labelling, one may largely suspend considerations of conceptual definition in achieving adaptation to the continuous stream of challenges posed by the social milieu.

Support for this last conclusion can be garnered from a variety of different locales. For example, the Zen Buddhist tradition maintains a firm distinction between conceptual and nonconceptual thought. While the former is placed under severe attack, the latter is celebrated as the path to wisdom. From the Zen tradition, conceptual thinking places severe restrictions over one's experience. For instance, the five colors will blind a man's sight. The five senses will deaden a man's hearing. The five tastes will spoil a man's palate. The implication is that by classifying (or conceptualizing) the world of experience, sensitivity is lost to its many nuances. Rather than attempting to understand the rapid and ever-shifting character of our sense data in a conceptual way, argues the Zen philosopher, one's reactions are far more adequate if one responds in a more organic or holistic manner. "The perfect man employs his mind as a mirror," argues the Taoist priest, Chuang-tzu. "It grasps nothing, it refuses nothing. It receives but does not keep." In effect, the individual who seeks continuously to place incoming experience into categories may lose importantly in his or her capacity to respond adaptively to this experience.

A somewhat similar message is echoed in much of the research into the differential functioning of the two cortical hemispheres (Gazzaniga 1971; Levy–Agresti and Sperry 1968). This work indicates that for most people the left cortical hemisphere is primarily responsible for solving problems employing discrete entities, including linguistic categories or concepts. According to Bogen (1969), the left hemisphere is a center for "propositional thought," and the right hemisphere appears to play a primary role in what is termed "appositional thought," that is, "thought based on the simultaneous grasp of related but differing phenomena." The right hemisphere is primarily responsible for solving problems of form or quality, not of logic or quantity. From this standpoint self-conceptualization may play a role in logical or analytic thinking. It may play but a minor part in the moment-to-moment adjustments necessary for effective action in most complex, ongoing relations.

THE FUNCTIONS OF SELF-CONCEPTION

If self-conception is essentially mythical with respect to its reliance on empirical data and does not serve as a major means of solving the problems of moment-to-moment adaptation, then what purposes does it serve? There are two major purposes to which attention may be fruitfully directed: (a) ontologic acceptability and (b) personal enhancement.

Ontologic Acceptability

At the outset it would appear that the individual must be centrally concerned with "making sense" within any given culture or subculture in which he or she participates (see Shutz 1967). If one's actions are unintelligible within a given conceptual framework, if they are "nonsense," then social supports may rapidly drop away. The individual may be criticized, ostracized, persecuted, locked away, or even extinguished. Goffman's (1959) concept of a "moral career" is relevant to this point. If the individual does not share the rules of meaning within a particular subculture, he or she is "morally suspect."

Failing to share in the common rules throws one's identity into critical question. The obvious case is the individual who believes himself to be Jesus Christ or Napoleon. Typically such cases are isolated from society; they are insane.

From the present standpoint, however, there is no way of proving objectively that such aberrant self-identifications are empirically incorrect. After all, our conceptions of such figures as Napoleon or Christ are themselves forms of mythical construction, and many people are wholly prepared to accept a second coming of at least one of these two personages. To press further, legend has it that one of these figures, namely Jesus, was executed in part for claiming that he was Christ. His self-conception disagreed with that of the mainstream culture of the times. Yet, millions have been willing to accept this claim quite readily since the early period, and have executed many who disagree. People who today claim to be Christ are frequently incarcerated, essentially because they do not share in the rules for generating meaning within contemporary culture. Should they be capable of renegotiating the rules of social intelligibility, they might gain broad veneration. There is more to challenge public concern in the fact that the individual is unable to explain satisfactorily his or her aberrant behavior in the behavior itself. The behavior itself is not essentially problematic. The individual's inability to gain others' agreement about its meaning is portentious.

Turning to the more common case, a person may be chastized for conceptualizing his or her own behavior as competent, while others view it as incompetent; labelling one's own actions as warm and friendly while others see them as remote and aloof; viewing one's own emotions as depression where others label them "self-pity." In all such cases, the individual is at social risk until he or she can either jettison the socially unacceptable practice of negotiating reality or convince others to accept an alternative view of "the way things are."

From these arguments it follows that one principal use to which self-conception may be put is that of gaining (or maintaining) a state of what may be termed ontologic acceptability. That is, one may adopt particular self-referring labels in the attempt to insure that his or her formulation of reality is not significantly discrepant from those toward whom one is vulnerable. In maintaining a given self-definition, the individual reinforces or substantiates the network of agreements within the culture (or subculture) concerning the nature of reality.

The present line of argument prompts a reconsideration of the traditional symbolic interactionist account of self-concept formation. As Mead (1934), Cooley (1922), and others maintained, the individual's self-concept is largely a reflection of the views that others share toward the individual. The present arguments first supply a motivational basis for this "looking-glass-self" phenomenon. They suggest that others' opinions may be relied upon, first, because people do not generally find themselves in possession of sufficient evidence to furnish broad confidence in their own judgments of self. Their personal doubts may thus be assuaged by falling back on social consensus. Second, people may primarily turn to others in order to gain ontologic acceptability. To throw in with others' account of one's actions is to gain an important increment in security. It is to participate in the common view of reality.

By the same token, the present arguments indicate that the individual *need not* accept the views of others toward self. The literature in this area has tended to treat the looking-glass-self phenomenon as fundamentally lawful, and perhaps even essential for the development of basic self-conception. In describing the normal process by which self-conception is acquired lies a subtle prescription as to the grounds on which one should come to understand oneself. However, as now seen, the individual is confronted with choice. One may avoid groups whose rules of meaning operate to one's disadvantage, or may attempt to change those rules. This latter choice has been made by those labelled sexually "queer" by mainstream society. In recent times such persons have banded together to redefine the character of their activities in a more positive light, and have coupled these activities with an attempt to change the typical structure of meaning more common in society. They have developed the "homophobic" label to derogate those whose rules of meaning are repugnant to them, and remove homosexuality from the traditional nosology of character disorders.

Finally, the present analysis has implications for the change agent, including the therapist, counselor, educator, and parent concerned with personal or social change. One is often faced with an individual who suffers from a particular view of self, who believes him- or herself to be incompetent, worthless, unlovable, sexually inadequate, deviant, and so on. Typically the change agent sets out to understand the validity of such accounts. How incompetent is the individual, in fact? What skills are lacking, what particular actions are unlovable, what is the nature of his or her deviance? From the present standpoint, such a search is fundamentally misleading. It assumes that such descriptive accounts can be validated or invalidated by reference to observable behavior or verbal accounts of emotions or thoughts. As we have seen, the attempt at validation or falsification cannot yield objective results. That which can be located is a mutually acceptable account.

The proper search under such circumstances may be for means of enabling the individual to reconceptualize him- or herself. New rules, support groups, or negotiation tactics for self-interpretation may be required. One may ask such questions as these: What reference groups are supporting a self-defeating manner of definition? Must the individual continue to participate in such groups? Are there other groups which do not share these particular rule systems? Does one as change agent have the skills to renegotiate the meaning of the individual's actions in a way that is more personally satisfying to the individual? The point is not to "get to the bottom" of such problems but to examine people's rules of meaning, their origin, arbitrariness, and implications.

Personal Enhancement

As the meaning of one's actions or feelings are negotiated within the social milieu, one's personal state may be enhanced or diminished. Praise or criticism, pride or depression, stereotypy or enriched opportunities may all be generated by the particular concepts one employs in understanding oneself. If one believes oneself a failure, little may be attempted; if one fancies oneself a struggling romantic, mounting frustrations may be transformed into existential ecstasy; if people believe they need another's love, then they may organize their lives around the search. However, given the fundamental subjectivity of social definition, the individual is free to select those forms of self-understanding or self-conception that yield positive as opposed to negative outcomes. Self-conception can essentially be viewed as a matter of desire, need, taste, or purpose.

From this perspective it can be seen that such terms as self-deception, rationalization, and false consciousness may represent unwarranted attempts to legitimatize personal taste. That is, in using such terms to discredit another's account of reality, one makes implicit reference to an empirical standard of truth by which certain accounts are obviously deceiving or can be proven false. The change agent may feel a client is engaging in self-deception and try to demonstrate the error of his or her ways; the glutton who says he or she can't help eating may be accused of rationalization; and the housewife who says she actually likes this role may be viewed as a victim of false consciousness. In terms of the present account, none of these attacks is warranted on empirical grounds. They may be legitimate as expressions of personal disapproval of a given pattern of action. They can make no claim, however, for empirical superiority. By the same token, it can be seen that the individual is free to accept or reject such accusations on grounds of personal preference.

This last statement also serves as a convenient point upon which to extend the earlier argument for viewing the impact of social appraisal on self-conception as subject to voluntary decision. As we saw, gaining one's concept of self from others may hardly be considered an immutable given of social life. One is free to do otherwise, and to the extent that the principle is supported through research it may only be reflecting contemporary social mores (Gergen 1973). By the same token, other processes said to be important in generating self-conception may be viewed as potential as opposed to fundamental. To illustrate, Festinger's theory of social comparison (1954) has provoked a substantial research effort over the years, an effort generally devoted to establishing its empirical validity and generality. It is argued that social comparison is a basic generator of self-conception. One learns who one is by comparing one's characteristics with those of others (Morse and Gergen 1971). On the present account, people need not compare themselves with others as a means of determining who they are; the results of such comparisons inevitably reflect the individual's initial labelling of the other according to a fundamentally arbitrary set of standards (i.e., in order to know that I am "bad" I must first apply the concept of "good" to another's actions). One is free not to engage in such practices if one's experience of self is thereby diminished. Thus, the enlightened individual will engage in social comparison primarily when it yields a result that is personally satisfying. In an enlightened society social comparison might cease to be the highly general phenomenon that it is currently believed to be.

Finally, turning once again to the change agent, there is a need to begin more steadfast inquiry into the issue of communication skills (Rommetveit 1974). The change agent faced with a person whose self-conception is maladaptive might wish to direct attention to ways in which this conception can be renegotiated. The suffering individual essentially occupies this unfavorable position because he or she lacks skills in (a) employing alternative rules of meaning from those thrust upon him or her by the immediate social milieu, or (b) making these alternatives intelligible (i.e., acceptable) to others. The change agent may help the needy person to see that his or her actions are not as others see them, but ultimately the individual's resilience will depend on personal capacity for what we may term *generative* conceptualization (Gergen 1978), that is, the capacity to develop alternatives to the ontologic givens of the culture (or subculture) and to communicate about these in such a way as to undermine others' confidence in their own interpretations. As change agent, one should not only enable others to find alternatives to damaging self-conceptions but to locate means of engendering conceptual and persuasive skills that enable subsequent emancipation from them.

CONCLUSION

As this chapter has attempted to demonstrate, to view the self-concept as an empirically stabilized structure is subject to serious limitations. Abandonment of the longstanding belief that the individual attempts to develop an empirically accurate conception of self—either of interior process or external behavior—would seem auspicious. It is now essential to give thorough consideration to those social processes in which self-conception is inextricably lodged. A recentering is necessary—from a concern with cognitive process to that of social interchange. In a fundamental sense, cognition does not essentially determine social activity as much as social activity determines what we believe to constitute cognitive process.

6 REFLECTIVE PROCESS

Stephen P. Spitzer

(One hears all too often that symbolic interactionism, rather than constituting a body of theory, represents a body of sensitizing concepts.) At least two reasons for this attribution can be cited. The first pertains to disagreement regarding what is meant when the term theory is used. Theory usually refers to one or more propositions amenable to empirical test. Here the implication is that the terms of symbolic interactionism are generally not operationally specifiable. A second pertains to what is meant by the phrase empirical test. If we think of empirical test as resting upon methodologies that exclude ethnomethodological procedures as a proper part, testable propositions entailed by symbolic interactionism are almost exclusively restricted to the Mead–Cooley proposition that a person's self-conception is in large part a function of other people's reactions, actual or imagined, toward him or her. Numerous studies employing self–other rating procedures and based on the Mead–Cooley proposition are reported in the literature (Miyamoto and Dornbusch 1956; Quarentelli and Cooper 1966; Reeder, Donohue, and Biblarz 1960; Sherwood 1965).

Would it in any way facilitate convergence within current symbolic interactionism if one could cite and bring to test at least one additional self-oriented symbolic interactionist contention? Here I do not have in mind reviewing and selecting for test those propositions which have already been enumerated in various known listings

(Burke 1980; McCall 1977; Rose 1962; Spitzer et al. 1970). Rather I have in mind directing attention toward a proposition central to symbolic interactionist theory which is omitted by such listings and which has yet to be put to test—by either empiricist or ethnomethodological procedures. Certainly, such an endeavor could not insure any measure of convergence within symbolic interactionism, but it would be unlikely to exacerbate its already divergent tendencies. And it might just help to bring about some convergence between symbolic interactionists and sources of the somewhat disparaging "sensitizing concept" allegation.

Accordingly, one purpose of this chapter is to focus on one additional proposition articulated by Mead in his major works (1934, 1936, 1938) which is included in other writings in the symbolic interactionist tradition (Cooley 1922; E. Faris 1940; R.E.L. Faris 1952; Lindesmith and Strauss 1968; Miyamoto 1970; Shibutani 1961). A second purpose is to examine this proposition by contrasting groups of subjects that would be expected to show a difference on the property on which the proposition rests. Then, it is my intention to draw the connection between the focal Meadian proposition and other dependent variables, which in some cases are scores from psychometric instruments in use among sociologically oriented social psychologists. Finally, I will cite the results of two investigations in which the construct validity of the proposition is examined.

Let me first state the proposition as simply as possible and then proceed to define my terms. Reflection, or the reflective attitude, is said to emerge when conduct is interrupted, thus rendering ongoing action incapable of automatic continuation. That is, when action becomes problematic, the reflective attitude is assumed. In classic Meadian terminology, reflection is said to signify the condition of an organism when its own delayed responses enter the field of its own selectivity so that the organism becomes an object to itself. Stated in the terminology of modern set theory, reflection is present if *the image of the thinker of a set of thought is an element of the set of thoughts thought by a thinker*. In narrative terminology and employing responses to the Twenty Statements Test (TST) as a source of indicators of reflection, the attitude of reflection is one in which reference to the agent of an assertion is subsumed within the assertion made by its agent. That is, in responding to the injunction of self-identification, that is, "Who am I?," the person invokes reference to his own subjectivity as a defining element of self.

There are three types of reflective assertions. One class of reflective assertion (*pronominal*) is denoted by the presence of (a) one or more singular or plural personal pronouns (of nominative, possessive, or objective case) or (b) the reflexive pronouns, that is, self terms. Another class of reflective assertion (*paranominal*) is denoted by (a) abstract nouns naming mental concepts that are used such that (b) the action of the verb of the sentence points to the assertor. The analog for a third class of reflective assertion (*autodescriptive*) is given in the machinery characterizing certain many-valued logics (Rescher 1969), and terms such as conscious, reflective, and so on, serve the function of autodescription on the metalinguistic level when self-reference without compounding of parts is entailed.

EXPLORING REFLECTIVE PROCESSES

Discriminant Validation

We have conducted several studies following the general strategy of contrasting "known groups" by dividing sets of TST protocols according to some criterion variable and then determining the proportion of protocols in each subset showing one or more indicators of reflection. For example, subjects displaying anxiety are more likely to show reflection than nonanxious subjects because it is intimated (see Mead 1895, 1936) and expressly stated (see Faris 1952; Shibutani 1961) that emotion may be understood as an aspect of the process which takes place in the blocking of the act. When activity is inhibited, effort is required to find a means of resumption. If the demand characteristics of a task call for self-identification, the degree to which the act of self-identification is problematic should determine the level of tension exhibited by the subject. Therefore, subjects manifesting a tension level sufficiently high to qualify as anxiety should show greater indications of reflection than subjects in which tension level is low. As can be seen in Table 6-1, this prediction is confirmed.

Other studies follow the general strategy of selecting groups in which the degree of problematicity in self-identification might be expected to differ while controlling for other relevant personal, social, and demographic variables. Consequently, we have contrasted groups for which the rationale is self-evident, such as migrant versus

Table 6–1. Proportion of Subjects Showing One or More Indicators of Reflection by Dichotomized Samples.

Sample	*Dichotomy*	*N*	*Proportion Reflective*	*Differential*	*Test*[a]	*p*
University students	Anxious	47	.72	.29	$z = 2.29$	$< .05$
	Nonanxious	21	.43			
Psychiatric hospital prepatients	Anxious	30	.77	.27	$z = 2.30$	$< .05$
	Nonanxious	44	.50			
Oriental university students	Asian birth	49	.90	.27	$z = 3.25$	$< .001$
	U.S. birth	68	.63			
Upper-income matched females	Career	10	.80	.47	$z = 2.31$	$< .05$
	Housewife	9	.33			
Student trainees	Pastoral counseling	8	1.00	.50	$z = 6.34$	$< .001$
	Business admin.	12	.50			
Psychiatric hospital	Prepatients	74	.61		$x^2 = 7.69$	$< .05$
	Inpatients	53	.48			
	Postpatients	45	.36			
Prison inmates—conviction	Personal crime	17	.53	.35	$z = 2.30$	$< .05$
	Property crime	22	.18			
Prison inmates—motivation	Provocative	30	.23	.37	$z = 2.14$	$< .05$
	Nonprovocative	10	.60			

a. With the exception of x^2 all comparisons are for the significance of the difference between uncorrelated proportions, $H_0: P_1 = P_2$, one-tailed test.

stationary populations, women with newly acquired occupational roles versus those who are still "housewives," as well as groups for which the rationale and methods require some elaboration.

For instance, it is a central contention of symbolic interactionist theory that a person's view of him- or herself is a consequence of other people's reactions toward that person. In a more specific context, labeling theories (Goffman 1959; Scheff 1968) contend that persons take on prescribed definitions of themselves as a consequence of ascription and other types of societal reactions, particularly when "locked into a role" as is the case in psychiatric deviance defined as sufficiently serious to require institutionalization. It seems then, that the act of self-identification may become less problematic as ascriptions are interiorized, and we would expect interiorization to accompany increasing exposure to the role of deviant. In order to examine this conjecture, TSTs were administered to first admission cases with functional disorders either applying for admission to a university psychiatric hospital, already admitted for inpatient treatment, or released from that hospital for a period of six to eighteen months. Except for a slight increase in age corresponding to mean length of incarceration and release, the cohorts were equivalent on diagnostic categories and demographic characteristics. It was found that indicators of reflection decrease according to progression through the patient career.

Although it may seem that the very character of life in total institutions such as mental hospitals and prisons would dictate negative attraction, total institutions have been shown to have positive attractions for individuals with certain kinds of dependency needs. For such people the total institution functions as "a home away from home" (Coser 1956; Townsend 1976). Consequently, it would not be surprising if some persons engineered their own incarceration, if not by actual design, at least by indifference to the obvious consequences of performing criminal acts wherein their identities are either public or only thinly disguised. Such an orientation may be labelled as provocative. Since nonprovocative subjects displayed no evidence of intention for arrest and conviction, it would seem that imprisonment represents a greater blockage or inhibition of action to them than it does to provocative subjects. Accordingly, nonprovocative subjects are more likely to show indicators of reflection than provocative subjects. The subjects were male inmates at the Minnesota State Prison, Stillwater, Minnesota, classified as provocative and nonprovocative, who received a routine individual administration of the TST shortly before parole (see Spitzer and West 1978). Comparison of the two types of offenders disclosed similarity on relevant demographic characteristics and length of sentence, and the results obtain for first-time as well as multiple offenders.

Criterion Validation

Table 6–2 summarizes the results of correlating the appearance of reflection with various psychometric instruments. All linear coefficients are statistically significant and in the direction that one would expect. For example, reflection is associated with the degree of life stress recently experienced by the respondent, with the degree to which the respondents view themselves as subject to internal controls rather than controls eminating from the environment, with high self-monitoring activity, with low ego-strength, with propensity to subscribe to Machiavellian methods of interpersonal control, and so on. Curvilinear relationships are observed for two of the three Activity Preference Questionnaire (APQ) subscales, and indicate that persons at the extremes of the reflection continuum (nonreflective or highly reflective) are those least likely to avoid personally and socially threatening types of situations.

Moreover, reflection appears independent of social desirability response set as assessed by the Crowne–Marlowe (1964) instrument. Point biserial coefficients averaging –.05 and product moment coefficients averaging –.11 are found for different college students samples. Similarly, coefficients of association between reflection and final course grade do not differ significantly from zero in any of the university student samples, thus suggesting that reflection is independent of intelligence, at least insofar as within-group analyses are concerned. It is also noted that when the TST is coupled with a self-rating technique (Mulford 1955), the relation between reflection and self-satisfaction is inverse, that is, the greater the number of reflective assertions, the lower the level of self-satisfaction.

Construct Validation

Unlike criterion–related validation strategies, construct validation strategies are grounded on establishing that test scores allegedly

Table 6–2. Relationships Between Reflection and Criterion Variables.

Instrument	*Sample*	*Coefficient*	*p*
Barron (1953) Ego Strength Scale	Community college (N = 35)	r = −.42	< .01
Christie and Geis (1970) Mach IV Scale	University upper division (N = 63)	r_{pb} = .28	< .05
Holmes and Rahe (1967) Social Readjustment Rating Questionnaire	University extension (N = 47)	r_{pb} = .24	< .05
Jesness (1970) Behavior Checklist Self-Appraisal Form "Insight" Subscale	Semi-delinquent special education jr. high (N = 14)	r_{pb} = .46	< .05
Lykken and Katzenmeyer (1968) Activity Preference Questionnaire			
Ego Strength Subscales	1st year university group 1 (N = 63)[a]	r_c = .32	< .01
Social Anxiety (Form A)	1st year university group 2 (N = 62)[b] males	r_c = .18	< .05
Physical Anxiety (Form A)		r_{pb} = −.21	< .05
Mulford (1955) TST Self-Satisfaction Rating	Upper division university (N = 67)	r = −.22	< .05
Rotter (1966) Internal-External Locus of Control Scale	University lower division females (N = 25)[c]	r_{pb} = −.43	< .05
Snyder (1974) Self-Monitoring Scale	Upper division university (N = 54)	r = .27	< .05
Troldahl and Powell (1965) Short Dogmatism Scale	University upper division (N = 63)	r = .22	< .05

a. Subjects at extremes of reflection continuum likely to have low ego-strength scores, that is, do not tend to avoid ego-threatening situations. Male (N = 29) correlation ratio, .44; female (N = 34) correlation ratio, .32.

b. Males at extremes of reflection continuum likely to have low social anxiety scores, that is, do not tend to avoid socially anxious situations. Female (N = 56) coefficients, n.s.

c. Males (N = 20), n.s.

"reflect" a specifiable underlying construct. As such, construct validation requires commitment to a theoretical position regarding the mechanism that would hypothetically (a) regulate the behavior of test scores under conditions of experimental manipulation, or (b) generate a particular configuration of data. Accordingly, three studies are presented to demonstrate that scores obtained by the method of reflective analysis behave and distribute in "proper" fashion.

One of the curious properties of tetrahydrocannibinol (THC), the active ingredient in cannabis substances, is that its effects are produced without interruption of the transmission of the nervous impulse. There is little question, however, about the fact the THC operates in such a way as to "de-automatize" the structures that regulate psychological functioning (Deikman 1966; Hochman and Brill 1971). If the reflective attitude emerges under conditions of interrupted action, one could expect the reflective attitude to emerge under conditions that de-automatize those structures on which the act of self-identification depends. Accordingly, it may be conjectured that indicators of the reflective attitude are more likely to be found under conditions of THC ingestion than under conditions of no THC ingestion. Subjects averaging 2.86 ($SD = 1.00$) years' experience with cannabis were randomly assigned to receive one of two treatments. The experimental group ($N = 91$) was allowed to self-administer a "desired" amount of cannabis substances (marijuana, hashish, etc.) about fifteen minutes before filling out the TST. Control subjects ($N = 90$) were required to refrain from ingestion of any cannabis substance for at least eighteen hours before completion of the TST protocol. Experimental group subjects average 18.38 ($SD = 3.50$) statements and 11.70 ($SD = 51.77$) words as compared to an average of 18.34 ($SD = 3.50$) and 109.71 ($SD = 50.42$) words among control group subjects. (Equivalence of statement ($t = .08$, n.s.) and word ($t = .13$, n.s.) counts by treatment condition provides assurance that the results obtained are not an artifact of a differential propensity to produce responses on the instrument from which the measure of reflection is abstracted.)

The results indicate that 89 percent of subjects in the experimental group but only 69 percent of subjects in the control group show one or more indicators of reflection ($z = 3.32$, $p < .001$; one-tailed test). It appears that reflection behaves in accordance with our major conjecture.

The Kierkegaard–Laing model of ontological insecurity (1965) is structured in such a way that while reflection brings about anxiety in a system as a whole, the act of reflection mitigates the emergence of anxiety at the particular points within the system at which reflection is deployed. This is observed from the paradox that the model poses: since it is the case that self-awareness is a precondition for the emergence of anxiety, how is it possible that self-awareness can also reduce anxiety? There is also a resolution predicated on the assumption that the function of self-awareness is twofold, creating anxiety at the same time (but not at the same place) as anxiety is reduced.

Specifically, the model asserts that the existential position of a self-conscious person is one of ontological insecurity, and is allegedly a consequence of the failure to achieve a secure sense of identity. Hence, the most fundamental characteristic of the self-conscious person is a state of anxiety. Equating the term self-consciousness with reflection, it follows that *reflective persons are more likely to display indicators of anxiety than nonreflective persons*. Furthermore, the model asserts that fear of nonexistence is the source of anxiety: "Not to be conscious of oneself . . . may be equated with nonentity." (Laing 1965, p. 119). The major security-enhancing strategy available to the anxious person is self-observation, since, by taking himself as his own object, the anxious individual maintains surveillance on himself and so assures himself of his existence. Permanence of state is therefore greater at those points within a system where existence is recognized than at those points which are not, so to speak, covered by the surveillance mechanism. And since anxiety is least likely to be present where permanence of state is greatest it follows that *persons are less likely to be anxious about those aspects of self on which reflection is shown than those aspects on which there is no indication of reflection*.

Referring to Table 6–1, it is again noted that the mark of the reflective person is anxiety, and reference to Table 6–3 (which is based upon the student data set) indicates that the proportion of subjects whose anxious statements are more frequently nonreflective than reflective significantly exceeds the proportion of students showing the converse pattern. A similar result is obtained upon analysis of the hospital prepatient data set appearing in Table 6–1. Anxiety is largely restricted to statements devoid of reflection (see Spitzer 1978). It appears that the distribution of reflection and anxiety

Table 6–3. Subjects Showing One or More Indicators of Anxiety Divided According to the Distribution of Reflection Within Their Anxiety Statements.[a]

Type of Subject	*Proportion*	*Differential*	*z*	p^b
Anxious statements mostly reflective (N = 15)[c]	.32	.26	3.48	< .01
Anxious statements mostly nonreflective (N = 32)	.68			

a. Single-sample test of proportions; Ho:P = .5.

b. One-tailed test.

c. Includes six subjects whose anxious statements are equally divided between reflective and nonreflective.

conforms to theoretical expectations: reflection entails anxiety in a space of n-spaces although any one given space is unlikely to contain them both.

DISCUSSION

Of the many concepts on which symbolic interactionist propositions are based, there is little question that the social self and the social act occupy positions of utmost centrality. Because of their importance to this paradigm, these two concepts are subject to periodic re-examination and subsequent interpretation. Insofar as re-examination of the social self is concerned, the approach presented here is no exception. But rather than being restricted to the contents of self-conception, the method of reflective analysis has allowed for the disassociation of form from content with a degree of precision not often found when attempting to disassociate one from the other in symbolic interaction research. As such, we are faced with yet another instance in which the test of a proposition awaited the development of an appropriate methodology. This might help to account for the length of time that elapsed before a test was conducted of the proposition that the disposition to view oneself as object is an inverse function of the degree to which action remains under the control of automatic regulations.

In conclusion, this chapter has attempted to operationalize the hypothesis of reflection and inhibited action as well as to demonstrate its tenability in current research. To the extent that the evidence presented is taken as convincing, the interactionist-oriented social scientist is provided with some additional justification for disclaiming the disparaging allegation that the paradigm to which he adheres suffers unduly from an inability to generate clearly articulated propositions amenable to empirical validation. Hopefully also, the study of reflective processes, as defined here, may have further implications. In particular, the study of reflective processes may provide information useful for resolving the trait-versus-situation controversy by suggesting an alternative perspective regarding the definition of nondemographic individual difference variables in social psychological research.

Unlike conventional traits and properties which are identified according to relatively stable and enduring presences across variable situations, such as transituational consistency, the property to which our attention has been directed derives a stable and enduring quality from predictable fluctuations concomitant with specifiable environmental variations. If regarded in this way, the appearance, disappearance, and subsequent reappearance of the reflective form is a function of situation. Consequently, the reflective form is as sociological as it is psychological and, as such, may serve to provide an interface between the now fashionable predilection to assign inordinate weighting to situational determinants in behavioral covariation and the equally prejudicial position that behavioral covariation is attributable to individual difference variables alone.

7 SELF-CONCEPTING
Another Aspect of Aptitude

Theresa J. Jordan
Philip R. Merrifield

Although self-concept literature has burgeoned since the 1960s, as a whole it remains markedly deficient in its attempts to articulate and investigate cognitive processes operating to develop, maintain, and alter this trait. The current lack of operational linkages between self-concept and its antecedents and consequences is criticized sharply by Wylie (1968) and emphasized by Spears and Deese (1974) who point out that this lack exists within a body of literature which nevertheless adheres tenaciously to a notion of self-concept as casually related to human activity.

The equivocal nature of the findings that have resulted from self-concept research casts serious doubt on the adequacy of the theoretical frameworks that have spawned the studies. Self-concept has been regarded as a composite self-description or self-portrait (Yamamato 1972); as a mechanism for regulating, guiding, and unifying behavior (Lecky 1969; Rogers 1951); and even as the motivational force for all human activity (Combs and Snygg 1959; Hayakawa 1963; Snygg and Combs 1949). Yet, the specific mechanisms through which an individual protects, enhances, and maintains this regulating, guiding, and unifying self-portrait have not been delineated.

In contrast to these approaches, Bannister and Agnew (1976) propose that one does not possess a concept of self at all but rather a construct of self which is continually undergoing validation and invalidation; they suggest that the experience of self-concept is a process of construing that continues throughout the lifespan. Epstein (1973) corroborates this view by indicating that what is generally referred to as the self-concept is, in fact, a self theory, a conceptual tool for assimilating knowledge and for coping with the world.

This notion of becoming as opposed to being precludes the existence of a self-contained, static self-portrait. It demands increased precision and specificity in the theoretical links that translate self-concept into a multitude of behaviors, and translate experience into self-concept. The model that follows focuses not only on the self-concept but also on the processes of *self-concepting.* As with the development of any other concept, these processes are primarily cognitive.

FOUR PROCESSES FOR ARTICULATION OF THE SELF

The foundation of this model consists of the notion that four cognitive processes operate on the thought content that is usually categorized as self-concept. The four processes, reminiscent of Guilford's (1967) model, are: remembering, evaluating, transforming, and generating. As basic components of the cognitive system, these processes are by no means restricted to operations on content categorized as self, but also operate on a variety of other contents of thought including meanings, forms, and persons (Merrifield 1978). When the object of thought is the self, one can consider the self alone, or one can consider the self in relation to meanings, forms, or persons.

In the present context, the process of remembering refers to classification and organization of input into the cognitive system, resulting in a data base that is accessible and retrievable in response to appropriate cues. Although remembering requires that simple paired-associate or stimulus-response learning has occurred, it further suggests that the learned elements do not remain disconnected and fragmentary but rather develop a degree of cohesiveness and articulation among themselves.

In existing self-concept literature, the role of remembering is indicated by referring to the self as a "datum" (Kelly 1955), as a "biography" (Bannister and Agnew 1976), and as self-related information (Marcus 1977). When the process of remembering is focused on the self-as-object, the result is awareness of one's unique identity (self-awareness). In more specific instances, remembering self-in-relation-to-persons leads to awareness of one's previous socializing, of groups to which one has belonged (or has wished to belong), and of interpersonal interactions of varying intensities. Remembering self-in-relation-to-meanings leads to awareness of one's vocabulary, one's degree of skill in recalling poems and plots, and the like.

Evaluating refers to the continuum of discrimination activities which involve varying degrees of judgment. Remembering is a necessary condition for evaluating: the cognitive system must have access to those criteria that apply to a given thought content, and may in fact be required to retrieve the thought to be evaluated.

The process of evaluating has been referred to implicitly by Kelly (1955) in his discussion of differentiating one's self from others. Duval and Wicklund (1972) propose that self-awareness cannot occur in the absence of self-evaluation, which involves measuring the self against mental representations of correct or appropriate goals, behaviors, traits. Internal tensions result from perceived discrepancies (evaluations) between self-concept and actual performance; and human behavior has been viewed as a mechanism for reducing those discrepancies (Rogers 1951), even when the attainment of congruity requires striving toward self-integration as an unworthy or inadequate person (Snygg and Combs 1949). Brookover, Erikson, and Joiner (1967) have offered support for the critical role of evaluative self-concepts in constituting limits or ceilings for the levels of achievement that individuals will attempt. Evaluating self-as-object involves the making of judgments upon which self-esteem hinges. One may evaluate the self-in-relation-to-persons, as when judging one's social acceptability and effectiveness; or the self-in-relation-to-meanings, as when judging one's virtuosity in choosing words for effective communication, or as a rational critic. In all these instances, accuracy in evaluation is requisite for self-perceptions which are consistent with external reality.

Generating begins when the individual engages in those behaviors that result in new learning, such as trying on new identities or roles. Generating initiates the process of distancing the self from that which is learned. Through generating, an individual reflects oneself outward on the environment and begins to gain the control and relative objectivity resulting when the learner can place that which has been experienced at a more external or distant status.

Generating is closely akin to Erikson's (1963) concept of the identity strivings which in his model occur primarily during adolescence. But generating oneself does not wait for this stage of development. Indeed, as Thomas and Chess (1980) point out, even the "infant is initiating behavior that has consequences . . . the beginning of that basic constituent of positive self-concept, that 'I' can produce changes in the external world . . ." (p. 189). Generating applied to self-as-object, inventing oneself, as it were, is critical for later initiative and self-development. With self-in-relation-to-others as the object of thought, generating leads to trying on new social roles, to initiating various group activities. Generating applied to self-in-relation-to-meanings might involve the degree of confidence in oneself as fluent in communication or as a good conversationalist.

Transforming is an act of restructuring or reorganizing elements that pre-exist in the processor's mental data base. This restructuring occurs in response to new information which does not at first fit readily into the existing self-structure. Thus, it is a response aimed at resolving a state of disequilibrium. Balance is achieved when the experiential field is organized or reorganized in a way such that new or different perceptions achieve maximum "fit" within the framework of previous learning.

Transforming is related to accommodation, as Piaget defines it. Yet, transforming is not restricted to childhood. (Of course, neither is accommodation!) It is exemplified by the reinterpretation of situations following negative evaluations. And it is central to problem-solving behavior, for if the intervention first produced is evaluated as adequate, one does not have a problem, just a solution. Applied to self-as-object, transforming is manifested in changing one's values or lifestyle (as in successful therapy). Transforming of the self-in-relation-to-others leads to insight about and reinterpretation of one's behavior. One's felt ability to solve problems, to paraphrase, to reinterpret situations, to use effectively the double entendre and the pun—all are manifestations of transforming the self-in-relation-to-meanings.

The processes of self-concepting discussed above are aptitudes essential for the development of realistic and adaptive self-concepts. To investigate the application of these aptitudes, one cannot attend to self-report data alone, but must instead consider the degree of accuracy with which these self-data reflect externally verified performance.

PROCESSES, CONTENTS, AND CAUSALITY: A SITUATION-SPECIFIC APPROACH

When remembering, evaluating, generating, and transforming are applied to the thought content categorized as self, they focus largely on the self *in relation to* a range of life experiences which are situation-specific in nature. Each individual possesses a unique data base regarding his or her past life; thus, remembering evokes the individuality of experience, an individuality predicated on the existence of situation-specific data. Each individual possesses not only a "conclusion" about the self in a given area of life but also manifold bits of information from which this conceptual conclusion was derived. Similarly, one's personal history is a determiner of how evaluating of the self will proceed: it dictates not only what will be ignored and what will be focused on for evaluation but also which criteria will be selected for making the evaluation. In generating new notions of the self, what will be attempted or risked depends greatly on the specific areas in which competence has already been attained and on areas in which a need for further growth is perceived as necessary or rewarding. And, finally, the extent to which transforming can occur will be heavily determined by the nature of the specific elements that already exist in the self-structure. Successful accommodation to new self-notions will necessarily involve the resolution of apparent conflicts of new information with a range of specific self-data residing in memory.

Wylie (1974) has discussed global self-concept as a self-view which may be regarded as content-free or content-general in nature. Rosenberg (1965), for example, has attempted to measure a content-free, global self-concept. If such a concept exists, it must involve an extremeness of abstraction which evokes no specific self-referent information. The content of thought must be *the self only*, and not the self in relation to other phenomena. The global approach that has pervaded self-concept literature has resulted in such constructs as global self-concept, identity, and self-esteem, which give little direction for intervention. The interventionist is left to measure and grapple with conclusions about the self, high-level abstractions, without a sense of which personal data to address as the causes of these products.

General or global self-notions are not, however, precluded by the model presented here. In fact, the likely outcomes of the four cognitive processes operating on self-content alone would involve self-awareness, self-esteem, self-enhancement, and self-transformation. However, as indicated previously, self-concepting also involves thinking about the self in relation to the other contents of thought—meanings, forms, and persons—either singly or in combination. One can, for example, think about the self in relation to the rubric of other persons; or about the self in relation to combinations, like meanings × forms as in mathematics, or meanings × persons as in history.

It is this focus on the self in relation to specific contents that is the dynamic core of self-concepting. Here, the individual is dealing not with a notion of self so abstract that it is removed from life experiences, but rather with the self in relation to these experiences. Thus, one is focusing on the continual, inductive process of inventing and elaborating a concept of self—a concept which is developed like any other, through the acquisition and assimilation of specific data.

The literature to date has proved markedly deficient in empirically establishing self-concept as either a cause or effect of behavior. It is a major contention of this chapter that the equivocal nature of existing self-concept research can be largely attributed to global formulations of the construct which have precluded precise and focused study of the processes involved. It is perhaps the movement toward greater specificity in conceptualization as well as measurement that has contributed to the relative success of situation-specific versus global notions of self-concept in predicting behavior (Brookover et al. 1962, 1965, 1967; Deese 1971; Jordan 1979; Mintz and Muller 1977; Stillwell 1965). The processes and contents involved in self-concepting have remained untapped in previous research; therefore, it is not surprising that studies of the antecedents and consequences of self-concept have been unimpressive and equivocal.

If self-concepting is, in fact, a series of dynamic processes, directions of causality may alter across varying points in development as well as across situations. Perhaps these phenomena have contributed to the acceptance of symmetrical causality which Calsyn and Kenny (1977) have found to be prevalent in current work. That is to say, the causal relation between two variables may be sometimes in one direction, and sometimes in the other, depending on the background of the person involved and the nature of the specific occasion.

The four cognitive processes discussed in the context of this chapter are conceived as operating both *on* and *with* the self, thereby implying two directions of causal flow. As James (1890) indicated early in the development of psychology, the self can act as both subject and object. In the present model, the self as subject is the self thinking about or behaving in relation to meanings, forms, or persons. In this mode of operating, conscious attention or awareness is not focused on the self in relation to these contents but rather on the contents themselves. Yet, the biases, limitations, and orientations existing in the self-structure mediate these thoughts and behaviors. Thus, the concepting is done with (and by) the self. In the present model, the self as object occurs when awareness is focused on how the individual relates to meanings, forms, persons. Here, the concepting is performed on (and of) the self.

Fluctuations in the extent to which experience will exert causal predominance over self-concepting, and vice-versa, will depend upon the person's individuality of experience that he or she brings to a given situation. Upon encountering a new situation, experience is likely to predominate over self-concepting. During infancy, for example, self-concepting is probably an experience comprised largely of remembering, with new learning constantly being assimilated into the self-structure. Thus, during infancy, experience may be causally predominant over self-concepting. Given a base of experience, the other direction of causal flow may become operative. For the adult with a data base of experience in a specific area, self-concepting is probably perceived most often as an evaluative experience, which can lead to both transforming and generating. While transforming implies that experience causally affects self-concepting, generating suggests the other direction of causality, that new notions of self are reflected outward onto the environment.

NEW DIRECTIONS FOR INTERVENTION: COGNITIVE MODIFICATION

The tendency to adhere to self-views that are inappropriately negative may not be a product of the need and striving to maintain the integrity of an existing self-structure, as per Snygg and Combs

(1949), but may instead be a stance adopted for lack of the proper cognitive tools required to generate new self-views. Would-be interventionists must, therefore, learn to teach the processes of self-concepting. In such interventions, individual differences must be seriously considered: self-structures are unique in the contents that have been assimilated; and individuals surely vary in the virtuosity with which they have learned to apply the processes of self-concepting.

A first step for intervention must be to determine the contents of thought which are to be the target for change strategies. Thus, one must determine whether, for example, a self-concept of mathematics ability, of social interacting, or of physical prowess is at issue. Once a situation-specific content has been identified, one might proceed to investigate whether deficits appear to exist in the processes or aptitudes of self-concepting in that content area. "Transfer" from one such content area to another is *not* to be expected.

When a perception of personal inadequacy in a specific area is advanced, the educator or clinician must consider the origin and accuracy of this viewpoint. For the child whose self-concept of mathematics ability is summed up by the statement, "I can't do arithmetic," one must attempt to assess whether this self-evaluation is an accurate reflection of actual experience (which would require skills development), or an inaccurate self-view based on gender stereotypes, overgeneralization of a single negative event, and so on. One must bring into focus those cognitive processes by which inaccurate notions of self have been derived, an awareness that is a necessary condition for change.

A series of questions can provide the framework against which the processes of self-concepting can be examined. To address the issue of remembering, one might ask if a given occurrence has been distorted or overgeneralized. Is the memory a realistic or correct reflection of an event or series of events?

The second process, evaluating, involves the making of distinctions between evidence or data and conclusions. One must ask whether conclusions about the self are based on adequate evidence, and whether the individual is aware that conclusions depend for their validity on an adequate body of data. Too frequently, conclusions about the self are adhered to tenaciously and are reified without the understanding that such judgments should be continually subjected to the test of empirical evidence. Through reliance on indiscriminate positive feedback, some attempts at self-concept enhancement have tended to provide children with ready-made conclusions, without developing adequate bodies of evidence to support these judgments.

It is clear that severe trauma may make a single case more impressive than a host of more ordinary events; the problem, in such an instance, is to question the evaluation of the severity of the trauma—while it may well have been serious and debilitating in the context of earlier experience, would its recurrence in the context of the child's current life space be more easily assimilated?

Critical questions related to the process of generating include: Is the individual effectively exerting efforts to be creative in the invention of the self? Is he or she aware that there are alternative identities or self-views that might be tested for goodness of fit? And, perhaps most critically, what are the limits or boundaries that the individual has set up for him—or herself? As indicated previously, Brookover and others (1967) have provided support for self-concept as a kind of ceiling for what an individual will attempt. Thus, the range of identities or of new selves which will be tried and tested is restricted by a self-imposed and not always conscious boundary condition.

Transforming is the actual cognitive modification of the concept of self: it is the process by which accommodation to newly generated self-notions occurs. Here, one might ask whether a supportive climate is provided so that the individual can afford to take the psychological risks inherent in changing his or her self-structure. One might consider the extent to which the Rogerian ideal of unconditional positive regard is approximated, in an effort to create an optimum climate for transforming to occur. Here, however, the interventionist might be concerned with creating a temporary state of unconditional positive regard in relation to a specific subsample of the individual's behavior. Thus, the interventionist would attempt to provide an assurance that risks may be taken, since the security of retreat back to old "selves" is likewise possible. One might also ask whether an intervention is geared to an acceptable level of specificity of self-information: considerably less risk is probably involved in attempting to accommodate to new notions about one's capacity to solve word problems in arithmetic than to new notions about one's total self as a "good person." Specific and focused interventions will be less likely to cause the individual to feel that the security of an existing self-structure is being invaded, or to avoid the necessity of coping with impending growth and change.

II THE DEVELOPMENT OF SELF-CONCEPT

Kenneth J. Gergen

In the beginning of this book our chief orientation was synchronic, that is, centering on the existing structure and functions of self-concept in ongoing relationships. However, a series of different but equally significant questions emerge from a diachronic orientation, one concerned with self-conception across time. For example, how are we to understand the formative bases of self-conception? Do early influences on self-concept have long-term consequences? Are there systematic alterations in self-concept across time, and if such changes can be discerned, to what are they attributable? To what extent is contemporary knowledge about self-concept dependent on the existing nexus of historical circumstances?

Such questions as these have long been critical to investigators in the developmental domain. As early as 1922 Cooley had begun to elaborate a theory of self-concept that traced its origins to early social experience. For Cooley, as well as in the later works of Mead (1925), the individual's self-concept was primarily a reflection of the views of significant others. This view, of course, later served as the cornerstone for the symbolic interactionist school. Contrasted with the symbolic interactionist view is the family of psychodynamic theories. These theories place major stress on the emotional or motivational needs of the child as they play themselves out in the early years of life. Freud's theory of the ego's emergence from id is seminal among these contributions. However, Sullivan's (1953) views on the development of the self system in early childhood, A. Freud's (1946) discussions of ego functions in puberty, and Erikson's (1959) analysis of the formation of identity in adolescence have added substantially to this line of thinking.

In the present volume are included important lines of departure from these early traditions. The first is represented in the advent of the cognitive perspective. It is often said that recent psychology has undergone a cognitive revolution. Many of the present chapters support such a contention. More importantly, these contributions point to significant new insights into self-concept development that are fostered by this perspective.

In Michael Lewis and Jeanne Brooks–Gunn's contribution (Chapter 8), self-concept development is cut away both from the reflective influence of others' opinions and from emotional dynamics. As it is argued, self-concept is learned through cognitive appraisals of the self and others in action. Reflecting an intriguing line of research into the child's recognition of its own visual image, the authors argue that children acquire rudimentary self-knowledge by nine months of age, and that by the end of the second year the fundamentals of self-knowledge are firmly established.

Mervin D. Lynch in Chapter 9 proposes a cognitive formulation of self-concept and presents descriptions of its development through childhood. According to Lynch, self-concept is a set of rules that play a central role as the executive monitor in human information-processing activities. Such rules are either inborn or acquired as individuals develop and are confirmed or infirmed by validational rules as the individual tests concepts against the contingencies supplied by real-world observations. Epigenetic stages in self-concept development are guided in part by biological considerations and in part by the child's confrontation with social institutions such as the family and the school. Lynch goes on to demonstrate the utility of this formulation in empirical research in applied settings.

Some of Lynch's view are reflected in Ardyth A. Norem–Hebeisen's notion of self-concept in adolescents and adults (Chapter 10). Her notion also incorporates the humanist tradition in its emphasis on the organism's fundamental and autonomous quest for survival, maintenance, and growth. At the same time the approach pushes further than many existing humanist conceptions as it suggests a variety of dimensions along which healthy development might be assessed. Consistency, differentiation, and its capacity to incorporate diverse experiences are all relevant.

Although retaining the cognitive perspective adopted by previous authors, William and Claire McGuire (Chapter 11) focus on cognitive inputs to self-concept that may be independent of specific developmental stages. Rather than tracing components of self-concept to various ontogenetically governed capacities, McGuire regards the social environment at virtually any stage; establishing such differentiation is critical from his perspective in supplying the content of self-concept. Of equal importance, McGuire's analysis emphasized the potential of the individual to discern, recall, or forget distinctive qualities of self in any given situation. This thesis adds additional weight to the argument for inconsistency in self-concept and raises additional question for those assuming stabilization in self-concept.

The emphasis on self-concept change is re-echoed in Morris and Florence Rosenberg's contribution (Chapter 12). They trace children's changing conception of their occupational future between ages of eight and sixteen. As in Lynch's work, these changes are traced both to ontogenetic and social influences. Younger children, whose cognitive processes are equipped to deal primarily with concrete observations, select professions in the observable environment. As gains are made in capacity for abstract thought, children begin to select professions that are removed from immediate observation. Unsettlingly, however, by the age of sixteen, female children show distinct preferences for occupations that are lower in status than those selected by males.

Gender differences in self-concept development also play an important role in Anne C. Peterson's research on adolescence (Chapter 13). Although there has been a long-standing belief that females possess a lower level of self-esteem than males, this research indicates that the picture is far more complicated. In certain respects adolescent males do manifest higher self-esteem (e.g., body image, external mastery), but in terms of moral evaluation and relations with others, the females enjoy an enhanced position. Interestingly, the most dramatic differences are found between urban and rural youth, with those living in urban areas manifesting higher levels of self-esteem in every area tested.

The final chapter in this section amplifies and elaborates on a theme implied by several of the earlier chapters. Rene L'Ecuyer

(Chapter 14) outlines the causal burden for self-concept development from the early periods of life and argues for developmental shifts in self-concept across the full life span. Based on a multifaceted view of self-concept organization, L'Ecuyer is able to show that body image is primarily important during the early and late periods of life, and that typically its importance is eclipsed by other aspects of self-concept. Similarly, the individual's concern with differentiation of self from others continues throughout the life span, but its modalities of expression change. Of particular importance in L'Ecuyer's work is his concern with multiple trajectories of self-concept change in life-span development. If recent work on the historical imbeddedness of life-span trajectory is an indication (see Baltes and Reinert 1969; Elder 1974; Gergen 1980; Neugarten and Datan 1973) a major shift may be anticipated in the way in which self-concept research is viewed. Rather than assuming that the conclusions of contemporary research are transhistorical in character, increasing attention needs to be given to the historical contingency of such work and its essential value in describing characteristics of the culture at a particular point in its own development.

8 THE SELF AS SOCIAL KNOWLEDGE

Michael Lewis[a]
Jeanne Brooks-Gunn

Like most investigators intrigued by the self, we are concerned with how individuals come to know themselves and what it means to have self-knowledge. Our interest, however, is in the origins and development of this knowledge, the beginning of self-discovery. We believe that such knowledge is acquired early, in the first months of life, and forms the basis for what today is known as social cognition. In fact, early social cognition in particular and development in general may best be understood through knowledge of self. In this essay, we will explore the relationship between self and social cognition, explain how the first notion of self might develop, present data relating to this development, and show how our data on self relate to social cognition.

SOCIAL COGNITION

Social cognition has been studied by many, including attributional, cognitive, personality, and phenomenological psychologists. It has been studied under the guise of recognition of various emotions exhibited by others, and the ability to judge others' emotional states

a. The writing of the paper from which this chapter came was supported in part by a grant from the Foundation for Child Development. The research reported here was conducted under National Institute of Mental Health Grant #MH 24849.

(Bruner and Tagiuri 1954; Darwin 1965; Tagiuri 1969), the reasons a person acts as he does and the perceptions of others' actions (Heider 1958; Kelley 1973) and role-taking, empathy, and person perception (Hoffman 1975). Recently, developmental psychologists have become interested in this topic, and a number of reviews of cognition in the preschool and middle childhood years have appeared (Chandler 1977; Shantz 1975; Youniss 1975). Shantz, for example, has defined early social cognition as "a child's intuitive or logical representations of others, that is, how he characterizes others and makes references about their covert, inner psychological experiences" (1975, p. 258). Unfortunately, this definition does not include other important aspects of social cognition, such as self-knowledge of relationships. Youniss (1975) has offered a more inclusive definition, adding a sense of self, knowledge of self vis-à-vis society, and a sense of values and principles, as well as knowledge of others and one's relationship to them.

Social cognition in the earliest years, however, has not been studied *or* defined. We would suggest that infants' social cognition includes knowledge of the self, knowledge of others, and knowledge of one's relationship to others, and that these three features are interrelated and have parallel developmental courses. Following the work of Mead (1934), Cooley (1972), and others, we believe that knowledge of the self and knowledge of others are dependent upon one another: "I cannot know another unless I have knowledge of myself." Further, the child's knowledge of self and others is developed through one's interactions with these others, social interaction being the basic unit out of which social cognition derives. Many who subscribe to an interactionalist position agree that knowledge of others (and the world in general) is derived through interaction: "To understand that a person is . . . involves understanding what sorts of relationships can exist between mere things and between people and things" (Hamlyn 1974, p. 7). However, knowledge of the self must also arise out of such interactions, a position advocated by only a few. Because what the child knows of the other through interaction (usually nonsocial "other," characterized by physical properties such as weight, length, etc.) has been our major focus, the fact that knowledge of other, gained through interaction, must provide information about oneself has been ignored. If I find one object hard and the other soft through holding them, then not only do I know something about objects (in this case, hardness) but I know something about myself (how hard the object feels to me). As the phenomenologist Merleau Ponty (1964) has indicated: "If I am a consciousness turned toward things, I can meet in things the actions of another and find in them a meaning, because they are themes of possible activity for my own body" (p. 113).

Because we have failed to attend to this parallel development between self and other and the role of interaction in this development, we have failed to understand social cognition. Our studies of cognition have concerned themselves with attributes of the physical world which often have little to do with social attributes or with self attributes, or at least are lower level attributes. While attributes of objects are acquired early, social attributes to which the child must respond for survival also are learned as early if not earlier. Lest you feel that the infant is too cognitively immature to acquire such information, just look at the expansion of our knowledge about the infant's cognitive abilities in the last decade (Stone, Smith, and Murphy 1973). The infant is an active and competent organism, one who at an early age already shows signs of planning and of intentional behavior (primary and circular reactions being just one example [Piaget 1952] and one who derives information from interactions with the world. Such an organism does possess the perceptual-cognitive ability to acquire early social cognitions, as we shall see.

Before turning to some of our data, we would like to offer three principles underlying early social cognition. These principles are a summation of our comments on the relationships among the three features of social cognition and are discussed at length in Lewis and Brooks-Gunn (1979a).

Principle I: That any knowledge gained about the other also must be gained about the self. Baldwin (1894) understood this principle when he wrote: "My sense of self grows by imitation of you, and my sense of yourself grows in terms of my sense of self. Both ego and alter are thus essentially social; each is a socius, and each is an imitative creation" (p. 338).

Principle II: What can be demonstrated to be known about the self can be said to be known about the other, and what is known about the other can be demonstrated to be known about the self. This principle can be used to infer early social cognition, specifically what knowledge the child possesses about self versus other as a consequence of interaction.

Principle III: Social dimensions are those attributes of others and self which can be used to describe people. While Piaget and those that have followed him have greatly increased our knowledge about some of the dimensions of the nonsocial world (such as weight, length, and volume), few have attempted to describe the equivalent social space or social dimensions. The categories of self and others that emerge from the infant's interaction with the environment allow us to generate social dimensions.

EARLY SELF-KNOWLEDGE

Before turning to our data, we need to consider the two aspects of the self that appear to develop in the first two years of life. The first, and by far the more primitive, is the *existential* self, I as distinct from other. It is the subjective self. The second is the *categorical* self, which includes the categories by which one is defined (I am female, I am big, etc.). It is the objective self.

Existential Self

The basic notion of existence separate from other (both animate and inanimate) develops as the infant differentiates self from other persons. The first social distinction probably involves the mother or caregiver, a position advocated by psychoanalytic theorists (Erikson 1937; Spitz and Wolf 1946). This primitive self develops from birth and therefore exists in some form in the early months. In fact, three- and four-month-old infants are able to differentiate between mother and female stranger as measured by a variety of infant responses (cardiac deceleration—Banks and Wolfson 1967; vocalization—Turnure 1971 and Rebelsky 1971; wariness—Bronson 1972; differential reinforcing properties—Wahler 1967). It is not unreasonable to assume that the self-other differentiation also occurs by this time. In fact, differentiation of self from other may be a precondition for differentiation of other persons.

This nonevaluative, existential self is developed from the consistency, regularity, and contingency of the infant's action and outcome in the world. The mechanism of reafferent feedback provides the first contingency information for the child; therefore the kinesthetic feedback produced by the infant's own actions forms the basis for the development of self. For example, each time a certain set of muscles operates (eyes close), it becomes black (cannot see). The action of touching the hot stove and the immediacy of the pain tells me it is my hand that is on the stove. This self is further reinforced if, when I remove my hand, the pain ceases. These kinesthetic systems provide immediate and regular action-outcome pairings.

Such contingent feedback is also provided by the environment. Infants' interactions with objects provide consistent information (a round object always rolls while a square object does not). In addition, social stimuli (especially the caregiver) provide extensive feedback and are potent reinforcers. First, social reinforcement may be the most effective behavior-shaping mechanism in infancy. Wolff (1963), in his intensive study of infant behavior in the first weeks of life, has found that social stimuli (such as vocalization and facial movement) elicit smiling responses more readily than do nonsocial stimuli. Social reinforcers (an adult smiling, talking, patting an infant) can also be used to condition smiling (Brackbill 1958) and vocalizing (Rheingold, Gewirtz, and Ross 1959) by the age of three months. Since social stimuli are such potent reinforcers, it is not surprising that differentiation between familiar and unfamiliar occurs early. The caregiver is the person who provides the bulk of social reinforcement in the first year of life.

Second, the contingency feedback given by the primary caregiver probably provides for generalized expectancies about the infant's control of his world. Such expectancies would also help differentiate the infant's actions from others' actions. The generalized expectancy model (Lewis 1977; Lewis and Goldberg 1969) proposes that a mother's responsiveness to her infant's cues determines the infant's expectations. The consistency, timing, and quality of the mother's responses create expectancies about control and competence. If the infant's demands (defined as his behavioral repertoire) are reinforced, they are, in a sense, controlling their environment. Thus, their actions may produce outcomes in the social as well as the kinesthetic realm. Such contingencies should relate to the development of self-other differentiation. Moreover, since self-other interaction always involves the other's relating to a specific locus in space, the interactive nature of self-other should facilitate a schema for self.

For example, action by the other directed toward self is always space-specific. Thus, not only is there interactive reciprocity in time but reciprocity in space as well.

The development of self is also related to the general issue of permanence. Permanence deals with the recognition that objects and people exist even when perceptually absent. Self-permanence may exist when the infant is aware that the existence of other objects is not contingent on their presence. That the self is distinct from other environmental events is a necessary condition for later development of self-identity (Guardo and Bohan 1971). The concept of self as identity is elucidated by Guardo (1968), who defines self "from the point of view of the experiencer as a phenomenological feeling or sense of self-identity" (Guardo 1968, p. 139).

If object and person permanence exists by eight months, it may not be unreasonable to suppose that self-permanence may also exist. In fact, we hypothesize that these processes probably occur simultaneously. Thus, the early differentiation of self and other should take place at the same time the child is differentiating mother from others and is acquiring object permanence.

Categorical Self

The categorical self, which refers to the categories by which the infant defines itself vis-à-vis the external world, is somewhat different. First, the categorical self is subject to many changes. Ontogenetically it should change as a function of the child's other cognitive capacities as well as with changing social relationships. The categorical self, then, undergoes a lifelong change. Some categories, like gender, remain fixed; others, like size, strength, and competence, change either by being added to or altered entirely. Historically and socially this categorical self should be expected to change. For example, different cultures have different requirements for their members. In one case the male is expected to be a good hunter, while in another being a good scholar is important. Given these different values, different categories of self will emerge and disappear. If this conceptualization is at all valid, it becomes necessary to consider what categories may be available to the infant and how they are altered.

Not only must infants differentiate between the social and nonsocial world, but they distinguish among different persons and between themselves and other persons. Thus, self-categories would be the same as the ones infants use for categorizing the rest of the social world. Research done on the origins of social categories suggest that familiarity, age, and gender are the first to be used consistently. Infants differentiate between parents and strangers; babies, children and adults; and men and women, mother and father, and boys and girls (Brooks and Lewis 1976; Brooks-Gunn and Lewis 1978, 1979; Lewis and Feiring 1978). Infants also, as we shall see, differentiate between pictures of themselves and others, categorize themselves as young, and as a member of one gender (Lewis and Brooks-Gunn 1979a). Thus, familiarity, age, and gender are used to categorize both self and others (Lewis and Feiring 1978).

THE DEVELOPMENT OF SELF-RECOGNITION

Self-recognition is only one part of the self-knowledge, but it is easy to define and to observe. The kinesthetic feedback produced by our actions is continuous, and such action-outcome contingencies must theoretically form the basis for self-recognition. However, observing self-recognition experimentally may be more difficult than defining it theoretically. For example, facial recognition should be universal in our society as a result of repeated exposure to mirrors and pictures. The only adults who would have difficulty recognizing their faces visually are psychotic patients and patients suffering from certain central nervous system (CNS) dysfunctions (Cornielson and Arsenian 1960; Frenkel 1964). Although self-knowledge and self-recognition are not synonymous, the demonstration of the latter may give us insights into the former. In addition, self-recognition itself may not be a unitary concept since recognition may occur in several modalities—visual, auditory, tactile, olfactory, proprioceptive. In fact, visual self-recognition, the aspect which we have studied, is probably not the first to develop. For example, proprioceptive recognition probably occurs much earlier. This being so, visual self-recognition may not be demonstrable in infants who do, in fact, already recognize themselves or have knowledge of self.

In order to study self-recognition and to examine both categorical and existential self-knowledge, our studies include infants from nine to thirty-six months of age. Given the needed motoric ability to demonstrate recognition, which appears around eight to nine months of age, and the obvious importance of language and personal pronoun usage, which occurs between twenty-four and thirty-six months of age, the age range we have chosen appears relevant. That is not to say, however, that the self does not develop gradually, nor that the self stops developing with the onset of personal pronoun usage, but that the origins of self may best be studied within this age period.

In choosing visual self-recognition as a method for exploring the development of self, three different procedures, using three different types of self-images, were studied (Lewis and Brooks-Gunn 1979a). We observed infants' responses to mirrors, videotapes, and pictorial representations of the self since all three sources present the child with different types of information and different tasks. Let us look at the information provided by each of these forms.

Recognition of pictorial representations of one's face requires prior experience with the face itself in a reflective surface or prior labeling of the face, as seen in a mirror or picture of oneself. However, an infant could conceivably learn to differentiate some features of self and other without specific visual experiences. For instance, if an infant learns that age is an important and discriminable feature of the social world and learns that he is a baby (young), not an adult (old), then conceivably he could differentiate between self and other. Since infants are able to respond differently to and correctly label babies and adults, self-adult differentiation without knowledge of one's own perceptual features would be possible. That is, given two pictures, one of self and one of an adult, the infants are able to differentiate between the two pictures and prefer looking at their own. The picture of self represents a category (baby) of which the infant may know he or she belongs, while the adult picture does not represent this category. This suggests that the infant has some attributes of self-knowledge ("I am a baby") but not others ("the specific facial features of the person in that picture are mine"). The same argument can be made for gender differentiation; if an infant differentiates among others on the basis of gender and knows his or her own gender, then differentiation of the self and an opposite-sex person should be possible without explicit knowledge of one's own facial features. However, in order to differentiate pictures of oneself and a same-age, same-sex person, the specific facial features which are unique to oneself must be learned. Thus, some prior experience with self-representations (e.g., pictures or mirrors) is necessary. In addition, the fact that self-attributes which are common social attributes (e.g., age and gender) can be known with specific visual experience suggests we should be careful in selecting the "other" with which to compare oneself and cautious in interpreting self–other differentiation when the comparison person's gender and age are different from the self.

The knowledge that a reflection in the mirror is oneself and not another seems an easier task than picture recognition. Mirrors possess special and unique properties, as they are three-dimensional, are relatively distortion-free, and reproduce one's actions immediately. The one-to-one correspondence of one's actions and the reflection of those actions is naturally present in light-reflecting surfaces. Such contingencies give infants valuable feedback, as they learn that other people do not produce behavior sequences identical to their own and that only a reflective image of self does so. An infant must discover the contingent nature of mirrors, making the inference that a reflection is not another, but is self. With this knowledge, the special features unique to oneself may be learned.

Videotape representations have features of both pictorial and mirror representations. Like mirrors, videotapes can present immediate, direct, and contingent self-representations, although these representations differ from mirrors in several important ways: most videotape systems utilize black and white rather than color representations, utilize television monitors which are clearly discriminable from mirrors, and are more distorted than a mirror image. Videotapes also may be presented after the fact rather than simultaneously, with the videotapes being similar to home movies and having feature similarity, but not contingency cues. Like pictures, they maintain feature similarity, but unlike pictures, they present it in motion. Moving pictures contain information (the nature of one's own movement) that may be important for proprioceptive recognition, but may not be so important for visual recognition.

In sum, pictorial, mirror, and videotape (both contingent and noncontingent) representations present different information about the self and allow us three uniquely different ways of representing the self. In the following discussion we shall examine each one, with the greatest emphasis placed on mirror representations since they have been studied most extensively and are most likely to be experienced in the child's natural environment.

Pictorial Representations

Our studies of pictorial recognition always involved the face, for as Schlossberg and his associates (Woodworth and Schlossberg 1954) have shown, adult subjects have considerable difficulty recognizing their features other than their face; for example, recognizing one's own hands or shoulders.

Preverbal children's ability to recognize their faces in pictures is best inferred through differential responses to pictures of self and other. The "other" that is used for comparison purposes should be as similar to the self as possible, since differential responding may be elicited by person perceptions other than self-perception. For example, infants respond quite differently to adults and children in live approach sequences (Brooks and Lewis 1976; Greenberg et al. 1973; Lewis and Brooks 1974) so that differential responses to pictures of self and adults or even to self and older children may not be indicative of self-recognition but instead may be indicative of age differentiation. Two methods of observing self–other differentiation were used, one of which involved studying the children's perceptual and affective responses to the pictures and one of which involved the children's verbal responses. Since personal pronouns appear late in the infancy period, anywhere from twenty-four to thirty months, a variety of other verbal responses had to be observed in order to find some that distinguished between self and other, with one's own name being most important at earlier ages. Using one's own name when viewing one's own picture usually means that a child knows that that picture is "self." However, this may not always be true as a child may know that the child in the picture is Amanda and that she is Amanda, but may not know that the two Amandas are the same person. Even so, the ability to label one's own picture with one's own name, and not labeling a same-age, same-self peer picture with that appellation suggests that the child has learned that a name (his or her own name) is coupled with a set of facial features. Such data in conjunction with other self-recognition observations, provides a more complete picture of the child's unfolding skill. The use of verbal self-referents in mirror studies has been used as a measure of self-recognition in many other studies (see Bertenthal and Fischer 1978; Bigelow 1975; Gesell 1928; Zazzo 1948).

In our studies, nine- to twenty-four-month-old infants were presented with 35mm slides of themselves, same-sex peers, and opposite-sex peers, with only the face and shoulder area being photographed. Affect, attention, and verbal labels were recorded. We find that children under two years and, in some cases, under one year, respond differentially to pictorial representations of self and other in terms of smiling, frowning, and fixation time differences. Infants respond differentially to pictorial representations having to do with gender and age, important dimensions of the social world. Several of our findings suggest that early self–other differentiation may require perceptual-cognitive support structures other than feature recognition. For example, some of our young infants differentiate between self and opposite-sex babies' pictures, but not between self and same-sex babies' pictures. The ability to differentiate early self from other may require featural differences that have categorical qualities such as age or gender. The presentation of strangers varying in age and gender attributes was an attempt to see whether this was the case. The data, at least in part, support our belief that self–other differentiation in the first year of life is dependent on additional perceptual structures and that not until the middle of the second year are children capable of recognizing their own pictures using only perceptual feature differences. In our first study, the ten- to eighteen-month-old infants did not respond differently to pictures of themselves and other infants. However, a small pilot sample of twenty-two-month-olds did so, smiling and looking more at their own pictures than at pictures of same-age babies. In our second study, nine- to twelve- and twenty-one- to twenty-four-month-old infants smiled more at the self than the same-aged baby while fifteen- to eighteen-month-old infants did just the opposite. In addition, the infants in the second study tended to frown more often at the peer than at the self-picture. These trends suggest that infants as young as nine to twelve months of age are capable of some differentiation between pictorial representations of self and other, even though the evidence for differentiation becomes stronger in the second year.

The children's verbal responses to pictorial representations also were studied using verbal comprehension and production. Both elicited as well as spontaneous verbalizations were used. In the verbal comprehension task infants were asked to point to their pictures given a set of pictures including their own and others. In the verbal labeling task, infants were shown pictures of themselves and others and asked to label the pictures. As many language studies have shown, comprehension preceded verbal production. This was true for the task of self-recognition. Comprehension as measured by the infants' correctly pointing to their own picture as opposed to another picture was observed by a majority of the infants as early as eighteen months of age. Correct labeling of their own picture did not occur in a majority of infants until twenty-one to twenty-four months of age. And personal pronouns, although appearing at the end of the second year, were not used by a majority until thirty to thirty-six months of age. Ames (1952) and Gesell (1928) also reported that personal pronouns were not commonplace until the third year of life. Use of one's own name for one's own picture, but not for the picture of another baby, appeared prior to personal pronouns and, in one case, in a child of sixteen months. In the first study, one-quarter of the eighteen-month-olds and two-thirds of the twenty-two-month-olds labeled their pictures correctly. As shown in Table 8–1, these data parallel the age increases seen for mark-directed behavior and illustrate the occurrence of correct picture labeling before the end of the second year, not in the middle of the third year, as others have assumed.

Mirror-Image Representations

Mirror-image representation is the one form of self-recognition that has received a great deal of attention. Given its natural occurrence in human experience, both from reflecting surfaces found in nature and its long history of technology, mirror representation is seen as ecologically valid, that is, it is a common, everyday event in the child's life. The use of bronze mirrors dates back to human's earliest records, while use of mirrors to study self-recognition dates back to Charles Darwin and William Preyer.

Infants' responses to mirrors have been observed in experimental situations. The most commonly used situation was developed by Amsterdam (1968) for infants and by Gallup (1970) for chimpanzees. In the Amsterdam procedure, the infant's face is marked, either by rouge or tape, and the infant's response to seeing the marked face in a mirror is observed. The operational definition of self-recognition is directing behavior toward the mark, since the infant must recog-

Table 8–1. Developmental Sequence of Self-Recognition.

Age in Months	*Self-Recognitory Behavior*
5–8	*No self-recognition but contingent play*
	Play with contingency
	No self–other differentiation
	Self- but no mark-directed behavior seen
9–12	*Contingency needed for self-recognition*
	Play with contingency
	Some self–other differentiation exhibited
	Self- but no mark-directed behavior seen
15–18	*Self-recognition with features and contingency*
	Play with contingency
	Mark-directed behavior begins
	Use of mirror to reach for objects seen
	Self–other differentiation emerges
	Self-conscious behavior emerges
	Verbal labeling of self begins
21–24	*Use of features for self-recognition*
	Play with contingency
	Mark-directed behavior seen
	Self-conscious behavior seen
	Clear self–other differentiation
	Verbal labeling of self seen
	(proper name usage common)
	(personal pronoun usage begins)
24–30	*Use of features for self-recognition contingency*
	Personal pronoun usage seen

nize that on the image's face, but on his or her own. In our studies, infants first received a no-mark trial, their faces were then marked with rouge (under the guise of wiping the face), and then received a marked trial in front of the mirror.

Self-directed behaviors as seen in mirrors are one of the most direct measures for inferring self-recognition. Imitation has some of the properties of self-directed behavior in that behavior taking place at one point in space (self) is replicated at another point in space (in the mirror). Since it is possible to imitate another, imitation is more likely to occur to one's own image than to another's image, suggesting that it is part of the self-recognition process.

We have observed two types of imitation with the first being less related to self-recognition than the second. The first type includes rhythmic movements, such as bouncing, waving, and clapping, and is most prevalent in infants between nine and twelve months of age. The second type, imitation proper, involves facial movements (e.g., making faces, sticking the tongue out) or playing with the contingency of the mirror (i.e., watching oneself disappear and reappear at the side of the mirror). These behaviors seem to indicate a growing awareness of the properties of reflections and perhaps are related to self-recognition. To our knowledge, these latter behaviors have only been observed in our studies, where they first occurred at fifteen to eighteen months of age, becoming prevalent at twenty-one to twenty-four months of age. These behaviors appear at the same time as mark-directed behaviors but not earlier, as some have proposed, suggesting that at least some forms of imitation are part of the self-recognition process.

The two types of behaviors typically studied and usually thought to infer self-recognition are body-directed and mark-directed behavior. In general, mark-directed rather than baby-directed behavior has been studied, the exception being Gallup's primate work. In our studies we have consistently found that one-quarter of the infants nine to twenty-four months of age touch their bodies or faces when placed in front of a mirror without their faces being marked. Moreover, the number of subjects who do this increases with age. Body-directed behavior increases after being marked with rouge, even in infants who did not specifically touch the rouge and even in our youngest infants. The increase in body-directed behavior after being marked is seen in all of our age groups and may be similar to chimpanzees' use of the mirror to locate visually and touch inaccessible parts of the body (Gallup 1973).

Mark-directed behavior in infants has been examined in at least four studies. All of the studies report surprisingly consistent results: mark-directed behavior was never exhibited by infants younger than fifteen months of age, while fifteen to eighteen months marked the beginning of self-recognition. One-quarter of our sample, 5 percent of Amsterdam's (1968), and none of Schulman and Kaplowitz's (1977) fifteen- to eighteen-month-olds exhibited mark-directed behavior. However, between eighteen and twenty months, a dramatic increase occurs, with approximately three-quarters of the eighteen- to twenty-four-month-olds in all three studies exhibiting mark recognition.

Videotape Representations

It is quite clear from the literature reviewed thus far that young children are able to recognize themselves in mirrors and in still picture representations. However, it is not clear what dimensions of self-representations are salient for the young infant and whether these change with age. As we have noted, infants could be responding to the social features that are common to the image and to the self (i.e., same-age, same-sex peer), to the contingent feedback offered by the mirror, to the familiarity of the perceptual features in the mirror (i.e., specific facial features common to self and image), or to some combination of these. By utilizing videotape feedback systems, it is possible to obtain information on the salience of various dimensions for self-recognition as well as age changes in their use.

The videotape studies were used to compare self and other. In the picture studies, both perceptual-affective and verbal behavior were used as measures while in the videotape studies just perceptual-affective measures were used. In our first videotape study infants were seated in front of a television screen and were presented three different stimulus conditions—contingent self (simultaneous condition), noncontingent self (a videotape of the infant in the same setting made a week earlier), and noncontingent other (a videotape of a same-sex, same-age infant in the same setting). Infants received approximately 25 trials. Affective, attentional, and imitative behaviors were coded. In the second study, the same procedure was utilized with one interesting addition. An unfamiliar person silently approached the infant from behind, with the approach being visible on the television screen. In the contingent conditions, the person was actually there; in the noncontingent conditions, she was on the videotape but not actually present.

In our first videotape study, infants exhibited more positive affect and attention to the other than the self, while they exhibited more imitation and contingent play to the self than to the other noncontingent condition. Thus, affect and attention were more likely to be directed to the unfamiliar peer, imitation to the self. In our second study, infants were more likely to turn to the stranger in the other than in the self noncontingent condition. Differentiation of self and other occurred at fifteen to eighteen months of age in our first study and at twenty-one to twenty-four months of age in our second study. Other studies report that this discrimination did not occur until about two years of age, at the same time that verbal self-referents began to appear (Bigelow 1975), or not at all in the first two years of life (Amsterdam and Greenberg 1977). Our data from both pictures and videotape studies suggest an earlier differentiation of self–other. Interestingly, our picture studies show that infants began to use their proper name only for their pictures and not peers as early as sixteen months. Thus, self–other differentiation in picture or videotape representations are most similar. That videotapes provide information about movement and pictures does not appear to affect the child's ability to differentiate self from other.

Infants also respond differently to contingent and noncontingent representations and do so very early. Papousek and Papousek (1974) report that five-month-olds discriminate between noncontingent eye contact and contingent no-eye contact representations of self, first preferring the latter. Rheingold (1971) found that five-month-old infants responded more positively to a mirror than to a moving picture of an unfamiliar baby. Given these findings with young infants, it is not surprising that we found differentiation between contingent and noncontingent representations in both of our studies, and during the first year of life.

Ontogenetic Sequence

Our studies, taken together with those of previous investigators, allows for general statements about the ontogenesis of self-recognition. This ontogenesis is related to contingency, feature recognition, and social category usage (Lewis and Brooks-Gunn 1979b). Table 8-1 presents a description of self-recognition's developmental sequence over the first three years of life. Contingency is used quite early in the child's life, but it is the ability to recognize and respond to self *independent* of contingency, to respond to feature-recognition, that represents the important developmental milestone in self-recognition. In contingent situations—mirrors and contingent videotapes—infants as young as nine months of age smile, watch themselves intently, move rhythmically, and touch their bodies. These behaviors change very little over the nine- to thirty-six-month period. In fact, some of these behaviors are exhibited even earlier than nine months of age, as Papousek and Papousek (1974) have demonstrated in five- to six-month-olds. At the same time, infants began to use the mirrors to reach for things, both the self (touching the body) and others (turning toward a person who is approaching or an object that is dangling behind). Around fifteen months of age, self- or mark-directed behavior appears in the mirror contingency situation, as does self-conscious behavior. By twenty months, almost all infants respond to contingent representations appropriately and may be said to recognize themselves.

Noncontingent recognition occurs in a parallel although slower sequence. At about nine to twelve months, self-recognition independent of contingency first appears. Support for this comes from our second videotape study (nine- to twelve-month-old infants turn to search for the stranger more often when the other child's videotape is on the screen) and from our second picture study (nine- to twelve-month-olds smile more at their own picture than at another infant's picture). Around fifteen to eighteen months of age, more infants exhibit self–other differentiation in our picture and videotape studies. And, by the time verbal self-referents appear, they are used consistently for self rather than other. By twenty months, self-recognition on the basis of features is clearly evident, as infants recognize their pictures and use social categories appropriately for self and other.

CONSTRUCTING THE SOCIAL WORLD

As we have argued earlier, the child's social cognition involves knowledge of self, of others, and of relationships with others. Indeed, knowledge of others, logically social knowledge (Lewis 1980), cannot be understood without referring to self-knowledge. Further, knowledge of self and others is derived through interaction with the world. In this chapter, we have presented evidence to support our belief in early self-knowledge, demonstrating that the child does acquire such knowledge early, around eight to nine months of age. By the end of the second year, this knowledge is firmly established.

Not only does the self develop during infancy but it influences the acquisition of knowledge of other. Social dimensions such as age and gender are salient for the infant, who uses them to categorize both self and other. The child uses these dimensions to construct an elaborate social world, one that includes various people, social functions, and social situations. Unless we reintroduce the self into this complex social world, we will not be able to understand how the child actually constructs it.

9 SELF-CONCEPT DEVELOPMENT IN CHILDHOOD

Mervin D. Lynch

Self-concept has generally been treated by psychologists as an affective variable that has implications for their own personal personality theory but not as a variable that has a theoretical formulation of its own. As a result, there are many singular and overly simplistic notions about self-concept but no unified theory that may be called a theoretical formulation of self-concept or of self-concept development. Such a developmental formulation is necessary before we can specify precise factors effecting changes in self-concept or specify self-concept—factors that can be measured at various ages of development.

The formulation of self-concept presented in this chapter is that of an information-processing model. It starts with the notion that concepts are rules or combinations of rules called algorithms used by an individual for classification or discrimination. This information-processing notion of concepts stems from writings of Hull (1970) and Piaget (1976) who describe concepts as explanatory rules by which a relation between two or more events may be described. These rules are cognitive processes performing regulatory functions in information-processing as described in writings by Bruner (1975), Schroder et al. (1957), and Hunt (1962). The rules also serve as antecedents to affective consequences such as an individual's self-esteem, empathy, or identification patterns.

The self-concept, like other concepts, is a set of rules for processing information; this particular set has a central regulatory function governing all information-processing and of monitoring sensory input. This set of rules operates as the executive monitor in information processing models similar to one suggested by Bruner (1973) and functions like the ego control processes proposed by Freud (1923), Hartmann (1964), and Klein (1932) in their theories of ego development. Hartman (1964) states that "the ego organizes and controls motility and perception—perception of the outer world but probably also of the self." The ego's "coordinating or integrating tendencies" as well as the "differentiating factor" comprise an "organizing function" representing one level of "mental self-regulation in man."

SELF-CONCEPT DEVELOPMENT

The self-concept originates as sets of inborn rules that support biological survival. Some self-concept rules, including equivalence, ordering, adaptation (assimilation and accommodation), transformation, efficiency, and abstraction, are present at birth. They provide the basis of interaction with environmental stimuli which results in more complex sets of rules for developing reciprocity, visual and motor skill coordination, linguistic and nonlinguistic forms of predication, temporizing, and combination of rules into algorithms.

Early Childhood

Of the rules which comprise the self-concept, some are inborn and others are acquired during infancy; but it is the acquisition of language that enables the rapid proliferation of rules and algorithms governing cognitive processing and resulting in the rapid growth of the self-concept. Research in language development in early childhood has shown that the child has available complex sets of language rules early in its developmental history. For instance, the child as early as eighteen months has rules for grammatically combining words into simple sentences (Braine 1963; Ervin and Miller 1963), rules for transforming sound to meaning (McNeil 1970), time rules for language acquisition (Lenneberg 1967), and perhaps most important, a set of syntax rules to effect the acquisition of vocabulary (Lenneberg 1967).

To account for the existence of language acquisition rules, Chomsky (1967) has proposed the existence of a linguistic acquisition device that develops rules about the regularities of language and rules able to exclude the nongrammatical. This device is inborn, contains the rules for syntax transformation, combination and classification of syntactic and semantic features; and it plays a regulatory role such as that attributed to self-concept. As such, the linguistic acquisition device can be viewed as a special self-concept algorithm, syntactically structured and probably communicated either as codes on a template or syntactically structured codes within the DNA. In either case, templates or structural codes, language acquisition may occur within the unfolding of the syntax by which the self-concept rules are structured.

As the child acquires the language in the early childhood stage, he or she also faces increased sensory input both of a positive and negative nature. Negative input such as unresolved discrepancies, contradictions, personal evaluations, or even denial of a pleasurable experience or aggressive actions would most likely prevail, and as a result the child needs a set of rules for protecting the rules of the executive monitor or self-concept. Ego psychologists have maintained that defense mechanisms are developed by the child to cope with negative or conflicting input, and these represent self-concept rules, such as rationalization, projection, denial, reaction formation, or defense processes such as displacement. This view of defense mechanisms as self-concept rules is consistent with the notion of the inhibitory as well as of the adaptive capacities and the synthetic integrating and organizing functions of the ego presented by writers such as French (1941), Hartmann (1964), and Nunberg (1930).

In early childhood the child begins to distinguish his awareness of a self apart from others, an awareness largely attributable to the development of language and expressed primarily in terms of physical body differentiation. Freud (1923) and Hartmann (1964) have each focused on the importance at this stage of the development of a body image leading to a differentiation of the self from the object world.

Between the ages of three and five the child grows rapidly, averaging about ten inches in height and about ten pounds in weight over a three-year period. During that time the child becomes increasingly more facile in psychomotor skills, so that by five, the child relies confidently on his motor behavior. In the early childhood stage reciprocity rules are formed, and the child develops and elaborates on the figure ground distinction between me and not me. Society impinges and this is accompanied by the growth of reciprocity rules which increasingly occurs with language acquisition. The child is expected to eat with socially accepted implements, drink from glasses, dress in sex-oriented ways, and delay gratification through restrictions such as toilet training.

At the same time the child is learning the societal rules, he or she is also learning to differentiate body parts from objects and others. The three-year-old child spends a large percentage of time exploring his or her body, an interest that decreases dramatically in mid-childhood. During this time there is a growing need to apply rules for validating the success of the child in interacting with the environment (see Freud 1923). The child in infancy seems to recognize its difference from others, but it is in early childhood that the child is able to isolate distinctive features in comparing body parts and motor performance to that of other children and adults.

Along with this intensive focus on body parts is the growth of self-evaluations, a belief about the goodness or badness of rules for solving problems. This self-evaluation or self-esteem probably arises because the child applies what are called validity rules. In early childhood these evaluations are simplistic, all-or-nothing beliefs about the goodness or badness of body parts—for example, I have pretty eyes or I have pretty hair—as reported in observations by Piers and Harris (1964). Such self-evaluations result from trying to validate rules learned at this stage about the use of body parts. They are indications of success or failure in applying self-concept rules; they are not the self-concept rules per se, as has been suggested in the literature.

These validity rules test the success of applications of other rules for adjustment purposes and play a central role in the development of the self-esteem and the general self-concept. As rules are validated, an individual becomes confident in their continued successful applications. Consequently, self-esteem is raised, and the individual can move on to acquire more complex sets of rules for processing information.

Where rules are not successfuly validated through application, an individual will likely experience frustration, heightened anxiety, and a loss of self-esteem. Such failure to validate is likely experienced quite often by individuals who have physical or mental deficiencies or disabilities because these persons may not have self-concept rules for successful application to solve problems or resolve conflict. Failure to validate applications of self-concept rules will lead the individual to search for new rules which an individual with a disability or deficiency may not be able to discover. As a result disabilities or deficiencies are likely to be accompanied by lower self-esteem and by impairment of self-concept development.

Children have the capacity to modify the rules governing their behavior. During the early childhood stage the child generates new rules or modifies old ones to produce algorithms for classification (conjunctions, disjunction, or relational), transition rules from stage to stage, and rules for abstracting features to use for purposes of classification, differentiation, discrimination, or integration. Attention is directed more toward graphic detail (Luria 1976; Vygotsky 1962) with an increasing but sporadic focus on the development of differentiation rules. Beliefs about objects, others, and the child's own self are formed on the basis of attempts to validate the rules which comprise the self-concept, using the self-concept rules for its own validation. Such validations may be against external standards, societal agreement, or rules based upon the child's own perceptual processes.

At the beginning of early childhood the child is relatively inflexible, tending to rely on simple self-concept rules for purposes of validation decisions. As the child progresses through early childhood, however, the child increasingly differentiates between validations based upon different stimuli, and the self-concept becomes more flexible.

Middle Childhood

As the child enters middle childhood he or she depends more on verbal, logical, or abstract rules for validating its self-concept rules, than the more inflexible graphic rules applied at an earlier stage, such as proposed by Vygotsky (1962) and Luria (1976), or simple classification schemes of edge matching, thematic, or key-ring groupings as those proposed by Bruner (1973).

The onset of the formal educational structure aids in self-concept flexibility. Education seems to lead to a reduction in the child's reliance on graphic detail from grades one to six, and to an almost linear decrease in dogmatism (Lynch and Grew 1974). Formal education leads to the acquisition of more abstract sets of representational rules during the middle childhood years as shown by Vygotsky (1962) and Luria (1976). In early childhood exceptions to the rule were not permissible because of the relatively singular rules available for validating reality; but in middle childhood, exceptions are allowed, and the child can now validate concepts formed in infancy, early childhood, and middle childhood.

As the child progresses from ages six to twelve, self-concept rules become constant, and the concepts of invariance and reciprocity rules are developed (Piaget 1926). The child moves from attention on functional means of classification to more analytic and relational forms of classifications such as those shown by Kagan and others (1964). The child is able to set expectancies, be selective in attentional focus, and devote sustained attention to activities such as those in the classroom. The child sets standards about the quality of his or her performance in activities with peers, in school, and at home. Given the availability of expectancy-setting and standard-setting behaviors, the child is able to formulate hypotheses and, through data collection, to evaluate them.

The development of standards and the setting of expectations is represented by the child's efforts to develop an idealized image and to self-actualize. The notion of self-actualization proposed by Maslow (1954) and Rogers (1954) holds that individuals form an expectation about self-development and then evaluate the extent to which they have validated that expectation. The idealized or actualized self-image is a consequence of self-concept, not self-concept per se. Expectations seem to be sets of rules for achieving the self-ideals that are set as standards, the successful validation of which will result in increased idealized or actualized self-judgments. These self-judgments may be more or less distorted indicators of how well the child is actually doing, and thus are more or less accurate indicators of the validation of self-concept rules.

The age level of six to nine seems to be the age when the idealized self develops and when measures of the self–ideal discrepancy can be applied with reliability. A recent study by Howell (1977) indicated that idealized self-discrepancy measures were unreliable when applied to preschool and first grade children, perhaps due to the fact that younger children don't have rules for setting expectations about the idealized self.

During the ages of six to twelve the child, through societal institutions and games, begins to develop social reciprocity rules that reach their peak in adolescence. Societal rules of fair conduct, winning and losing, sportsmanship, courtesy, etiquette, and social rules for interacting with personnel in schools, churches, police departments, government, and with families, friends, and peers are formally developed. Limit-setting is applied more extensively as the child explores the stimulus environment to determine his or her available choice options or psychological degrees of freedom.

Self-concept rules seem to become more differentiated during this period so that children find multiple meanings in response to the same stimulus and have not yet developed the rules for validating the correct one. Findings in a study by Bruner and Kenney (1965) showed the extent of the problem of differentiation that children experience at this age level. It was found that seven-year-olds made more errors than five-year-olds, ostensibly because five-year-olds attended to only one feature, whereas seven-year-olds attended to two or more. Effects on increased differentiation have also been shown in factor-analytic studies of ratings of self-judgments. For instance, Lynch and Chaves (1977) subjected semantic differential responses on the concept myself to factor analysis for second, fourth, and sixth grade children. They found that second graders had as many dimensions for judging the self as did fourth and sixth graders, but the dimensions obtained for second graders were not as differentiated as those for fourth or sixth graders.

The increase in differentiation and acquisition of rules during middle childhood is accompanied by the development of rules for judging how the individual is evaluated by others. This judgment of how others view me has been described by Cooley (1922) as the "looking-glass-self" and by Mead (1934) as the "interactionist self," and represents what may be called the empathic self-judgment. Empathic self-judgments result from the application of the self-concept rules but are not self-concept rules per se.

The end of the childhood period is accompanied by the development of puberty and adolescence. The child begins to grow dramatically, and attention is largely directed to the achievement of fertility and social acceptance of new physical characteristics. Rules acquired by the child are cultural ones for validating the desirability or undesirability of the new body characteristics. The individual forms questions which they will ask in adolescence such as "how they can make the rules and skills learned earlier jibe with what is currently in style" (Erikson 1951). The child's concern for how others view me "becomes progressively more important with the approach of purberty and reaches a peak in adolescence. Successful or unsuccessful applications of rules for attaining social acceptance results in increasingly more dramatic shifts in empathic self-judgment, and a search for different and often more complex self-concept rules for achieving social acceptance and independence. It is through the successful acquisition and application of such rules in adolescence that the child acquires an ego identity associated with maturity (Erikson 1968).

SOME IMPLICATIONS OF THIS SELF-CONCEPT FORMULATION

The definitional framework and developmental sequence of rules presented here provides a particularly useful and meaningful basis for conducting research on self-concept. The specification of levels at which self-concept rules are developed should provide a basis for selecting measures of self-concept to use at each age. Instructional procedures may be directed toward developing appropriate rules for each age level. The absence of rules where expected at a particular age level may provide useful indicators of the possible presence of learning disabilities, described as errors in self-concept rules in accordance with Cobb (1970) and Bobroff (1956).

The redefinition of self-concept as a cognitive variable provides a basis for eventually resolving some problems associated with approaches to measuring self-concept. Some writers have criticized available measures of self-concept in that they often have "undemonstrated, inadequate, or even entirely unexplored construct validity" (Shavelson et al. 1976; Wiley 1974). In the theoretical framework presented in this chapter, self-concept tests such as those currently available are viewed as tests of the consequences of attempts to apply and validate self-concept rules and *not* tests of self-concept per se. This situation is analogous to that of memory and retention, where memory is measured in terms of its consequences, such as retention. Self-concept will have multiple consequences such as self-esteem, idealized self-judgments, and empathic self-judgments; and such consequences should provide useful constructs against which to validate present measures.

One should expect to find that changes in validation of the self-concept rules will lead to changes in consequences specified by the rules. If an individual successfully validates rules for achieving self-idealization then available measures should show an increased self-idealization. Likewise, successful validation of rules for achieving empathy should be measured by increased congruency of the individual's judgment of the self as expected by others and increased empathic self-judgments. It should be possible to design experimental studies where validations of construct-specific rules are made, and measures are tested. A major problem, however, is that descriptive items used in available self-concept tests are situationally specific, that is, they apply differently in different contexts, as shown in studies reported by Bridgman and Shipman (1975) and Norem–Hebeisen (1978). This problem will have to be remedied before descriptive measures can accurately test self-concept through its consequences.

APPLICATION OF THIS THEORETICAL FORMULATION TO RESEARCH

Applications of this theoretical framework for self-concept as a cognitive variable to the study of situational specificity in self-concept measurement provide useful examples of how this cognitive formulation of self-concept works with a meaningful research problem. In the present formulation, situational specificity in measurement is considered a consequence of differential levels of individual exposure to self-concept-related frustration. An individual likely will exhibit shifts in self-evaluation as a consequence of exposures to potentially frustrating events, with the level of shift in evaluation judgments corresponding to the level of frustration experienced.

This notion of self-concept-related frustration stems from considerations basic to the present redefinition of self-concept as a particular set of rules governing information-processing behavior and operating to monitor and to control behavioral functions. As one function, the self-concept has rules for validating other concepts in the behavioral system, rules which confirm the adequacy of the rules for processing information. This is most likely what is measured by existing tests of self-concept. These evaluations depend in large part upon the extent and quality of the prior experiences individuals have had in validating these rules, and of course are subject to change, given variations in contextual stimuli.

A likely source of variation in evaluative judgments will be the frustration an individual experiences as a result of exposure to situations leading to potential disconfirmations of the available rules for central processing. Self-concept-related frustration is defined the same as general frustration; an "interference with the occurrence of an instigated goal-response at its proper time in the behavior sequence" (Collar et al. 1969). Frustration events are those which block the individual's goal-seeking behavior, threaten his self-esteem, or deprive himself the opportunity to gratify some salient motive (Barker et al. 1943; Mussen et al. 1963; Sears 1958).

Self-concept-related frustration may result from the interposition of obstacles, deficiencies in the environment or the person, and personal or interpersonal conflicts that prevent an individual from achieving a goal—specifically, the validation of rules which are part of the general self-concept. Frustration will also most likely be accompanied by anxiety which an individual may reduce by successfully applying rules developed for overcoming obstacles or deficiencies or conflict resolution; validation of the success of rule applications should lead to ego enhancement. Likewise, an individual may escape from or avoid frustration by applying one of many defense mechanisms such as rationalization, projection, or identification. Successful application of defense rules will be ego-enhancing or at least provide the individual time to develop rules for resolving problems or conflict resolution.

When a rule application is not validated after exposure to a frustrating event or frustration stimulus concept, the individual will experience either frustration or anticipation of frustration, and will respond accordingly. Heightened anxiety or drive state which accompanies this self-concept-related frustration may lead to consequences usually associated with frustration in general such as restlessness, aggression, apathy, fantasy, stereotypy, and regression; hence an individual is motivated to resolve, escape, or avoid this frustration.

When an individual experiences frustration and its consequences, the individual will also probably experience a shift in self-judgment. If an individual has had extensive experience with frustration, he or she may exhibit frustration tolerance and show little shift in self-judgment as a function of the exposure to a frustration stimulus. If, however, the person has little prior exposure to the frustration stimulus, then the individual may exhibit high frustration, and such frustration may also lead to sizeable temporary shifts in self-judgment. The extent of the shift in self-judgment should be directly related to the extent of frustration or of the heightened anxiety or drive state accompanying the frustration experience. As a result, a measurement on the shift in self-judgment resulting from an exposure to a frustration stimulus provides an index of self-concept-related frustration, whether the frustration is real or anticipatory.

MEASUREMENT OF SELF-CONCEPT-RELATED FRUSTRATION

Pattern analysis procedures with the semantic differential and *D* statistic measures are used here to index shifts in self-judgment as a measure of self-concept-related frustration. Several research applications are presented, explaining the measurement methodology. The purposes in these applications were twofold: (a) to propose a pattern analysis approach using the semantic differential and *D* statistic as a methodology which will index self-concept-related frustration; and (b) to present the results of three applications of this measurement methodology to problems of indexing individual reactions to potentially frustrating situations.

Measures of self-judgment are obtained with the semantic differential, as has been the case in more than eighty studies of self-concept (Wiley 1973). Selections of semantic differential items for use in this measure are made from other applications of the semantic differential to obtain adult measures of self-judgment. These have been generated with factor analysis in studies reported by Osgood (1957) and Snider and Osgood (1969). Semantic differential items for children were chosen from those isolated in a factor analytic study by Lynch (1970).

The generalized distance measure *D* is used as a pattern analysis measure with the semantic differential to obtain a measure of shifts in self-judgment. Its application is similar to other applications in studies of identification, idealized self-concept, and empathic self-concept (for example, Lazowick 1955; Lynch 1970; and Nugent 1970). In those studies ratings were obtained on semantic differential items on the concept myself and on other concepts such as mother, father, how I would like to be and how other persons see me, with the same set of semantic differential items for each concept. The *D* statistic measure was applied to scores on ratings on each concept pair, and this *D* statistic provided measures of identification, self-idealization, or empathic self-concept.

In the present studies measurements were obtained on the concept myself and on a selection of potential frustration stimulus concepts presented in writing in a "suppose" framework. This accommodated the possibility that individual subjects may not have experienced the frustration stimulus situation. For example, a study was made of frustration situations experienced by quadriplegics. In that study ratings were obtained on a frustration stimulus concept such as "Suppose you were in a good restaurant and you had to go to the toilet but you couldn't because your wheelchair wouldn't fit in the bathroom. How would you feel about yourself?" Ratings were obtained on the concept myself and on each of the suppose potentially frustrating stimulus concepts. The *D* statistic was computed between scores on these ratings, and these *D* statistic scores provided measures of self-conception-related frustration. The larger the *D* statistic, the larger the shift in self-judgment the individual experiences, given exposure to the frustration situation specified in the concept.

SOME APPLICATIONS OF THIS METHODOLOGY

To date we have carried out a number of applicational studies using this measurement methodology in which frustration stimulus concepts are chosen representing different levels of potential frustration. These studies provide some face validity evidence that this methodology of measurement is discriminating as it should be and, hence, that it is validly measuring self-concept-related frustration.

One such application was the previously mentioned study of quadriplegics. Stimulus concepts were chosen which represented a wide variation in potential frustration levels. Highly personalized and likely high frustration male–female situational concepts were generated such as "Suppose you were out on a date and your date wanted to have sex with you, but you wouldn't because you felt you couldn't have sex, how would you feel about yourself?" and "Suppose you meet a person whom you would like to date, but they turn your offer down based on their explanation that you are in a wheelchair, how would you feel about yourself?" Less personalized and potentially less frustrating situations were represented by concepts such as "Suppose you are entering a city building to meet with the mayor and you must be carried up a long flight of stairs, how would you feel about yourself?" Mean *D* statistic frustration scores varied from 11.39 for the having sex frustration concept to 6.07 for the low frustration being carried up the stairs situation, with the differences significant, $p < .01$.

These results lend support to the validity of this procedure for measuring self-concept-related frustration in that the measure is discriminating in expected ways. One other finding of this study was interesting to note in terms of the value of the measurement approach. These quadriplegics had all received extensive work on independence training. On the basis of behavioral measures of their ability to perform various daily activities on their own, it was possible to split the twenty-four individuals into high and low independence groups. Although the groups differed on behavioral measures of independence, they did not differ in degrees of frustration experienced given exposure to the various stimulus situations. It is likely that the independence exhibited behaviorally was not internalized conceptually, and that while some quadriplegics appeared to have shown independence adjustment behavior, it was most likely only superficial. These results indicate that substantially more training is needed with these quadriplegics to enable them to cope with emotional problems before real independence will be achieved.

A second application was a study of fourth grader reactions to potential frustration experiences associated with failure. High frustration situations included those associated with failure due to personal inadequacy such as "Suppose your friends were playing tag in the water but you couldn't because you didn't know how to swim, how would you feel about yourself?" and "Suppose you were taking a math test and you were the only one who didn't finish, how would you feel about yourself?" Lesser frustration situations included common experiences toward which children have likely developed some frustration tolerance such as "Suppose your teacher called on you and you gave a wrong answer and the other kids laughed, how would you feel about yourself?" and "Suppose your parents expected you to do well in school and you came home with an unsatisfactory report card, how would you feel about yourself?" Mean frustration scores varied from 7.05 for the playing tag situation, 6.82 for the math test example, 6.43 for the wrong answer example, and 6.21 for the report card case; the means for high and low situations differed significantly, $p < .01$.

Finally, a third application was a study designed to explore the possibility of relationships between three self-concept-related frustration measures and truancy behavior. In this study 180 seventh and eighth grade students—half truants, half nontruants—were administered a questionnaire including measures of attitudes toward the teacher and three self-concept-related frustration measures. Scores on measures of intelligence were available on all students. A linear discriminant analysis was made on this data with truancy as the dependent variable, and the three best estimators of truancy behavior were identified as the IQ measure and two of the three *D* statistic measures of self-concept-related frustration. These were "Suppose you had to go to the bathroom and the teacher wouldn't let you go because she thought that you were faking it, how would you feel about yourself?" and "Suppose you had cut class with some friends and you all decided to 'borrow' some bicycles to get downtown—and were caught, how would you feel about yourself?" The going to the bathroom concept likely represents a trust factor which is positively associated with truancy. The greater the frustration experienced due to a lack of trust as indicated by the bathroom example, the more likely a student is to be a truant. In contrast, being caught borrowing someone else's bicycle is likely "old hat" for the truant. Compared to the nontruant, the truant seems to have developed a tolerance for getting caught. It is the nontruant who would probably experience frustration in this situation.

In addition to these studies, we are currently completing a number of other studies using the self-concept-related frustration measure for purposes of studying situations involving failure, consequences of abuse, and other problems of learning disabilities, all of which present problems in measuring self-concept in situationally specific contexts. The definitional framework of self-concept, its development, and the notion of self-concept-related frustration presented in this chapter seem to provide both a meaningful theory and a useful methodology through pattern analyses for study of these and other related problems.

10 A MAXIMIZATION MODEL OF SELF-CONCEPT

Ardyth A. Norem–Hebeisen

Self-concept is subject to a common central organizing principle: selection of rules and processes which are consistent with enhancement of the survival, maintenance, and growth of the organism. It is generated from observations of oneself and one's relationship with the environment and includes self-related definitions, expectations, and interpretations of the linkage of related events. It is a component of the continuous reciprocal interaction between behavior, environment, sensory input, and thought. The following series of propositions elaborate on the role of self-concept in human functioning. The conceptual forebearers of these propositions are found in general systems theory, cognitive consistency theory, and cognitive developmental theory, while much of the self-concept research was gleaned from the field of social psychology.

Proposition 1: *The human organism functions in a purposive manner, demonstrating patterns of behavior that support its own survival, maintenance, and growth.* This maximizing principle also includes conceptualization in general and self-conceptualizing in particular. Given a multitude of external inputs, the organism constructs meanings which, within the matrix of events and realities perceived, supports the individual's survival and growth. This view of human functioning is consistent with proposals from several scientific disciplines including evolutionary biology, social psychology, and systems theory (Dawkins 1976; Heider 1958; Lecky 1945; LockLand 1973).

Explicit documentation of this proposition is not possible at present because its support lies in logical analysis of broad patterns of behavior, in the demonstrated survival of living systems, and in scientific support for more narrowly defined implications of the propositions. Each of the following propositions are logical extensions of this first one, and because of their more limited scope, empirical data related to their support are more readily available.

Proposition 2: *The human organism seeks self-oriented concepts and meanings that (a) evidence consistency across the diverse elements of a given segment of experience, (b) evidence consistency with established internal organization of the individual, and (c) are maximizing to the individual's experience and functioning.* Sources of information for concept development may include currently held concepts, personal objectives, rules of causality, and environmental constraints. Identification of consistent elements across these inputs facilitates the acquisition of pragmatically valid concepts which are (a) consistent with one's experience, (b) a reasonable reflection of "objective" reality, and (c) provide a reasonable basis for judgments and decisions. This identification of consistent elements supports the growth, maintenance, and survival of the organism. Thus both conceptual schema and behavior may be broadly interpreted as products of the rules for selecting, maximizing, and interpreting outcomes. Self-concept also functions in this manner.

The processing of information across diverse aspects of experience is fundamental to a mastery of the causal network of the environment, and some minimal level of such consistency across information sources is essential as a basis for action (Davies 1968; Heider 1958; Lecky 1945; Rosenberg 1968; Tannenbaum 1968). Historically, efforts to describe and document balance, consistency, or "goodness of fit" have been carried out by social psychologists in the pursuit of the principle of "cognitive consistency" (Abelson 1960, 1968; Brehm and Cohen 1962; Katz 1968; Kelman and Baron 1968; Newcomb 1968; Rosenberg 1968). A review of the rich diversity of data related to these efforts leads to two inferences: (a) there are varied components of consistency, ways of attaining it, and levels at which it may be attained, and (b) consistency issues appear to be relevant only when the purposive or goal-directed aspects of the individual are involved. The second inference suggests that optimization of personal functioning may be served by the consistency-seeking process.

Recent research provides empirical evidence in support of a more broadly defined consistency-seeking process. Three studies provide evidence that organization of perceptions is influenced in the direction of enhanced personal well-being. First, Rogers and others (1977), in their review of their experimental data, note that self-reference provides an integrated encoding device which is very powerful as a facilitator of recall; they suggest in light of such data that the self is a "well structured and powerful schema which, in order to function as demonstrated in the study, must be a consistent, uniform, well structured, and powerful schema." Second, subjects in a study by Miller and others (1978) made more observations and interpretations about other people's behavior when they anticipated that they would deal with them again. This finding suggests a self-serving interpretation of the attribution process, wherein information is processed in ways to better increase our own prediction and control. Finally, Marcus (1977) identified self schemata in subjects which function as cognitive generalizations about the self derived from past experience. These schemata organize and guide the processing of self-related information contained in the individual's social experiences and can then be used as a basis for future judgments, decisions, and predictions about the self.

Proposition 3: *The development of conceptual structures consistent with the survival, maintenance, and growth of the organism is multifaceted and developmentally progressive.* Self-concept is a function of (a) the meanings and consequences of past experiences, (b) current experience originating in the external environment, (c) conditioned emotional responses to the environment, and (d) the internal cognitive processes used for selecting and making meaning from the matrix of data available. Developmentally it reflects qualitative changes similar to other aspects of cognitive development. Thus, self-concept varies in degrees of organization and complexity and ranges along continua from fragmentary to cohesive, concrete to abstract, simple to complex, and specific to general. The fragmentary, concrete, simple, and specific ends of each continuum are most characteristic of the self-concept of young children, while their opposites are more characteristic of mature persons. With the passage of time, shifts along the continua reflect consistency based on accommodations of an increasing body of diverse experiences. On the basis of the "best-fit" rule, the individual must periodically review and reformulate self-concept as new input is available and as needs and circumstances of the individual change.

The multifaceted, developmentally progressive quality of concept development may be observed in several theoretical camps. These include sociology, cognitive developmental psychology, social psychology, and ego psychology. A brief review follows of some aspects from each of these fields relevant to self-concept.

According to Mead, self-concept evolves through changing qualities of interaction with the social environment (Meltzer 1967). At the earliest stages in life a child has only observation of others and imitation as a means to derive information about him- or herself. Thus the small child's self-concept is likely to be highly consistent with a given experience in time, but highly fluid and changing across situations. Later, as the child moves to a role-taking mode, self-concept will reflect consistency with a given role, but continuity across roles or classes of situations may vary.

Later the child abstracts a generalized self. This later stage reflects self-concept at a higher level of abstraction. A more unified sense of self is under construction as the individual accepts concepts of self that fit appropriate roles and experiences, and rejects those that seem less suitable.

As the level of generality and focus for which conceptual consistency is sought progresses from one phase of development to another, the total organism encounters a wide variety of factors that may require accommodation. Among these are social constraints as brought to bear by significant others such as teachers, peers, and parents; the pressure of the broader community and general expectations to produce; one's own judgment of what one ought to be and what is good; the degree to which the meeting of specific needs is dependent on achievement of specific kinds and levels of performance; the need to be accepted by others; attributions of effort, ability, and effectiveness; and estimates of efficacy, potential, and expectations for future outcomes. Thus one would expect issues salient to self-concept to shift for adolescents and adults as a reflection of their primary social rules and functions.

Cognitive developmental psychology places great emphasis on the study of qualitative changes in internal organization as individuals mature. Meticulous description of such changes in logical functioning has been provided by Piaget (Inhelder and Piaget 1958). Following Piaget's pioneering work, other researchers have investigated the nature of such qualitative changes. Thus, Loevinger (1976) has focused on ego or character development in human personality, claiming the ego as the central organizing factor in human functioning. Kohlberg (1969) has focused his research and theory on the development of moral reasoning. Common across all such cognitive developmental perspectives is the claim that the individual progresses along an invarient hierarchical sequence of qualitative change. The changes reflect transformations characterized by shifts along continua from the simple to complex, specific to general, concrete to abstract, and fragmentary to cohesive. They develop through reciprocal interaction between genetically determined developmental sequences and life experiences.

More explicit attention to the developmental qualities of adolescent and adult cognitive development introduces a shift in emphasis from Piaget's work. While retaining concepts of hierarchical development across childhood, there is greater emphasis on interaction with the social environment. The influence of current life experiences on the cognitive development of adolescents and adults is discussed by Piaget (1972), Riegel (1973), and Schaie (1977). While these authors describe cognitive changes in adolescents and adults in the context of current life experiences, the structural change implicit in Piaget's theories on cognitive development in childhood serve as a foundation from which specialization and elaboration of later cognitive development may merge.

Within the area of social psychology, several theorists describe cognitive consistency processes from a developmental perspective. Kaplan and Crockett (1968) propose that modes of dealing with inconsistency differ systematically in a developmental sequence. More primitive modes of resolution are characterized by an exclusive single factor with no consideration of multiplicity of sources. In the intermediate modes the process moves to one other factor beyond those immediately involved to resolve the apparent incompatibility of elements. In advanced modes of resolution, explicit consideration is given to a multiplicity of factors. Kelman and Baron (1968) outline a similar hierarchy in consistency processing. Their model proposes movement from compartmentalization, to restructuring the context in which the inconsistency occurs, to transcendence through introduction of a superordinate principle. The models provided by Kaplan, Crockett, and Kelman and Baron parallel the cognitive developmental theories in the manner in which they outline qualitative changes in the cognitive processing of the available data.

Another line of related research and theory development is focused on the quality of self-knowledge. Research by Alschuler and others (1977) supports the hypothesis that self-conceptualizing is characterized by hierarchical cognitive structure. The finding of this research parallels other theories of hierarchical change in conceptual functioning. Alschuler and others propose four levels of self-knowledge: elemental, situational, patterned, and transformational. In a replication of their original work, the stages correlate substantially with age ($r = .61$) and ego level ($r = .77$).

Other research is also consistent with the thesis of hierarchically ordered changes in self-concept. Van den Daele (1968) has identified such a developmental organization in description of ego ideal, while Monetmayor and Eisen (1977) have found that self-descriptions are characterized by increasing abstraction with age and a tendency for children and adolescents to describe areas of particular salience for their age group. Here again is a repetition of the theme: fixed sequence of developmental change *and* high salience of current life experience as a focus of the level of achieved functioning.

If subsequent research into developmental qualities of self-concept development reinforces the observation of isomorphism across various dimensions of cognitive functioning, the following assertions may be strengthened. Many of these specify the unique qualities of self-concept among adolescents and adults as contrasted to that of children.

1. An ongoing task in self-conceptualization is to integrate increasingly wider sets of information into a concept of self. At higher levels of development the self-concept will incorporate a broader data base.
2. Prior to developmental change, the perceived body of data about self will always be greater than is currently integrated into the self-concept.
3. As development progresses, self-perceptions will become more differentiated, and contain more subcategories and conditions under which a particular self-attribution might be made.

4. As development progresses, self-concept will be more stable, anchored as a generalization across situations, and less vulnerable to change on the basis of single episodes.
5. As development progresses, measured self-concept will reflect greater internal consistency. Where self-concept of young children will be highly unstable, self-concept of mature persons will have some optimal level of consistency across self-descriptions.
6. Adult self-concept will integrate some apparent contradictions in self-description. The superordinate principle of opposites as part of the whole will serve to unite widely differing behavior.
7. Aspects of self-concept most salient to the individual will be those which are a function of current life circumstances.
8. Self-concept evolves through a recursive process involving acquisition of new data, matching the new data against current concepts, and revision of current concepts where this is required to support an integrated and realistic sense of self. Conclusions about self which are estimated to be most conducive to a stable perception and supporting well-being will be preferred, selected, and defended.
9. In earlier stages of development, data derived from external events will be the raw material from which self-concept is constructed. As development progresses, internal points of reference, values, and personal perceptions will have an increasing salience in the formulation.
10. Self-concept is a central component within a larger belief system about the nature of the world and people in it. As development progresses, concept of self, while nested within broader concepts of the nature of the world in general, will become increasingly explicit.

Proposition 4: *Specific content of the self-concept is generated within the constraints of the "goodness of fit" or consistency rule, thus serving the purpose of maximizing gain and minimizing loss for the individual as a living system.* This is a fairly obvious and readily acceptable position with respect to a positive sense of one's own work, a sense of efficacy, confidence, and self-respect. That enhanced or positive self-concept should function to support organismic functioning seems almost a truism; however, there are considerable complexities to such a claim.

Persons have a tendency to process information and to behave in a way that is most enhancing to self-concept. Several recent studies make this point with respect to self-presentation, effort expended in a task, and social action behavior. In a reanalysis of their earlier study, Rokeach, Grube, and others (1977) interpreted obtained behavioral changes as an effort to secure and maintain a positive self-concept. In this study subjects participated in social action activities subsequent to being confronted with the discrepancy between their current behavior and their self-concept on such issues. Sigall and Gould (1977) found that high and low self-esteem subjects chose to expend effort in "easy" and "hard" evaluation conditions on a basis that would be experienced as maximally enhancing of self. Low self-esteem subjects would choose to expend more effort for an easy evaluator as this would maximize successful outcomes. For a difficult evaluator they would choose to expend little effort; any subsequent failure or criticism could be attributed to their relative lack of effort in that situation. High self-esteem subjects would expend less effort for an easy evaluator, assuming that they would expect to be evaluated well anyway; they choose to expend greater effort for the difficult evaluator as such effort was more likely to win positive outcomes and support self-enhancing attributions. Subjects in another study (Baumeister and Jones 1978), when confronted with unfavorable information about themselves, were likely to avoid refutation but to emphasize other enhancing information about themselves. Persons receiving highly positive evaluations were more modest in their self-presentations. The authors summarize by suggesting that the "results might be taken as further support of the notion that people are motivated to gain approval after failure and to avoid disapproval after success" (p. 617). In each of these studies those choices which were supportive of self-concept may also be interpreted as consistent with broader organismic well-being.

However, it is conceivable that an individual's need for an interpretable, predictable, or safe environment may supersede the possible advantages of enhancing self-concept. Self-concept may include attributions which serve the need of the total system at the cost of a subjective sense of personal value or efficacy. Psychological survival for some persons, for example, may require that they relinquish a sense of competence in deference to needs of another person (parent, peer, lover) who is important in other ways to their well-being. In daily life, and in the research literature, we clearly see people choosing patterns of behavior and making judgments of themselves which are denigrating. Does this challenge the principle of facilitation of organismic functioning? The position of this chapter is that well-being of the total organism, not enhanced self-concept, is of higher priority for the individual. Carl Rogers (1959) cites the hypothetical case in which a child's need for a parent's approval and support may cause the child to go against that which the child perceives as appropriate. In this situation, the child abdicates his or her own sense of judgment and sense of what is worthy for gains which may be interpreted as broader survival needs: the acceptance, continued nurturance, and care by a parent.

Negative self-judgments may or may not enhance total organismic well-being. There are at least two patterns. The first pattern is use of negative self-judgments which are consistent with a broader sense of well-being. This is illustrated in a case where it is more optimizing to make choices consistent with objective reality than choices that make undue claims of success, thus assuming a maintenance perception of self as an objective thinker. The second pattern is observed in negative judgments, which serve as markers that broader organismic needs are being shortcut. In this pattern broader organismic well-being is precluded by homeostatic processes that serve limited needs and functions of the organism. An example is the self-critical but "helpless" attributions of an overweight person who continues to overeat in order to serve short-range goals of anxiety reduction. Perseverating negative self-judgments under these circumstances are indications that other aspects of organismic well-being are not being met.

A body of research related to negative self-concept is that which investigates the "helplessness" phenomenon and its counterconcept, "efficacy." Subjects' sense of efficacy is highly predictive of actual performance in some settings (Bandura 1977b). Furthermore, attributions of helplessness may be induced with a model paralleling common classroom procedure (Dweck et al. 1978). Given a predisposing series of life situations, the attribution of helplessness may be a tenable response. However, difficulty occurs when the individual fails to be open to new data that could suggest better probabilities or alternative directions. This may lock the individual into a pattern of interpreting and responding which is counterproductive to optimal functioning. When this happens, a process of selection begins to function to the disadvantage of the individual; such persons tend to drop out, leaving new frontiers of growth to those who have more supportive rule systems. Persons who are better able to cope as expressed in their positive sense of efficacy have a better chance of psychological and physical survival.

If the individual experiences helplessness through repeated or profound failure, there appears to be at least one pattern of response toward better functioning. This response entails reassessment of the situation and making choices on a basis that will opt for the greatest probability of well-being. In the case of repeated or profound failure, a reassessment of oneself and one's subsequent behavior may be the key to salvaging a maximally supportive and protective outcome in a situation which is, in other respects, profoundly negating or invalidating of the individual's assertion toward desired outcomes. The dynamic tension between despair and assertive commitment to change is dramatically portrayed in Hamlet's soliloquy:

> To be or not to be: that is the question.
> Whether 'tis nobler in the mind to suffer
> The slings and arrows of outrageous fortune,
> Or to take arms against a sea of trouble,
> And by opposing end them.

The complexity inherent in the functioning of negative self-concept is reflected in this series of hypotheses.

1. Negative self-concept is often an indication that some aspect of one's experience is inconsistent with one's survival-maintenance-growth. It is often accompanied by feelings of inadequacy which serve as a signal that the individual must make some kind of action in defense of or in assertion of his or her well-being.
2. Situations or behavior at the time when feelings of inadequacy are experienced may often be characterized by adaptive or defensive behavior. Such adaptive or defensive behaviors provide short-term support toward fuller functioning; they are often insufficient, however, to fulfill more broadly defined organismic well-being.
3. Adaptations are characterized by responses that maximize achievement of broad organismic well-being; defenses are characterized by responses that secure some approximation of balance in some area of focus while preventing or interfering with

accommodation to broad organismic goals. Avoidance, denial, rationalization, acceptance, and assertion may all function as either adaptation or defense, depending on the outcome for the organism. An example of adaptation is seen in an able person searching for ways to build more effective study habits. An example of defense is illustrated by an able person who gives up academic pursuits to avoid implications of anticipated failure.

4. As persons mature, they tend to insulate themselves from tasks and relationships that they experience as denigrating. They select lifestyles that minimize chronic feelings of unease and become more adept at identifying and circumventing derogating events.
5. Adaptive and defensive behaviors may become established as self-perpetuating closed processes in which other alternatives appropriate for even broader organismic growth are less likely to occur. In this case, unresolved feelings of inadequacy reflect the failure to advance toward more broadly defined organismic goals.
6. Life experiences sometimes lead persons to the conclusion that they can make minimal progress toward meeting their needs and goals. When this position of helplessness is adopted, errors made tend to lower or confirm the already decimated self-concept; each error is given excessive credibility as confirmation of the position of helplessness.
7. If, in a position of helplessness, the individual continues to reexamine conditions surrounding the issues at hand with the purpose of arriving at patterns of behavior conducive to the well-being of the organism as a whole, the attribution of helplessness will be reassessed. Then areas of behavior in which greater efficacy may be expressed can be identified, and behavior in areas containing greater probability of success can be pursued. Failure to renegotiate apparently helpless situations in this manner may lead to more constricted functioning. In extreme conditions it may result in death.

Proposition 5: *In concurrence with the principle of complimentarity (borrowed from theoretical physics), the rule that dictates consistency with organic well-being sometimes implies implementation of the antithesis of survival, maintenance, and growth; withdrawal, diminution, and death.* Given certain conditions in the organism's environment, regression or death may sometimes be selected as maximizing. This is analogous to the pattern observed in physics and philosophy (Capra 1977); the cyclical giving up of current existence and coming into new existence. In psychological development examples of this include the relinquishing of childlike ways for new patterns of adulthood, and the relinquishing of rigidly adult behavior for a synthesis of child and adult patterns.

This principle augments the consideration of negative self-concept. When organisms are overwhelmed, the most constructive or compassionate choice for the experience of well-being for a given life may be to end it. In human beings, the giving up of existence is best documented in the literature on suicide and studies of psychosomatic medicine. Suicide may sometimes be perceived as the best alternative to a bleak future, and research in psychosomatic medicine points to unresolved personal loss and despair as concomitant with malignancies. There are also increasing reports of clinical case studies in which reframing a cancer victim's self-concept with respect to self-blame and despair precedes marked remission or disappearance of the physical pathology. Such thereapeutic approaches deal with multiple levels of meaning for the concerned person and imply multiple levels of information-processing at which the self makes decisions to thrive or to sicken.

IMPLICATIONS OF THE MODEL

Given the framework outlined in this chapter, what is a probable network of relationships among the self-concept variables? Here are some possibilities:

1. Self-concept is not the product of a simple sum of experiences. With advancing development, self-concept reflects increasing interaction and integration within an organized network of relationships.
2. Developmental changes in self-concept are reflected in the breadth of the context and quality of conceptual organization reflecting increasing abstraction, generalizability, and complexity.
3. Self-concept is one variable among several which serves to influence behavior and preferences.

4. There is likely a reciprocal feedback network between the concept of the world-at-large and self-concept and capacity to perceive, respond to, and integrate complex concepts and data matrices.
5. The concepts held by an individual at any point in time will be a product of past learning experiences and affective and cognitive processing.
6. Some component of the self-concept will be challenged whenever an event occurs which does not fit within the constraints of the present self-concept. At such a point, an altered concept will be sought which is consistent with new data and the integrity of the organism.
7. In situations that are perceived to threaten or denigrate the individual's concept of worth, choices will be made which maximize gains or minimize losses first to an immediate state of internal balance, and second to the total organismic balance.

The broad theoretical construct outlined is a framework for viewing research on the relationship between behavior and self-concept. Both children and adults have been subjects in studies suggesting that self-concept functions in a causal role (Miller et al. 1973; Shrauger and Rosenberg 1970; Wattenberg and Clifford 1962), while another cluster of studies points to behavior as an antecedent to changed self-concept (Bandura et al. 1977; Calsyn and Kenny 1977; Koocher 1971). The multivariate, interactive concept of human cognition and behavior outlined in this chapter would predict that in these studies the antecedent variable which inputs either new self-concept or new behavior introduces inconsistency in the current conceptual-behavioral matrix. Thus behavior which is inconsistent with the self-concept is a potential stimulant to self-concept change, while self-concept shifts which are inconsistent with current patterns of behavior are a potential stimulant to behavioral change. Such relationships may ultimately prove to be cyclical or spiral in nature when appropriate measures and data analysis become available to test such a pattern of interdependence.

The tendency toward consistency with organismic well-being is a megatrait extending across multiple modalities and multiple categories of situations involving cognition, affect, and behavior. The configurations of a more broadly defined consistency process may clarify as we study its implications for the promotion of organismic well-being.

Recent calls to scientists for research and data-processing methods which better take into account the multifaceted, interactive qualities of the human system have been made by Kenneth Gergen (1976), Urie Bronfenbrener (1977), and Fred Kerlinger (1977). The model outlined here provides a conceptual framework that requires an accounting of such variables.

11 THE SPONTANEOUS SELF-CONCEPT AS AFFECTED BY PERSONAL DISTINCTIVENESS

William J. McGuire
Claire V. McGuire

Taking the self-concept trip is hardly a lonely voyage. Wylie's (1974, 1978) new two-volume edition of the *Self-Concept*, despite being selective, summarizes over a thousand studies. These studies having consumed so much social resources, we researchers have an obligation to evaluate whether the resulting advancement of knowledge regarding the self-concept has been proportionate to the considerable effort put into its investigation.

APPROACHES TO SELF-CONCEPT STUDY

In this introductory section we shall first describe strengths and weaknesses of the published self-concept work, and then describe an alternative, relatively neglected approach that we have adopted in our own research work. Following these considerations, we shall report the results of three of our experiments that utilize this alternative approach.

Has the Self-Concept Research Trip Been Worthwhile?

First, the good news: we are studying the right topic. People's phenomenological musings about themselves are an interesting subject—

the self, after all, being everyone's favorite topic. Indeed, laypersons often think that what constitutes psychology is the study of the contents and form of the human's conscious awareness, and consciousness of self should lie at the heart of this phenomenological domain. Since it is laypeople who supply (through their elected representatives) support for psychological research and who constitute the population from whom we hope to recruit talented new researchers, it seems reasonable that we professional psychologists should give appreciable research attention to this topic which society thinks it supports us to investigate. But perversely, most psychological research has focused on behavioral manifestations rather than phenomenological experience. Psychologists, especially the most prestigious, have shied away from studying the contents of awareness and from using phenomenological experiences for explanatory purposes. One of the few exceptions to this neglect has been the self-concept research (along with the related topic of person perception) where study of a frankly phenomenological topic has generally been accepted even within mainline psychology. But if we who have been investigating the self-concept have been exerting ourselves in the right ballpark, have we been playing the right game?

The bad news comes when we consider the output of these several thousand studies of the self-concept. It would be ungraceful here (and perhaps unfair) to deny that the vast input of effort has yielded a modest success (leaving room to quibble about how our emphasis should be distributed between "modest" and "success"), but I do not discern a basis for confidently making any greater claim than this. One problem with the vast number of self-concept studies is that, as Wylie (1961, 1974, 1978) continuously complains, they have demonstrated so few firm relationships; to paraphrase Brecht, so many questions, so few answers. But a more serious complaint arises not from the tactical disappointments of how poorly questions have been answered but rather from the more fundamental strategic worry that the provocative questions have not been asked. Even if nature had responded univocally to the questions that self-concept researchers have been putting to her or him, I fear that the layperson would be left with the disappointed feeling that our output is interesting as far as it goes, but that it does not go very far.

Of course, a researcher must begin somewhere and should not be expected to answer all questions simultaneously. The issues selected and the methods generally used in self-concept research are respectable. A partisan might even argue that the approach usually taken by self-concept researchers is the optimal starting point, but I believe that in science (as well as in the biological environment) there is a tendency to overconcentrate at optimal points. It is my judgment that the conventional issues and methods used in the thousands of past self-concept studies are too narrow and should be broadened in at least two major respects.

Causes for the Modesty of Our Past Successes

The basic limitation that I see in the past research is that it has focused on the *reactive* rather than the *spontaneous* self-concept. A corollary limitation is that these reactive studies have almost always focused on the single dimension typically called self-esteem or self-evaluation. By the reactive self-concept approach we refer to the usual procedure of asking the person to respond by placing him- or herself on a dimension presented by the experimenter. Since the person is simply reacting to a dimension chosen by the researcher, no information is obtained about the salience of that dimension in the self-concept, about whether the person is at all concerned about this aspect of her- or himself. It merely indicates where the person would think of him- or herself as being on that dimension if thoughts of the dimension ever spontaneously arose. We feel that the reactive self-concept approach is seriously deficient in that it provides no information on the more interesting question of what are the dimensions in terms of which people tend spontaneously to think of themselves, what the aspects of the self are, in other words, that concern the person. To provide information on this more basic question, we have been presenting a lower profile to the participant so the person can choose the dimensions in terms of which to describe him- or herself, eliciting the person's spontaneous self-concept by asking a nondirective question such as "Tell us about yourself."

The loss of information inherent in the past overuse of the reactive approach is further aggravated by the unfortunate uniformity in the choice of the dimension they have presented to the person. Over 90 percent of the self-concept research is, according to my analysis of a sample of references in the Wylie (1974) volume, on the one evaluative dimension of self-esteem. Indeed, the three review volumes by Wylie might have been more specifically titled *Self-Esteem* rather than *Self-Concept*. It can be argued that self-esteem is an interesting part of the self-concept, but it is far from the overwhelming part. Our data (McGuire and Padawer-Singer 1976) suggest that only 7 percent of the material that occurs to children in response to a "Tell me about yourself" question consists of self-evaluations, including 2 percent physical evaluations ("I'm a pretty good-looking fellow" or "I'm not a fast runner"); 2 percent intellectual evaluations ("I'm not very good at math"); 2 percent moral evaluations ("I'm better behaved than most of the kids in this class"); and 1 percent emotional self-evaluation ("I cry too easily"). It does not seem appropriate to concentrate over 90 percent of all the self-concept research on this one dimension of self-esteem that constitutes only 7 percent of the self-concept.

This narrow channeling of the vast effort expended on self-concept research within this double constraint of asking the person only to react to self-concept dimensions chosen by the researcher and the researcher's uniform choice of the evaluative dimension is, I believe, the main cause for the rather disappointing yield. My colleagues and I during the past several years have tried to supplement the narrowly channeled past research by going beyond the self-esteem dimension and by utilizing the spontaneous self-concept approach.

An Alternative Approach for Studying the Self-Concept

The Spontaneous Self-Concept. By asking the person to respond to such open-ended questions as "Tell us about yourself," we have measured the spontaneous self-concept to explore what aspects of the self are spontaneously salient in consciousness and to identify the factors that determine what is salient. The usual reactive self-concept approach, on the other hand, provides information only regarding where the person would place the self on the experimenter-chosen dimension if the person were ever to think of the self in terms of that dimension. Past neglect of the more information-rich, spontaneous self-concept approach has not been complete. Two instruments, Kuhn's Twenty Statement Test and the Bugental and Zelen's "Who Are You?" test, have long been available for this alternative approach, and over a hundred studies using such instruments have been reviewed in Spitzer, Couch, and Stratton (1971). The Twenty

Statement Test (TST) asks the person to list twenty different statements answering the question, "Who am I?" The Who Are You? (WAY) instrument uses a similar approach of presenting the person with this question and asking him or her to respond freely. Unfortunately, these instruments have typically not been used to exploit their greatest potential, investigating the relative salience of various dimensions, but rather to measure the people on some specific a priori chosen dimension (often self-evaluation once again), thus employing these information-rich procedures for a purpose for which they are not particularly efficient. A better example of the efficient use of this open-ended approach comes from research on the perception of others rather than on the self-concept, preeminently Rosenberg's (1972, 1978) person perception approach that allows people to describe others in words of their own choice.

Distinctiveness Postulate Predictions. Our long-run intention is to depict the content and form of the self-concept during the years of childhood, describing first how this content and form of self-consciousness matures over the school years, and then the antecedents and consequences of such self-concept developments. Toward this end, we have developed an elaborate content analysis system that we are currently using to score the content and form of the spontaneous self-concept responses by a large sample of school children. Within the next year we should be reporting on the initial results of this work.

In this chapter we shall describe the results of three more specialized studies, all designed to test a specific theoretical insight, the "distinctiveness postulate," as to what determines the salience of characteristics in the person's self-concept. Our underlying assumption is that humans chronically operate under a perceptual limitation (or information-overload) economy, in such a way that the person receives more information through the senses than he or she can effectively encode: only a subset of the information received by our senses reaches the level of consciousness. Humans have developed a variety of modes of coping with this information-processing economy (McGuire et al. 1979) such as chunking, temporary storage, selective noticing, and so on. There are a number of bases on which aspects of complex stimuli (such as the self) are selected for noticing: for example, one tends to notice aspects of complex stimuli that one has been reinforced for noticing in the past, or be attentive to aspects relevant to one's present wants. We postulate that one important determinant of what gets selectively noticed is distinctiveness; that is, one tends to notice aspects in the environment that are different (and thus information-rich), resulting in our encoding complex stimuli in terms of their peculiarities. Applying this distinctiveness postulate to the spontaneous self-concept, we predict that a given dimension will be salient in a person's self-concept to the extent that the person's characteristic on the dimension in question is peculiar (that is, distinctive from the characteristics on that dimension possessed by the other people in the person's usual reference groups).

The three studies reported in the following sections apply the distinctiveness postulate to predicting the salience in the spontaneous self-concept of three different kinds of characteristics. The first study tests hypotheses that when we ask children to "Tell us about yourself," they will reply in terms of their physical characteristics on any given bodily dimension to the extent that their characteristics on the dimension are different from those of most of their schoolmates. The second study focuses on self-perception in terms of one's ethnicity, predicting that ethnicity will become a more salient part of children's self-concepts to the extent that their school is more heterogeneously integrated. The third study predicts that the salience of gender in the child's spontaneous self-concept increases to the extent that his or her gender is in the minority in the child's household.

SALIENCE OF PHYSICAL CHARACTERISTICS IN THE SPONTANEOUS SELF-CONCEPT

A previous study (McGuire and Padawer-Singer 1976) indicated that a half-dozen physical characteristics are mentioned as part of the spontaneous self-concept by at least 10 percent of the children, a frequency sufficient to allow adequate tests of salience hypotheses. The six characteristics are height, weight, hair color, eye color, birth date (age), and birthplace. To these six we added a seventh, wearing eyeglasses, which, though rarely mentioned, provides an "acquired" physical characteristic with which to test the distinctiveness postulate. For each of these seven dimensions, we predicted that the likelihood that a person would mention it as part of his or her spontaneous self-concept increases to the extent that the person's characteristic on the dimension is peculiar in his or her social milieu.

Methods Used in the Physical Characteristics Study

General Procedure. The children were asked the "Tell us about yourself" question in a group situation calling for written responses (rather than by the individual administration, oral-response procedures we used in the next two studies) in order to increase the base rate mention of physical characteristics which in the face-to-face interview might be screened out by the child as too obvious to mention.

The interviewer entered the classroom at an hour designated by the teacher as convenient and gave each child in the class a booklet, with the instruction that they not write their names in the booklet so that their answers would be anonymous. The interviewer explained that there were no right or wrong answers but that the child should respond to the question with the first thing that came to mind. The children were then asked to turn to the first page headed "Tell us about yourself," and the following instructions were read to them by the interviewer: "On the lines below tell us each of the things that you think of in answer to the question, 'Tell us about yourself.' Write down during the next five minutes all of the thoughts that you have about yourself. You can use just one word, or a couple of words, or a whole sentence to tell us each thought about yourself that comes to mind. Write down each thing as you think of it. We shall tell you when the time is up. Now start your answer to the question, 'Tell us about yourself.' "

After five minutes the interviewer told the students that the time was up and asked them to turn to the following pages which included a structured questionnaire headed "Your physical appearance." It explicitly asked their height, weight, hair color, eye color, age, birthplace, whether they wore eyeglasses, and how tall and how heavy they felt themselves to be compared with the other children in their class.

Scoring the Variables. To score the independent variable (salience of the physical characteristics in the spontaneous self-concept), judges other than the interviewers, unfamiliar with the hypotheses and without any other information on the children, read each child's response protocol to the "Tell us about yourself" question. They tallied any mention of height, weight, hair color, eye color, eyeglass wearing, birth date (or age), and birthplace. The salience of each characteristic in a given child's protocol was scored as 1 versus 0, depending on whether the child did versus did not, respectively, mention that characteristic.

Participants. We elicited the spontaneous self-concept from a hundred boys and a hundred girls at each of five grade levels—fifth, seventh, ninth, eleventh, and twelfth—with fifth grade being the youngest group because children in lower grades had difficulty in giving written responses. These 1,000 participants were selected from the school system of a medium-sized industrial city in inland New England. Within the system we arbitrarily selected one of its two high schools to furnish our eleventh and twelfth graders, and then selected at random two of the junior high schools that fed into this senior high school to furnish the seventh and ninth graders, and randomly selected three of the elementary schools that fed into these two junior highs to obtain the fifth graders. To obtain the hundred boys and hundred girls at each grade level, we tested virtually all the students in those schools at the given grade level, except those absent on the day of testing and those in classes of exceptional children.

Results Obtained in the Physical Characteristics Study

Base Rates. Before presenting the results bearing on these distinctiveness predictions, we shall report some base rate scores regarding the length of the protocols and the frequency of mention on the dimensions under study. The length of the spontaneous self-concepts could be measured rather exactly since they were all rewritten slightly in the form of three-unit (subject-verb-modifier) segments as part of a content analysis procedure suitable for computer analysis. Over all five grade levels, the mean response length was 16.1 of these three-unit segments. The girls' responses are 22 percent longer than the boys', and eleventh graders' are 27 percent longer than seventh graders', both group differences significant at the .01 level (by a 2 × 2 analysis of variance).

The baseline levels of the physical characteristics are worth reporting because of their ad hoc interest even though they do not bear directly on the distinctiveness postulate being tested. Height was mentioned as part of their spontaneous self-concept by 19 percent of the children, while only 11 percent mentioned their weight, a difference significant at the .01 level. (All significance levels reported henceforth are based on chi-squares.) There was no sex difference in the mention of height or weight and no age difference in salience of height, but weight was mentioned by twice as many eleventh and twelfth graders as by fifth and seventh graders, indicating an increasing concern about weight in late adolescence. Hair color was mentioned by 14 percent of the respondents and eye color by 11 percent. Both of these characteristics were mentioned almost twice as often by girls as by boys ($p < .01$); and both are mentioned more often ($p < .05$) by younger than older children. Birthplace is a less salient characteristic, being mentioned by about 6 percent of the children, without significant gender or grade differences; while age is highly salient, being mentioned by 31 percent of the respondents, twice as often ($p < .01$) by the younger than the older children but without a sex difference. Eyeglasses were mentioned by 1.5 percent of the respondents (significantly more often by younger and by female students) making this characteristic marginally suitable for testing, considering our large sample size. These baseline levels, as well as the differential levels relevant to the distinctiveness postulate, are summarized in Table 11-1.

Distinctiveness Effects on the Salience of Height. Since each child was asked his or her height and weight, it was possible to calculate an objective distinctiveness score for these two characteristics; and a subjective distinctiveness score was also available since each child was asked to judge whether his or her height (and weight) was below average, average, or above average. Hence for height and weight, it was possible to test the distinctiveness postulate prediction in terms of both objective and subjective measures of distinctiveness.

As our objective measure of each child's height deviation, we calculated the deviation of his or her own height from the mean height of those of the child's gender and grade level at the school. The results show that the height deviation scores calculated in this way are related to salience of height in the spontaneous self-concept as predicted by the distinctiveness postulate: only 17 percent of children of average height (within one inch above or below the grade level mean for their sex) spontaneously described themselves in terms of their height, while 27 percent of the very tall and short children (five inches below or above the mean height) spontaneously men-

Table 11–1. Sallence of Physical Characteristics (Percentages of Children Mentioning the Characteristic as Part of Their Spontaneous Self-Concept) as a Function of Its Distinctiveness Within the Child's School Group.[a]

		Respondent Group								
		By Sex			*By Grade*			*By Distinctiveness*		
Characteristic	*Overall*	*Male*		*Female*	*12, 11*		*7, 5*	*Unusual*		*Common*
Height	19	21		17	18		18	27	**	18
Weight	11	11		11	13	**	8	12	**	6
Haircolor	14	10	**	18	11	**	17	17	**	13
Eyecolor	11	8	**	15	9		13	13		11
Age	31	28	**	33	24	**	38	33		30
Birthplace	6	6		6	7		6	10	**	4
Eyeglasses	1½	½	**	2½	0	**	3	3	**	½

a. Percents separated by "**" are significant above the .05 level by chi-square.

tioned their height, a difference significant at the .05 level. Both the very tall and the very short children described themselves in terms of their height more often than those of average stature: 25 percent of those five inches above average and 31 percent of those five inches below average mentioning height, in contrast to the 17 percent mention by those within one inch of the mean height.

The subjective as well as the objective distinctiveness measure showed the predicted relationship to salience of height in the spontaneous self-concept. Of those who later judged their height to be average, only 17 percent had spontaneously mentioned it, while 22 percent of those who judged themselves as taller and 22 percent of those who judged themselves as shorter than average mentioned their height spontaneously, this difference between the 17 percent and 22 percent spontaneous mention being significant at the .05 level.

Distinctiveness Effects on the Salience of Weight. The distinctiveness predictions regarding weight were similarly confirmed. In regard to the objective distinctiveness score, only 6 percent of the children of average weight (within six pounds above or below the class mean) spontaneously described themselves in terms of weight; while weight was mentioned as part of the spontaneous self-concept by 12 percent of the heavy and light children (those whose weight deviated by fourteen pounds above or below the grade level mean for their gender). Overweight children were significantly ($p < .05$) more likely spontaneously to mention their weight than were underweight children.

The distinctive postulate is also confirmed when weight deviation is defined in subjective terms. Only 8 percent of those who judged their own weight as average defined themselves in terms of this characteristic, while significantly ($p < .01$) more spontaneously mentioned weight among those who considered themselves thinner than average (13 percent mention) and fatter than average (22 percent).

Distinctiveness Effects on Hair Color and Eye Color Salience. The distinctiveness factor operated less strongly in affecting the spontaneous salience of hair color and eye color. The effect of hair color just barely attained the .05 level of statistical significance: Of the black- and brown-haired majority, only 13 percent spontaneously mentioned their hair color as part of their spontaneous self-concept, while 17 percent of those with the atypical blond and red hair colors spontaneously mentioned it.

There was no significant confirmation in the case of eye color. Of the brown-eyed majority, 11 percent spontaneously mentioned their eye color as part of their spontaneous self-concept, only trivially less than the 13 percent mention by the blue-eyed minority.

Distinctiveness Effects on Birth Date and Birthplace Salience. The results on birth date (age) did not confirm the distinctiveness prediction, but the data on birthplace did. From the children's report of age, we calculated the age in months for each grade level and gave each child a deviation score in terms of number of months above or below the mean age for grade level. Of those near the modal age (within seven months of the grade-level mean age) 30 percent spontaneously mentioned their age as part of their self-concept; and of the atypically young and old children (more than seven months above or below the mean for their grade level), 33 percent spontaneously mentioned their age. While this slight 3 percent difference is in the predicted direction, it is of trivial statistical significance.

The results for spontaneous mention of birthplace lend strong support to the distinctiveness hypothesis. Subsequent to giving their spontaneous self-concepts, the children were asked explicitly to list their birthplace, thus allowing us to partition the children on the basis of birthplace commonality at a variety of cutoff points. Contrasting the great majority who had been born within the state in which the study was done versus the minority whose out-of-state birthplaces made them more peculiar in this regard, we found that 3 percent of those born within the state had spontaneously mentioned where they were born as compared with a 15 percent mention of birthplace by those who were born outside of the state ($p < .01$ for the 3 percent versus 15 percent difference). For a more extreme partition point, we contrasted the U.S.–born with the foreign-born and found that of those born in the U.S., 5 percent spontaneously mentioned their birthplace as compared with 18 percent of the foreign-born ($p < .01$).

It is worth noting that the distinctiveness postulate predictions are confirmed by these birthplace-salience results (and also by results on other dimensions, such as weight) even though this outcome goes against opposite predictions derived from other plausible hypotheses such as social desirability and environmental frequency.

Distinctiveness Effects on Eyeglass Salience. The distinctiveness prediction is also confirmed by the outcome regarding spontaneous mention of eyeglass wearing, even though the low base rate of salience (only 1.5 percent of the children's mentioning this dimension) is barely sufficient to allow testing the hypothesis. Overall, 31 percent of the children subsequently reported that they did wear eyeglasses; hence, to test the distinctiveness prediction, we partitioned the children into those from classes in which fewer than 30 percent of the children wore glasses versus those from classes in which 30 percent or more wore glasses. In those classes where wearing glasses is rarer (less than 30 percent of the classmates using glasses), 8 percent of the wearers spontaneously mentioned their glasses, while in classes where eyeglass-wearing is more common (over 30 percent of the classmates wearing them), fewer than 1 percent of the wearers spontaneously mentioned them, a difference significant at the .01 level.

Conclusions Regarding the Distinctiveness Postulate's Predictions Regarding Physical Characteristics' Salience. In regard to the seven physical dimensions mentioned with sufficent frequency to allow testing the predictions, the distinctiveness postulate proved respectably powerful. All seven outcomes were in the predicted direction, five of these above the conventionally acceptable .05 level of statistical significance. For the two characteristics, height and weight, on which there were both objective and subjective measures of distinctiveness, the predictions were confirmed by each measure. Significant confirmations by the objective measures were obtained for the hair color, birthplace, and wearing eyeglasses dimension. For each of the three, as one's characteristic became more distinctive from one's classmates' characteristics on the dimension, the dimension became more salient, that is, more likely to be mentioned as part of the spontaneous self-concept.

The results with the other two dimensions, eye color and age, are in the predicted direction, but the relationships fall short of the conventionally acceptable level of statistical significance. Our post-factum conjecture to explain away these two failures of confirmation is that eye color may be a rather subtle characteristic so that one is not as easily aware of one's own or another's eye color as one is of one's hair color, height, and so on. Likewise, exact age is not as apparent as the other physical characteristics, and the classes are so homogeneously age-grouped (over one-third of the children being within three months of the grade level's average age) that it might be hard for the children to become aware of the small age differences among the classmates.

SALIENCE OF ETHNICITY AS A FUNCTION OF THE GROUP'S ETHNIC HETEROGENEITY

The salience of physical characteristics study was described above in some detail since it has not been previously reported; the next two experiments, on salience of ethnicity and salience of gender, can be described more briefly below since full reports on each are in print (McGuire et al. 1978, 1979).

Distinctiveness Theory and Ethnic Consciousness

General Theoretical Considerations. The distinctiveness postulate implies, as regards salience of ethnicity in one's self-concept, that one's ethnic consciousness develops only as one moves into ethnically mixed situations where one's own ethnicity becomes distinctive. Students in an all-black or all-white school are unlikely to think of themselves as black or white because the ethnic characteristic does not contain enough information (distinctiveness) in a racially homogeneous, social environment to be worth noticing. On the other hand, the person in a racially mixed setting is more likely to develop a concept of the self and of other people that includes ethnicity, and this salience will be particularly pronounced for people in the ethnic subgroup that is in the minority in that setting. The relationship can be derived and even quantified by the Equation 1 formalization of the distinctiveness postulate.

$$P_{ij} = \frac{N - n_{ij}}{\sum_{i=1}^{N} \sum_{j=1}^{M} \left(N - n_{ij} \right)} \qquad [1]$$

Where P_{ij} is the probability that individual i will think of self in terms of his or her characteristics on dimension j; N is the number of people in individual i's reference group; and n_{ij} is the number of people in the reference group who share i's characteristic on dimension j.

As an example of how this formulation is applied, consider the situation illustrated in Table 11-2, each of whose columns describes one of the N people in the group who include, successfully from left to right, a black female, a white female, and four white males. The row headings in Table 11-2 name the n dimensions—in this case, gender and ethnicity—that distinguish the group members. The cell entries give the number of discriminations for the column person on the row characteristic. Questions about the salience of gender and ethnicity in the self-concepts of the people in this group can be answered by examining row totals, column totals, and the cell entries of the table. If we look at the row totals, we see that the distinctiveness postulate as formalized in Equation 1 predicts that in the spontaneous self-concept of the people in this group gender should be mentioned 60 percent more often than ethnicity. If we look at the column totals, we can see that the probability that the black female will think of herself in terms of these two characteristics is three times as great as the probability that any of the white males will think of himself in these terms. By considering the cell entries, we can derive the prediction that for the black female, it is 25 percent more probable that she will think of herself in terms of her blackness than in terms of her gender; while for the white female, it is 400 percent more likely that she will think of herself in terms of her gender than of her ethnicity.

We are stressing in this example and in the present study that distinctiveness is to some extent situationally determined: a black female who finds herself with ten black males is likely to think of

Table 11-2. Number of Discriminations on the Bases of Gender and Ethnicity for Each Individual in a Hypothetical Six-Person Group.

	Person						
Characteristic	*Black Female*	*White Female*	*White Male*	*White Male*	*White Male*	*White Male*	Σ
Gender	4	4	2	2	2	2	16
Ethnicity	5	1	1	1	1	1	10
Σ	9	5	3	3	3	3	26

herself as a female; if she then moves to a group of ten white females, she will become conscious of herself as a black. We conjecture that there is also a chronic component to the distinctiveness postulate so that a characteristic tends to become persistently salient in one's self-concept if the other people in almost all of one's reference groups are continuously different from oneself on a given characteristic. This chronic aspect of the distinctiveness postulate will be tested in the third experiment on the salience of gender described later.

Specific Hypotheses. From the distinctiveness postulate we derived three hypotheses about salience of ethnicity in the students' self-concepts as a function of the school's racial mix. First, we predicted that in ethnically mixed schools, members of minority groups are more conscious of their ethnicity than are members of the majority group. Secondly, it was predicted that within any ethnic group, members become progressively less conscious of their ethnicity as their ethnic group becomes increasingly preponderant numerically in that group. A third prediction is that for members of the minority group, ethnicity is more salient in the affirmation self-concept (in response to "Tell us about yourself") than in the negation self-concept (in response to "Tell us what you are *not*"); whereas, for the ethnic majority group, the reverse is the case, with ethnicity more salient in the negation than in the affirmation self-concept. The derivation of these three hypotheses from the distinctiveness postulate is discussed in more detail in McGuire and others (1978).

Methods Used in the Salience of Ethnicity Study

In this study we obtained the spontaneous self-concept responses to the same "Tell us about yourself" probe, but by an individual oral interview of each child that allowed the interviewer unostentatiously to judge and record the child's ethnicity. Eliciting the spontaneous self-concepts in the oral rather than written modality had the added advantage of allowing us to get responses even from the youngest schoolchildren. Hence, the present study is based on individual oral interviews of 70 boys and 70 girls at each of four grade levels (first, third, seventh, and eleventh) so that a total of 560 students participated. In addition, "negation self-concepts" were elicited from each child by a "Tell us what you are *not*" probe. After the tape-recorded oral responses were typed out verbatim, coders not familiar with the hypotheses read each response protocol and scored the dependent variable (spontaneous self-descriptions in ethnic terms such as one's being black, white, Hispanic, Caucasian, Puerto Rican, Afro-American, etc.), so that each of the 560 affirmation and negation self-concepts was scored 1 versus 0, depending on whether or not there was at least one self-description in terms of ethnicity in that protocol. The independent variable measure, the child's actual ethnicity, was scored by the judgment made by the interviewer prior to the self-concept response, based on the child's appearance, name, and accent.

Results on the Salience of Ethnicity Study

Baseline Results. The interviewers' judgments of the ethnicity of the 560 children classified 82 percent ($N = 460$) as white, English-speaking; 9 percent ($N = 48$) as black; 8 percent ($N = 44$) as Hispanic; and 1 percent ($N = 8$) as uncertain or other. Hence, in this school district the white, English-speaking students constituted the majority ethnic group, while the black and the Hispanic students constituted the minority groups.

Ethnicity was not a highly salient characteristic among these children; only 3 percent spontaneously mentioned their ethnicity during the five minutes allowed for the affirmation self-concept. There was no sex difference in salience of ethnicity, but there was a decided age effect with progressively more mention of ethnicity in the higher grades ($p < .01$).

Differences Among Ethnic Groups in Racial Consciousness. The first hypothesis derived from the distinctiveness postulate is that members of minority groups would be more conscious of their ethnicity than members of the majority group. This prediction was confirmed ($p < .01$) in that 17 percent of the black and 14 percent of the Hispanic students spontaneously mentioned their ethnicity as compared to only 1 percent racial mention by the numerically preponderant English-speaking whites.

Within-Ethnic Group Numerical Preponderance. The second prediction derived from the distinctiveness postulate is that the members of any one ethnic group become less conscious of their ethnicity as their proportionate representation in the group increases. The prediction was confirmed on the overall data when we partitioned students of each ethnicity into those from schools in which their ethnic group was represented above versus below their group's overall median representation in the school system. For all three ethnic groups combined, only 2 percent of the students spontaneously mentioned their ethnicity when in classes in which their own ethnic group was present in numbers exceeding their overall numerical median in the school system; while 6 percent spontaneously mentioned their ethnicity when their group's preponderance fell below the overall median. This 2 percent versus 6 percent spontaneous mention level is significant at the .05 level.

The Negation Versus Affirmation Self-Concept. The affirmation self-concept focuses one's attention on the self and therefore, according to the distinctiveness postulate, should cause one to notice peculiarities that characterize the self. The negation self-concept, on the other hand, focuses one's attention on other people's characteristics that one lacks oneself, causing one to notice other people's distinctive characteristics that one does not share. Hence, it is predicted that for the majority ethnic group, ethnicity should be mentioned more often in the negation than in the affirmation self-concept, whereas for the minority black and Hispanic students, ethnicity should be more often mentioned more in the affirmation. This prediction is borne out by the data. For the white English-speaking students, only 1 percent spontaneously mentioned ethnicity as part of the affirmation self-concept, while 5 percent mentioned nonmembership in another ethnic group as part of the negation self-concept. Among the black and Hispanic students, on the other hand, 15 percent mentioned their ethnicity as part of their affirmation self-concept, while only 7 percent as part of their negation self-concept mentioned not having other groups' ethnicity. This contrast between the minority and majority groups' ethnic salience in the affirmation versus negation self-concept is significant at the .01 level.

SALIENCE OF GENDER AS A FUNCTION OF HOUSEHOLD SEX COMPOSITION

The third study tested distinctiveness postulate implications regarding the salience of one's gender (spontaneous mention of being a boy or a girl in response to the "Tell us about yourself" question) as a function of whether members of one's own gender are numerically preponderant in one's household. Its description here will be brief since its method is similar to the ethnicity study just discussed and because a fuller report is already available (McGuire et al. 1979).

Theory and Method of the Gender Salience Study

Hypotheses. The distinctiveness postulate prediction is that children are likely to think of themselves in terms of their gender to the extent to which the other sex is numerically preponderant in their households, since as the proportion of household members who are of the other sex increases, one's own gender becomes a more peculiar, distinguishing characteristic within this household reference group. This prediction might seem to go against the Establishment's "social learning" or "modeling" theorizing yielding the seemingly opposite prediction that adherence to own-sex behavioral stereotype is greater when one's own sex is numerically preponderant, thus providing more role models and environmental reinforcers for behaving in accord with prescriptions for one's own gender. Our dependent variable, however, is a phenomenological one, gender consciousness, while the seemingly opposite social learning theory prediction is made with respect to another kind of variable, namely, sex-role behavior. We are predicting that children from households in which people of their own gender are rare become more aware of themselves as being a member of that sex and define themselves in terms of gender. Distinctiveness theory yields no derivation about whether these children whose sexual distinctiveness has made them preoccupied with being a boy or a girl may, as social learning (modeling) theory predicts, have a less clear knowledge of the behavioral patterns conventionally ascribed to that gender role.

Method. To test our prediction, the dependent variable (salience of gender in the spontaneous self-concept) was scored by having coders analyze the 560 affirmation self-concepts, scoring each 1 versus 0, depending on whether the child did or did not describe him- or herself in terms of gender at least once during the five-minute response to "Tell us about yourself."

The independent variable of household sex composition was measured on the basis of data obtained by the interviewers after the child had responded to the spontaneous self-concept probes. Each child was asked first to name all of his or her brothers and sisters, and to indicate whether each sibling was or was not presently living at home; then to give the first name of mother and father and to indicate whether each was currently in the home; and finally to give the first name of each other person in the household and to indicate that person's relationship to the family. Follow-up questions were allowed to clarify ambiguities (unless the child seemed reluctant to discuss the matter). Subsequently, coders unfamiliar with the hypothesis were able to score the number of males and females in the home for all but 6 of the 560 respondents. A second independent variable measure, needed to test the distinctiveness postulate corollary that father-absence enhances boys' consciousness of being male, involved scoring each participant on whether the father was present or absent from the household, a scoring that was possible for all but 3 of the 560 respondents.

Results of the Gender Salience Study

Base Level of Gender Salience. Gender proved to be a moderately salient characteristic in that 9 percent of children described themselves in terms of their gender at least once in their five-minute oral response to "Tell us about yourself." Gender becomes progressively more salient with age ($p < .01$), its being mentioned by 3 percent, 6 percent, 10 percent, and 19 percent, respectively, of the children of first, third, seventh, and eleventh grades. There is no appreciable difference between boys and girls in percent who describe themselves in terms of gender.

Effect of Other Sex's Numerical Predominance in the Household. To test the distinctiveness postulate prediction that spontaneous mention of one's gender becomes more likely to the extent that people of one's own sex are a minority in one's household, the children were partitioned into those coming from households with male majorities (33 percent), those with equal number of males and females in the household (29 percent), and those with female majorities (38 percent). As can be seen in Figure 11-1, boys are more likely spontaneously to mention being male as we go toward households with increasing proportions of females; while conversely, girls are more likely to mention their being female as the proportion of males in the household increases. The trend in each sex separately is

Figure 11–1. Spontaneous Salience of Gender in One's Self-Concept as a Function of the Other Gender's Numerical Predominance in One's Household.

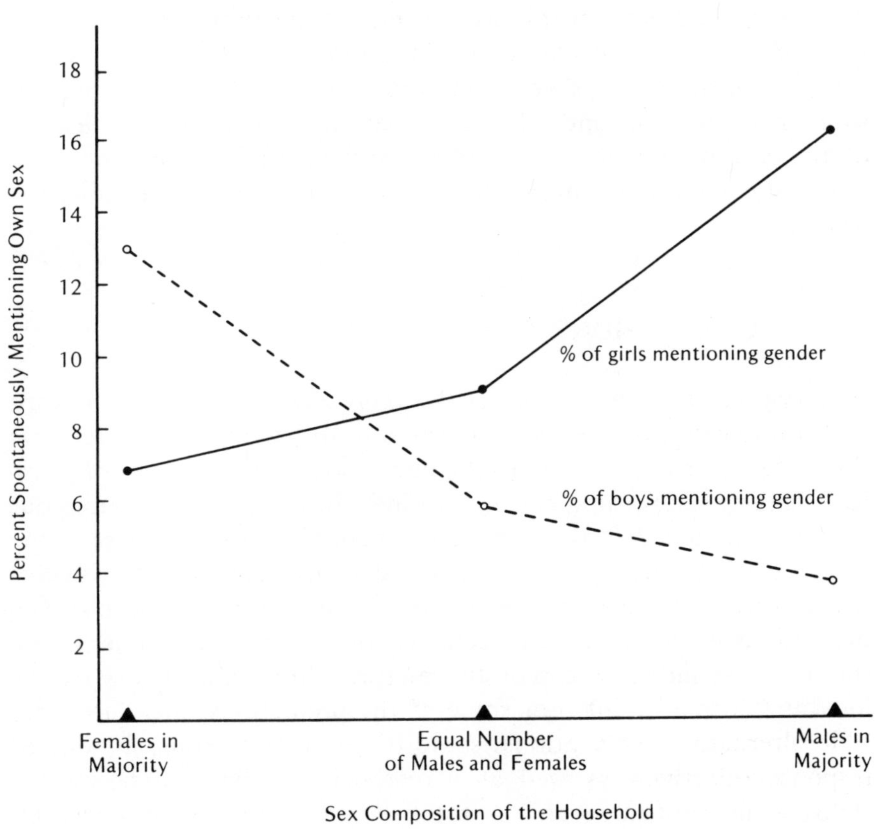

significant at the .05 level and, for the two sexes combined, at the .01 level.

Effect of Father's Absence on Gender-Salience in Boys. A corollary prediction drawn from the distinctiveness postulate is that boys will be more conscious of their maleness if they come from father-absent households. Thinking in this area (for example, the "Moynihan Report" conjectures about effects of the prevalence of father-absent households in the black community) has been dominated by social learning theory that makes an opposite-sounding prediction that father's absence interferes with boys' learning of the conventional male sex role. The results support the distinctiveness hypothesis: when the boys are partitioned into those from households with both mother and father present (the home situation for 227 of the 280 boys in this study) versus those with the mother but not the father present (the home situation for 33 of these boys), we find that of the 33 boys who came from fatherless homes, 18 percent spontaneously mentioned that they were boys, while only 7 percent of the 227 boys whose mothers and fathers are both present spontaneously mentioned their maleness, a difference significant at the .05 level.

CONCLUSIONS

Evaluation of the Distinctiveness Postulate Research. The score card of confirmations of the distinctiveness postulate predictions in these three studies is respectable. In the new study on the salience of physical characteristics, the data on all nine of the predictions came out in the predicted direction, seven of them significant at least at the .05 level. The three predictions tested in the salience of ethnicity study were confirmed at the .05 or .01 level, as were both of the predictions made in the salience of gender study. A cautionary note should be sounded here that the picture blurs somewhat when we look at the small print. For some of the predictions, there are plausible alternative explanations; some of the effects could be due to response selectivity as well as perceptual selectivity; some predictions, while confirmed on the total data set, are not supported by some subsets of the data. These limitations are discussed more fully by McGuire and others (1978, 1979).

Methodological Implications

In regard to the future of self-concept research, we have two general proselytizing aims in this chapter. First, we are urging that more researchers investigate the spontaneous rather than the reactive self-concept. We admit that spontaneous self-concept probes evoke unwieldy data and provide a lower information-to-noise ratio regarding any specific a priori dimension; however, these disadvantages are outweighed in many cases by the fact that the spontaneous self-concept provides information regarding an important neglected area of self-concept inquiry, namely, the issue of what is salient in the person's self-concept. It allows investigating the extent to which people think of themselves on various dimensions, rather than just (as with the reactive self-concept) where people would place themselves on a researcher-specified dimension were they ever to think about it.

Secondly, we are urging that research on the self-concept, whether reactive or spontaneous, shift from exclusive preoccupation with self-evaluation to a study of other aspects of the self-concept. We urge this shift not because self-esteem is uninteresting, but rather because the narrow preoccupation of past and present research with this one evaluative dimension has been excessive.

Theoretical Implications

Both the theoretical point of departure of the research reported here (the distinctiveness postulate) and its innovative method (the spontaneous self-concept approach) redirect attention to a generally neglected dependent variable, phenomenological awareness. An example of this neglect is provided by the conventional research being done on the currently popular topic of sex-typing. In almost all of the current sex-typing research, the dependent variable is either behavioral or affective, measuring either the degree to which one's behavior conforms to the conventional stereotype of how those of one's gender should behave or how much the person likes one's own gender or objects or roles ascribed to this gender. The distinctiveness postulate calls attention to a different aspect of sex-typing, namely, the phenomenological or cognitive variable of gender salience in one's awareness and perception of the self.

Consider, for example, previous sex-typing research on the independent variable used in our third study, household sex composition variables such as having an older sibling of same versus other sex, or having father present versus absent from the home. This past research has been dominated by social learning (imitation, modeling) theory whose predictions focus almost exclusively on behavioral sex-typing as their dependent variable. The distinctiveness postulate corrects this overpreoccupation with behavioral indices by predicting seemingly opposite relationships for an alternative awareness index.

Social Relevance

The distinctiveness postulate as applied to the spontaneous self-concept has appreciable social policy implications. The second study demonstrates that people's awareness of their ethnicity as part of their self-concept increases with school integration and, by implication, ethnic mixture in other settings. According to the distinctiveness postulate theorizing, this heightened salience occurs as an information-processing phenomenon, regardless of the conditions under which the integration occurs. The finding creates an internal contradiction for people of good will who would like to see the development of a culture in which the person's perception of him- or herself and others would de-emphasize ethnicity and who feel that ethnic integration should be promoted. The outcome of our studies suggests that these two goals, ethnic de-emphasis and integration, involve an internal contradiction. Perhaps one could conjecture that even though in the short run, integration increases salience of ethnicity, in the long run it might decrease salience. Or perhaps a rethinking would reveal that increased awareness and acceptance of ethnicity of self and others has attractive aspects that should be encouraged as well as unattractive ones that should be discouraged.

The second and third studies reported here suggest that decisions on two important social policy issues during the past decade have been made on an incorrect psychological assumption. One of these has to do with the Moynihan (1965) report on "The Negro Family," conjecturing that the prevalence of fatherless homes in the poorer black socioeconomic sector of the population may have interfered with the masculine sex-typing of black males, producing various socially and personally undesirable consequences. Our studies do not refute the social-learning prediction that coming from fatherless homes might interfere with mastery of the male sex-role stereotyped behavior; but the confirmation of the distinctiveness postulate predictions indicates that awareness of and preoccupation with being a male may actually be enhanced by the father's absence.

A second social policy controversy of relevance involves interracial adoptions. In the early 1970s, black social worker groups protested the adoption of black children by white parents with the result that this practice, which had risen sharply during the 1960s, has fallen drastically during the past several years (Ladner 1977; Simon and Alstein 1977). Among the arguments for opposing interracial adoption was the assumption that the black child brought up in a white household would tend to lose ethnic consciousness, a loss that opponents of interracial adoptions considered undesirable to the child, to people who are black, or to society in general. However, the distinctiveness postulate implies quite the opposite, namely, that children brought up in a household with members of a different ethnicity would be more conscious of their ethnicity than would those brought up in own-ethnicity households. The results of our second and third experiments lend some support to this implication.

In conclusion, we shall reiterate the hope that in coming years more of the self-concept research will utilize the spontaneous rather than reactive self-concept approach and will shift from the overstudied evaluation (self-esteem) dimension to other neglected dimensions such as awareness of one's gender, ethnicity, physical characteristics, and so on. Also, we hope that future work might draw inspiration from newer information-processing theorizing such as the distinctiveness postulate used here, in preference to the traditional, relatively overworked social learning (modeling) theorizing.

12 THE OCCUPATIONAL SELF
A Developmental Study

Morris Rosenberg
Florence Rosenberg

How do children's views of their desired future selves change as they grow older? Compared to the developmental work in such areas of social cognition as moral development (Kohlberg 1976; Piaget 1948), role-taking (Damon 1977; Flavell 1974, 1968; Schantz 1975), or person perception (Livesley and Bromley 1973; Secord and Peevers 1974), research on the development of children's desired self-concepts is relatively sparse. Yet the child shares with the adult the remarkable and somewhat mysterious ability to imagine himself as other than he is, to create in his mind's eye a picture of a self that is attractive and appealing. This desired self represents both a standard against which the extant self is evaluated and a goal to be realized.

Our present concern is with one important component of this future desired self: occupational status. This future desired self represents what Piaget (1970), in a rather different context, has referred to as an "anticipatory image." How does the occupational component of the desired self change with age? It will become apparent that, as in the case of moral development (Kohlberg 1969), both developmental and social processes are involved: that the fundamental process is a matter of cognitive development, but that the content is a matter of social learning.

This chapter addresses three questions: First, in envisioning the future desired self, is the occupational realm more salient to older or to younger children? Second, do occupational aspirations change as children grow older and, if so, what developmental processes underly this change? Third, to what extent are these changes governed by a pattern of occupational sex-typing which influences the desired occupational selves of boys and girls?

SAMPLE

The data for this report are based on a sample of 1,988 school children from grades three through twelve collected in twenty-five Baltimore, Md. public schools in 1968. Each school in Baltimore City was initially stratified by two variables: (a) proportion of nonwhite students, and (b) median income of its census tract. Twenty-five schools falling into the appropriate intervals were randomly selected. From each school, 105 children were selected by random procedures from the central records.

Some children had withdrawn from school after the central records were compiled and were no longer available. We were, however, able to interview 79 percent of the sample children still registered in the school or 73 percent of all children originally drawn from the central records. Closely reflecting the population, the present sample is 63 percent black and more heavily working class than the national average.

SALIENCE OF OCCUPATIONAL STATUS

The self-concept is a complex structure whose parts or components are organized in a hierarchy of prominence. Some of these components are at the center of the individual's phenomenal field (McCall and Simmons 1966; Rogers 1951; Snygg and Combs 1949; Stryker 1968)—in the forefront of consciousness—whereas other elements are more peripheral—on the fringe of awareness. The question we wish to raise is the following: in envisioning his future desired self, will occupational position be more prominent in the mind of the older child, who is rapidly approaching actual entry into the world of work, or of the younger, who is still remote from it?

In order to examine this issue, we asked our respondents the following questions: "Now I would like to ask what kind of person you would like to be as an adult. What kind of life would you like to lead? How would you like to spend your time? What kinds of things would you like to do when you are an adult?"

Contrary to expectation, it is the younger children who are much more likely than the older to cite an occupation as their first response. This is true of both boys and girls, and in equal measure. Table 12-1 shows that among boys, 64 percent of the eight-year-olds and 52 percent of the nine-year-olds responded in terms of some job or occupation compared with only 28 percent of those sixteen or older. For the girls the corresponding figures are similar: 65 percent of the eight-year-olds and 52 percent of the nine-year-olds conceptualized their future selves specifically in occupational terms compared with only 23 percent of those sixteen or older. In the words of some of the younger boys: "I want to drive a bull-dozer." "I'd like to be a middle rate lawyer." "Like to be a fireman." "A policeman, riding cars." "Be a professional baseball player." "A doctor taking care of people." The young girl, too, thinks of jobs, though different ones: "I hope I get to be a teacher." "I want to live in Virginia, want to be a teacher down there." "I'd like to be a nurse—helping people." "A nurse. Work at my job and spend my spare time dancing." "I want to be a secretary and I want to work in a big company."

If the younger child is much more likely to conceptualize the future desired self in occupational terms, the older is more likely to characterize it in terms of some overarching theme or value. For some adolescents, the future desired self involves a life of ease and self-indulgence. For one, the dream is to be a "Millionaire, easy, resting, [doing] anything I want to do." For others it is a life of dedication and service: "I would like to devote most of my time to helping people, and in useful clubs, and if I can be in certain civil rights movements, and working in, helping, the community." "Would like to lead a full and useful life." For some adolescents the dominant theme is one of excitement and adventure: "Travel to the moon." "I'd like to travel from state to state and country to country." To others the central theme is one of satisfaction and contentment: "Peaceful life. Together with a family. Travel and settle down." "Plain simple conservative life, spending time on things that are personally important." For some adolescents, conformity is the ideal. "Just an average person who goes to work and returns home—get married and have children." "Average life. Have a nice house, regular

Table 12–1. Kind of Life Child Wishes to Lead as Adult, by Age.

	Age of Boys[a]						*Age of Girls*[a]					
	8	*9*	*10–11*	*12–13*	*14–15*	*16+*	*8*	*9*	*10–11*	*12–13*	*14–15*	*16+*
Job, occupation	64	52	52	37	28	28	65	52	47	39	29	23
Education	2	—	1	2	3	2	3	1	2	—	1	1
Family, home	2	1	2	5	10	15	—	7	7	9	17	9
Traits, dispositions	10	16	15	16	19	13	15	18	19	22	20	25
Social, political	—	1	3	1	1	2	2	5	3	4	4	5
Recreation	5	18	10	13	7	6	2	5	10	8	6	5
Central life theme	12	11	14	23	31	32	13	11	13	17	21	31
Adult orientation	5	1	3	2	2	1	—	2	—	1	1	1
N = 100%	(42)	(90)	(202)	(195)	(152)	(173)	(40)	(103)	(241)	(211)	(158)	(150)

a. $p < .001$.

family, keep my children in clothing, spend time with my family, go on picnics and trips. If I have boys, take them to the ball game." For others the self envisioned has a life of success and achievement—successful, famous, prosperous, "good achievement in goals." Still others are concerned with being in the swing or up-to-date: hip, want to be modern, not square. As Table 12-1 reveals, 32 percent of the older boys but 12 percent of the younger boys conceptualized their ideal future selves in terms of one of these themes; for girls, the corresponding figures are 31 percent and 13 percent.

In summary, specific occupational position appears to be a more salient feature of the young child's future desired self than of the older child's. Insofar as occupation enters the older child's imagined future self, it does so as part of some broader overarching theme. Before deciding how seriously to take these data, it is first necessary to ask whether the occupational realm has any real meaning to the younger children. Our data (Simmons and Rosenberg 1971) suggest that by the age of twelve, children have acquired a rather remarkable amount of knowledge about the occupational realm. Our respondents were asked to rate fifteen of the better-known occupations of the ninety appearing in the National OpiWion Research Corporation measure of occupational prestige. It turns out that the rank order assigned to these occupations by our Baltimore sample of elementary school children and a 1963 nationwide sample of adults (Hodge, Siegel, and Rossi 1964) were almost identical; the Spearman rank correlation was .93 and the Pearson *r* was .96. By middle childhood the youngster has evidently acquired a considerable amount of knowledge about occupational stratification.

Occupational Aspirations Among Boys

Asked to envision an ideal future self, then, occupational status is much more likely to loom large in the mind of the younger child than of the older. But younger and older children also tend to choose different specific occupations.

Our respondents were asked the following question: "What job do you want to hold when you are grown up or older?" These age-related responses are examined for boys and girls separately, not only for their substantive interest but because this procedure helps us to separate out the predominantly developmental component of occupational aspirations from the predominantly social learning component. Insofar as the occupational choices of boys and girls differ at equivalent age levels, this difference is a reflection of social learning. But insofar as boys and girls are alike at the same ages but differ from those of different ages, developmental processes may well play a role. Hence, it is relevant to compare younger and older children within each sex and sex differences within each age group.

Table 12–2 examines the relationship of age and occupational aspirations. The occupational classification is based on the Hollingshead scale. Several points deserve comment.

The most striking finding is the degree to which the younger boys, relative to the older, choose one of the manual-level occupations—skilled, semi-skilled, and unskilled. Fifty-five percent of the youngest boys but only 22 percent of the oldest selected one of these occupations. The younger boys, on the other hand, are much less likely to choose higher executive or major professional occupations as their future desired selves. Only 19 percent of the youngest compared with 41 percent of those sixteen years of age or older selected one of these fields.

We also examined our subjects' *idealized* occupational images by asking the following: "You have been telling me what you might want to be like when you become an adult. But what if you could be anything in the whole world, anything at all, what would be the most wonderful thing you'd want to be as an adult?" This question was followed by others dealing with more specific aspects of the future self, including, "If you could have any job in the world when you are an adult, what would it be?"

Despite our open invitation to allow their imaginations to soar, only about 10 percent of the boys chose some grandiose or fantasy position: millionaire, president of the whole world, member of the Supreme Court, a bather in money. An additional 18 percent selected what might be called the "special talent" or "entertainment" occupations. These include the performing arts (movie star, dancer, musician), the fine arts (writer, painter, composer), and athletics (baseball, basketball, football player). With the exception of a striking propensity among twelve- to thirteen-olds to dream of being sports figures, no linear age trend is discernible.

Because the Hollingshead categories were not used in coding this idealized image question, the answers are not precisely comparable to the earlier findings. Nevertheless, the data again show the striking

Table 12–2. Job Wanted When Grown Up or Older, by Age.

Hollingshead Occupational Classification	*Age of Boys*[a]						*Age of Girls*[a]					
	8	*9*	*10–11*	*12–13*	*14–15*	*16+*	*8*	*9*	*10–11*	*12–13*	*14–15*	*16+*
Higher executive, large proprietor, major professional	19	19	30	29	30	41	2	5	5	6	5	6
Managers, medium proprietors	2	6	—	—	2	2	—	—	—	—	—	—
Lesser professional	2	5	8	7	11	10	56	61	54	47	32	27
Administrative, small proprietor	—	1	2	—	3	—	6	5	10	17	25	20
Semi-professional	11	8	17	25	19	15	2	7	7	13	16	17
Clerical, sales, technical	9	5	3	6	7	9	6	5	7	8	14	20
Skilled manual	32	35	25	21	17	15	10	6	5	4	2	3
Semi- and unskilled	23	17	15	12	8	7	15	10	11	4	6	7
Other	2	3	1	1	3	2	2	—	1	—	—	—
N = 100%	(47)	(96)	(196)	(189)	(149)	(177)	(48)	(111)	(262)	(224)	(174)	(158)

a. $p < .001$.

propensity of younger boys to choose one of the manual occupations: 54 percent of the eight-year-olds but only 12 percent of those sixteen or older cited some such occupation. On the other hand, only 18 percent of the youngest boys, given the choice of any job in the whole world, opted for one of the major or lesser professions, compared with 47 percent of the oldest. In addition, 12 percent of the oldest chose business or government compared with 5 percent of the youngest. Even when encouraged to ignore reality, the younger boys continue to select the lower status manual occupations; the older boys, the higher status professional and managerial occupations.

What accounts for the fact that the younger boy is so much more likely than the older to center his aspirations on the lower status manual occupations and so little on the higher status professions? The answer, we suggest, is fundamentally rooted in the *exteriority* of youthful cognitive processes. By exteriority we refer to an alertness to the visible surface features of things or people rather than to their underlying properties. In Piaget's words (1928), "The child's attention is wholly turned toward the external world, toward action . . ." (p. 213). Young children, whether thinking of themselves or others, are oriented toward that which is overt, visible, and palpable rather than to the elements of a psychological interior (Dymond, Hughes, and Raabe 1952; Flapan 1968; Livesley and Bromley 1973; Rosenberg 1979). The same process of cognitive development, we believe, helps to structure the future occupational self. At least four characteristics make an occupation particularly visible to a child: (a) motor activity; (b) concrete matter; (c) distinctive appearance; and (d) flesh-and-blood exemplars.

Motor Activity. It is certainly not surprising to find that one thing attracting the young boy to the manual occupations is that they involve motor activity—the visible manipulation of matter or machinery. The young boy wants to be a "bulldozer operator," "mechanic," "roofer," "work in a bakery," "building cars," "bus driver," "cement finisher," "airforce mechanic," "drive a tractor trailer," "construction worker," "electrician." In addition, he is attracted to such occupations as policeman, fireman, soldier, cowboy, or football player, in part because they are perceived to involve physical action—running, shooting, riding, climbing, throwing.

Concrete Matter. The young child is also attracted to occupations involving work with things because his thinking tends to be concrete. Piaget (1970) has pointed out that early thought tends to involve concrete operations, as in thought about classes, relations, and numbers bound to objects. Similarly, the bulldozer operator, butcher, glassblower, bricklayer, stevedore, and welder are exciting because they entail the physical manipulation of material objects, whereas the accountant, bacteriologist, chemist, engineer, lawyer, and psychologist are uninteresting because they do not.

Distinctive Appearance. Occupations involving distinctive dress, such as uniforms, are exterior visible components of an occupation. Unfortunately, in our study, we did not code occupations as uniformed or not uniformed. However, we randomly selected fifty elementary school boys in our sample and re-examined their specific responses to the question of what they would like to be when they grew up. Fully eighteen, or 36 percent, chose some uniformed occupation. Heading the list was policeman, but also included were fireman, baseball player, Navy, Marines, Air Force, railroad worker, and ice cream man. It may be noted that certain high-status uniformed occupations are *not* mentioned—for example, judge or clergyman—but it may also be observed that these are rather somber uniforms.

Exemplars. A fourth indicator of the exterior orientation of the young child is his attraction to occupations whose incumbents constantly enter the child's experience as flesh-and-blood exemplars, directly or in the media. The young boy actually sees and recognizes policemen, firemen, or baseball players in the flesh or on the screen much more than lawyers, accountants, engineers, or bank presidents.

We thus suggest that the young child is attracted to occupations involving work with things because, in general, he is oriented to the external and visible aspects of the world rather than to internal or underlying components. But it is relevant to ask why he is *not* attracted to those occupations involving work with data and with people.

One reason why the young child is uninterested in those professional or managerial occupations involving work with data has already been suggested by our earlier discussion of the concrete thought of young children. The higher-order abstractions and formal logical operations (Inhelder and Piaget 1958) that constitute the occupational imperatives of work with data exceed his grasp.

But there is also little indication that the young boy is attracted to occupations involving work with people. This fact may appear surprising since young children enjoy being with playmates and are accustomed to associating with adults. However, what these higher level occupations require, as occupational imperatives, are interpersonal skills and sensitivity; the incumbent must be interested in other people's thoughts and feelings. Insofar as the child is in the stage of egocentrism, he lacks such interpersonal sensitivity because he has not yet learned to take the role of the other and to see matters from the other's point of view (Flavell 1968; Piaget 1926; Schantz 1975). As long as the child has not reached the stage where he is conscious of the invisible thoughts, feelings, and motives of others, the exercise of interpersonal skills and sensitivity holds little attraction for him.

In summary, asked to envision his future occupational self, the young boy is attracted to those lower-status occupations involving work with things because he is in general responsive to the exterior aspects of people or objects. The invisible inner world of thought and feeling that constitute the essence of the higher-status occupations involved in work with data or people is largely alien to him. One reason work with data or people is so much less attractive than work with things is that all the occupational incumbents do is think or talk; they don't *do* anything.

These observations may also help to explain the earlier finding that occupational activity is so much more salient to the young child's future desired self than to the older child's. The child sees adults either at work, going to work, or coming home from work. That such work is governed by an underlying system of motives or constitutes one segment of a more fundamental life theme or value system escapes him. All the young child knows is that most grown-ups work at jobs, and that is how he envisions his future desired self.

It is relevant to ask whether these occupational preferences may be more matters of social learning than of cognitive development. Little boys, after all, are given cowboy hats and sailor suits to wear and they play with toy guns or trucks; they are not garbed in judges' or clergymen's robes, are not given toy legal briefs, slide rules, or double-ledger books. In opting for manual occupations, they are apparently attracted to that which they are taught to want. We would suggest, on the contrary, that they are taught to want that to which they are attracted; in other words, the social learning follows the cognitive development. We expect that experience has shown adults that young boys enjoy playing cowboy, fireman, and policeman but not playing astronomer, economist, engineer, or executive. For why else would adults encourage these activities? The adults are no more likely to want their younger sons to be policemen, firemen, or bulldozer operators than their older sons. In this regard, then, the adults are probably following rather than leading their children, stimulating interest in those activities intrinsically appealing to the young boy, given the nature of his cognitive development.

Occupational Aspirations Among Girls

The younger girls, like the younger boys, are also more likely than the older to choose a manual occupation. Twenty-five percent of the eight-year-old girls but 10 percent of those sixteen or older selected one of these fields. But the younger girls are also more oriented than the older to what Hollingshead has described as one of the "lesser professions." Among the eight-year-olds, 56 percent choose such an occupation but, by the time they are sixteen or older, the proportion has declined to 27 percent. On the other hand, as the girls grow older, they are increasingly drawn to administrative positions, semiprofessional posts, and clerical, sales, and technical work. Combining these three categories shows 56 percent of the oldest girls aspiring to these occupations compared with only 15 percent of the eight-year-olds.

When we compare the younger girls with the younger boys, the most striking difference is that nearly three out of every five girls are apparently attracted to the lesser professions, whereas only one out of twenty-five boys chooses such an occupation. Since these occupations primarily involve working with data and with people rather than with things, it would appear to contradict the earlier claim that young girls are also attracted to what is external and visible. A closer look at the specific responses, however, reveals that a large proportion of the young girls are actually choosing the occupations of nurse and teacher, with a scattering selecting librarian. Unfortunately, these occupations were not coded separately but were lumped together in Hollingshead's "lesser professional" category. For this reason, we returned to the original questionnaires and recoded the responses of all the female respondents in one predominantly black and in one predominantly white elementary school. The results show that of thirty-one girls in the black elementary school, six chose nurse, seven chose teacher, and two selected librarian. In other words, nearly half of all occupational choices were confined to these three categories. Similarly, of the twenty-eight girls sampled in a white elementary school, fully ten chose teacher and two selected nurse—nearly two-fifths of the total in these two categories.

A similar pattern appears in response to the question of what the girls would like to be if they could have "any job at all in the world." Like the boys, about 8 percent of the girls mentioned some grandiose or fantasy position: movie star, First Lady of a Negro President, Mother Goose, and so on. About 11 percent of the girls also chose one of the "special talent" or "entertainment" occupations, that is, in the performing and fine arts. Little systematic variation by age is discernible in these choices. For the rest, the young girls, like the young boys, are again more likely than the older to select one of the manual occupations: 22 percent of the eight-year-olds compared with 7 percent of those sixteen or older. Conversely, 27 percent of the oldest girls chose a white-collar (chiefly clerical and sales) occupation compared with only 3 percent of the youngest. The manual orientation of the younger girls and white-collar orientation of the older girls is expressed in responses to both questions.

A number of interesting points of similarity and difference in boys' and girls' future occupational selves may be noted. First, the same principles of cognitive development apparently direct the occupational choices of young girls and young boys. Like the boys, the young girls are attracted to physical, visible, and overt occupations. As with the boys, younger girls are more likely than older ones to select manual occupations, such as "a cook in a hospital like my mother," "work in a bakery," "waitress," "cooking, sewing," "a cleaner," "sweeping the floors or washing windows," "beautician." Similarly, they are attracted to such lesser professions as nursing. The nurse, like the policeman and fireman, is recognized by a uniform. Finally, they are drawn to teachers and, to a lesser extent, librarians—people who enter the child's experience as flesh-and-blood exemplars. Furthermore, these occupational incumbents are visibly identified with certain occupational settings, props, and paraphernalia. The teacher stands in front of the room behind a desk, equipped with chalk, eraser, and notebook, and the librarian also is to be found in a fixed location operating certain exotic equipment.

The second point relates to boys' and girls' occupational status levels. It is sometimes contended that a major reason for the occupational status disparity of adult men and women is that young girls are socialized to set low aspiration levels, whereas young boys are socialized to aim for the top. Our data suggest, on the contrary, that in the early years the reverse is the case. In terms of general occupational prestige, the aspirations of eight- to nine-year-old girls is actually considerably *higher* than that of eight- to nine-year-old boys. This difference, we believe, is an accidental byproduct of occupational sex-typing. It is true that both young boys and young girls are attracted to what is overt and external, but it so happens that the visible occupations attracting boys are manual, whereas the visible occupations attracting girls turn out to be the lesser professions. To be a nurse, teacher, or librarian requires a college education and commands relatively high status, whereas to be a cement-finisher, bulldozer operator, tractor-trailer driver, policeman, fireman, or soldier requires much less education and commands a lower rank in the status hierarchy. These data clearly demonstrate that if girls end up in lower occupational statuses, this outcome is definitely not a result of early socialization.

The third point to note is that the occupational aspirations of boys and girls move in opposite directions; with advancing age, the boys' aspiration levels rise while the girls' aspiration levels decline. The boys start out with an interest in the manual occupations but in the course of time are increasingly attracted to the major professions—doctor, lawyer, engineer, architect, and, to a lesser extent, managerial and executive positions. Girls, by contrast, start out aspiring to lesser professional positions (nurse, teacher, librarian) but with increasing age move in the direction of what Hollingshead calls "administrative position" (chiefly a secretary), a semi-professional activity (such as an airline stewardess, interior decorator, model, or piano teacher), or a sales or clearical activity. With increasing age, there is a striking increase in the proportion of older girls who reply that they wish to become a "secretary," "stenographer," "typist clerk," "office work (typing, filing, etc.)," "bookkeeping." Although we are unable to provide exact figures for the sample as a whole, it may be noted that when we looked at the questionnaires of a random sample of twenty-five senior high school girls in a working class neighborhood, fully thirteen chose one of these office work occupations. Among the remaining twelve, three chose social work, two chose airline stewardess, and three selected computer operator or programmer.

To recapitulate, the occupational aspirations of boys and girls are governed by similar cognitive processes but follow opposite status trajectories. In the early years, girls heavily aspire to the lesser professions (particularly teacher and nurse), whereas boys aspire to manual statuses (truck driver, machinist, bulldozer operator) or their uniformed status equivalents (fireman, policeman, soldier). With increasing age, however, the status aspirations of the sexes move in opposite directions, the boys' aspirations rising to technical and administrative levels at the junior high school period and to the major professions—doctor, lawyer, engineer—in senior high. Girls, on the other hand, start out aspiring to be teachers, nurses, or librarians but, although these aspirations persist to some degree, in general they decline to secretary, office workers, or sales workers.

The fourth point is that by the end of high school, occupational aspirations of boys are much more widely dispersed than aspirations of girls. Specifically, boys are much more likely to aspire to the higher levels of the major professions and top executive positions but are also more likely to aspire to the lower levels of blue-collar work; the girls, on the other hand, are concentrated largely in the middle of the occupational hierarchy, engaged in white collar jobs. By the age of sixteen or older, fully 41 percent of the boys aspire to one of the major professions or an executive status compared with only 6 percent of the girls. At the same time, older boys are about twice as likely as older girls—22 percent to 10 percent—to envision themselves in manual jobs. Girls, on the other hand, are concentrated in the center of the status hierarchy—in the lesser professions of teaching, nursing, and social work; in administrative positions such as secretary; in semi-professional roles such as airline stewardess, model, or beautician; and in other white-collar work such as sales person or clerk-typist.

The fifth point is that the amount of occupational sex-typing is little short of astounding. This sex-typing is clearly apparent even among the youngest children in our sample and continues unabated throughout their educational careers. Although similar cognitive development attracts the youngest boys and girls to the manual occupations, social learning insures that these are very different occupations. Few girls opt for such occupations as tractor-trailer driver, roofer, electrician, or baseball player, and equally few boys choose nurse, librarian, beautician, or secretary. So extreme is this pattern, so early is it in evidence, and so persistent is it over time that it is difficult to evade the conclusion that these youthful aspirations are governed in large measure by observed empirical reality.

Consider the occupational sex-typing of the adult world. Although adult women currently represent a large segment of the work force, they tend to be concentrated in a small number of predominantly feminine occupations. For example, in 1960 fully one-third of all employed women were concentrated in only seven occupations—secretaries, bookkeepers, elementary school teachers, nurses, household workers, waitresses, and salespersons—and this proportion had actually increased by 1970. In 1970, 98 percent of the secretaries and 94 percent of the typists were women compared to only 4 percent of the architects and 2 percent of the engineers (Lecht 1976; Lyle and Ross 1973). This occupational reality must inevitably influence youthful aspirations; the upshot is that boys and girls end up aspiring to those occupations that they will actually enter.

But this occupational sex-typing may represent more than an unreflective mimicry of the adult occupational structure; it may also be rooted in a more fundamental sense of sex-identity. In today's world, of course, the biological basis of occupational sex-typing is trivial. There is nothing in the actual work activity of the nurse, teacher, librarian, or secretary that should render it unattractive to the young boy, or of a doctor, engineer, or dentist that should make it unappealing to the girl. If they fail to hold these aspirations, it can only be because they interpret them as sex-inappropriate.

Nor does actual exposure to the living embodiments of these occupations explain these differences. The little girl sees as many policemen and firemen as the little boy, the little boy sees as many teachers and librarians as the girl. These choices obviously have nothing to do with exposure to living flesh-and-blood exemplars. Something more fundamental evidently plays a role.

We suggest that occupational sex-typing is rooted in the very process of sex-identity development. The concept of gender is probably no different from any other concept and is learned by the child in much the same way. Conceptual development is fundamentally a classificatory process which involves assigning all units characterized by one or more common features into the same category. According to Kohlberg (1966), it is through such a classificatory process that the young child develops a concept of male and female. Early on, the child's attention is directed to certain visible features which serve as a basis for sex classification, particularly such overt features as dress, hair, and form. Particularly pertinent in the present regard is that men and women are defined not only by how they look but by what they do. To be a policeman is not only to be of the police but to be a man; the term soldier calls forth the image of a man; the sex of a nurse is communicated by the term. Thus it is not simply a matter of the child assigning an occupation to one sex or the other; rather, the concepts of male and female are themselves organized partly in terms of sex-typed occupational activities. In the mind of the child, occupational activity becomes one of the defining characteristics of sex-identity, just as short hair and long hair does, dresses and trousers, football or dolls. For a girl to think of herself as a machinist or a boy as a nurse is to violate their sense of femininity or masculinity. The choice of an occupation thus deeply implicates a more fundamental sense of sex-identity. Even among the youngest children in our sample, then, fundamental sex differences regarding occupational selves are evident, despite common processes of cognitive development.

SUMMARY

In this study, we have asked our youthful respondents to perform a remarkable imaginative leap: to envision a self that has no current existence but is seen to arise out of some vaguely conceived process of the transmutation of the current self into some future being. In particular, we have been concerned with how the occupational component of the desired self changes as children grow older.

It is apparent that processes of cognitive development and of social learning are both involved. Younger children, it has been found, are much more disposed to conceptualize the self and other people in terms of a social exterior; they are attuned to the concrete, visible, surface aspects of things and people. They tend to select occupations whose primary tasks involve physical action, include the manipulation of matter and machines, are publicly announced by uniforms, and whose incumbents directly enter their experience. The future desired self of the young child is constrained by the level of his cognitive development. Older children, on the other hand, are more oriented toward occupations involving work with data and people.

But social learning also plays a very important role in the formation of the desired future self, best exemplified by the powerful tendency toward occupational sex-typing that characterizes the American occupational system. Though the fundamental processes of cognitive development follow the same course, boys and girls start out aspiring to different occupations, change their occupational aspirations as they grow older, and end up aspiring to different occupations. One reason it may be difficult to change such choices is that they are integral to the child's gender identity.

13 THE DEVELOPMENT OF SELF-CONCEPT IN ADOLESCENCE

Anne C. Petersen

Self-concept is an especially salient construct during the adolescent years. Theoretical and empirical work has suggested that adolescence is an important time for changes in self-concept. In this chapter, we provide a framework for conceptualizing the development of self-concept in adolescence and then review existing evidence for its development at this stage. Previous studies are reviewed and new data presented that describe influences on the development of self-concept at adolescence.

EXISTING DEVELOPMENTAL THEORIES

Currently there is no theory that specifically addresses the development of self-concept during adolescence. Erikson's (1968) theory of the development of identity comes closest, yet Erikson considers self-image[a] as only one of the eight part-conflicts in the development of identity at adolescence (see Petersen and Offer 1979). Other psychoanalytic theorists (for example, Blos 1979; A. Freud 1958) have presented perspectives that would have implications for the development of self-concept at adolescence (see Adelson and Doehrman 1980, for a review). These perspectives propose that psychologi-

a. The terms self-concept and self-image will be used interchangeably.

cal turmoil at adolescence is necessary and universal, a stance not supported by empirical research (for example, Douvan and Adelson 1966; Offer and Offer 1975).

Piaget's theory of cognitive development also is highly relevant to the development of self-concept. The capacity for formal operational thought (Inhelder and Piaget 1958), first emerging at adolescence, ought to enable the adolescent to think about the self as an abstract entity. While Piaget dealt primarily with the individual's capacity to think about objects and their relationships, others (for example, Selman 1976; Shantz 1975) have extended these concepts to include the development of understanding of persons and their relationships. Research in this area, now termed social cognition, shows promise of expanding our understanding of the development of self-concept (see Hill and Palmquist 1978; Keating 1980).

Preliminary results from our laboratory (Hurtig 1980; Jarcho 1980) suggest that measures of cognitive development and social cognition are similar, but show enough dissimilarity to question hypotheses of a single underlying construct or a single stage sequence. No research, to our knowledge, has linked either cognitive development or social cognition to self-concept in adolescence.

A HYPOTHETICAL MODEL

In lieu of a theory, we will describe a model for the development of self-concept at adolescence. While models do not typically generate hypotheses, they are useful in providing a framework within which existing research can be evaluated. In addition, models can draw attention to areas needing research.

Two aspects of the development of self-concept will be addressed: (a) changes in the quality and quantity (e.g., positiveness) of self-concept, and (b) factors influencing changes in the direction or nature of self-concept. Our model for the development of self-concept is a transactional one (Sameroff 1977). Theories for the uniform development of any psychological characteristic are likely to fail when tested empirically because of the varied environmental factors that influence development. On the other hand, it is not appropriate to abandon the study of development since there are aspects of adolescence as a stage of life that influence the course of development.

Puberty, for example, generally considered as the beginning of adolescence, is a process that affects development profoundly for all young people experiencing this normal biological change (Petersen and Taylor 1980.) Because of this maturational change, developing individuals change dramatically in appearance and, hence, are perceived and responded to differently by self as well as others. This transformation to adult appearance and mature reproductive capacity is associated with a series of role changes—for example, from child to potential parent and from student to worker. Thus, the biological change in appearance together with the ensuing social changes in role expectations are likely to have extensive impact on one's self-concept at adolescence.

QUANTITATIVE CHANGES IN SELF-CONCEPT

Most of the available evidence suggests that self-concept becomes less stable and more negative in early adolescence (roughly, the junior high school years) compared to earlier and later periods. The major source of evidence here is from the research of Simmons and colleagues. Simmons, Rosenberg, and Rosenberg (1973) identified the movement from sixth to seventh grade as a stressful period for self-image. Early adolescents, especially girls (Simmons et al. 1979; Simmons and Rosenberg 1975), showed heightened self-consciousness, greater instability of self-image, and lower self-esteem as compared to younger children. Older adolescents improved on most of these dimensions. Other cross-sectional studies have obtained similar results showing self-image disturbance in early adolescence (for example, Long, Zeller, and Hendersen 1968; Offer and Howard 1972; Piers and Harris 1964). Studies of adolescents in high school or older also report increases in self-esteem (Nichols 1963). Some investigators, however, have concluded that the self-image is relatively stable over adolescence (Carlson 1965; Engel 1959).

Data on changes in self-image over the high school years are shown in Table 13-1. Self-image is measured with the Offer Self-Image Questionnaire (OSIQ), a 130-item questionnaire with eleven scales: Impulse Control, Emotional Tone, Body and Self-Image, Social Relationships, Morals, Sex Attitudes, Family Relationships, External Mastery, Vocational and Educational Goals, Psychopathology, and

Table 13–1. The Offer Self-Image Questionnaire (*OSIQ*).

OSIQ Scale[a]	*Means and Standard Deviations by Grade and Sex*							
	Freshmen		*Sophomores*		*Juniors*		*Seniors*	
	M(N = 28)	*F(N = 53)*	*M(N = 24)*	*F(N = 39)*	*M(N = 36)*	*M(N = 63)*	*M(N = 31)*	*F(M = 29)*
Impulse Control	4.13 (.63)	4.25 (.66)	4.05 (.68)	4.45 (.78)	4.47 (.68)	4.34 (.75)	4.29 (.81)	4.38 (.69)
Emotional Tone	4.60 (.49)	4.30 (.90)	4.52 (.54)	4.38 (.71)	4.54 (.60)	4.35 (.76)	4.52 (.73)	4.39 (.66)
Body/Self Image	4.48 (.61)	4.16 (.72)	4.38 (.62)	4.27 (.61)	4.57 (.60)	4.33 (.72)	4.56 (.82)	4.39 (.67)
Social Relations	4.49 (.61)	4.59 (.74)	4.52 (.73)	4.71 (.68)	4.75 (.55)	4.70 (.62)	4.61 (.69)	4.74 (.70)
Morals	4.36 (.66)	4.62 (.45)	4.19 (.53)	4.82 (.45)	4.47 (.65)	4.61 (.50)	4.44 (.56)	4.85 (.49)
Family Relations	4.65 (.55)	4.79 (.67)	4.53 (.77)	4.64 (.72)	4.52 (.78)	4.68 (.95)	4.88 (.62)	5.06 (.62)
External Mastery	4.64 (.69)	4.46 (.59)	4.52 (.63)	4.55 (.53)	4.64 (.60)	4.40 (.65)	4.74 (.65)	4.69 (.58)
Vocat/Educ Goals	5.01 (.55)	4.91 (.45)	4.93 (.61)	5.14 (.53)	5.05 (.55)	4.99 (.67)	5.81 (.65)	5.33 (.47)
Psychopathology	4.55 (.53)	4.29 (.67)	4.43 (.50)	4.42 (.61)	4.50 (.61)	4.36 (.69)	4.49 (.57)	4.49 (.56)
Superior Adjustment	4.40 (.47)	4.33 (.43)	4.30 (.54)	4.48 (.48)	4.48 (.49)	4.44 (.61)	4.52 (.59)	4.74 (.43)
Total Score	4.53 (.41)	4.47 (.46)	4.43 (.39)	4.59 (.41)	4.60 (.43)	4.51 (.54)	4.61 (.47)	4.71 (.44)

a. Scale responses range from 1 to 6. A higher score indicates a better self-image.

Superior Adjustment.[b] A multivariate analysis of variance examining changes between successive grades showed no significant multivariate effects. There were some univariate effects; juniors had poorer self-images than seniors on Family Relations ($p < .01$), External Mastery ($p < .05$), Vocational and Educational Goals ($p < .05$), and Superior Adjustment ($p < .05$).

Changes over the high school years were also examined by fitting a straight line (linear polynomial), a curved line (quadratic polynomial), and a curved line with two "humps" (cubic polynomial). Again, there were no multivariate effects, suggesting that no systematic trends were apparent in the data overall. The only significant ($p < .05$) univariate effect was on the Superior Adjustment scale, showing a positive self-image with increasing grade. This result ought to be viewed with caution, however, as we would expect by chance to find one significant result in these analyses.

While few of these comparisons show significant differences across the high school years, note that with all but two instances for both males and females, self-image is enhanced by the senior year relative to the freshman year. In comparisons across sex, three scales showed significant increases in self-image over the high school years: Family Relations, Vocational and Educational Goals, and Superior Adjustment.

QUALITATIVE CHANGES IN SELF-IMAGE

In an analysis of the connotative structure of self-concept, Monge (1973) concluded that the self-concept is continuous through the pubertal years and that the structure of self-concept remains similar

b. The OSIQ scales and the items measuring them were conceptually derived and were based upon theories of adolescent self-concept as well as previous research (Offer, Ostrov, and Howard 1977). The content validity of most items seems quite high. The inter-item (interclass) correlations are uniformly high for this type of construct ranging from .41 to .88, suggesting that the scales are relatively homogeneous (Offer and Howard 1972.) Each item in the OSIQ consists of a statement to which the adolescent responds with a Likert-type scale ranging from "describes me very well" to "does not describe me at all." This sort of response format has the advantage at providing variability in responses (assuming that the statement is not so extreme as to preclude variation in response.) The disadvantage, of course, is that the response scale is an abstraction whose interpretation is left to the respondent. Response style, including the tendency to use more versus less extreme categories as well as the tendency to be more or less positive, becomes confounded with the extent to which the adolescent in fact is described by the statement.

from sixth to twelfth grade. Similarly, Michael, Smith, and Michael (1975) concluded that three major dimensions of self-concept were invariant over cross-sectional samples of elementary, junior high, and high school students.

In contrast, Montemayor and Eisen (1977), in their examination of the development of self-concept from a cognitive–structural perspective, found that age-related changes in the categories used to describe oneself depended upon the kind of category. From age ten to age eighteen there were significant increases in the use of the following categories: occupational role, existential or individuating, ideological and belief references, sense of self-determination, sense of unity, interpersonal style, and psychic style. References to self in relation to place of residence, possessions, and physical body decreased over the same period. A curvilinear *U*–shaped function best describes the references to gender, name, kinship role, membership in an abstract category, and interests. The authors conclude that self-concept development, like cognitive development, proceeds from the concrete to the abstract, with a few exceptions.

These seemingly discrepant conclusions about changes in self-concept during adolescence can be integrated by examining the constructs studied. Monge, for example, studied semantic differential scales to which individuals' attributions are more likely to be stable. Montemayor and Eisen, on the other hand, examined self-descriptive categories that are more likely to change during the adolescent transition because of changing cognitive capacity as well as changing roles. In our own current research with early adolescents, we have found it necessary to modify the OSIQ so that it is valid for younger adolescents (Petersen, Jarcho, and Offer 1980). The items requiring deletion or change fell mainly into two groups: (a) items that demanded abstract thinking and (b) items with inappropriate role content.

INFLUENCES ON SELF-CONCEPT OVER ADOLESCENCE

In early adolescence, there are two major influences: puberty and changes in expectations due to the youth's entry into an adolescent status. In our society we expect pubertal youth to become concerned with their bodies, and there is some evidence that they do (for example, Montemayor and Eisen 1977). In addition, school structure changes to a more complicated and demanding format at this age, which caused disturbances in self-image (Simmons et al. 1973). Some evidence suggests that peer pressure is greatest in early to middle adolescence (Coleman 1977; Costanzo 1970). Though there is a paucity of research on parental influences at this age (for example, Hamburg 1974; Lipsitz 1977), our preliminary data suggest that some parents experience anxiety when their children reach puberty (Solomon et al. 1980).

At mid-adolescence, Coleman (1977) suggests that parental pressure peaks, and the peer group increases in relative importance. The adolescent is making course choices in school that have implications for later occupational choices (for example, Fennema and Sherman 1977).

By late adolescence, the post-high-school years, youth "should" be integrating their selves; though the studies of identity status (for example, Marcia 1966, 1980) suggest that this task does not come until later (if at all) for many youth. Many young people struggle with issues of separation from their families of origin (Blos 1962). Heterosexual relationships (Coleman 1977) and occupational issues (Havinghurst and Gottleib 1976) become important for many youth.

DEMOGRAPHIC FACTORS ASSOCIATED WITH SELF-CONCEPT AT ADOLESCENCE

In addition to developmental influences on self-concept at adolescence, several demographic factors have been identified that could have differential impact on self-concept at adolescence.

Sex

Many studies have found that girls have poorer self-images than boys at adolescence (Gove and Herb 1975; Offer and Howard 1972; Offer, Ostrov, and Howard 1977; Simmons and Rosenberg 1975). Figure 13-1 shows sex differences on the data appearing in Table 13-1. Though there is a significant multivariate sex difference, only four scales show sex differences, with males showing better self-image on Emotional Tone, Body and Self-Image, and External Mastery, and females looking better on the Morals scale. The sex difference in self-

Figure 13–1. Sex Difference in Self-Image.

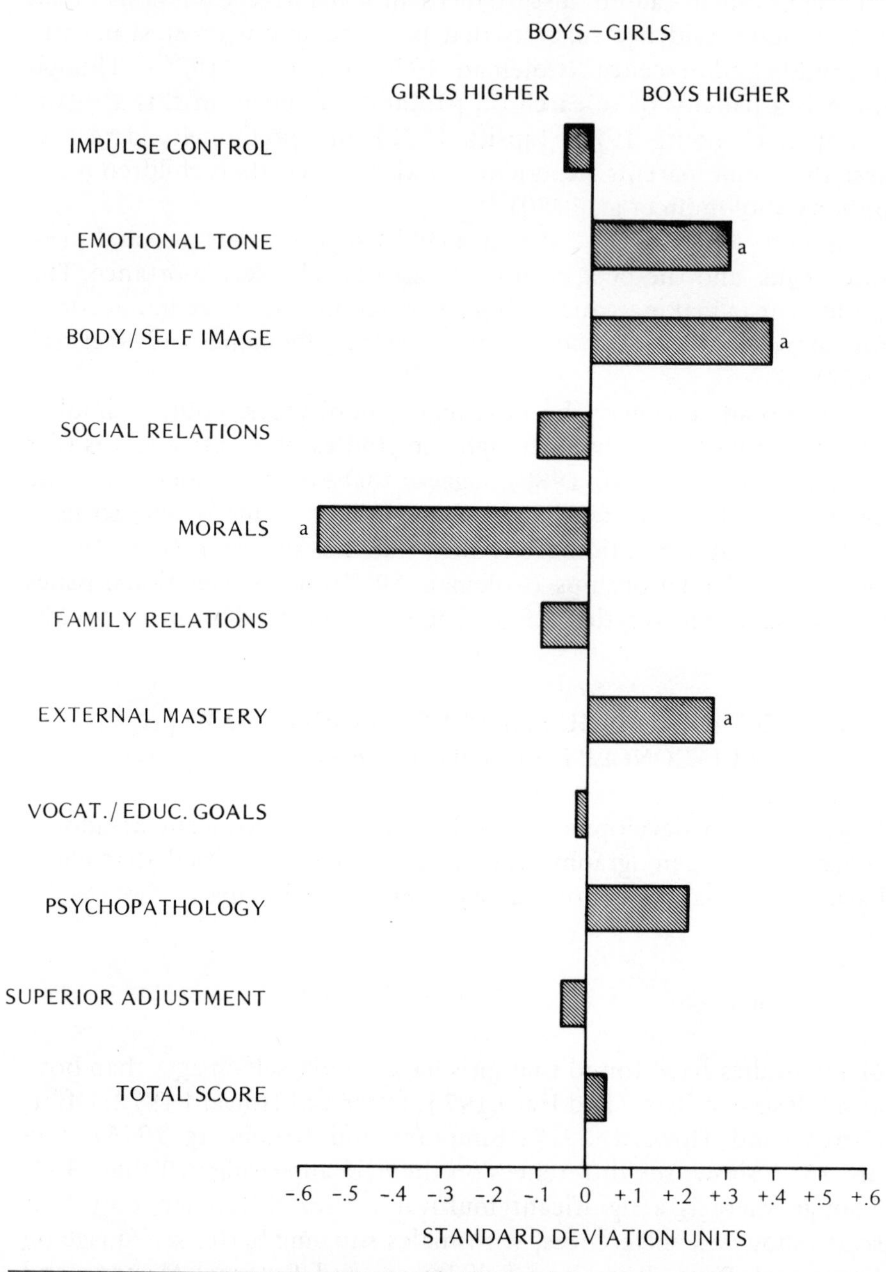

Note: Sample = 113 boys and 181 girls.

a. Difference Significant ($p < .05$).

image seems to persist into adulthood (for example, Rosenkrantz et al. 1968), though there is some evidence that this difference may be disappearing (Srole and Fischer 1980).

Cohort

Nesselroade and Baltes (1974) found that cohort or historical effects are important variables to consider in studies of adolescent development. Figure 13-1 shows cohort differences obtained by averaging results of four independent comparisons of samples drawn in the 1960s compared with the one described earlier in Table 13-1, drawn in 1978. The 1978 younger (freshman-sophomore) and older (junior-senior) males and females were compared with samples drawn from the same urban area and similar in religion, socioeconomic status, and ethnic background. Despite the fact that the 1960s comparison samples were drawn from 1962 to 1969, the four comparisons produced similar results, represented by the averages in Figure 13-2. The 1970s youth showed lower self-image than the 1960s youth on every scale. With most scales, the differences were sizable. The largest average effects are seen with Impulse Control (two-thirds of a standard deviation and Morals (one-half of a standard deviation). Cohort effects are not unique to adolescence, though we might argue that they would be more extreme, precisely because of the development of self-concept during these years.

Urbanicity

Previous research (Petersen; Offer, and Kaplan 1979) showed that rural youth tended to report lower self-image than their more urban counterparts. Figure 13-3 shows average effects over samples obtained within a six-month period (1977-78). With every scale, suburban youth report higher self-image. On three scales, these differences are at least one-half of a standard deviation: Morals, Psychopathology, and Superior Adjustment. The effect size for the total (average) score is half a standard deviation as well.

Figure 13–2. Cohort Differences in Self-Image from 1960s to 1970s.

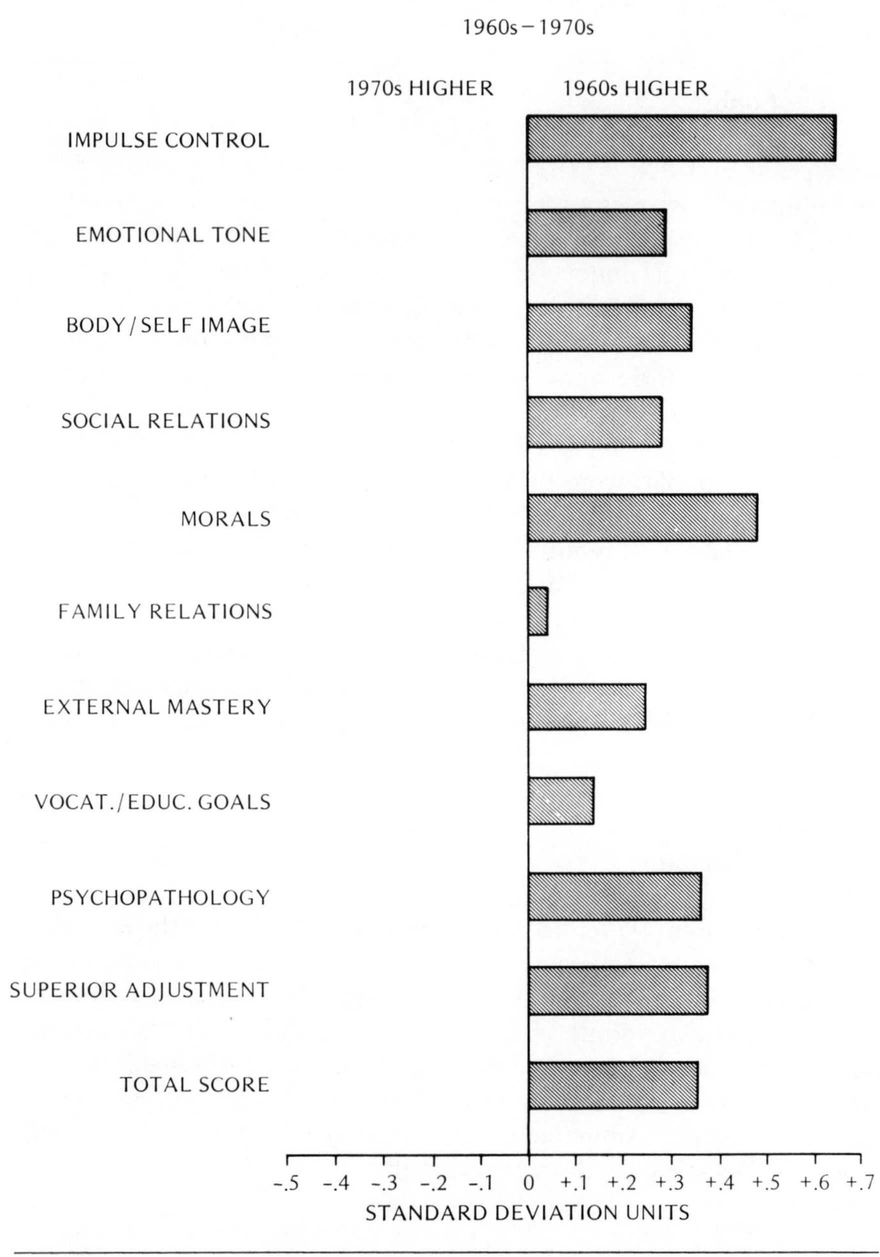

Figure 13–3. Urbanicity Differences in Self-Image.

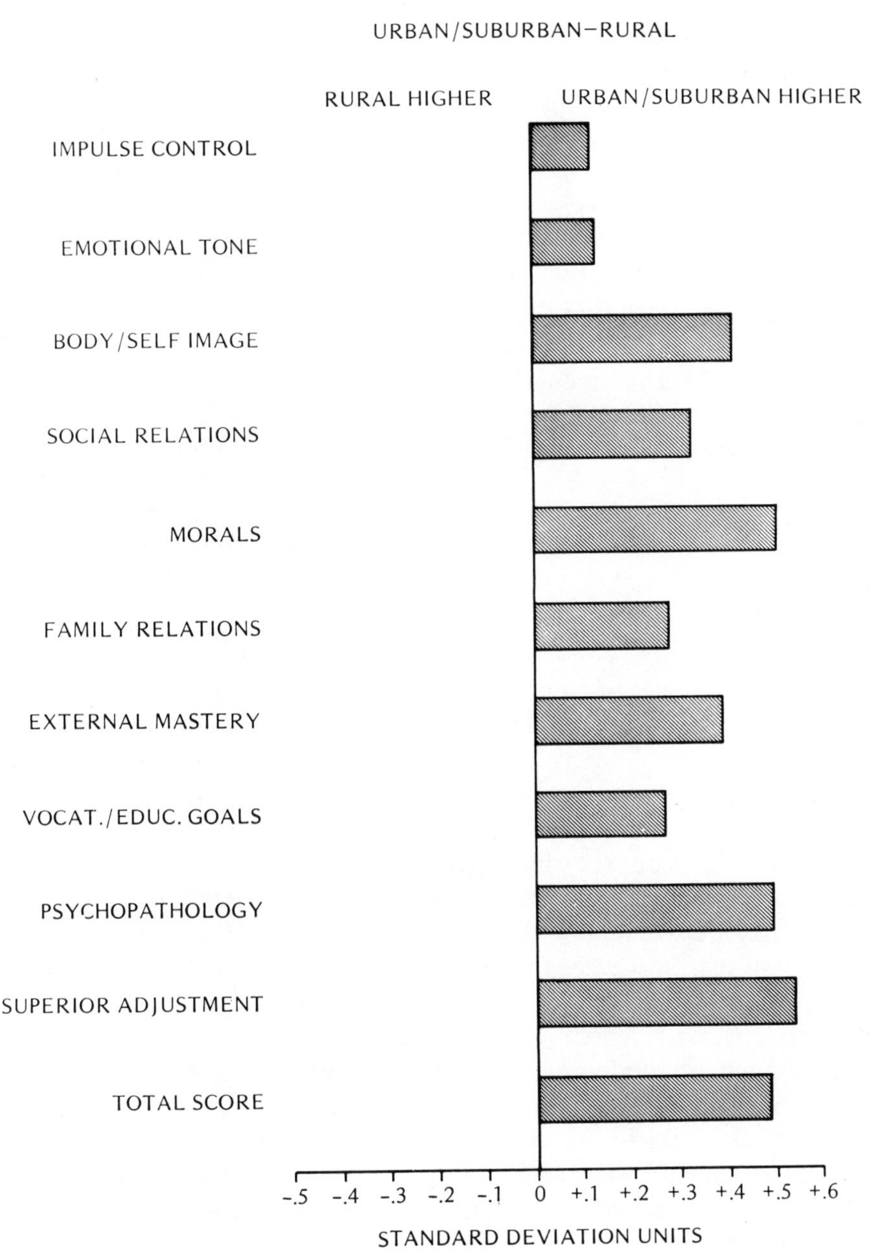

SOCIOECONOMIC STATUS AND ETHNICITY

The major research on socioeconomic status (SES) in relation to self-concept has been done by Rosenberg (1965). He suggests that the self-concept is at least partly dependent upon the adolescent's reference group. While his data support this hypothesis, other research on the relation of SES to self-concept shows mixed results. Some studies have found that youth with higher SES have better self-image, while others have obtained the reverse result, and still other studies suggest that SES has no significant influence on self-concept (see Petersen, Offer, and Kaplan 1979, for a review). Like SES, the effects of ethnicity on self-concept are ambiguous. These studies have focused on difference between blacks and whites; some studies have found that blacks have more positive self-concept than whites, while others find the reverse (reviewed in Petersen, Offer, and Kaplan 1979).

SUMMARY

While adolescence seems to be a good time of life at which to study the development of self-concept, few developmental theories or empirical studies exist. The available evidence suggests that self-concept declines in early adolescence, perhaps due to some combination of pubertal changes and related changes in expectations. Other research on influences on self-concept at adolescence suggests that girls may fare poorer than boys. Similarly, rural youth may feel worse about themselves than their more urban peers. The adolescent years may be worse now than a decade or so ago. Race and socioeconomic status, however, are probably not important factors for adolescent self-concept.

The existing research on self-concept at adolescence supports the importance of models or theories that consider both maturational and environmental or situational factors. Adolescence involves the mastery of specific maturational changes. In addition, other kinds of stresses such as historical times, urbanicity of community, or gender role may exacerbate or diminish the difficulty of developing a self-concept.

14 THE DEVELOPMENT OF THE SELF-CONCEPT THROUGH THE LIFE SPAN

Rene L'Ecuyer

Since William James' famous writings on the self-concept (1890), a great amount of research on this topic has been conducted. It still remains difficult, however, to work in that field. At the level of the definition of the self-concept, the tentative distinction between the ego and the self, the self-as-object and the self-as-process, raised much confusion and brought nothing very useful (Hall and Lindzey 1957; L'Ecuyer 1978; Murphy 1968; Patterson 1961). Another difficulty lies in whether to consider the self as a single, unitary, or unidimensional concept (Bertocci 1945; Cooley 1902; Lecky 1945; Mead 1934; Rogers 1951) or to see it as a multiple, complex, or multidimensional concept. This last conception seems to be the one presently preferred (Allport 1955; Gergen 1971; L'Ecuyer 1975a, 1978).

Allport (1955), Combs and Snygg (1959), Gordon (1968), James (1890), and others also proposed the hypothesis that the self is composed of "vital" or "central" and less important or "peripheral" elements; in other words, they point out the existence of a hierarchical organization between the different elements constituting the self-concept. Few things have been done in that direction, except Fitts's remarkable works for diagnostic purposes (1965, 1969–72) and Gordon's research (1968).

As to the hypothesis of the development of the self-concept all through the life cycle (Allport 1961; James 1890) very few researches exist on so large a scale, with the same framework and from the individual's point of view. Furthermore, such works are based on mathematical scores so that we neither know what exactly varies nor the psychological nature of such variations (Bugental 1964). The certainty is too great that children and older people are unable to explore and communicate the experience of their selves; this capacity is even strongly denied for normal adults (Hilgard 1949; Snygg and Combs 1950).

Consequently, research on the self-concept is limited to specific areas or directions: reactions of the child in front of a mirror; the origins of the self through the study of language development or behavior observations; and an important amount of research showing only the correlations of the self with just about everything: learning, creativity, school adaptations, job satisfaction, success in therapy, teachers' attitudes, and what else. Therefore, we know better and better the size of the correlations of the self with other phenomena, but we still do not know the nature or quality of what is related within the self to these phenomena.

Briefly it can be said that the variety of definitions of the self and the wide-ranging use of very different methodologies led to the impossibility of really understanding the evolution of the self; and that the current use of *inference techniques* and mathematical scores often banishes all possibility of being in real contact with the true self, that is, with the way the individual experiences his own self.

All these facts lead to the necessity of long-term research conducted with the same theoretical and methodological (especially autodescriptive) framework. Such kind of research is rather rare; in that way, Gordon's (1968), Kikuchi's (1968), Perron's (1971), Bianca Zazzo's (1972), and few other works are interesting.

AIMS

We founded the Self-Concept Research Laboratory at the Department of Psychology at the University of Sherbrooke in order to try to find some solutions to the different problems cited above. The main purposes of this laboratory are: (a) the development of a multidimensional model of the self-concept useful for the classification of the results and flexible enough to incorporate new elements derived from experimentations; (b) the elaboration of a technique suitable to both children and adults, allowing the subject to describe him- or herself the way he or she perceives that self, and allowing the experimenter to stay in direct contact with the perceptual contents of these self-descriptions; and (c) the study of the development of the self-concept through the life span, comparing males and females in terms of the evolution of the patterns of organization of the self (modification of central and secondary perceptions through age), and in terms of the evolution of the psychological contents characterizing the experience of subject's own self.

The experiments began in 1967. Since then, results have been obtained from three- to one-hundred-year-old subjects. Of course, it is impossible to describe here the forty-three developmental curves representing the different dimensions of the self-concept.[a] According to that, we will discuss the different stages of development through the life span and different developmental hypotheses in the light of our results and their consequences. A few discussions conclude the chapter. Before this analysis, it is necessary to describe briefly the conceptual framework of our research, the technique used, and to give a few details related to the experiments as such.

THE CONCEPT OF SELF

One of the important consequences of the great variety in the definitions of the self is the necessity of rebuilding this concept. The final conceptual model adopted in the laboratory is mainly derived from the following authors: Allport (1955), Gordon (1968), James (1890), Jersild (1952), Mead (1934), Sarbin (1952), Staines (1954), and Symonds (1951).

From this analysis derives the firm belief that the self must be considered as a concept consisting of three levels of organization or generalization which are: the structures, the substructures, and the

a. Detailed analyses of central and secondary perceptions and of psychological content for children aged three to eight are made in L'Ecuyer (1974a, 1974b, 1975a). General descriptions of the development of central and secondary perceptions at ages three to twenty-one and sixty to one hundred are made in L'Ecuyer (1978). Content analysis is made on the elderly's self-concept (L'Ecuyer 1977) and on the phenomenon of reminiscence (1979).

categories. The structures of the self constitute its main fundamental regions and are the material self, the personal self, the adaptative self, the social self, and the self–non-self. These five structures are divided into different areas called the substructures. The substructures are in turn subdivided into more restricted elements, the categories, designing the multiple aspects of the self-concept and directly derived from the very intimate individual's experience which is felt, then perceived, and finally symbolized or conceptualized by him (L'Ecuyer 1975a, 1978). Figure 14–1 shows the internal organization of these different constituents of the self-concept.

This model makes possible the analysis of profiles and their development: profiles of structures, of substructures, and of categories. Each profile can also be analyzed in terms of central and secondary perceptions, and in terms of their modifications throughout the life span. Finally, a detailed content analysis can be made for each category derived from subject's own description of him-or-her self. More complete details are available concerning the origin and development of this model, and the definitions of each dimension of the self (L'Ecuyer 1975a, 1978).

METHOD OF INVESTIGATION

The method used to investigate the self-concept is derived from Bugental and Zelen's Who Are You? (WAY) technique (1950). The final form obtained is now called the GPS method (Self-Perceptions Genesis) and is suitable to any age level, starting from two-year-old children up to the elderly. Such a choice of an autodescriptive technique was made with full knowledge of the problem of inference methods versus self-reports (Combs and Soper 1957; Hilgard 1949; Wylie 1974). For a complete discussion on this methodological problem and for more details on the GPS method, see L'Ecuyer (1975a, 1975b, 1978).

EXPERIMENTAL DESIGN

All the subjects from three to a hundred years of age were normal, that is, in physical and mental fitness. Age criteria—children three, five, and eight years old and adolescents twelve, fifteen, eighteen,

Figure 14–1. Constituents of Self-Concept: Internal Organization[a].

Structures	Substructures	Categories
Material Self (SM)	Somatic Self (SSo)	physical traits (tra) physical condition (cph)
	Possessive Self (SPo)	possession of objects (obj) possession of persons (per)
Personal Self (SP)	Self-Image (ImS)	aspirations or ideals (asp) enumeration of activities (ena) emotion (sem) interests (int) capacity, aptitude (apt) quality-defect (def)
	Self-Identity (IdS)	simple denomination (nom) role and status (rol) consistency (con) ideology (ide) abstract identity (ida)
Adaptative Self (SA)	Self-Esteem (VaS)	competence (com) personal worth (vap)
	Self-Activity (AcS)	adaptational strategy (sta) autonomy (aut) ambivalence (amb) dependency (dep) actualization (act) lifestyle (sty)
Social Self (SS)	Preoccupations and Social Activities (PaS)	receptivity (rec) domination (dom) altruism (alt)
	Reference to Sex (RaS)	simple reference (res) sexual attractiveness and experience (sex)
Self-Non-Self (SN)	Reference to Others (ReA) Others' Opinion on Self (OpA)	nil

a. Translated from: L'Ecuyer, R. (1978), *Le Concept de Soi*. Paris: Presses Universitaires de France, p. 80.

and twenty-one, with a variation of plus or minus six months around each age—have been met. There were fifteen boys and fifteen girls at each age level for children, and about twenty to thirty for adolescents. Adults between twenty-five and fifty-five years of age were selected according to a five-year interval (25, 30, 35, . . . 55). Each age level is represented by twenty to thirty individuals for each sex. Samples of sixty- to one-hundred-year-old people were also selected according to a five-year interval and with a variation of plus or minus one year around each age level. Each group includes fifteen to twenty-five men and fifteen to twenty-five women. There were, unfortunately, no men at age one hundred and only two women (due to our criteria of mental and physical fitness).

Individual interviews with the GPS were conducted with children and elders. Group testing was made for ages twelve to fifty-five.[b]

The results are classified according to Van Kaam's general methodology (1959) with few adaptations. Each statement is classified according to the meaning given by the subject during his or her self-report, not to its latent signification. Central perceptions are those expressed by 70 percent or more of the subjects in a sample, and secondary perceptions by 30 percent or less. Perceptual contents refer to what is specifically said during the self-reports under the final identified categories. For example, do males and females say the same things and with the same signification in their statements classified into somatic self, self-esteem, adaptative self, and so on, at ages five, twenty-five, fifty-five, seventy-five?

THE SELF-CONCEPT AND THE LIFE SPAN

We have divided the life span into six phases or stages of development: the emergence of the self, the assertion of the self, the expansion of the self, the differentiation of the self, the maturity of the self, and the longevous self. These stages will be described briefly, and a few developmental hypotheses and processes reviewed in the light of our results.

b. This research was supported by grants by the Department of Education of the Province of Quebec, the Ministry of Social Affairs of the Province of Quebec, and by the Council of Arts of Canada.

Stage I: Zero to Two Years Old: The Emergence of the Self

Two aspects will be pointed out in discussing the emergence of the self: the self-non-self differentiation and the body image.

During this first stage, the formation of the self begins through a variety of experiences that happen to the child: physiological, cognitive, affective, social. This emergence of the self is realized via the process of differentiation called ego-non-ego by the psychoanalysts, the self-not-self by Bugental (1949), the I and the not-I by Harding (1965) and Symonds (1951), the self-not-self by L'Ecuyer (1975a, 1978), the self-other differentiation process by Rodriguez Tomé (1972) and Ziller (1973). This differentiation is generally considered as the first fundamental distinction in early childhood, and after that point is mentioned irregularly except during adolescence.

The formation of a body image occurs during this first stage and is an important aspect of differentiation. According to several authors, the body image is the nucleus of self-consciousness (Fisher and Cleveland 1968; Schilder 1935; Symonds 1951; Zazzo 1948), and is sometimes considered as one of the most important—if not *the* most important—dimensions of the self in its development. Every perception of self is then said to stem from the perception of one's own body.

Our results, then, seem to demonstrate that the self-concept is far from being overwhelmed by (and, of course, limited to) the body image at different steps of the life cycle, and that the process of self-non-self differentiation occurs all through the life cycle.

The Vanishing Importance of the Body Image. When the development of the body image is analyzed in terms of the degree of importance of the different dimensions of the self-concept (central, intermediate, and secondary perceptions), the following considerations appear: globally, from ages three to twenty-one and sixty to one hundred, the body image is a central perception in only eight samples out of twenty-nine (that is, at ages five, seventy, seventy-five, ninety to a hundred for males, and three, eight, eighty, ninety-five to a hundred for females); when the body image is central at any given age, there are always between eight to fifteen other dimensions of the self-concept that are central at the same time (L'Ecuyer 1975a, 1978).

In fact, the following dimensions are usually more central than the body image: possessive self (central at every age from sixty to one hundred), self-image and self-identity (always central from three to twenty-one, and sixty to one hundred), adaptative self (quite always central), social self (always central from three to twenty-one and intermediate only three times from sixty to one hundred). The structure self–non-self is even more often central than body image from sixty to one hundred.

Our results prove that the importance of the body image seems to have been overemphasized in dealing with general (or normal) development. Greater importance of the body image seems then to be mainly related to special events (culture, illness, education, religion), and not necessarily to development as such. These results confirm Allport's (1961), Cooley's (1902), and Hall's (1898) thinking that the body image is far from being unique, and that it is an important element only within the early ages, and that this importance is gradually declining in favor of other self-concept dimensions over the years.

Self–Non-Self Differentiation and the Life Cycle. Theories also insist on the process of differentiation within the early years, particularly through the discovery of the child's own body as different from his or her mother's. Other kinds of differentiation are also mentioned during adolescence. Our results clearly show that the process of self–non-self differentiation is not limited to specific stages of development; rather, it is going on all through the life cycle. This process is always active, but its modalities are changing from stage to stage.

Our results give a sort of *U* curve in the self–non-self differentiation through the life cycle. In other words, the structure self–non-self is a central perception from ages three to eight, varying between intermediate and secondary during ages twelve to twenty-one, rising again to the intermediate level of importance during ages sixty to seventy-five, and coming back to a central perception at ages eighty to one hundred. This process seems, then, to be more active during childhood and old age.[c]

c. Caution must be observed on the *U* curve description because the results have not yet been analyzed within the twenty-five to fifty-five age range.

The changing modalities of expression of this process appear in the dimension self–non-self at different ages: children (ages three to eight) show a constant shifting from identification and differentiation through possessive aspects—"This is mine" or "My friend has a nice bicycle"—and through others—"My father works in a factory" (L'Ecuyer 1974a, 1974b, 1975a); during adolescence (twelve through twenty-one) it is manifested by the self's comparison of others' opinions on him or her to his or her own opinions. This fact is greatly confirmed by Tomé's works on self–other differentiation process (1972) and Ziller's individuation process-identification process (1973). Finally, during old age (sixty to one hundred), it is illustrated through a constant comparison between the elderly's present and past life and more frequently, through their children: how many they have, whether they are living, what their situations are, and so on.

Stage II: Two to Five Years Old: The Assertion of the Self

A phase of widening, consolidation, or assertion of the self seems to follow the first establishment of a diffuse sense of self. This is the construction period of the real bases of the self-concept. Literature says it appears through the development of the language and particularly through the progressive use of the pronouns "I" and "me" (Ames 1952; Goodenough 1938), through the growing sense of possessiveness ("This belongs to me"), through identity construction via differentiation (negativism), and through identification (imitation, role-playing) without forgetting the effect of environmental interactions and reactions (L'Ecuyer 1978). Two features are important here: the kind of material obtained as such, and the degree of organization of the self during this stage.

The Autodescriptive Material. Scientists are so sure that young children are unable to describe themselves that nobody ever really tried. Our results clearly demonstrate that even three-year-old children, when asked, are able to verbalize freely how they perceive themselves. This gives a new look in considering the processes of self-assertion, of self-expansion, and the development of the self as such because it comes from the point of view of the child himself. This material can be used to re-evaluate and validate the inferences made from the development of language, child's behavior observations, and projective tests.

The Organization of the Self-Concept.. Our results also show that the child's self-concept is surprisingly well organized as early as age three (L'Ecuyer 1975a). All the main dimensions of the self are already present: the five fundamental structures (the material self, the personal self, the adaptative self, the social self, and the self–non-self), nine of the ten substructures, and seventeen of the twenty-eight specific categories of the self.

All these elements of the self-concept present during the second stage are organized into hierarchical profiles presenting several similarities among boys and girls but revealing many differences, not only in quantity but also in the psychological contents of same dimensions (see detailed analyses in L'Ecuyer 1974a, 1974b, 1975a).

To sum up, children's own verbalizations can fruitfully be analyzed as important indices in learning about the development and the internal organizations of their own selves.

Stage III: Five to Twelve Years Old: The Expansion of the Self

With the entrance into school, the already established perceptual system rapidly becomes incomplete and must be enlarged to incorporate and integrate all these new experiences. The child must adapt to new social experiences, new roles and status quos, new ways of evaluating competence and aptitudes, new interests, and so on.

Our results suggest that this process of self-expansion can be observed three ways:

1. An increasing number of categories. New categories appear during this stage demonstrating that the antecedent self-organization becomes insufficient. These new categories are: the perceptions of self in terms of emotions, aptitudes, quality and defect, dependency, altruism, and references to sex.
2. New psychological contents inside the same category. The content of a given category of the self is not necessarily the same at

each age, showing an expansion of the experience of oneself for each dimension of the self.

3. Variations of the degree of importance of certain categories. The integration of all these new experiences has an incidence on the hierarchical organization between the different elements of the self.

Stage IV: Adolescence: Ten Through Twelve to Fifteen Through Eighteen Years Old: The Differentiation of the Self

All researchers consider adolescence as a special moment to make complete revisions or reformulations concerning one's own self. Theories and research suggest an increasing importance of the body image, modifications in the self-esteem (moral value, competence), revisions of one's own identity (role and status), increasing autonomy, and new perceptions of the self.

Our results show that the process of expansion of the self observed throughout the third stage is still going on along with the process of differentiation during adolescence. New dimensions of the self appear which are perceptions of themselves in terms of ideologies, abstract identifications, self-consistency, and ambivalence. Similarly, several new psychological contents appear inside the pre-existing categories of the self such as: self-esteem, many new interests, refinements in perceptions of their qualities and defects, and in perceptions of their autonomy, ambivalence, and dependency.

Secondly, several dimensions of the self present variations in their degree of importance. The hierarchical profiles are changing. Some dimensions decrease in importance (somatic self, possessive self, enumeration of activities, and self–non-self), while others are increasing: quality and defect, role and status, competence, dependency, altruism, and reference to sex. There are occasional differences between boys and girls that should be investigated further.

Thirdly, the process of differentiation can also be observed through the number of links or interrelations consciously made by the adolescent between different perceptions. This phenomenon is very rare at earlier stages.

Fourthly, the process of differentiation is also manifested through the self–non-self structure by reinforcing consciously the self–other distinction. For example, "My friends think I am very easy, but in fact I am not."

Finally, it must be noted that this process of differentiation during adolescence is wider than the one described for self–non-self differentiation at the first stage and that it is not limited to this fourth stage: new elements of the self, numerous interrelations between these different elements, and changes into the hierarchical profiles appear until a hundred years of age (L'Ecuyer 1977, 1978).

Stage V: Twenty to Sixty Years Old: The Maturity of the Self

We have to be more theoretical concerning this stage because this is the only one where our results are not yet available; the experiments, just concluded in May 1980, were not ready for publication in this book.

According to the existing literature, three main hypotheses seem to be in confrontation: the plateau-like curve, the peak-like curve, and the multiple changes hypothesis. Let us examine each of them.

1. The adult maturity as a *plateau*. Several authors have proposed that the adult maturity reaches a sort of plateau. The main bases of the personality have been previously acquired, and no important changes are to be expected or observed during that stage. Consequently, the characteristics of the self are supposed to be relatively stable during this stage. For example, with the Tennessee Self-Concept Scale, Thompson (1972) found considerable consistency of the self between ages twenty to sixty contrary to other ages.
2. The *peak-like* developmental curve. According to this hypothesis, the personality characteristics increase till ages 40 or 50 and then decrease gradually (Back and Gergen 1968; Bischof 1969; Henry 1968). Few results on social interest and self-esteem tend to support this hypothesis where the forty to fifty year age range constitute a kind of hinge-phase during the development, from the outer processes (zero to forty) to internal processes (forty and over).

3. The *multiple changes* hypothesis. Other recent experiments, those using more multidimensional approaches, such as the work of Chiriboga and Thurnher (1975), tend on the contrary to demonstrate the presence of numerous changes in the personality within the twenty to sixty year age range. They discern no plateau, no general peak-patterned curve, no considerable consistency within the personality structures during this period of development.

If we consider the nature of life itself, it seems very natural that many changes occur during the twenty to sixty year age span. Adulthood, similar to any other stage of development, brings the individual face-to-face with several new experiences and sometimes challenging events: the adaptation to work or professional life; the variation of the feeling of competency and adequacy according to professional success or failure; adaptation to marriage, celibacy, divorce, paternity, maternity; the evolution of physical capacity; the socioeconomic status; the social value of one's roles played in society; and so on. It is difficult to imagine that such events and many others would not have affected the personality so that certain changes would appear over this long period representing half of the mean life.

Maybe these three developmental pattern curves are occurring differentially during this period according to different kinds of experiences and variables which are interacting at every moment. Certain dimensions would attain a plateau, others evolve in a peak-like pattern, and still others present several kinds of changes during this time from twenty to sixty years. The different ways of measuring such dimensions (inferential or autodescriptive material) or of computing them may influence the patterns of the obtained curves.

Stage VI: Sixty to a Hundred Years Old: The Longevous Self

As pointed out by Bischof (1969), the direction of development in gerontology is still debated. Several theories exist: continuous development, decrement effect with age, theory of the repetition of anterior developmental phases but in a reverse direction starting at sixty, and disengagement theory. The most popular thinking in old age involves an intensification of declining. The self-concept of the elderly is then supposed to be mainly negative: negative body image due to diminishing capacities, loss of identity due to retirement, negative self-esteem, poor social contacts, and so on.

Our results suggest that every kind of curve appears within the forty-three different dimensions of the self-concept included in our model between ages sixty to one hundred: *increments* (the perceptions of one's own emotions in women between ages sixty to one hundred); *decrements* (category interests in women and men, the social self in women, strategies of adaptation in men), *stability or plateau-like curves* (role and status in women from sixty-five to one hundred); *oscillations* through ages (somatic self in men, perceptions of self in terms of quality and defect in women, competence in women); and *peak-like curves* (role and status in men with a lower peak at age seventy; competence in men with a higher peak at seventy-five; self-esteem in men with a lower peak at seventy). Note that these curves are compiled as to the degree of importance that these dimensions represent and not as to their positive and negative tone.

At the present time, the interpretation done would just seem to be a matter of the preferred hypothesis at the beginning. Globally the developmental pattern of these forty-three dimensions shows that reality is multiple and very well balanced around a nucleus of stability within the elders:

- In men: seven increasing directed curves plus three high peaks;
  seven decreasing directed curves plus three low peaks;
  twenty-three relatively stable curves;
- In women: eleven increasing directed curves plus one high peak;
  eleven decreasing directed curves plus three low peaks;
  seventeen relatively stable curves.

Which hypothesis is the right one? The majority of the developmental interpretations on adult and old age are derived from mathematical scores only. There is a need to go beyond the scores to reach the very essence of the psychological contents in order to analyze the real negative and positive perceptions as felt and experienced by the elders so they can get a better knowledge of themselves (L'Ecuyer 1977). But even then, the psychologist is still faced with many problems: is a content negative from his point of view as a psychologist or from the point of view of the elders? Examples:

- Reformulation in the line of social (and scientific?) prejudices: "I was someone but now I am nothing anymore."
- Reformulation according to reality: "I must recognize the changes which are occurring in me."
- Reformulation in the way of a resistance to prejudices: "We are supposed to admit we are no more anything because we are old, but it is not true. I remain the one I have always been."

The emergence of new dimensions during old age (actualization, style of life, etc.)[d], the refinement of many psychological contents, and the reorganization of the degree of importance of many dimensions demonstrate that the self of the elderly is still developing and not necessarily into a declining direction.

SUMMARY AND CONCLUSIONS

The aim of this chapter was to discuss few problems and hypotheses concerning the development of the self-concept through the life cycle in view of the results obtained in our Self-Concept Research Laboratory. To attain this goal the model of the self-concept developed in our laboratory has been presented with a few details as to the methodology and the experimental design.

The results obtained clearly demonstrate that the self-concept is developing all through the life cycle. The different developmental processes present during infancy and adolescence (expansion, differentiation, refinements, and profile patterning of the self-concept) are still active through the entire life cycle including old age up to hundred-year-old people. Our results also suggest that different kinds of

d. It has to be taken into account here that the new dimensions observed between ages sixty and one hundred may not be new when the results at twenty-five to fifty-five are analyzed.

patterns of developmental curves seem possible during the entire development through life: no single hypothesis can pretend to offer the entire truth.

The field of adult development, particularly that of aging, cannot be studied solely at the light of the hypotheses built from the study of children's and adolescents' development. Furthermore, as pointed out by Butler (1975), researchers must be aware of social and even scientific prejudices toward these categories of people. We have so intensively boosted the aptitudes, intelligence, creativity, and adaptability of youth that we now seem unable to evaluate other modes of development of physical fitness, intelligence functioning, creative activities, and adaptation to reality as being sane and positive with regard to the other specific stages of development. Research designs and scientific attitudes have to be revised to be able to get a better understanding of the last three-quarters of the developmental curves, to point out not only the declining characteristics (which exist and cannot be denied) but also trace the positive ones which also exist and should not be denied.

III THE SELF IN APPLIED SETTINGS

Kenneth J. Gergen

For many investigators of self-concept, the ultimate crucible against which theory and research is to be assessed is the context of everyday life. Will investigation into self-concept enable people to solve the pressing problems of daily life? Many investigators also believe that an answer to this fundamental question should not await the emergence of a fully elaborated and empirically substantiated theory of self. Because any active field of knowledge undergoes continuous change, postponing application to the point of full theoretical fruition would obviate application altogether. And, such postponement would likely prevent the discipline from drawing from one of its richest sources of information: the dialectic relationship between theory and practice. As theory develops and the practitioner presses its implications into service, the outcomes may be elucidating. In the face of ongoing experience, the practitioner may find that existing theory is insufficiently rich or differentiated; novel distinctions are essential to account for ongoing events. Existing measures may also be lacking, and new methods developed that may subsequently be incorporated into the empirical pursuits within the academic. Findings within the applied setting may also furnish needed support for existing theory, or raise challenges to existing conceptualizations. In sum, many believe the processes of generating and applying knowledge most fruitfully proceed as an interdependent endeavor (see Gergen and Basseches 1980).

The interrelationship of theoretical and applied interests has a long and illustrious history in self-concept work. Perhaps the most widely celebrated of these endeavors has occurred within the therapeutic setting. The theoretical work of Horney, Lecky, Sullivan, and Schilder informed a legion of later practitioners that both the etiology of and therapeutic intervention into problems of psychological distress must take into account the individual's conception of self. The systematic studies later undertaken by Rogers and his colleagues (see Rogers 1951, 1954, 1961; Rogers and Dymond 1954) furnishes perhaps the most dramatic illustration of the catalytic potential underlying the collaboration of theoretical and applied concerns. This tradition has continued to bear important fruit. Yet, the therapeutic context is only one in which the dialectic between theoretical and applied interests has proved productive. Of substantial importance has also been research using self-concept theory to make inroads into problems of the aged (Gordon 1976); prejudice (Kardiner and Ovesey 1951; Rosenberg and Simmons 1971); poverty (Berser 1965; Sarbin 1970); drug dependence (Davison and Valins 1969); and suicide (Diggory–Farnham 1964).

The present volume has selected the educational process as its major focus of applied concern. Educators have long been interested in problems of student motivation and in the effects of education on various aspects of human functioning. Many have also realized that the individual's conception of self may play an integral role in the educational process (see Hamachek 1965). The contributions within this section reflect the state of the art at the present time. The first three papers principally focus on the relationship between self-concept and academic performance. As indicated, investigators have long believed that performance in the educational setting is virtually dependent on one's concept of self.

As the theoretical contribution by Richard J. Shavelson and Kenneth R. Stuart (Chapter 15) makes clear, however, previous research on this issue has often been too simplistic in its approach. Through causal modelling they demonstrate the importance, first, of distinguishing among components of self-concept; in this case, it becomes apparent that various aspects of self-concept may be related to academic achievement in different ways. It is further seen that the relationship between self-concept and academic achievement may be a reciprocal one. Early research has often failed to tease apart the reciprocal relationships, and has seldom explored the influence of exogenous factors on the ostensible relationship between the two.

Both Chapter 16 by Stanley Coopersmith and Ragnar Gilberts, and Chapter 17 by Bonnie Ballif shift the concern from the conceptual to the operational level. Coopersmith and Gilberts demonstrate the advantages of employing a multifaceted measure of self-esteem, and demonstrate as well the potential in using observer ratings of self-esteem in lieu of self-ratings. Correlations between various subscales and intellectual achievement tests prove robust.

In Chapter 17 Ballif reasons that conceptualizing oneself as a successful learner is a critical thought pattern responsible for motivation to learn. Correlation data from large samples lend support to her contention. Ballif demonstrates that it is possible to design training experiences that boost the individual's concept of self. While the correlational data reported in this and the preceding chapter are subject to the various problems of interpretation discussed by Shavelson and Stuart, Ballif's concern with the effects of self-concept on motivation suggests that the Shavelson and Stuart model be expanded. In particular, a motivational construct should be inserted between the variables of self-concept and academic achievement. Required are causal models of even greater complexity than Shavelson and Stuart propose.

William H. Fitts (Chapter 18) shares observations garnered from a professional career devoted largely to problems of understanding, measuring, and changing self-concept. As he argues in the present case, the major issue facing the practitioner is that of self-concept change, whether it be in the therapeutic, educational, or any other applied setting. If certain configurations of self-conception are dysfunctional, how can one go about aiding the person in altering these conceptions? As he further argues, an understanding of change will require a concomitant increase in theoretical clarity and elaboration, and a further development of methodological skill. His concern with the potential interaction between self-concept and behavior echos a theme voiced in the two preceding chapters.

Many of Fitts' concerns are, in turn, revivified in Lorin W. Anderson's (Chapter 19) subsequent discussion of change in academic self-concept. His specific focus is on change in academic self-concept between elementary and high school. As he finds, there is little overall change in academic self-concept between grades three and eight.

This finding would support Fitts' belief in the difficulties of altering self-concept. However, closer inspection of the data indicated that distinctions are necessary between evaluative and non-evaluative aspects of self-concept. Males and females show different patterns of change on differing subdimensions. To return to the Shavelson and Stuart offering, this is to suggest that a full causal model must also distinguish among various subcomponents of academic self-concept (over and above more general self-concept) and must be prepared for differing causal patterns in various subpopulations.

The work of Wilbur B. Brookover and Joseph Passalacqua (Chapter 20) further demonstrates the necessity of looking at more complex relationships between academic aspects of self-concept and achievement. In their chapter, Brookover and Passalacqua provide research evidence suggesting that the relationship between academic aspects of achievement and self-concept is, in large part, determined by the social context in which self-concept is developed. In their research Brookover and Passalacqua found that the relationship between academic self-concept and achievement is significantly different for blacks and whites, and they attribute this difference to differential effects of expectations introduced during the child development within these two races.

Last but by no means least, Lawrence Dolan (Chapter 21) has attempted to identify some determinants of self-concept development of children in educational settings. Dolan, as with Anderson (Chapter 19) and Brookover and Passalacqua (Chapter 20), focuses on the importance of contextual as well as classroom factors as determiners of academic self-concept, and his work illustrates the complexity that should be considered in causal models such as the one proposed by Shavelson and Stuart in Chapter 15.

15 APPLICATION OF CAUSAL MODELING METHODS TO THE VALIDATION OF SELF-CONCEPT INTERPRETATIONS OF TEST SCORES[a]

Richard J. Shavelson
Kenneth R. Stuart

The need to validate interpretations of self-concept measurements has been well established (for example, Crowne and Stephens 1961; Shavelson, Hubner, and Stanton 1976; Wylie 1961, 1974). Such methodological research has potentially important benefits for building a theory of self-concept and applying it to critical areas of social research such as education, juvenile delinquency, and counseling. This happens because in the methodological research, theoretical conceptions of self-concept (for example, explicit definitions, implicit interpretations) and the methods used to measure it are systemically examined, and logical and empirical evidence is brought to bear on the measurements, the theory, and their application.

Methods for examining self-concept interpretations of measurements have been available for at least thirty years. They include correlational techniques such as factor analysis and the multitrait-multimethod matrix, experimental techniques (randomized experiments), and logical analysis. (For a review and application of these techniques, see Shavelson et al. 1976.) While the methods of construct validation are as applicable today as they were thirty years ago, a re-examination of some aspects of construct validation and the

a. The authors wish to acknowledge the help and constructive criticisms of Leigh Burstein, Frank Capell, David Rogosa, Noreen Webb, and Phil Winne in the development of this paper.

introduction of some methods not previously used to validate construct interpretations appear timely. The purpose of this chapter is to build a framework for and to introduce the application of causal modeling to the examination of self-concept interpretations of measurements. This is not merely a methodological exercise but an attempt to advance substantive knowledge about self-concept and its application to important areas of personal and social concern.

CONSTRUCT VALIDATION THEORY[b]

A construct is a psychological concept reflecting some postulated attribute of people such as their self-concepts. It is assumed to be reflected in performance on tests when these tests represent some facets or aspects of the construct. A construct is defined by setting forth the laws governing its occurrence; "the interlocking system of laws which constitute a theory [of self-concept is called] a *nomological network*" (Cronbach and Meehl 1956, p. 290; italics in original).

Construct validation begins when scores from a test are interpreted as reflecting facets of a particular construct. The proposed interpretation leads to hypotheses and counterhypotheses which research either confirms or disconfirms. While construct validation often begins with an informal, intuitive definition, the ultimate goal of the process of validating a construct is to build a logically and empirically verified theory and instrumentation.

In examining self-concept interpretations of measurements, correlational techniques have been used (for example, correlation coefficients, factor analysis, and sometimes the multitrait-multimethod matrix). The data are often collected on a *convenient* sample of subjects who have undergone a series of experiences in a particular setting, usually with only one measure of self-concept. The logic of this approach, then, is one of direct inference from the convenient sample to a population like the sample ("available population") in similar settings with similar experience using similar instruments.

b. In this section the brief presentation of traditional construct validity theory draws heavily on the work of Cronbach and Meehl (1955) and Cronbach (1971). The ideas about current issues were, in part, suggested by Cronbach either directly or indirectly through his criticisms of an earlier paper by the first author (Shavelson et al. 1976). The authors, of course, are responsible for any distortion of these ideas here.

In present-day application, several limitations of construct validation theory are apparent. One limitation is the time needed for the process of construct validation. While a complete specification of a nomological network for self-concept is an admirable—if unreachable—goal, measurements with valid self-concept interpretations are needed now, especially in evaluating social action programs. With a potentially infinite number of counterinterpretations to a proposed construct interpretation, the best that researchers can do is to examine the most telling counterinterpretations for the purpose of their substantive research.

A second limitation of this approach is its reliance on formal statistical models in making inferences from samples to available populations. In examining statements about self-concept, however, interpretations generalize beyond the findings to other persons, settings, and so on. Construct validation, then, must take into account not only the inference from sample to available population but also the inference from available population to the broader "target" population of interest.

In examining the *causal* relation between achievement and self-concept, for example, the most defensible method would be a true experiment in which subjects are randomly assigned to treatments representing variation in achievement. After receiving the treatment, their self-concepts would be measured. Several problems with this approach are obvious. First, the study would have to be conducted in a laboratory, or in classrooms willing to participate in such a study. Second, the treatment would probably have to be contrived in that students would randomly receive treatments in which they were more or less successful in achievement. Finally, even if the study were run, evidence of the generalizability of the findings to the world of education would be demanded. These problems and this demand for replication represent an issue of external validity, that is, generalizability to the population of people and conditions of interest.

An alternative approach to the true experiment is to collect data in, for example, naturally occurring educational settings in order to examine the causal relation between achievement and self-concept. This approach, called causal modeling (or structural modeling) is taken here (see Bentler 1978). It substitutes substantive knowledge (the nomological network) for statistical control in examining counterinterpretations to the proposed construct interpretation. While this approach represents a possible weakening in statistical inference when applied to informal theories such as self-concept, as substantive knowledge about the construct grows, the substitution of this knowledge for statistical controls leads to increasingly strong inferences about causality. Moreover, it seems to meet the criticisms of the experimental approach.

In updating construct validation theory, then, attention must be paid to conducting research on the most telling counterhypotheses to the proposed interpretations in a particular area of research. In the remainder of this chapter, a causal modeling approach is presented. This method permits an examination of causal interpretations while providing a reasonable trade-off between direct inference and generalization.

CAUSAL MODELING AND THE VALIDATION OF SELF-CONCEPT INTERPRETATIONS OF TEST SCORES

In this section, we describe the interplay between counterhypotheses to a proposed construct interpretation and the construction of alternative causal models for testing rival hypotheses. This approach is guided by research and theory on self-concept in academic settings.

Self-concept theory posits a causal relation between academic achievement and self-concept, usually with achievement causing self-concept (but see Anderson and Evans 1974). Moreover, interpretations of substantive findings in self-concept research and the application of those findings in educational settings assume this causal relationship. Counterhypotheses to this causal argument might posit that there is a reciprocal causal relationship or that the two constructs are independent. Thus, if measurements are interpreted as reflecting a facet of self-concept, they should support this causal link. If not, the instruments, the theory, or both need modification (see Cronbach and Meehl 1955).

In making inferences about the causal effect of achievement (X) on self-concept (Y), three general conditions have to be met. First, X and Y must co-vary; that is, X and Y must be related. Second, X and Y should be ordered in time so that X preceeds Y. This temporal asymmetry indicates that the presence of X leads to the presence of Y. And third, no other variable (Z) causes the relation between X

and *Y*. The first two conditions pose little problem for correlational or experimental research, although temporal asymmetry has sometimes been ignored in drawing causal interpretations in self-concept research (for example, Purkey 1970). The third condition is troublesome, especially for correlational research. In experimental research this condition is approximated in any one study, and overall it is assured by randomly assigning subjects to levels of *X*. With correlational research, however, in order to rule out the counterhypotheses that *Z* caused the relationship between *X* and *Y*, all variables which may, plausibly, affect the hypothesized relationship between *X* and *Y* must be incorporated and measured in the research design. The choice of variables to include in the model depends on theoretical insights into the construct under investigation and past research. Clearly, the choice of variables should reflect the counterhypotheses to the proposed interpretation that *X* caused *Y*. As evidence consistent with the proposed interpretation is amassed, confidence in the proposed causal interpretation increases.

Simplest Case of Causal Modeling

In order to see how the logic of causal modeling works, consider the simplest case of the proposed causal relationship between achievement and self-concept. There are four possible alternative specifications of the causal relationship. The first is that achievement causes self-concept ($ACH \rightarrow SC$, the arrow denoting direction of causality). The second is that self-concept causes achievement ($SC \rightarrow ACH$). The third is that causality is reciprocal ($ACH \rightleftarrows SC$). And the fourth is that some other variable (Z) causes the observed relationship ($Z \begin{smallmatrix} \rightarrow ACH \\ \rightarrow SC \end{smallmatrix}$: the curved, double-arrow line denotes joint association). In order to rule out some of these alternatives, theory is brought into play. For example, suppose that a self-concept theory leads to the causal model shown in Figure 15-1. In this model, the arrow from *ACH* to *SC* indicates that achievement causes self-concept; reciprocal causality and the possibility that self-concept causes achievement have been ruled out on the basis of theory. The coefficient, β, is a measure of the strength of the causal relationship between achievement and self-concept. The term, R_v, is an error term or a "disturbance" term. It represents random variation *and* syste-

Figure 15–1. Hypothesized Model of Causal Relationship Between Achievement and Self-Concept.

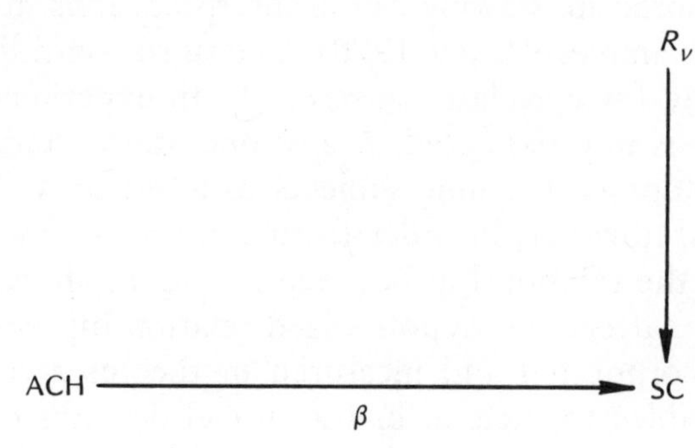

matic variation of variables (Z) not measured in the study. The absence of a line from R_v to ACH is also based on theory; it rules out the possibility that some third variable causes the relationship between achievement and self-concept.

In examining the causal relationship between achievement and self-concept, attention is focused on β, the coefficient from the regression of SC on ACH. If the (very restrictive) assumptions of this model hold, β can be interpreted as the strength of the causal relationship between achievement and self-concept.

Clearly, this two-variable example is not plausible with respect to the causal relationship between achievement and self-concept since the assumption that both are unrelated to some third variable, Z, is untenable. For example, self-concept and achievement are both related to grade point average (for example, Torshen, 1969). In order to remedy this situation, several options are available. One option is to incorporate other variables that might reasonably account for the apparent causal relation between achievement and self-concept (for example, Anderson and Evans 1974).

Causal Model: Two Variables Measured at Two Points in Time

A second option, taken up here, is to measure achievement and self-concept at two (or more) points in time. One possible causal model is shown in Figure 15-2. With this causal model, covariation between achievement and self-concept can be examined, as can the time-ordering of the two variables. The curved, double-arrow line between ACH_1 and SC_1 indicates that they are correlated and not simultaneous causes of one another. The two coefficients, β_1 and β_4, are stability coefficients. The two path coefficients, β_2 and β_3, may be termed cross-lagged coefficients; they represent the sole sources of causation in the model. This is due to the absence of a relation between the disturbance terms, R_u and R_v, which indicates that the systematic factors influencing ACH_2 and SC_2 are unrelated. That is, we assume that the relationship between achievement and self-concept is not caused by some other variable Z. Finally, the absence of a direct path between ACH_2 and SC_2 rules out simultaneous causation between these two variables.

In the analysis of data from this two-variable (2V—achievement and self-concept), two wave (2W—time 1 and time 2) design, $ACH2$, for example, would be regressed on $SC1$ and $ACH1$. The coefficients (βs) would be unstandardized, partial regression coefficients. A comparison of the cross-lagged coefficients would provide data bearing on the predominant causal relationship—from achievement to self-concept or vice versa. "These estimated causal effects may be sound-

Figure 15–2. An Alternative Causal Model of the Relationship Between Achievement and Self-Concept.

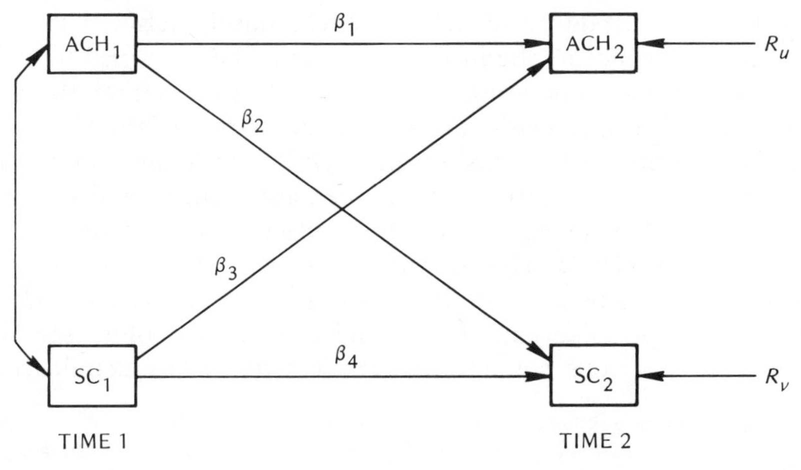

ly interpreted *when the restrictions (assumptions) of the model are satisfied*" (Rogosa in press, p. 22; italics ours).

In order to examine the causal relation between achievement and self-concept of ability, Calsyn and Kenny (1977) used a cross-lagged design to re-analyze data collected by Brookover (1962). Data on achievement (grade point average) and self-concept (a composite of scores on Brookover's measure of self-concept of ability and measures of perceived evaluation of parents, teachers, and peers[c]) were collected at five points in time. (For detailed exceptions, see Calsyn and Kenny 1977.) This produced a 2V5W design which was treated as a 2V2W design with replications.

In examining these data, Calsyn and Kenny used a cross-lagged panel correlation analysis which differs slightly from the 2V2W causal model presented above. Rather than comparing βs, they compared correlation coefficients in order to determine the causal predominance of self-concept or achievement. (For a cogent criticism of the use of cross-lagged correlations instead of regression coefficients, see Goldberger 1971 and Rogosa in press.) On the basis of a summary of their results of comparisons between cross-lagged correlation coefficients,[d] Calsyn and Kenny found achievement to be a stronger cause of self-concept than vice versa for females but not for males. However, data from other cross-lagged panel correlation studies (for example, Bixler, 1965; Trickett, 1969) cast doubt on this finding, so causal predominance of achievement (or self-concept) has not been established. This suggests that in order to identify the limits of the generalizability of the causal relationship between achievement and self-concept, the instruments should be examined to make sure that they are operating as expected, to see whether the self-concept theory needs revision, or some combination of the two.

In interpreting the results of the Calsyn and Kenny study and others on the causal relationship between achievement and self-concept, an important question is whether self-concept of ability (*SCA*) differs from academic achievement. It might be that *SCA* is merely another report—albeit the students'—of grade point average (*GPA*), other indices of achievement, or some combination of these. This amounts to a serious counterinterpretation that bears examination.

c. This composite was justified on the basis of a confirmatory factor analysis. Causal models incorporate this notion of multiple indicators of one construct into the analysis directly.

d. Unfortunately, the sample correlations were not presented (probably due to limitations of journal space), nor were example sets of correlations.

If supported, it suggests the need for revising the definition of *SCA*, the methods of measuring *SCA*, or both.

Causal Model Incorporating a Counterinterpretation

The two-variable designs discussed so far do not permit us to untangle the proposed self-concept interpretation of *SCA* from a counterinterpretation that *SCA* is another measure of achievement. An expanded causal model is needed which would test the proposed counterinterpretation by introducing a third variable into the two-wave design. One possible causal model, shown below, incorporates general self-concept (*SCG*) as the third variable.[e]

Not only can the structural relationships between achievement and self-concept of ability be studied but so can the relationship of these two variables to the newly introduced variable of general self-concept. While a number of additional hypotheses may be considered, our focus still remains with achievement and self-concept. In this 3V2W model, three questions, critical to testing construct interpretations, can be examined. The first question is the same as that posed for the 2V2W panel design: is achievement of self-concept of ability causally stronger? A comparison of the lagged coefficients, β_3 versus β_7, provides data bearing on this question.

The second and third questions refer to general self-concept. Shavelson and others (1976) argued that general self-concept is influenced by behavior and evaluations in specific situations. In the present context, this means that while self-concept and achievement have reciprocal effects on one another, the predominant direction of causality should be from achievement to self-concept of ability to general self-concept. This leads to the second question: is self-concept of ability causally stronger than achievement with respect to general self-concept, as theory predicts? A comparison of the lagged coefficient, β_2 versus β_8, provides data bearing on this question. The third question is: is the causal relation between achievement and self-concept of ability stronger than the relation between achievement and general self-concept as theory predicts? A comparison of the lagged coefficients, β_2 and β_3, provides data bearing on this question.

e. The curved lines in this model represent joint association between pairs of variables, with ρ representing the magnitude of association between the variables of time 1 and ψ representing the magnitude of association between the disturbance terms at time 2.

Figure 15–3. Structural Equation Model of the Causal Relationship Between Achievement and Self-Concept.

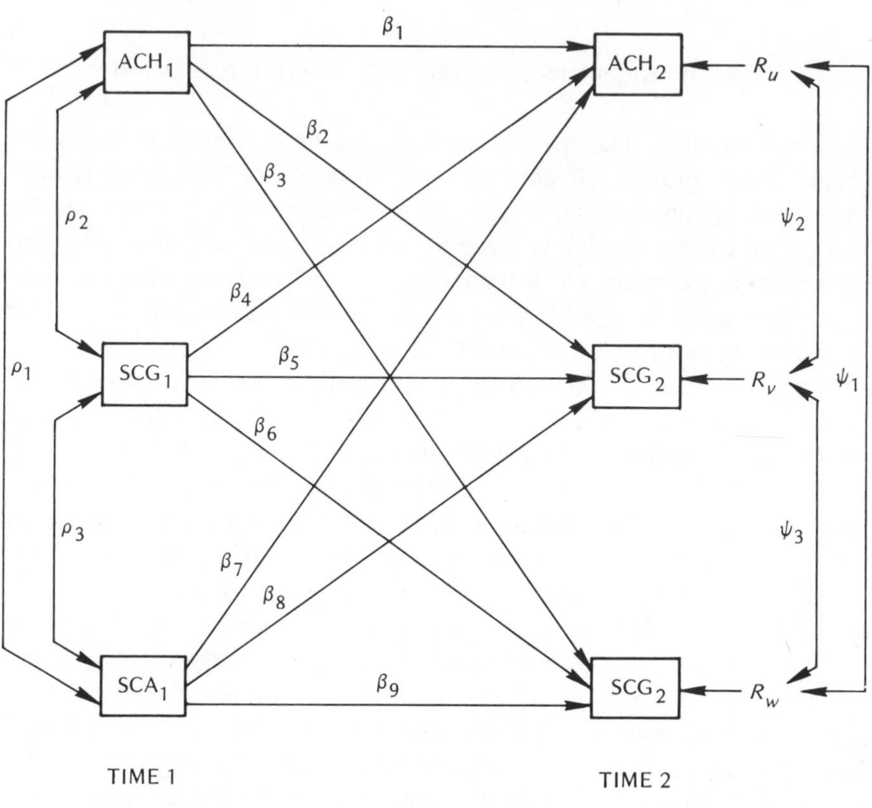

Causal Model with Multiple Measures of the Same Construct

There are, however, both conceptual and statistical limitations of the model in Figure 15-3. Statistically, the number of parameters to be estimated (all correlations and regression coefficients) is equal to the number of observed variances and covariances (twenty-one). Thus, Figure 15-3 presents a just identified model which cannot be tested for goodness of fit (for example, chi-square) to the observed data. In order to test the model, the number of observed variances and covariances must exceed the number of parameters in the model (for example, Duncan 1975).

Conceptually, the last model assumes that each construct is reliably and validly measured by only one test. A more persuasive model, one akin to the multitrait-multimethod matrix (Campbell and Fiske 1959), would show that several measures of each construct converge on the construct and are distinct from measures of other constructs in the model. Fortunately, the statistical and conceptual limitations of the last model can be avoided by incorporating multiple measures of each construct in the model.

Figure 15-4 presents one possible revision of the previous model with multiple measures (the boxes) of each construct (the circles). At each of two points in time, there are two measures of achievement such as test scores (*ACH* 1) and grade point averages (*ACH* 2), two measures of general self-concept such as the Piers-Harris (*SCG* 1) and Coopersmith (*SCG* 2) instruments, and two measures of self-concept of ability such as the Brookover (*SCA* 1) and Sears (*SCA* 2) instruments (Shavelson et al. 1976).

The model in Figure 15-4 incorporates a measurement model including reliability estimates and factor analyses with a structural equation model. With respect to the measurement model, the delta's (δ) and epsilon's (ϵ) represent measurement error (unreliability) in the observable variables. The lambda's (λ) are factor loadings of the observed measures on the constructs. (In addition, the phi's (Φ) represent the correlations among the underlying construct, and the psi's (ψ) represent unidentified influences on the constructs.)

With respect to the structural model, the path coefficients (β) have a similar interpretation to the paths between observed variables in previous models. In interpreting the paths in Figure 15-4, however, it is important to remember that they connect underlying constructs and not observed variables. The influence of achievement upon self-concept (for example, *ACH* 1 → *SCA* 2) may be contrasted against opposing alternatives by a study of the coefficients. For example, if coefficient β_3 were significantly greater than coefficient β_7, our hypothesis that achievement causes self-concept would be supported. Additional support would come from the finding that β_7 is significantly greater than β_4.

SUMMARY

At this point, we have traced an application of causal modeling to the validation of self-concept interpretations from its simplest form

Figure 15–4. Structural Equation Model of the Causal Relationship Between Achievement and Self-Concept Utilizing Multiple Indicators.

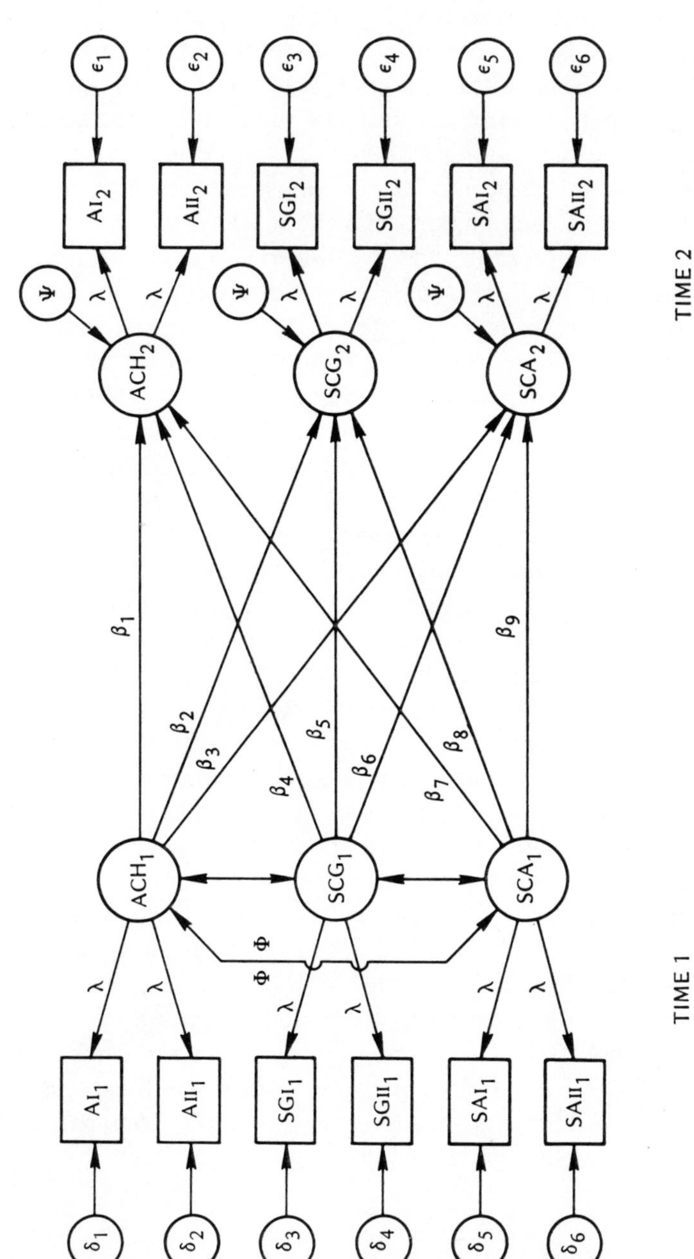

to a complex form. The use of manifest variables as multiple indicators of latent constructs is methodologically sophisticated while providing flexibility in hypothesis testing. Perhaps this approach will assist researchers in building models and testing them empirically against crucial counterinterpretations to the proposed self-concept interpretation.

16 BEHAVIORAL ACADEMIC SELF-ESTEEM

Stanley Coopersmith
Ragnar Gilberts

Self-esteem theorists, including Coopersmith (1967), Jersild (1952), Purkey (1978), Rogers (1951), and Wiley (1968), are in general agreement that self-esteem is both a private or subjective matter as well as a public matter since it is displayed in overt behaviors and therefore open to evaluation on both levels. Instruments for detecting subjective self-esteem usually have relied on self-report. Shavelson and others (1976) have reviewed some of the more frequently used self-report measures, including Brookover (1967), Coopersmith (1967), Piers and Harris (1969), and Sears (1963), and found them to have varied effectiveness in assessing subjective self-esteem. On the other hand, self-esteem as measured by inferences from overt behaviors appears to be less well established. Measures of observed self-esteem based on overt behaviors have been developed largely for the specific situation of the classroom.

These efforts include Cowan and others (1973), Purkey and Cage (1973), and Shannon (1976). Limited efforts were noted in the foregoing behavioral scales in establishing relationships between inferred self-esteem and school achievement in children; study of this relationship appears to be more suitable for establishing predictive validity. For instance, Cowan's scale, entitled the Aggressive, Moody, and Learning Disability (AML), confined its validity to concurrent validity or the discriminatory power between high and low inferred self-esteem students. Purkey's instrument, the Florida Key, found his factors of Relating, Asserting, Investing, and Coping to be related to the Coopersmith Self-esteem Inventory. In contrast, Shane (1976) found a significant relationship using an adjective checklist between teachers' ratings of self-concept and the children's achievement in reading and mathematics ($r = .33$).

Limited research efforts in establishing predictive validity parallel the paucity of research contributing to construct validity of self-esteem measures and difficulties associated with reliably measuring self-esteem in young children.

The level of concept development, coupled with the response set of social desirability, appear to contribute to the unreliability of measurement of self-esteem in young children. Crandall and Crandall (1965) suggested that children as early as grade three and younger are vulnerable to social desirability factors which serve to confound the results of self-report measurements. Attempts to assess self-esteem through observations of behavior avoids the aforementioned problems inherent in self-report methods of measurement.

The Behavioral Academic Self Esteem (BASE) scale was developed to improve the quality of measurement of self-esteem and to meet the following criteria: (a) to infer self-esteem based on observations of behaviors; (b) to establish valid and reliable measures at early age levels; (c) to establish measures situationally specific to the classroom; and (d) to establish construct and predictive validity related to common measures of school success.

The theory on which BASE was constructed was derived from Coopersmith (1967). This theory and the research on which it was formulated indicated that children who were functioning at high levels of self-esteem were active, exploratory, persistent children who participated fully in daily activities at home and at school. These children had experienced a great deal of care and affection in their early lives, and were provided with a clear social structure through rule-setting and rather authoritarian parental practices. The children demonstrated traits of self-confidence and social attraction, were generally successful in their efforts yet were able to cope with failure, and their verbal behaviors were acceptable and appropriate to the social setting. While limited in organization and scope, the Coopersmith Behavior Rating Form (BRF) was constructed to tap these traits. BASE is a revision and reorganization of the Coopersmith BRF.

BASE emerged as a result of a revision and repeated factor analysis of the Coopersmith BRF. It also reflected a decision to focus on self-esteem behavior specific to the academic environment and effective school performance. The factors emerging from the analysis of BASE data reflected the Coopersmith theory of self-esteem. These factors emphasized the traits pertinent to self-esteem of children as reflected in effective academic performance. The construct of *academic* self-esteem became apparent in the factor organization stemming from teacher judgments of children's behavior. The BASE factors are listed as follows: (a) Student Initiative (SI); (b) Social Attention (SA); (c) Success/Failure (S/F); (d) Social Attraction (SAT); and (e) Self-Confidence (SC).

METHOD

The Sample

The data were collected between 1974 and 1978 in the Bay Area of California which includes the peninsula to the south of San Francisco and the East Bay, both suburban areas. These children came from families ranging in socioeconomic status from low to upper middle class. The children were in grades ranging from preschool and kindergarten to grade eight. Included in the sample were children from both extremes of the distribution of school achievers, including students categorized and placed in state-funded programs for educationally handicapped (EH) and mentally gifted minor (MGM) students, as well as regular education students, the latter making up the majority of children. Over 4,000 records comprised the data base.

Reliability

Estimates of internal consistency were collected and observed following the initial administration of BASE. Items were scored simply by reversing the negative items on BASE and summing the teacher ratings of student behaviors. The total score was used as a criterion for correlating individual items. Single item-total score correlations may be seen in Table 16–1, together with item means and standard deviations. All single item-total score correlations were found to be signifi-

Table 16–1. BASE Item–Total Score Reliability Coefficients, Means, and Standard Deviations.

Item No.	*Behavior*	*Mean*	*S.D.*	*Item–Total Score Correlation*
1	Undertakes new tasks	3.98	.85	.75[a]
2	Makes decisions	3.98	.83	.70[a]
3	Child's company sought	3.62	.89	.59[a]
4	Seeks attention	4.04	.96	.54[a]
5	Acts as leader	3.24	1.03	.61[a]
6	Copes with failure	3.80	.89	.48[a]
7	Shows self-direction	3.75	.98	.75[a]
8	Asks how he or she is doing	3.54	.96	.26[a]
9	Copes with criticism	4.15	.91	.57[a]
10	Refers to self	3.84	.76	.69[a]
11	Expresses opinion	3.83	.89	.37[a]
12	Asks questions	3.82	.88	.59[a]
13	Initiates new ideas	3.19	.96	.66[a]
14	Appreciates own products	4.24	.70	.62[a]
15	Avoids bragging	4.09	.89	.50[a]
16	Adapts to change	4.03	.75	.76[a]
17	Avoids bullying	4.28	.85	.44[a]
	Total score	65.44	8.65	

a. Significant at .001 level.

cant at the .001 level. The correlations ranged from a low of .26 to a high of .76, with a mean *Z* transformation of the correlation coefficients of .61. The level of relationship suggested the items and the total scale scores were measuring common elements. The size of these correlations indicate a degree of redundancy which is necessary for factor clustering, yet is not dominated by any set of items accounting for most of the variance.

An estimate of reliability between teacher ratings of common children was estimated on an average of .71 level on several classes of students ($N = 142$).

Validity

The acid test of an instrument to assess accurately perceived social behavior is its level of relationship with a significant social criterion.

While the ratings of student behaviors by classroom teachers was the social event, the socially significant criterion was the level of achievement obtained by their pupils on norm-referenced academic achievement tests. Therefore, the predictive validity, or the level at which school achievement may be predicted by outcomes from student behaviors in the classroom, was established at a moderately strong level. As discussed later, the BASE correlated moderately (r = .50) with school achievement.

A second level of validity—namely, construct validity (Chronbach and Meehl 1955)—was purported. The primary hypothesis presupposed that six major factors were likely to occur in the first revision of the scale. Suffice it to note at this point that the criterion of construct validity, or an organization of preconceptualized factors, was present on virtually all three occasions, attesting to a substantial degree of congruence of the findings with the theoretical factors reported a priori to the study.

Construct validity was tested by application of factor analysis, computation of Pearson correlation coefficients, and means and standard deviations. The factor analysis program used on the three samples was the principal component routine (PAI) included in Nie and others (1975), designed to account for as much variance in the data system as possible with the smallest number of components. The program used unity as eigen values. The principal component matrix was rotated using an orthoganal rotation with a varimax criterion. The resulting factors were considered uncorrelated and, therefore, measures of unique aspects of inferred self-esteem.

RESULTS AND DISCUSSION

Male-Female Comparisons

Teachers rated the girls in the sample higher than they rated boys at a statistically significant level. Variances for boys and girls were virtually even, with a slightly higher standard error of measurement occurring on the boys' ratings. Separate norms were computed for boys and girls enrolled in grades kindergarten through eight to reflect the significant differences between the sexes in BASE scores (see Table 16-2). Differences between the sexes were virtually nonexistent in the teacher ratings of preschool children (Table 16-3).

Table 16–2. BASE Norm Data Showing Means, Standard Deviations, *N*s, and Standard Errors of Measurement of Kindergarten Through Grade Eight Students.

Sex	*Mean*	*S.D.*	*N*	*S.E.M.*
Boys	51.63[a]	13.57	461	7.31
Girls	55.25[a]	13.61	440	7.33
All	53.40	13.70	901	7.38

$t = 4.00$, $p < .001$.

Table 16–3. BASE Norm Data Showing Means, Standard Deviations, *N*s, and Standard Errors of Measurement for Preschool Students (*Four-Year-Olds*).

Sex	*Mean*	*S.D.*	*N*	*S.E.M.*
Boys	58.99	7.92	88	4.26
Girls	60.56	8.51	61	4.58
All children	59.63	8.61	149	4.64

The shapes of the distributions for both sexes approached the normal deviate with a slight tendency toward negative skewing.

Factor Analysis

After a factor analysis of three samples, shown in Table 16–4, the items factored consistently into five components in the following descending order of power: Student Initiative, Social Attention, Success/Failure, Social Attraction, and Self-Confidence. The first three factors emerged identically in the three samples, with one exception. Minor discrepancies were observed in factor configurations on two of the samples with respect to factor loadings on Social Attraction. While Self-Confidence collapsed as a factor on sample three, it should be noted that Self-Confidence and Success/Failure essentially traded places with respect to factor order on sample two, yet retained the same item compositions. Since the underlying structure of the three samples consistently retained their fundamental structure as hypothesized, the stability and construct validity of BASE was confirmed.

One of the most powerful features of the factor analysis was the comparative strength of the Student Initiative factor compared to the remaining components. For example, on sample one, the first factor accounted for 34.4 percent of the total variance, while on samples two and three, the Student Initiative factor accounted for 45.7 and 59.7 percent, respectively.

To test the predictive validity of BASE showing that teacher-rated, inferred academic self-esteem would correlate moderately strong with school achievement, correlations computed between the BASE and school achievement (Comprehensive Test of Basic Skills, Forms [CTBS] scores) are shown in Table 16–5. From the table it is clear that the teacher ratings of student behaviors resulted in moderately strong relationships with the level of academic achievement of their students. For example, the total composite scores on the CTBS correlated .50 with the BASE total score on sample two. It was curious to see that the Student Initiative factor correlated somewhat higher than the total BASE score, as the total score has more power in its larger number of items. The second most predictive relationship among the subfactors on the BASE was the Self-Confidence correlation with the total CTBS. The remaining subscales correlated approximately at a .30 level with the CTBS composite score.

Additional correlations were computed on sample three data which supported the strength of the BASE–CTBS correlations. Table 16–6 shows the results. While the mean *Z* transformation correlation coefficient was .55 for total BASE–CTBS correlations, it correlated .58 with Student Initiative scores. Again, the Student Initiative scale was mildly more predictive of school achievement than the total BASE scores.

To test the relationship between inferred academic self-esteem of students and grade in school, separate mean values were computed for grade levels two through eight. A trend was clear showing a steady decrease in mean values on the total and SI scores of BASE as grade levels increased from grades two through seven on the third sample. Tables 16–7 and 16–8 show this slight decline in BASE scores over grade increments. The decreasing trend leveled at grade seven with a slight increase at grade eight. The decreasing trend was also observed on many samples which were omitted for sake of brev-

Table 16–4. Factor Analysis of the BASE on Three Samples Showing Loadings, Percentage of Variance, and Total Variance Accounted For.

		Sample 1 (Fall '75)					Sample 2 (Fall '76)					Sample 3 (Spring '77)				
Factor No.	*Behavior*	*I*	*II*	*III*	*IV*	*V*	*I*	*II*	*III*	*IV*	*V*	*I*	*II*	*III*	*IV*	*V*
I	Student Initiative															
	1. Undertakes new tasks	.82					.65					.58				
	2. Makes decisions	.76					.77					.70				
	3. Shows self-direction	.74					.77					.73				
	4. Initiates new ideas	.73					.59					.76				
	5. Asks questions	.70					.77					.65				
	6. Adapts to change	.61					.63					.47				
II	Social Attention															
	7. Quiet in class		.77					.84					.86			
	8. Positive talk re: school		.77					.54					.55			
	9. Cooperates with children		.77					.71					.77			
III	Success															
	10. Copes with failure			.88							.82				.70	
	11. Copes with criticism			.73							.87				.74	

IV	Social Attraction															
	12. Child's company sought				.85					.80				.73		
	13. Acts as leader				.65					.76				.79		
	14. Refers to self as positive				.52				.84							.70
V	Self–Confidence															
	15. Expresses opinions					.72			.50			.71				
	16. Appreciates school work					.57			.60							.74
	Percentage of Variance	34.4	14.1	7.7	5.5	5.2	45.7	11.0	7.0	5.7	5.2	59.7	7.9	6.0	4.0	3.0
	Total Variance	Sample 1 66.9					Sample 2 74.6					Sample 3 81.0				

Table 16–5. Predictive Validity of BASE BASE-CTBS Achievement Correlations.[a]

BASE Subscales	*Reading*	*CTBS[b]–Form S* *Language*	*Math*	*Total*
Student Initiative	.425	.463	.513	.517
Social Attention	.256	.310	.360	.359
Success/Failure	.278	.258	.255	.297
Social Attraction	.267	.255	.280	.292
Self-Confidence	.331	.377	.390	.402
Total score	.408	.442	.483	.496

a. *N* of 126 sixth grade students, autumn 1976.

b. CTBS—Comprehensive Test of Basic Skills.

Table 16–6. Predictive Validity of BASE Total and Student Initiative Scores, BASE-CTBS Achievement Correlations (*Spring 1977*).

	Total BASE-CTBS[b] Correlations							
	Reading		*Language*		*Math*			
Grade	*SI*[a]	*TS*	*SI*	*TS*	*SI*	*TS*	*SI*	*TS*
2	.48	.41	.54	.50	.46	.38	.59	.52
3	.41	.37	.33	.35	.36	.37	.43	.43
4	.53	.47	.51	.54	.42	.46	.57	.57
5	.37	.36	.38	.38	.55	.53	.49	.48

a. SI—Student Initiative Factor.

b. CTBS—Comprehensive Test of Basic Skills, Form S.

ity. The mildly declining scores were consistent with Barclay (1973) who reported gradual declines in teacher evaluations of children from second to fifth grades. He, too, found similar plateau effects at the middle grade levels.

To complement the general decreasing trend in academic self-esteem with increasing grades, correlations were computed between grade level and BASE scores. Significant negative correlations were

Table 16–7. Means of BASE Total and Student Initiative Scores by Grade Level.

Grade	*N*	*Total BASE Score*	*SI Factor Score*
K	49	61.69	22.62
1	38	64.50	24.18
2	42	59.26	21.90
3	48	58.42	21.42
4	39	51.90	19.20
5	30	59.44	21.96
6	48	52.16	20.02
7	45	51.33	19.16
8	41	52.94	20.72

Table 16–8. Means and Standard Deviations of BASE Total and Student Initiative Scores by Grades (*Spring 1977*).

Grade	*N*	*Total BASE Score*	*SI Factor Score*
1	34	66.21	24.91
2	37	59.43	21.95
3	41	59.00	21.85
4	24	53.17	20.04
5	25	60.64	22.60
Mean	161	60.01	22.37
S.D.		8.66	3.79

found on three subscales and the total BASE scores with grade level on sample one. Near zero correlations were found on a non-MGM sample between BASE factor and total scores with grade level. A mildly declining trend of inferred self-esteem with increasing grade level was demonstrated.

Correlational Data

Additional data are reported to assist in interpreting BASE scores. Inter-teacher reliability, ratings of the same children by different teachers, was found to be moderately strong (r = .71). In contrast, ratings between teachers and parents of the same children were moderately weak (r = .36). At the kindergarten level the data suggest somewhat of a decline in the relationship between BASE and school achievement scores (r = .36). However, the relatively short length of the achievement test (approximately twenty-two items) may have spuriously affected the size of the BASE–Wide Range Achievement Test reading correlation. Further investigation is needed before kindergarten and preschool student data can be used comfortably.

Program Evaluation

A preschool program for four-year-old students used BASE to assess the effects of a set of activities to increase self-esteem of the children in classrooms. Results of the pre- and post-test evaluation are shown in Table 16–9. The results indicated that the children were rated by their teachers significantly higher on the post-test than on the pretest. The differences in mean ratings were significant on the five subscales of BASE. While the largest gains were shown in the SC ratings, the least amount of change was shown in the S/F sub-scale. These data tend to indicate that BASE is useful in estimating differences that may occur in academic self-esteem within a particular program.

Table 16–9. Differences Between Means of Pre- and Post-BASE Scores and t–Test for Four-Year-Old Preschool Children.

	BASE Post–Subscale		*BASE Pre–Subscale*		
Subscale	*Mean* *(N = 149)*	*S.D.*	*Mean* *(N = 150)*	*S.D.*	t
SI	22.28	3.63	19.45	4.26	6.18[a]
SA	11.27	2.03	10.07	2.35	4.73[a]
S/F	7.02	1.70	6.12	1.67	4.62[a]
SAT	11.01	1.92	9.57	2.35	5.80[a]
SC	8.11	1.34	6.75	1.57	8.05[a]
Total	59.69	8.61	51.97	10.80	6.78[a]

a. Significant at .001 level.

Teacher-Student Comparisons

One interesting comparison was made between teacher ratings of students and student ratings of themselves on the BASE scale. The results indicated consistent higher ratings of the students as compared to the teachers' ratings. The differences were significant at the .05 level. These data are shown in Table 16-10. Correlations between the teachers' ratings of the students and the students' self-ratings on the BASE scale are shown in Table 16-11. A consistent and positive significant relationship was found in the Social Attraction scale which indicated that students and teachers have a propensity to agree on their SAT ratings of peer relationships. The other consistent pattern was a negative, however nonsignificant, relationship between the way the students and teachers rated the S/F subscale. In other words, the students tended to rate themselves in a reverse direction than that of their teachers on all of the areas of academic self-esteem. This may indicate that the S/F subtest is the most sensitive and possibly controversial scale with respect to agreements between teacher and student perceptions of self-esteem.

Table 16-10. Comparisons Between Teachers' Ratings of Students and Students' Self-Ratings on BASE Scores.

BASE Scale (N = 27)	*Teacher Ratings*		*Student Ratings*		
	Mean	*S.D.*	*Mean*	*S.D.*	t
SI	17.56	4.56	20.07	2.60	
SA	9.26	2.03	10.89	1.31	
S/F	6.41	1.58	6.26	1.75	
SAT	8.81	2.56	9.37	1.80	
SC	6.15	2.20	6.59	1.52	
Total	48.19	10.96	53.19	4.92	2.16[a]

a. Significant at .05 level.

Table 16–11. Correlations Between Teachers' Ratings of Students and Students' Self–Rating on BASE Scores.

Teacher Ratings	*Total Student*	*Student Ratings*				
		SI Student Initiative	*SA Social Attention*	*S/F Success Failure*	*SAT Social Attraction*	*SC Self-Confidence*
Total teacher	.25	.09	.28	-.15	.43[b]	.04
SI	.20	.03	.30	-.11	.36[a]	.04
SA	.06	-.02	.16	-.26	.30[a]	.01
S/F	.08	-.11	.32	-.25	.39[a]	-.02
SAT	.34[a]	.27	.21	-.01	.44[b]	.34[a]
SC	.29	.21	.12	-.08	.34[a]	.17

a. Significant at .05 level.

b. Significant at .01 level.

17 THE SIGNIFICANCE OF THE SELF-CONCEPT IN THE KNOWLEDGE SOCIETY

Bonnie L. Ballif

Progression is a primary moving force in human behavior. The human being continually seeks to improve and maximize capacities (Maslow 1954; Rogers 1963) and to have dominion and competence in the environment (de Charms 1968; White 1959). Although each individual tries to overcome challenging situations by his or her own means (de Charms 1968), effectiveness in doing so depends greatly on how much correct information he or she has at hand. With appropriate information and essential skills, premature discouragement, failure, and depression can be avoided (Klinger 1975). Thus it becomes critically important for people to learn things that will help them to be effective in their daily lives. Even so, not all people are motivated to learn to the same degree. In fact, motivation to learn varies tremendously, from one to another.

FIVE PATTERNS OF THINKING

Initial investigations (Adkins and Ballif 1970, 1972) identified five patterns of thinking that determine motivation to seek knowledge and pursue learning in schools. First, the individual must think that learning will be pleasurable or beneficial in some way. This decision is based on associations he or she has made between affective states and similar situations in the past. These affective associations are processed as information (Posner and Snyder 1975) and structure expectations of what can be expected affectively in the future (Bolles 1975; Zajonc 1980).

Second, the individual will not engage in learning without the thought that he or she has some possibility of being successful (Atkinson 1964), and that it is one's own actions that will bring about success (Hardy 1964; Rotter 1966). Once again, previous situations associated with success and failure structure predictions for future probabilities for and control over success (Jones 1977).

Third, the individual must know how to set up personal goals and how to use these established goals to direct behavior. Fourth, the individual must have some knowledge of the instrumental steps that will be effective in accomplishing these specific goals. Fifth, the individual must have internalized standards for performance against which he or she can evaluate his or her work (Aronfreed 1968; McClelland et al. 1953) and acquired ability to use these standards in determining how well the work has been done.

Each of these five patterns of thinking must be present in some degree if motivation for learning is to occur. It also appears likely that these patterns of thinking are constantly interacting with and influencing each other. Within this context of interactive thought patterns, aspects of the self-concept that involve the individual's estimate of his or her capabilities to be a successful learner are examined here.

SEEING SELF AS SUCCESSFUL IN LEARNING

Several studies provide evidence that conceptualizing the self as a capable learner is a pattern of thinking that is critical to the presence of motivation for learning. Adkins and Ballif (1972) obtained data on 1,813 four-year-old children from ten ethnic and cultural groups. Subject distributions were approximately even by sex, with 29 percent from middle and 71 percent from lower socioeconomic backgrounds. The data were obtained using an objective–projective test originally called Gumpgookies (Ballif and Adkins 1968), now revised and known as Animal Crackers (Adkins and Ballif 1975). This instrument has been standardized on several thousand preschool and primary-age children and evidences KR–20 reliability coefficients typically in the .90s, and test–retest reliability coefficients ranging from the high .60s to the low .70s. Chi-square tests of independence of classification, high or low ratings by teachers and high or low test scores indicated significant relationships. A series of other studies correlating test scores with teacher ratings on several scales of motivation resulted in coefficients from .48 to .72 (Adkins and Ballif 1970). Findings by Bridgeman and Shipman (1978) indicate that Gumpgookies contributed significantly to the prediction of academic achievement for 404 children from low income areas. In each of these studies, one of the components of motivation for learning focused on conceptualizations of the self as a successful learner. Evidence comes from items describing gumpgookies who see themselves as always doing well and performing at the top of their class. Through factor analyses, a factor reflecting this pattern of thought was obtained with a KR–20 reliability estimate of .41 (Adkins, Payne, and Ballif 1972).

The purpose of the following three studies was to determine whether seeing the self as a successful learner is one of the critical thought patterns responsible for motivation for learning in three additional populations. The first (Ballif and Kramer 1978) studied 381 seventh, eighth, and ninth grade students in a low socioeconomic urban area. The subjects were almost evenly divided by sex, with 203 black and 178 hispanic. Motivation Components for Learning in School (MOCOS) was used to measure students' self-concepts as learners. This measure consists of five twenty-item subscales designed to measure adolescent thought patterns essential to the presence of motivation for learning. The alpha index of internal consistency is .91 for the total test, with subtest alphas ranging from .60 to .76 (Ballif 1977).

Aptitude was determined by the Metropolitan Achievement Test for Reading. Grade point ratios were calculated on the basis of current grades in academic subjects. Norms were then established for aptitude and achievement scores, and standard scores were determined for each subject. Students motivated to learn were differentiated from those unmotivated to learn, generally on the basis of one-half standard score discrepancies between aptitude and achievement scores. Subjects not falling into these categories were eliminated. The findings showed that students' concepts of themselves as successful learners significantly discriminated between those students who were and those students who were not motivated to learn, suggesting that this aspect of the self-concept does contribute to motivation for learning and gaining knowledge (see Table 17-1).

The second population consisted of 455 tenth, eleventh, and twelfth grade students in a small middle-class town (Eklof 1972). The subjects were all white and almost equally divided between males and females. Affective Conceptual—Propulsive Instrumental and Evaluative Components of Motivation (AC-PIE), a test of motivation for learning in school (Ballif 1976), was used to measure confidence in ability to learn as a component of motivation. Total test internal consistency is .93, and test-retest coefficients are .98 for the total score and from .70 to .93 for the subscales. Validity coefficients for correlations between two subscales and the Education Acceptance and Work Methods subscales of the Brown and Holtzman Survey of Study Habits and Attitudes (SSHA) scale (1964) were .64 and .60. Aptitude scores were obtained on the Otis Quick Scoring Test. Procedures were identical to the first study, and once again confidence in ability to learn significantly ($p < .001$) discriminated between motivated and unmotivated students.

The subjects in the third study were 160 college sophomores in an urban liberal arts college. All students were from low socioeconomic backgrounds and were of either black or white parentage. AC-PIE was used to measure expectations of success in motivation for learning. Aptitude scores were taken from the American College Test. Again, the results showed that the manner in which students think about their abilities to learn differentiates between those motivated to learn and those not so motivated (Hill 1977).

In a further study of the role of the self-concept as a learner in determining motivation for continued learning, Dewey (1978) interviewed forty retirement-aged adults, twelve males and twenty-eight females, enrolled in a College-at-Sixty Program in a private, urban

Table 17–1. Comparisons of Mean Scores of Motivated and Unmotivated Students on Total MOCOS and on the Self-Concept Subscale (*N = 381*).

Scale	*Total M*	*Motivated M*	*Unmotivated M*	t	F	P
Total	58.14	64.11	49.11	9.40	88.44	.0001
Self-concept	8.84	10.09	7.48	7.07	49.97	.0001

university. The subjects were white, from middle- and upper-middle-class socioeconomic backgrounds and were active in education, the community, and the arts. Evidence obtained supported the previous findings that self-conceptions of effectiveness in learning significantly contributed to motivation for learning and obtaining knowledge.

In combination, these studies suggest that the self-concept is a significant component in motivation for learning in students from four to seventy-five years of age, in students from low to upper middle socioeconomic backgrounds, for students in ghetto and private schools, for students in urban and rural areas, and for students from a variety of ethnic backgrounds. Clearly they argue that an individual's efforts to obtain knowledge and skill is dependent on how effective that person thinks he or she will be in doing so.

THOUGHT PATTERNS REGARDING ABILITIES TO LEARN

These critical thought patterns are nothing more than everyday attitudes. Close examination of one subscale used to measure the self-concept in learning demonstrates the patterns specifically: one question asks, "Can you learn most subjects in your classes . . . (a) with the same amount of trouble as most students in your class, (b) more easily than most students in your class, or (c) with more trouble than most students in your class?" Another item asks, "If an assignment is hard, you usually . . . (a) know that you can do it, (b) think you can't do it, or (c) are not sure that you can do it." Data from this revised seventy-five-item form of MOCOS given to 654 primarily black and Hispanic junior high school students from low socioeconomic backgrounds show that 10 percent see themselves as incapable of learning, getting worse grades than others, not being able to finish assignments or do a good job, and possibly failing classes and college. An additional 35 to 57 percent of the students are not sure that they can do an assignment if it is hard, and would feel lucky if they finished college or might not finish college at all. These two groups together constitute 45 to 67 percent of the student body, a sizeable section of the population who anticipate difficulty and failure in learning experiences. In a society that is run primarily on knowledge and skill, it is frightening that so many have such unsure views of themselves in knowledge-dominated situations.

The remaining students see themselves as capable of learning easily, getting the highest grades, and usually doing a good job; they are those students who are motivated for learning because their everyday thoughts about themselves are confident of success. In the long run, learning, gaining skills, and living an effective life may depend on such seemingly insignificant thoughts as whether or not you think you will be able to finish your homework!

THE EXPANSION OF KNOWLEDGE

Although it is now important for individuals to become educated in order to find employment and provide for their needs, the future promises to require that people be able to handle far greater amounts of knowledge than is necessary today. Toffler (1970) points out that the output of books on a world scale approaches 1,000 titles per day. The number of scientific journals and articles is doubling about every fifteen years, and the United States government alone generates 100,000 reports each year plus 450,000 articles, books, and papers. On a worldwide basis, scientific and technical literature mounts at a rate of some 60 million pages a year.

Progress in technology is also increasing the availability of large amounts of information. For example, information comes into most newspaper offices on teletype at a rate of forty-five words per minute. A new generation of machines is presently available that can transmit at 2,400 words per minute, and shortly it will be possible to transfer words, computer to computer, at a rate of 86,000 words per minute. Computers will also be able to store and retrieve this formidable quantity of information at the rate of about 12 million words per minute, and turn them into usable microfilm at about 700,000 words per minute, and into printed documents at 180,000 words per minute (Bagdikian 1971).

Even though our cables and computers can deliver millions of words and images, the final recipient is a human being who can only process between 250 and 1,000 words per minute. The disparity between the capacity of machines and the capacity of the human nervous system is not a small matter. If a large segment of our present population cannot cope with the existing information structure, it would be reasonable to assume that that percentage will increase as the information structure expands. To keep pace with the society of the future, lifelong learning will become necessary to update competencies. This will require that individuals be motivated to continue to learn long after the formal educational period is completed. Clearly it will be necessary not only for more people to be motivated for learning but for more people to see themselves as more and more capable of learning large quantities of information.

SELF-CONFIDENCE IN ABILITY TO ACQUIRE KNOWLEDGE

Because of the need for people to be confident in their abilities to learn so they can survive in an increasingly complicated and sophisticated environment, it is important to find ways to increase this pattern of thinking. Inasmuch as the self-concept is influenced by interactions with the environment (Cottrel 1969), a starting point is to design specific experiences that would facilitate confident thinking by structuring situations in which the individual is regularly stimulated to think that he or she is capable of successful learning. As the individual expects success, he or she will persist and thereby likely improve performance, thus increasing the probability of actual success (Atkinson and Raynor 1978; Jones 1977). The success will, in turn, most likely increase expectations of success in the future.

Apparently, principles of learning responsible for increasing the occurrence of confidence in personal ability are the same as those involved in increasing the occurrence of any acquired response. Thus in order to increase self-confidence in ability, the individual must first be given an opportunity to observe a model which would provide visual and verbal structures of confidence in personal ability to achieve in learning. Second, the individual must be given an opportunity to actually experience feeling confident in learning. And third, the individual must be reinforced for each successive approximation of the desired response made. Following these guidelines, curricular classroom games and activities were created to increase conceptualizations of the self as competent in learning and handling information.

Preschool Children

Preschool games and activities were designed, according to the principles of learning outlined, to increase expectations of successful learning (Ballif, Adkins, and Crane 1972). These games and activities were then organized into a sequence beginning with teaching thought patterns very much like the child's own thinking, and progressing in successive approximations toward thinking that success in learning in school was generally possible and success on specific school tasks was also likely. In each experimental session, one child worked alone with one experimenter. Careful records of the children's responses and other indications of their thinking were obtained. Each child met with the experimenter on three different occasions during the week for a total of six weeks. Four children from an inner-city parochial school served as subjects. Their ages ranged from fifty-one to sixty-seven months, and all were from low socioeconomic backgrounds.

Changes in the self-concept were evident in scores on several instruments. The first was the Pictorial Self-Concept Scale (Bolea, Barnes, and Felker 1971) which consists of fifty cartoon-like picture cards with a weighted score for each. A split-half reliability estimate of .85 (N = 1,813) has been reported as well as a validity estimate of .42 based on a correlation with the Piers–Harris (1964) self-concept measure. Second, structured observations were obtained by using a series of slides depicting interactions between the child and other children and activities in the classroom. These were then used to elicit stories about school, learning, and achieving. These stories were recorded in detail and scored for indications of the presence of confidence in ability to do well in school. Third, Gumpgookies was used as well as, fourth, the Motivation Rating Scale (Adkins and Ballif 1971) which consists of fifteen items with three items designed to measure each of the five patterns of thinking considered to be responsible for motivation for learning. The teacher is asked to rate the child on each statement on a scale from one to four. The ratings are summed to obtain a total score.

As shown in Table 17–2, these experiences increased confidence in being successful in learning for three of the four subjects. These increases in confidence in school abilities also increased motivation to learn in general. Furthermore, these findings support the idea that those aspects of the self-concept involved in how one sees one's ability to handle learning and increase knowledge can be altered through careful environmental design. Not only is it possible to begin to create such experiences for groups of children, particularly those who may lack sufficient motivation to realize their potentials, but it is also important to ask what kinds of experiences children are now

Table 17–2. Scores on Pictorial Self-Concept Scale, Structured Observations, Gumpgookies, and Motivation Rating Scale.

	Pictorial Self-Concept Scale		*Structured Observations*				*Gumpgookies*		*Motivation Rating Scale*	
S	*Pre-*	*Post-*	*1*	*2*	*3*	*4*	*Pre-*	*Post-*	*Pre-*	*Post-*
1	64.09	73.91	0	2	3	3	90	122	49	51
2	66.11	72.13	0	2	2	2	90	127	47	50
3	69.41	74.96	1	6	2	4	75	117	47	52
4	66.45	64.64	2	2	1	0	106	107	42	52

being exposed to that are resulting in so many of them losing confidence in their abilities to learn in school. Individuals around children can have an impact on the kinds of experiences children have that lead to their sense of effectiveness. Such interactions should be carefully studied and developed.

Adolescents

Encouraged by the effects of the curricular materials for preschool children, forty tasks were designed to increase the constituent thought patterns of motivation for learning in adolescents (Ballif and Kramer 1977). Corroborating effects of these tasks in increasing confidence in academic capabilities in eighth grade students have been obtained (Kramer 1979). The subjects for this study were seventy black and Hispanic teenagers from low socioeconomic backgrounds. In the experimental design, the subjects were divided into three treatment groups. First was the experimental group who received the forty tasks designed to increase motivation for learning in general and for the following specific subjects: English, reading, arithmetic, science, and social studies. The second group was a control group who played with thirty-five games that dealt directly or indirectly with the same educational subjects. The third group received no treatment. A series of chi-square analyses were used to confirm equality among the groups in terms of number of males and females, and blacks, Hispanics, and other subjects. Analyses of variance were used to affirm the comparability among the groups in terms of age, aptitude, and achievement. Evidence of changes in thought patterns contributing to motivation for learning were obtained on MOCOS. The analysis of variance for the conceptual subscale on the post-test showed differences significant at the .001 level. The Newman-Keuls post-hoc analysis indicated that the curriculum group yielded mean post-test scores on the conceptual subscale significantly greater than those of the games group or the test-only group. These latter two groups did not differ in their performance on this scale. It appears that students exposed to the experimental tasks showed significant increases in their abilities to see themselves as successful in learning and as personally responsible for their academic success (see Table 17-3).

INCREASING CONFIDENT THINKING INCREASES MOTIVATION

These initial steps show that patterns of thinking about the self can be identified, measured, and increased, and that they are critical contributors to motivation for learning. Unfortunately, large numbers of students see themselves as disadvantaged in their abilities to learn, and this number will likely increase as the demands for more learning in an extended-knowledge society become greater. Through increasing the presence of confident thinking and concepts of self that include expectations for success, motivation to seek new information and knowledge will also increase. Perhaps the concept of a capable self will be more essential to the progression of an individual as information multiples—will be, in fact, one of the most significant contributions that can be made to the knowledge society.

Table 17–3. Post-test Analysis of Variance for Conceptual Subscale Among Three Treatment Groups ($N = 70$).

Source	*df*	*ss*	*MS*	*F*	*P*
Between groups	2	154.218	77.109	7.885	.001
Within groups	67	655.225	9.780		
Total	69	809.443			

18 ISSUES REGARDING SELF-CONCEPT CHANGE

William H. Fitts

Lively discussion is current regarding the self-concept—how it develops, what its correlates are, how it can be measured. Each of these issues is important in its own right and fraught with many difficult problems. Even if all of these issues were settled to the satisfaction of everyone (an unlikely accomplishment), then the most critical issue would still remain.

As I see it, this most crucial issue is that of self-concept *change.* In understanding human beings and their behavior, it is essential that we have reliable and valid means of measuring the self-concept, that we have sound and empirically tested theories as to how the self-concept develops and how it relates to behavior; these factors alone, however, are not sufficient for those of us who are concerned with enabling people to grow and change. As a clinician and a researcher, my chief concern has moved from being able to understand people to helping them grow and change.

THE IMPORTANCE OF SELF-CONCEPT CHANGE

I have visualized the issue of self-concept change as central to all of our society. To me, this is the real issue underlying many others that plague us—crime and delinquency, mental illness, racial conflict, alcoholism, drug abuse, marital misery, and many other people-related problems. In that sense, it is easy for me to view the institutions, agencies, and movements who deal with those problems as essentially concerned with self-concept change. I also have no difficulty in extending this view to other broad areas like education and religion.

It is also felt at times that those who believe in the self-concept as an important psychological construct may have oversold it to human service workers and the public. If that be the case, and it may well be, then a real disservice has been done. In selling the notion that self-concept is important in *understanding* people, a second, implicit assumption has often been associated with the first: namely, that the self-concept can also change. The implication has also been that the individual's self-image can be *readily* changed. I have learned that this is not the case, and that the self-concept is, in fact, rather resistant to change.

THE NEED FOR BETTER ANSWERS

Numerous service programs, demonstration projects, and research studies have been justified as elements that will enhance the self-image, elevate self-esteem, or improve the self-concept. Aware of the importance of changing the self-concept, those who hold the purse strings have also bought the idea that the self-concept is amenable to change and have, therefore, willingly funded these projects. Many such projects make no attempt to measure or assess the actual self-concept change that does occur. Some projects do attempt to do so, but the findings are in no sense clear or consensual. We have relatively little solid data to answer the pressing question: how can you best enable people to change their self-concepts?

When concerned parents, teachers, or therapists ask me, "What can be done to help this person change his or her self-concept?", one is usually at a loss as to what specific suggestions to make. As a therapist, one can respond to this question with two answers, neither of which is very popular for those who seek specific handles. The first answer is:

> You can't! There's no way you can reach into someone else's psyche and rearrange their self-perceptions. The real issues are what do *they* have to do in order to perceive themselves differently, and how can you help them to define and implement those steps?

The second answer is:

> Don't try to change it! The more you can understand people as they are and accept, value, and respect them, then the more they *and* their self-concepts will change.

But these answers, stemming from a therapist self, do not fully satisfy a researcher self. They are too vague and general, not operational enough, and actually extremely difficult to carry out—as those of you who have tried will probably agree. So now let me switch to a researcher self and share with you the issues encountered as one who has struggled with this same question over the last twenty-five years.

WHAT DO WE MEAN BY SELF-CONCEPT CHANGE?

The first issue is the question of what we mean by self-concept change. This question can't be answered until others are answered. One must define the self-concept and develop reliable and valid ways of measuring it. One needs also to specify the variables one is concerned about when considering self-concept change. This is a continual issue, for people conceptualize the self-concept in many different ways. For example, many people conceptualize the self-concept solely in terms of self-esteem. There have now been hundreds of studies reported which employed my Tennessee Self-Concept Scale, or TSCS (Fitts 1965) in interventions aimed at changing the self-concept. It has been a source of great frustration to me that so many of these studies have only utilized one score from the TSCS—the overall self-esteem or total positive score. Is this all there is to be concerned about—one single index of self-esteem—when one talks about self-concept change? It is not what I am concerned about, so let me explain more about what is meant.

When one considers self-concept change, one's first question is: change from *what?* Self-theory places great emphasis upon the individual, and we all at least pay lip service to the principle of individual differences. And yet, one often tends to ignore the individual when research is carried out on self-concept change. Some are so eager to demonstrate the effectiveness of some new intervention—be it transcendental meditation, transactional analysis, physical fitness, or art therapy—that everybody is lumped together into a single group, pre- and post-measures taken, and all conclusions based on differences in two group means. Sometimes, the group means are not even reported, only the change scores. Sometimes means or medians are reported but no standard deviations or other information about the variance of the group. We theorize that the individual's self-concept influences the manner in which any situation is perceived, approached, and experienced. At the same time we approach research about self-concept change as if everyone coming into a given experience is going to perceive and experience it in the same manner and thus show the same kind of self-concept change.

GROUP VERSUS INDIVIDUAL CHANGE

Two different issues are considered here, so let's try to separate them. The first is dealing with the individual instead of groups, and the second concerns the limited data about self-concept. The two issues tend to interact with each other, but the focus here is mainly on the first issue. One should not be content to collect data from a group of people, feed them into a computer, then report and interpret the group findings. It is more important to get one's hands on the data and see what is really there—what's happening to the *individuals* there. When this has been done, one often finds that there is a great deal happening with individuals that is completely obscured or confounded by the group data. Some individuals are showing no change, as if the experience had no impact at all. Others show moderate changes in both directions, while still others demonstrate impressive changes although these too may be in both positive and negative directions.

This is one of those studies where the group statistics indicate no significant change, and the conclusion is that the intervention had no impact—nothing happened. Some of these frustrated researchers concluded instead that the problem was in the test. Something had happened to the people, but the test just wasn't sensitive enough to reflect it. And yet a close look at the individuals shows that a great deal may have happened, that there was much self-concept change and the test did reflect it, but their analyses didn't catch what was really there.

One problem that arises when trying to capture the significance of what is happening with individuals is the question: "What is a statistically significant difference, or change, with an *N* of 1?" Research is so locked into quantification and group statistics that this question is rarely asked and seldom answered. The answer is not given here, but it is still a very important question. It is always awkward to deal with individual data, especially from large groups, because it is hard to quantify, hard to interpret, and the data are going in all directions. However, it is also exciting and challenging to think that some day one may reach a point where one can say that a person with an *XY* type of self-concept is most likely to benefit from a type 277 experience, whereas a person with a *PQ* self-concept will not. The *PQ* self-concept will most likely respond to experiences like 23 or 149. This point will not be researched as long as researchers look for interventions and experiences which affect everyone the same way.

My work has moved beyond looking at individuals to two subsequent steps. One is to take the data from a change study, ascertain which individuals showed positive changes, which negative changes, and which no change. They can then be grouped accordingly into three or more groups, depending upon the size of the sample, and one can then work backwards. We can then ask, "What kinds of self-concepts did these groups have initially?" The opposite approach is to classify subjects into groups according to their initial self-concept and then examine the differences in the changes that occurred. Both approaches have been fruitful, and both have led to the same conclusion—that the kind of self-concept an individual brings to a given experience makes a big difference in how that self-concept will change during the experience. This doesn't sound surprising at all when one stops to think about it, but how often are such things thought about?

WHAT ARE THE VARIABLES?

The second major issue which was mentioned earlier is that of limited data regarding the self-concept. This author's first research on self-concept involved the use of the *Q*-sort technique where the person's self-concept is correlated with something else, such as his or her ideal self. That approach resulted in a correlation coefficient, of .69 or .87 or whatever, to work with, and what does that really tell about the individual's self-image? Even when some other score was computed, to provide an index of how positive or negative the self-concept was, that was not a lot better. One could tell when self-esteem rose or fell, but that was about all; and the morass of individual items was, again, too great to provide any other clues. Further information was sought about the self-concept, more variables that would help describe it and reveal how and where and in what respect it changes. The more this issue was covered, the more other aspects of the self-concept were identified which seemed significant.

In devising the Tennessee Self-Concept Scale, measures of these other aspects of the self-concept were included. Some of these measures have not satisfied the psychometric critics, who in turn have not always understood them. This is not the place to defend the TSCS, nor is that the purpose of this chapter. The most extensive and thorough factor analyses of the TSCS have been done in Israel, and they support the basic structure of the test right down the line. A frequent criticism has been that there are insufficient data as to its internal consistency. The critics have failed to note, however, that the TSCS provides measures of internal consistency regarding each person's self-concept, and collectively these measures provide relevant data about the scale itself.

DEFENSIVENESS

At any rate, when one speaks of self-concept change one thinks of the self-concept as a multi-variable entity which cannot be adequately depicted by a single score or correlation coefficient. A desirable self-concept is one that is both positive and realistic. The problem here is in determining how realistic or valid the self-concept is. One can never determine precisely the nature of another person's real self, and I will not venture into all the philosophical and measurement issues of that problem. Instead one may speak of defensive distortion. Studies of the self-concept are still primarily dependent upon the person's *report* of his or her self-concept, or the self-report. Fortunately, there are ways to measure defensive distortion in self-reports, and without these measures, positive scores alone can be quite misleading. For example, people who are suffering with paranoid schizophrenia or extreme manic states often report the most positive self-concepts of anyone. However, the measures of defensiveness, apart from their other deviant behavior, usually suggest that their grandiose level of self-perception is unreal and defensively distorted.

The problem of defensiveness has confounded and obscured the truth in many change studies. One example is an unfinished study which was initiated several years ago with a class of graduate students. Self-concept measures at the beginning and end of the year first seemed to indicate substantial gains in self-esteem. They had weathered a year of stress, demonstrated their competence, and elevated their self-regard. Closer inspection, however, indicated that these were artificial gains which in turn were clouded over and apparently accounted for by marked increases in defensiveness. Subjective exploration of this phenomenon led us to conclude that the extremely stressful year, characterized by inordinate work demands, cutthroat competition, and strife within the faculty, had simply made the students more paranoid.

There is another way in which defensiveness obscures self-concept change and sometimes completely confounds small sample studies in particular. This is the situation where there are one or two subjects within a sample of ten or twelve who have quite positive self-concepts but are what I call "defensive positives." Their high positive scores are clearly the product of defensive distortion—like the manics and paranoids. If the treatment intervention is successful, then their self-esteem should *drop* as their defensiveness also decreases. That, to me, would be desirable self-concept change. Unless one predicts or expects that or deals with it in analysis, then all that results is confounded data. The changes in these subjects are opposite to the changes in the other subjects—though perhaps just enough to cancel out any significant trend for the group as a whole. One concludes that the intervention had no effect, that nothing happened, but in reality there was a strong and demonstrable impact.

In addition to self-esteem and defensiveness, there are other qualities or aspects of the self-concept that are considered important. There is not time here to discuss all of these in detail, but some will be described briefly. Attempts to measure these variables are built into the Tennessee Self-Concept Scale. Some of them are crude, but apparently the TSCS is the only instrument that attempts to deal with them at all.

CLARITY OF THE SELF-CONCEPT

One of these additional variables is the clarity of the self-concept. This variable is largely independent of either defensiveness or self-esteem. As in a black and white picture, the images may be all black, all white, or all gray, or various combinations of these. The person may present a very clear, well-differentiated picture of himself or herself—someone who knows and clearly sees who and what he or she is as a person, be it a positive or negative image. Or, the image may be all gray, a vague and uncertain picture. Sometimes the image consists of nothing but stark blacks and whites with no tolerance for the ambiguity or ambivalence of gray. Research with the TSCS (Fitts 1972; Fitts et al. 1971) shows that troubled and disturbed people tend to fall at both extremes in regard to clarity. Their self-concepts tend to be fuzzy, uncertain, and undifferentiated on the one hand or overly differentiated, fixed, and rigid pictures on the other hand. In comparison, well-integrated people tend to present clear, well-differentiated pictures characterized by a rich mixture of black, white, and gray.

The clarity of one's self-perceptions seems related to the clarity of one's other perceptions, and significant experiences can alter this variable. It seems important to include this variable when one speaks of self-concept change. Even without significant changes in self-esteem or defensiveness, changes in the clarity of the self-concept may be significant in their own right.

INTERNAL CONSISTENCY

Another variable important to look at in the self-concept is internal consistency, which was mentioned earlier. Some persons have self-concepts which are filled with dissonance or contradiction and thus conflict. Such conflict is associated with turmoil, confusion, and anxiety as to who and what persons really are; it can be the source of much psychic distress. It may result from a highly fluid, unstable, and constantly shifting self-image. It may be attributable to a lack of self-awareness or to an inability to own and thus see certain aspects of self. Whatever the cause, it is nevertheless dissonant and contradictory if one views oneself as totally good but at the same time totally bad. Research shows that such conflicting self-perceptions are clearly associated with ineffective or deviant behavior, with emotional distress, and with psychopathology. It therefore seems appropriate that one consider internal consistency or conflict when speaking about self-concept change.

PATTERNS VERSUS LEVELS

There are perhaps other variables that one could and should examine when the self-concept is concerned, but these will not be pursued further here. Instead, this chapter will switch to a different issue, one rarely heard about or mentioned by others. This issue, labelled "patterns versus levels," is entangled with the preceding one, for unless there is more than one variable to consider, patterns of self-perception cannot be considered. One can only speak of the degree or level of that one variable. It is like looking at a picture where we are only concerned with one quality—like the degree of redness, for example. In that situation, we could say that the picture is 14 or 71 percent red or that it correlates .51 with maximum red, but that would not give us much information about what is in the picture.

Many self-concept studies have been solely concerned with the *level* along some positive–negative continuum and have made no attempt to look at the patterns and configurations that make each self-image unique. Many individuals may report the exact same *level* of self-esteem, yet have entirely different *patterns* across other aspects of their self-concepts. Some of the other variables have already been mentioned. In addition, the system of subselves which comprise the total self-concept is included. The theorists differ as to the number of and labels for these subselves, and the factor analysts come up with differing conclusions as to their purity and independence.

Nevertheless, the fact remains that with tests which attempt to deal with more than one variable, it is possible to look at patterns as well as levels in self-perception. It is fruitful to study these patterns both in understanding individuals and in looking at self-concept change. For example, early work with the TSCS identified rather different patterns of self-concept with people who were sociopathic personalities. Later, it became apparent that most alcoholics and juvenile delinquents showed the same pattern with a few slight variations. Still later, it became clear that the same thing is true for drug abusers. In the meantime, however, it was discovered that most adolescents present much the same pattern but with different levels of the pattern. All of this has generated much interesting speculation. The point here is that patterns of self-perception may be more important than levels, but both are important and warrant attention.

A good illustration of this point is people with the sociopathic personality. They rarely report extremely deviant self-concepts in terms of level, but a great majority of them (as well as criminals, alcoholics, and drug addicts) show the same *patterns.* In considering self-concept change in such populations, it is more impressive to consider interventions that change the configuration of their self-concepts rather than those that raise their self-esteem.

Once a basis for establishing patterns in self-concept is obtained, many other things can be done. One can determine how variable the pattern is or how consistent it is from one aspect of self to another. One can ascertain how deviant the pattern is or how similar it is to others which characterize certain types of people. Most of all, one can study how patterns shift and change through certain experiences. Once again, however, self-concept change cannot be understood as long as everyone has been lumped together and has disregarded the question of: "Change from what?"

WHICH CHANGES FIRST—SELF-CONCEPT OR BEHAVIOR

Now, to change directions completely, many have struggled with an issue separating self theorists and behaviorists: which changes first, the self-concept or behavior? Perhaps self-concept influences behavior, but behavior also influences self-concept. One could discuss this issue endlessly. There seems to be a constant interaction between self-concept and behavior, but without both, neither change will be very important or enduring. One may somehow distort one's self-concept and see oneself as a nonsmoker, but unless one's behavior changes and one actually quits smoking, a lot of dissonance will exist in one's self-concept. Which one has to change first—self-concept or behavior—is open to question, but I'm inclined to lean toward the latter. Thus, as a therapist, one is continually trying to help people find something they can *do* that will make them like themselves better.

THE "SO-WHAT?" QUESTION

Still another issue is what may be called the "so what?" question. So one is successful in helping people change their self-concepts, so what? What difference does that make, and how good a job has one done in demonstrating the results of such changes? Therapists are usually preoccupied with trying to accomplish change to the point that it becomes an end within itself. Many do not bother to follow these subjects and determine whether their changed self-concepts continue over time or whether they generate the other changes in their lives which are hypothesized. Inherent in this issue lies an assumption which has not been fully tested: if a person changes from a type *X* to a type *K* self-concept, does it follow that thereafter they will function like any other person with a type *K* self-concept? Or does having previously been a type *X* somehow make this person different from the usual type *K*? I would like very much to see more attention devoted to follow-up studies, and perhaps this "so what?" question will be answered.

THE NEED FOR SYNTHESIS

Several issues have been addressed which are important because self-concept change is itself so important. There is now one final point. The state-of-the-art regarding self-concept is such that one now needs more synthesis and integration of previous research worse than we need additional research. Some of the best work carried out is the synthesis and integration of widely diverse studies, and the same thing is needed with the area of self-concept change. There are now hundreds of change studies with the TSCS alone that could provide many answers. A synthesis of all these findings could make a real contribution and help us to see what is most effective with what kinds of people. This has not been accomplished because the fund grantors have not considered it important and thus it has not been provided.

One never gets far in any self-concept discussion without getting into measurement issues, and they certainly arise in multiplicity in the kind of synthesis proposed. The myriad array of instruments used to measure self-concept makes it very difficult to integrate findings across instruments. Perhaps it would therefore be more fruitful to begin such a synthesis with each instrument separately and examine every bit of evidence available as to what experiences and interventions generate desirable self-concept change. Perhaps these separate analyses would crossvalidate each other, perhaps not. There will be time enough to weave the threads together after we have found the threads.

19 AN EXAMINATION OF THE NATURE OF CHANGE IN ACADEMIC SELF-CONCEPT

Lorin W. Anderson

The concept of change has been an important part of educational and psychological thought for some time. Schools have as their major goals the facilitation of change in a variety of student characteristics, most notably, cognitive learning. Developmental psychologists attempt to describe changes that occur in various human characteristics. Psychometricians attempt to measure these changes.

One student characteristic that has received increased attention over the past two decades is self-concept. The desire for students to develop positive academic self-concepts is perhaps the most popular affective goal in schools today. Research on academic self-concept has flourished since the pioneering work of Brookover and his colleagues (1964). Research reviewed by Bloom (1976) and Shavelson and others (1976) attests to the number of studies conducted on academic self-concept.

Despite the increase in popularity, the nature of change in academic self-concept has seldom been explored. The present study was undertaken as an initial exploration into the nature of change in academic self-concept.

THE NATURE OF ACADEMIC SELF-CONCEPT

Self-concept can be defined in general terms as the set of beliefs people have about themselves. Academic self-concept is a subset of general self-concept and refers to the set of beliefs people have about themselves as students in academic or school settings.

Beliefs, in turn, can be defined as associations between attributes and objects. The statement "That flower is very small" is a belief associating "that flower" (the object) with "very small" (the attribute). Within this context, then, academic self-concept can be redefined as the set of *attributes* people associate with themselves as students in academic settings (the object). Two general categories of attributes may be considered: evaluative and non-evaluative. Evaluative attributes are those which indicate a judgment of oneself: for example, good worker. Non-evaluative attributes are more objective or factual in nature; for instance, dark hair.

This distinction between evaluative and non-evaluative attributes helps to clarify the difference between academic self-concept and academic self-acceptance (Shepard 1979). Whereas a person's self-acceptance is defined in terms of only evaluative attributes, a person's self-concept is composed of the entire set of attributes a person associates with himself or herself. Thus, self-acceptance is a subset of self-concept. For completeness we may refer to the non-evaluative subset as self-perceptions.

THE ACADEMIC SELF-CONCEPT SCALE

Items for inclusion on the Academic Self-Concept Scale (ASCS) were written in order to conform to the definition of academic self-concept described in the previous section and to be applicable to students from approximately eight to seventeen years of age. Lists of attributes used by students to describe themselves as students were compiled from discussions held with them. Additional attributes were identified from a review of existing scales. Both evaluative and non-evaluative attributes were considered.

Since the object of the belief was to be the student, statements were composed linking the previously mentioned attributes to the pronouns "I" or "me." For example, "I am a good student" is a statement linking the attribute "good student" to the object "I." Ten items were written in this manner. Five items contained evaluative attributes; the other five contained non-evaluative attributes (see Table 19–1). Students were instructed to read each statement and to

Table 19–1. The Academic Self-Concept Scale.[a]

Item Number	*Statement*		
1	Schoolwork is fairly easy for me.	YES	NO
2	When I try to do things I usually make mistakes.	YES	NO
3	I forget most of what I learn.	YES	NO
4	Most things are too hard for me to do.	YES	NO
5	I can do good work only if someone helps me.	YES	NO
6	I am slow in finishing my schoolwork.	YES	NO
7	I can give a good report in front of my class.	YES	NO
8	I am proud of my schoolwork.	YES	NO
9	Other students look to me for ideas.	YES	NO
10	I am a good student.	YES	NO

a. The first five items contain non-evaluative attributes; the second five contain evaluative attributes.

respond "yes" if they agreed with the statement or "no" if they disagreed.

SUBJECTS

Four samples of students took part in the study, one sample at each of four grade levels. All students were enrolled in an elementary, junior high, or high school in a midwestern city. The elementary school was a "feeder school" for the junior high school which, in turn, was a feeder school for the high school. Thus, the design of the study is quasi-longitudinal in nature.

The breakdown of the sample by grade level, number, sex, race, and average grade received in school is presented in Table 19-2. All students were administered the scale by their homeroom teachers during the spring of 1978.

TECHNICAL QUALITY OF THE ASCS

The validity of the ASCS was examined in several ways. First, correlations between scores on the ASCS and school marks received by

Table 19–2. Race and Sex Composition and Average School Marks of Samples Used in Study *(by Grade Level)*.

Grade	*N*	*Sex (Percent Male/Percent Female)*	*Race (Percent White/Percent Nonwhite)*	*Average Marks[a] Received*
3	107	47/53	70/30	3.60
6	147	56/44	68/32	3.15
8	147	54/46	80/20	3.33
11	150	45/55	81/19	3.44

a. The scale used for reporting student marks ranged from 1 (F) to 5 (A).

the students were computed. Previous research reviewed by Bloom (1976) suggested that these correlations tend to approximately 0.50. Second, correlations between scores on the scale and teachers' perceptions of students' academic self-concepts were calculated. Research (Dolan 1978) indicates that self-reports of academic self-concept are related to teachers' reports of students' academic self-concepts. Finally, a factor analysis of the scale responses was performed. Based on the design of the scale, two orthogonal factors should emerge. One factor should consist of the evaluative items; the other should be comprised of the non-evaluative items.

The correlations of academic self-concept scores with school marks and teachers' ratings of students' academic self-concepts are presented in Table 19-3. The correlations between academic self-concept and school marks range from 0.41 to 0.58. All are statistically significant, and the median correlation 0.45 is quite close to the median correlation reported by Bloom (1976).

The correlations between academic self-concept and teachers' ratings also are statistically significant at all grade levels. The correlations tend to be somewhat higher at grades three and six than at grades eight and eleven. This difference in magnitude seems reasonable given that the ratings of the third and sixth grade students were made by teachers who were with the students approximately six hours per day, while the ratings of the eighth and eleventh grade students were made by teachers who were with the students approximately one hour each day.

The results of a varimax rotation of a principal components factor analysis are summarized in Table 19-4. Two factors were extracted at each grade level based on the two categories of attri-

Table 19–3. Correlations of Academic Self-Concept Scores with School Marks and Teacher Ratings.

Academic Self-Concept Scale	*School Marks*	*Teacher Ratings of Self-Concept*
Grade 3	0.48[a]	0.50
Grade 6	0.58	0.60
Grade 8	0.41	0.26
Grade 11	0.42	0.25

a. All correlations are statistically significant at the .01 level.

butes "built into" the scale. The items loading on each factor at each grade level are indicated in the cells of the table. Items with correlations greater than 0.40 were said to load on a factor.

In general, the results of the factor analysis lend support to the validity of the scale. The first factor at grade levels three, six, and eight is clearly a non-evaluative factor. All five non-evaluative items load on this factor. The second factor at these grade levels is clearly an evaluative factor. Four of the five evaluative items load on this factor.

The results at grade eleven are less clear-cut. The first factor tends to be a non-evaluative factor. The second factor tends to be a "mixed" factor, with two evaluative and two non-evaluative items loading on it. Three items (8, 9, and 10) failed to load on either factor. A subsequent factor analysis of the grade eleven data with no constraints on the number of factors yielded four factors. Items 8 and 10 loaded on the third factor, while item 9 loaded on the fourth factor.

In sum, then, the correlational and factor analytic results tend to support the validity of the ASCS, especially at grades three, six, and eight. What's more, the validity of the ASCS tends to be quite similar at each of these grade levels.

The reliabilities of the ASCS at each grade level were also examined. Internal consistency estimates (alphas) were completed for (a) the total scale, (b) the non-evaluative subscale (items 1 through 5), and (c) the evaluative subscale (items 6 through 10). The alphas for the total scale were 0.74 for grade three; 0.69 for grade six, 0.67

Table 19–4. Results of Varimax Rotation of Academic Self-Concept Scale (*by Grade Level*).

	Factor Number	
Grade Level	*I*	*II*
3	1, 2, 3, 4, 5, 8	1, 4, 6, 7, 9, 11
6	1, 2, 3, 4, 5, 9	3, 6, 7, 8, 10
8	1, 2, 3, 4, 5, 8	6, 7, 9, 10
11	2, 4, 5	1, 3, 6, 7

for grade eight, and 0.54 for grade eleven. For the non-evaluative subscale the alphas were 0.73, 0.70, 0.65, and 0.38, respectively. Finally, for the evaluative subscale the alphas were 0.53, 0.50, 0.50, and 0.33, respectively.

In general, the internal consistency estimates were quite satisfactory given the nature of the scale and the number of items per subscale. The alphas for the non-evaluative subscale scores are quite similar to the alphas for the total scale scores. This would suggest the presence of subscales, a suggestion already verified by the factor analysis. The alphas for the evaluative subscale scores were lower at all grade levels. The alphas for the eleventh grade sample are quite low. As a result of the factor analysis and internal consistency estimates the grade eleven data will be excluded from further consideration.

DIFFERENCES ACROSS GRADE LEVELS

The major purpose of this chapter is best accomplished by examining the differences in ASCS scores across grade levels. Since the design of the study is quasi-longitudinal in nature, differences cannot be equated with changes. An examination of such differences, however, may shed some light on the possible changes in academic self-concept which might occur in future research.

Three dependent variables were used in the analysis: total scale scores, non-evaluative subscale scores, and evaluative subscale scores. The decision to examine differences in the total scale scores was based on the belief that the magnitude of the reliabilities warranted such an examination. That is, given reliabilities of 0.70, many researchers may choose to use the total scale scores as the sole dependent variable.

The results with total scale scores as the dependent variable are displayed in Table 19-5. As can be seen, the mean ASCS scores are virtually identical at all three grade levels. Based on these results, one could conclude that students' academic self-concepts do not change from grade three to grade eight.

The results pertaining to the non-evaluative subscale scores are presented in Table 19-6. The means on the non-evaluative subscale tend to increase over grade levels. The results of the analysis of vari-

Table 19–5. Means, Standard Deviations, and *F*-statistic for the Total Scale Scores (*by Grade Level*).

Grade Level	*N*	*Mean*	*S.D.*	*F-statistic*	*Significance*
3	107	17.10	2.34	0.03	n.s.
6	147	17.08	2.19		
8	147	17.04	2.10		

Table 19–6. Means, Standard Deviations, and *F*-statistic for the Non-evaluative Subscale Scores (*by Grade Level*).

Grade Level	*N*	*Mean*	*S.D.*	*F-statistic*	*Significance*
3	107	8.20	1.60	4.52	.01
6	147	8.48	1.56		
8	147	8.76	1.36		

Table 19–7. Mean, Standard Deviations, and *F*-statistic for the Evaluative Subscale Scores (*by Grade Level*).

Grade Level	*N*	*Mean*	*S.D.*	*F-statistic*	*Significance*
3	107	8.91	1.08	11.69	.001
6	147	8.59	1.00		
8	147	8.27	1.05		

ance indicated significant differences among the means. Subsequent Sheffé post-hoc comparisons indicated that the mean score of the eighth grade students was significantly *higher* than the mean score of the third grade students ($p < .05$). None of the other mean differences were significantly different.

Results pertaining to the evaluative subscale scores are presented in Table 19–7. The means on the evaluative subscale tend to decrease over grade levels. The results of the ANOVA indicated significant differences among the means. Subsequent Sheffé post-hoc comparisons indicated that the mean score of the eighth grade students was significantly *lower* than the mean scores of the third and sixth grade students ($p < .05$). The difference between the means of the third and sixth grade students was not significant.

DISCUSSION

The results of this study should be interpreted rather cautiously given the nature of the design (that is, quasi-longitudinal) and the rather moderate internal consistency estimates for some of the subscales. Nonetheless, several interesting findings emerge. First, differences among, and possible changes in, students' academic self-concepts are quite complex. When differences in a general academic self-concept are explored, none are found. When two separate, but related, components of academic self-concept are considered, however, differences among students of varying ages did emerge. The differences in the two components, self-perception and self-acceptance, were found to exist in different directions. Older students tended to indicate that they made fewer mistakes, remembered what they learned, and were able to learn on their own more so than did the younger students. On the other hand, older students indicated that they were less proud of their schoolwork, were unable to give good reports in front of their classes, and were poorer students in comparison with the younger students. Put simply, older students indicated they learned fairly well in school in comparison with the younger students, but they were more negative in their self-evaluations.

What can be made of this apparently discrepant result? Perhaps the older students evaluate themselves according to more stringent criteria than do younger students. That is, older students set higher standards for themselves which must be met before they are willing to accept themselves. Perhaps the older students make use of criteria other than schoolwork and school learning in making their self-evaluations. Peer perceptions and reactions, for example, may have a greater impact on adolescents' self-evaluations or self-acceptance than the more objective criteria of task difficulty, memory, and mistakes.

The difference between self-perception and self-acceptance has implications for the statement of affective goals in schools. Frequently affective goals are stated in the context of becoming more positive. For example, a goal concerning self-concept may be stated as follows: students will develop *positive* self-concepts. As such, this goal clearly focuses on the self-acceptance component of academic self-concept. An alternative, parallel goal may be useful in certain situations. Such a goal would be similar to the following: students will develop more *realistic* self-concepts. Perhaps the real goal of schools in this area is that students will develop positive, but realistic, academic self-concepts. If this is, in fact, the goal, difficulties in achieving it are apparent. It is possible for students to develop realistic and negative self-concepts.

Finally, the results of this study suggest that considering total scores on tests and scales may, in fact, hide important findings. This may be true even when the test or scale yielding the total scores is quite adequate technically (that is, from a validity and reliability perspective). As a consequence, the structure of affective scales should be examined routinely if such misinterpretations are to be avoided. This examination would involve both logical and empirical means.

20 COMPARISON OF AGGREGATE SELF-CONCEPTS FOR POPULATIONS WITH DIFFERENT REFERENCE GROUPS

Wilbur B. Brookover
Joseph Passalacqua

During the past twenty years there has been a rapidly increasing interest in the phenomenon of self-concept. The high level of interest in self-concept and the general recognition of its importance in education has specifically affected educational theory and practice. The demonstration by Brookover and others (1962, 1965, 1967) that individual self-concept of academic ability is significantly and highly related has led many educators to focus on the enhancement of self-concept as both a goal in itself and a means of achieving other educational objectives (Purkey 1970). Many innovations have been designed to improve educational outcomes by focusing on the improvement or development of the self-concepts of disadvantaged students (Scheirer and Kraut 1979). Belief in the importance of self-concept has been reinforced by evidence that individual self-concept, particularly self-concept in academic roles, is positively related to achievement (Shavelson 1976).

Much of the interest in academic self-concept is based upon the assumption that the enhancement of the self-concept of students in a given class or in a given school will generally improve the achievement of students in that class or school.

A recent study of elementary schools reveals a negative relationship between aggregated self-concept of academic ability and aggregated school achievement. The correlation between school mean self-concept of academic ability and mean achievement in reading and mathematics in a random sample of Michigan schools is −.547 (Brookover et al. 1979). This illustrates the "ecological phenomenon" described by Robinson (1950). Nearly thirty years ago Robinson startled the users of aggregated data with his proof that statistical associations for such populations could differ in magnitude and even in sign from those for individual population members. The purpose of this chapter is to examine the ecological phenomenon as it occurs in Michigan elementary schools and possibly in other social groups.

To understand this phenomenon in this context, it is essential to give a brief description of the data collected in a study of elementary school social climate in Michigan and its relationship to basic reading and mathematics achievement (Brookover et al. 1979). The data were obtained from randomly selected samples of fourth and fifth grade students in Michigan elementary schools. The representative state sample was composed of sixty-eight such schools, seven of which were predominantly black. For the purposes of this and other analyses it was necessary to augment the number of black schools. An additional twenty-three schools were randomly selected in order to have a subsample of thirty predominantly black schools. From this total of ninety-one elementary schools, subsamples of white schools, black schools, and higher socioeconomic and lower socioeconomic status white schools were identifiable.

The Self-Concept of Academic Ability data were obtained by means of a student questionnaire which included the Self-Concept of Academic Ability Scale (see Appendix A). This questionnaire was read to the students by a trained field researcher, and the students marked responses on the questionnaires. The school achievement data were obtained from the Michigan Department of Education Assessment Tests that were administered to all fourth grade students in the state. The mean school-level achievement score is the mean percentage of students mastering the forty-nine reading and math objectives measured by the Michigan Objective-Referenced Test. The racial composition of the student body of each school, reported as the percentage of whites, was obtained from the state department of education. These figures are based on the school principal's report. The mean socioeconomic status of the schools is based upon the main breadwinner's occupation as reported by the students in the fourth and fifth grades or as obtained from a sample of the school records in which the parental occupational data were available. The parent's occupational data were coded according to the Duncan Occupational Scale and the mean socioeconomic level for each school was calculated from those data.

Individual achievement test scores were not available for this population. It is therefore impossible to report within-school correlations between individual self-concept of academic ability and individual achievement. This relationship, however, has been consistently demonstrated in other studies, including numerous studies using the Michigan State Self-Concept of Academic Ability Scale as the measure of self-concept. These studies have demonstrated this relationship in various populations and over time reporting correlations in the range of .45-.70 (Auer 1971; Brookover et al. 1967; Haarer 1964; Vortuba 1970). Many other studies have confirmed the significant positive relationship between the individual Self-Concept of Academic Ability and various measures of individual school achievement as well (Bloom 1976).

RELATED RESEARCH

It is important to recognize that self-concept research has been based on many different measures and somewhat varied definitions of the construct. Therefore, we are not able to generalize across many studies involving self-concept, self-esteem, or other diverse measures of self. The phenomenon with which we are dealing refers specifically to Self-Concept of Academic Ability. We have no evidence or relevant research with regard to the ecological phenomenon in other self-concept measures.

Several reviews of research on self-concept and its relationships to school achievement have verified the existence of the positive correlation between individual self-concept and achievement (Henderson 1973; Morse 1963; Purkey 1970; Yamamotto 1972).

There is some evidence that mean self-concept differs for various populations. Coleman and others (1966) reported that the self-concepts of ability among black students in segregated black schools were higher than the self-concept of black students in integrated schools. Katz (1968) reported that the self-concept of students in schools declined as the proportion of white students increased. Henderson (1973) reported that the self-concepts of students in black elementary schools were higher than the self-concepts of students in white elementary schools in Michigan. Hara (1972) found that black students in Detroit area schools had higher self-concepts of academic ability and higher self-esteem than white students in Detroit area schools. Both white and black students' self-concepts were higher than that of Tokyo students. There is some evidence that students from different socioeconomic levels have somewhat different mean self-concepts (Trowbridge 1972). There has been some analysis of the difference in self-concept of randomly selected or matched groups within schools and other social systems (Borg 1966). We have not, however, identified any research that specifically examines the relationship between the aggregate self-concept of academic ability in specific schools and the aggregate achievement of those schools.

SELF-CONCEPT THEORY

Our examination of the negative relationship between school mean self-concept of academic ability and school mean achievement is based upon the symbolic interactionist frame of reference. The basic theory is that human beings assess themselves in terms of their perceptions of others' evaluations of them. Self-concept of academic ability, as any other aspect of self, is thus perceived to originate in the interaction with other persons who are relevant to the actor (Lindesmith and Straus 1968; Mead 1934; Sheriff 1967). We recognize there are other theories of self which frequently involve the conception that self is a permanent, fixed and, perhaps, even inherited aspect of human personality (Maslow 1962). In the interactionist context we perceive that each person has many selves and assesses him- or herself in many roles or statues. Self-concept or self-assessment at any particular time or situation varies from any other time or situation depending upon the social role the actor plays. Thus, the reference group to which he or she is referring in self-assessment varies from one social context to another. This is well illustrated by the finding that the self-concept of academic ability of blind children varied with the comparison or reference group to which they were asked to respond—seeing children or other blind children (Erickson et al. 1967).

With this frame of reference in mind, we turn to a possible explanation of the negative correlation between mean self-concept of academic ability and mean achievement. As will be noted in Table 20–1,

Table 20–1. Correlation Between Mean School Achievement and Mean Self-Concept of Academic Ability in Samples of Michigan Public Elementary Schools.

Samples	*N*	*Pearson Correlation*
Representative state	68	-.549
Total white	61	.039
High socioeconomic status white	31	.012
Low socioeconomic status white	30	-.233
Majority black	30	.004

the correlation between the mean self-concept of academic ability and mean school achievement in a randomly selected representative sample of Michigan elementary schools is -.549. This negative correlation between the school means is about as high as the typical positive correlation between individual student self-concept and individual achievement. It is this particular finding that led us to examine further the ecological phenomenon which it represents.

The most obvious explanation of the phenomenon is that students in high-achieving schools are comparing themselves to predominantly high-achieving peers and thus evaluating themselves less favorably than would students in a low-achieving school. Although this explanation has some merit, further examination of Table 20–1 reveals that it does not hold in the subsamples. It should be noted that within the sample of white schools, where there is considerable variation in the mean school achievement (see Table 20–2) there is essentially no correlation between mean self-concept of academic ability and mean school achievement. When the white schools are divided into two categories on the basis of the mean socioeconomic status, there is no correlation indicated between mean self-concept of academic ability and mean school achievement in the higher socioeconomic status white schools. Neither is there any correlation between self-concept of academic ability and mean achievement in the sample of black schools. However, there is a low, but possibly nonsignificant, negative correlation between mean self-concept and mean school achievement in the sample of lower socioeconomic status white schools.

The negative correlation might be explained by the simple differences in the level of achievement of the various schools' student

Table 20–2. Mean and Standard Deviations of Achievement and Self-Concepts of Academic Ability in Samples of Michigan Public Elementary Schools (*Means of Schools Mean Unweighted*).

	State Representative Sample		*Majority White Schools*						*Majority Black Schools*	
			Total White		*High Socioeconomic Status*		*Low Socioeconomic Status*			
	M	*S.D.*	*M*	*S.D.*	*M*	*S.D.*	*M*	*S.D.*	*M*	*S.D.*
Achievement	74.88	9.53	77.36	6.11	80.13	5.08	75.50	5.83	56.83	7.77
Self-concept	28.77	1.08	28.51	.77	28.75	.39	28.27	.79	30.81	.84

bodies to which the students are comparing themselves if the negative correlation was evident in each of the subsamples. Since it is found in only one of the four subsamples, at a marginal level of significance, this explanation does not seem viable. The lack of correlation in these subsamples might result from lack of variance, but the variance in both mean self-concept and mean achievement is sufficient in each subsample to provide some correlation between these variables (see Table 20-2). The table also shows the difference in the mean self-concepts of the students in the majority-black-school sample, 30.8, and those in the white-school sample, 28.5. Thus, the mean level of self-concept in the majority-white schools is decidedly lower than that in the majority-black schools. There is little difference in the mean self-concept of academic ability in the high socioeconomic white schools and the low socioeconomic white schools—28.7 compared to 28.3. This suggests that students in predominantly black schools assess their academic ability in a different social context than students in predominantly white schools. In a similar fashion we should note that the mean level of achievement in the black school sample is strikingly *lower* than the level of achievement in the total white school sample or in either of the white subsamples (Table 20-2).

Since all but three of the black schools are 98 percent or more black, it appears that black schools and the associated school community in which black students acquire their self-concepts of academic ability are decidedly different social systems than are characteristic of white schools, which are nearly all, 98 percent or more, white. Both the self-concepts and achievement in the two sets of black and white schools are the products of different social systems.

Although the majority of the schools among the ninety-one studied are essentially all white or all black, there is some variance in the percentage of white students in both subsamples. When the mean socioeconomic status and the mean achievement are controlled by entering them first in a multiple regression analysis, the percent of white students in the school contributes significantly to the explanation of variance in mean self-concept in the representative state sample (Table 20-3). The percentage of whites adds little to the explained variance in mean self-concept when mean socioeconomic status and mean achievement are controlled in the black and white subsamples where racial composition has already been controlled.

Table 20–3. Multiple Regression Analysis Showing Contribution of Percent White to Variance in Mean Self-Concept of Academic Ability, When Achievement and Socioeconomic Status Are Entered Prior to Percent White in a Representative State Sample and Two Subsamples of Michigan Elementary Schools.

Independent Variables	*State Sample*			*White Sample*			*Black Sample*		
	R^2	R^2 *Added*	*Zero Order* r	R^2	R^2 *Added*	*Zero Order* r	R^2	R^2 *Added*	*Zero Order* r
1. Socioeconomic Status and achievement	.370			.094			.174		
2. Percent white	.563	.192	-.697	.128	.034	-.080	.262	.088	-.245

It should also be noted that the simple correlation between percentage of white and mean self-concept of ability, -.70, is decidedly higher in the state sample than in the white subsample, -.08, or in the black subsample, -.25.

Our general conclusion from these simple analyses is that self-concept of academic ability is based on interaction within particular social groups. Self-concept of academic ability is therefore determined by the evaluations which are communicated in the group and the norms which characterize the group. The evaluations communicated within the black schools would appear to be decidedly different than are communicated in white schools. The black school norms of achievement are also different than the achievement norms in white schools. Data from this study also reveal that the mean student self-concept of academic ability has a high positive correlation with student's mean perceived evaluations and expectations held for them (see Table 20-4). This relationship is found in both white and black subsamples. The correlation is similar in magnitude and direction to that found between individual self-concept of academic ability and individual student perceived evaluation (Brookover et al. 1962, 1965, 1967). This positive correlation reflects the fact that students in predominantly black schools perceive higher mean evaluation and expectations than do students in white schools (Table 20-4). The mean perceived evaluations are thus positively associated with mean self-concepts which are also higher in black schools (Table 20-2).

Table 20–4. Means and Standard Deviations of Students' Perceived Evaluations and Expectations in Samples of Michigan Elementary Schools and the Zero Order Correlation Between Mean Perceived Evaluations and Expectations and Mean Self-Concept of Academic Ability in the Samples of Michigan Elementary Schools.

Samples	*Perceived Evaluation and Expectation* *N*	*M*	*∝*	*Sample Correlation Mean Perceived Evaluation and Expectation Subject Mean Self-concept of Ability*
State	68	23.11	.81	.879
White	61	22.95	.67	.794
Black	30	24.50	.66	.861

This further supports the conclusions that norms of evaluation and achievement are different in the black-school social systems than in the white-school systems (Passalacqua 1979) (see Table 20-4). Observations of some schools in our study and other research (Fernandez, Espinosa, and Dornbusch 1975) indicate that teachers praise black and other minority students for academic achievement more than they praise white high-achieving students. This also suggests that the norms characterizing black schools and the patterns of interactions communicating the norms and evaluations may not be comparable to those of white schools. Self-concept of academic ability as expressed in one social system is therefore not comparable to the self-concept expressed in another social system.

If the findings of this study are confirmed by other research, it is clearly not appropriate to compare self-concepts of academic ability across schools when the social contexts are different. Although self-concept is significantly and positively related to achievement on the individual level within a given school context, these variables may not be related at the aggregate school level. Although we do not have evidence, we could hypothesize that there are subgroups within schools that represent essentially different social systems. If groups within a school, such as tracks, are segregated in a way that minimizes interaction between members of different subgroups, while significantly different norms, expectations, and evaluations are communicated within each of the subgroups, we hypothesize that negative correlations between self-concept of academic ability and mean achievement will occur. If this were verified, it may explain some of the differences in findings regarding self-concepts of black students in integrated schools (St. John 1975).

Although enhanced self-concept of academic ability on the individual level is necessary for higher achievement by individuals within a given school social system, high aggregate self-concept of ability in a given school's social system is not a sufficient condition to guarantee high achievement. In our judgment there is no universal or common referent across school social systems to which students may compare themselves. Therefore, self-concept of academic ability is meaningful as a predictor of achievement only within the context of a specific school's social system.

APPENDIX A

Items Composing Self-Concept of Academic Ability Scale

1. Think of your friends. Do you think you can do schoolwork better, the same, or poorer than your friends?

    Better than all of them . . . . . . 1.
    Better than most of them . . . . . . 2.
    About the same . . . . . . 3.
    Poorer than most of them . . . . . . 4.
    Poorer than all of them . . . . . . 5.

2. Think of the students in your class. Do you think you can do schoolwork better, the same, or poorer than the students in your class?

    Better than all of them . . . . . . 1.
    Better than most of them . . . . . . 2.
    About the same . . . . . . 3.
    Poorer than most of them . . . . . . 4.
    Poorer than all of them . . . . . . 5.

3. When you finish high school, do you think you will be one of the best students, about the same as most, or below most of the students?

    One of the best . . . . . . 1.
    Better than most of the students . . . . . . 2.
    Same as most of the students . . . . . . 3.
    Below most of the students . . . . . . 4.
    One of the worst . . . . . . 5.

4. Do you think you could finish college?

    Yes, for sure . . . . . . 1.
    Yes, probably . . . . . . 2.
    Maybe . . . . . . 3.
    No, probably not . . . . . . 4.
    No, for sure . . . . . . 5.

5. If you went to college, do you think you would be one of the best students, same as most, or below most of the students?

One of the best ...... 1.
Better than most of the students ...... 2.
Same as most of the students ...... 3.
Below most of the students ...... 4.
One of the worst ...... 5.

6. If you want to be a doctor or a teacher, you need more than four years of college. Do you think you could do that?

Yes, for sure ...... 1.
Yes, probably ...... 2.
Maybe ...... 3.
No, probably not ...... 4.
No, for sure ...... 5.

7. Forget how your teachers mark your work. How good do you think your own work is?

Excellent ...... 1.
Good ...... 2.
Same as most of the students ...... 3.
Below most of the students ...... 4.
Poor ...... 5.

8. How good of a student do you think you can be in this school?

One of the best ...... 1.
Better than most of the students ...... 2.
Same as most of the students ...... 3.
Below most of the students ...... 4.
One of the worst ...... 5.

21 THE DEVELOPMENT OF SELF-CONCEPT IN THE ELEMENTARY SCHOOL
A Search for the Determinants

Lawrence Dolan

Most would agree that the affective consequences of school experience are wide and varied, whether they result from the magnitude of evaluation that occurs in school settings, the fulfillment of the expectations of those close to us, or the socialization press from both adults and peers in the academic setting. They nonetheless have an impact on how we negotiate new experiences and how we structure and evaluate our self-views. Unfortunately for science, the basis for such a belief is primarily formed by reflection on the implicit data of our life experiences, rather than the accumulation of rigorous evidence. This chapter attempts to improve our understanding of how varied school experiences contribute to the affective lives of elementary school children, more specifically to the development of self-conception.

This research effort also confronts a major problem of recent studies that analyze the effects of schooling experiences. It is based on the belief that these investigations have a limited perspective on the range of outcomes necessary to understand the impact of schooling, that is, a focus on cognitive criteria. It has become popular to suggest that the amount and quality of schooling are not as crucial to advancement in life as they were once proclaimed to be. The mood of pessimism about schooling that has emerged in the past decade is quite unprecedented in this century.

The faith placed in the conclusions concerning the negligible effects of schooling, the resultant loss of confidence, and growth of pessimism are mistaken in their premises and often destructive in their consequences. The position of this chapter is that the effects of schooling encompass far more than cognitive gains. The isolation of cognitive outcomes as the single contribution of schooling does not adequately reflect the student's complete response to a prolonged educational environment. The basic argument that will be developed is that given the intensity of evaluation that occurs in early schooling and the stresses placed on the student which parallel those in other life roles, the educative environment of the school, the home, and the degree to which they are congruent should be considered potent determining variables for the student's developing conception of self.

Contrary to the general belief of most educators that little research exists on the affective domain within the educational context, there is, in fact, a large research base. In spite of this research and the importance of such questions, it would be rare to find policymakers basing any of their decisions, whether directed toward teacher accountability or student advancement, on anything other than cognitive criteria. The research on the affective consequences of schooling is plagued with problems, most of which minimize the possibility for generalizations and make the field entirely too speculative for concrete decision-making.

To date, the majority of research has centered on one causal agent, achievement. What is needed is the simultaneous study of self-concept development of the same person in more than one context. Research that stresses the joint impact of two or more settings will avoid the often artificial and emphemeral conclusions of single-context investigations. In Bronfenbrenner's (1979) recent parlance, more focus on ecological experiments is required. Research on the interplay and reciprocity within different configurations of education such as the home, school, and achievement history are basic if we are to propose interventions or policies to promote growth.

The research on self-conception within the school setting has been plagued by inadequate assessment techniques, particularly when compared to the sophistication of cognitive measurement procedures. Brim (1976), in his report on national policy for children, stresses that well-validated measures of this construct are rare, and that changes over time must rely not on the careful analysis of scientific data but on inferences made from institutional records such as number of contacts with psychiatric facilities. It is believed that advancement of research in this field has been inhibited by the haphazard approach to the selection and assessment of such affective characteristics. The specific problems of assessment have been well documented, most recently by Shavelson's (1976) discussion. Research on self-concept could greatly benefit from a multi-trait and multi-source approach. Although this concern is frequently discussed, it is rare to see research that utilizes such techniques.

Finally, one of the main problems of the research on the self-concept correlates of school experience is the lack of attention to developmental issues. The majority of research has not focused on affective development under the fifth grade, in spite of the fact that the most likely period of growth occurs in the early years of the student's interaction with school. If we are to obtain evidence on when and how much schooling factors affect self-conception, there is a need to study a wide range of early school experience. The history of the learner must be considered a key variable. Are home support, instructional quality, and achievement equally important at all stages of elementary school? Are there optimal periods where specific factors are critical for development? To date, policy-makers have little data to support any period when intervention might be necessary, and if so, how much is enough? Intervention programs designed to have a positive impact on self-concept are often short-lived, and the fade-out effects so common to cognitive criteria apply equally to the affective outcomes. Affective variables such as self-concept which are products of successful interventions need time to grow and stabilize. Research is needed both at the early levels of schooling and on the effects of prolonged intervention.

DEVELOPMENT OF A RESEARCH STRATEGY

It was decided that some useful data might emerge from the study of very similar students under relatively extreme conditions of the quality of instruction received, ranging from brief treatment periods to treatment over the first six years of primary schooling. The hope was to meet a major shortcoming of past research: the isolation of student achievement from its instructional context.

Using criteria developed from the evaluation of systematic, mastery-based instruction (Bloom 1976), the successful components identified in the studies of early childhood intervention strategies (Anderson 1977; White 1972), and surveys of the most successful inner-city educational interventions for the improvement of cognitive skills (Havinghurst and Levine 1977), three instructional programs were selected for study. Representing the high quality of instructional treatment was an experimental program known as a child-parent center. Typically, the child-parent centers receive children from Title I areas who meet all the conditions of being labeled "educationally disadvantaged." In reality, these children are the most needy of the population within such specified regions. The children begin school at the age of three and typically continue through the first and, for some, the third grade. The one group of students under investigation had the unique opportunity to continue in this intensive program through the sixth grade, that is, receiving eight years of positive intervention. At the sixth level, students were reading at national norms. This program, which exists in an urban, black, poverty area, met most of the requirements of high quality of instruction, at least to a far greater extent than any known existing program that allows for suitable control comparisons. These features include:

- *Early intervention, program length, and continuity*—Treatment began at age three and continued through the sixth grade. With few exceptions, entry was not permitted after the prescribed entry age. This avoids a major problem of metropolitan areas, that of child mobility with children permitted entry at any age.
- *Parental involvement*—Parents are involved at a variety of levels of program operation, from administrative decisions to direct involvement in the classroom. Most important is the expectation that one parent will devote about one-half day per week to involvement in the center's activities.
- *Systematic, mastery-based inst uction in basic skills*—The continuity of the program allows for careful control of the cognitive entry level of the students from one year to the next. The center utilizes the DISTAR Instructional System (Becker 1978), which stresses the utilization of cues, participation opportunities, rewards, and a major emphasis on feedback and correctives.

Two contrast schools were included in the study's design. The first had a strong emphasis in systematic instruction (Contrast I) and the second being a typical urban elementary school, having a variety of special programs, but lacking any continuity in their implementation (Contrast II). The three schools were comparable at the classroom level by geographic location, race, parent education, poverty level, student mobility, and attendance. Due to the controls on student mobility and attendance, four of the nine control classrooms were the top ability groups at their grade level. The cross-sectional design of the study is presented in Table 21-1, which specifies the numbers of students and parents who participated in the study, as well as the student's current reading achievement.

The second contextual variable in the development of the model was the student's achievement within the instructional group. Using school records, achievement was assessed both in terms of current achievement within class (teacher's rating of students relative to class peers) and standardized achievement in reading (Iowa Test of Basic Skills).

Table 21-1. Student and Parent Sample Sizes, Reading Achievement Percentiles, and Home Concern and Support Statistics.

School Membership	*Data Designation*	*Grade Level* 1	2	3	4	5	6
	Student *N*	20	21	19	25	25	29
High	Parent *N*	18	18	19	25	21	29
quality of	Reading %tile	–	54	55	48	49	49
instruction	HCS[a] $\overline{X}$	148.8	151.5	145.4	150.4	145.2	150.4
	HCS S.D.	20.3	12.5	15.2	18.4	16.1	13.9
	Student *N*	–	25	–	26	–	28
Contrast I	Parent *N*	–	–	–	–	–	–
(systematic	Reading %tile	–	79[b]	–	40[b]	–	23
instruction)	HCS $\overline{X}$	–	–	–	–	–	–
	HCS S.D.	–	–	–	–		
	Student *N*	25	26	16	16	24	29
	Parent *N*	22	24	14	15	23	22
Contrast II	Reading %tile	–	–	50[b]	35	31[b]	21
	HCS $\overline{X}$	123.7	127.8	130.6	128.3	130.8	133.5
	HCS S.D.	25.2	19.0	19.6	24.5	25.6	25.5

a. HCS = home concern and support.

b. These classes were the highest ability group for this grade level.

The third and final explanatory context was the amount of home concern and support for the child in school. Home concern and support was assessed in each of the six grades for the high quality of instruction and the second contrast group. A semi-structured inventory was developed, focusing on the alterable characteristics of the home environment. To use a recent distinction, the stress was on the process rather than static characteristics. Parents were asked to complete the inventory either by coming to school or through a visit to the home. The thirty-nine-item instrument was designed to tap four factors—the parents' knowledge and interest in school-related activities, the parents' interaction with the child on school activities, the supportive aspects of the home environment for academic activities, and the parents' belief in the utility of schooling for the child.

In sum, the design permits the investigation of a variable-instructional quality, variable achievement, and variable-home support model. Obviously there exists dependence in this causal network, but the hope was that it would considerably expand the explanatory power of the existing research base which attempts to explain the impact of early school experience on the development of self-concept.

The question now presented concerns the selection of the most appropriate self-concept assessment given the objective of the study. The overriding concern was that a few measures of self-conception should be linked to a broader network of affective variables and indicators from significant others in the student's environment.

Three measures of self-concept were given to all students in the study. Academic self-concept was assessed by both a reference-based and behavior-based approach. The reference-based instrument was Brookover's Self-Concept of Ability Scale (Brookover et al. 1964). It centers on how the student views himself against present and future reference units. The behavior-based scale centers on the specific behavior and feelings within the classroom, not overtly linked to reference standards. An adaption of the School Mathematics Study Group's measure of general academic self-concept was used (Crosswhite 1972). In addition, an assessment of self-concept in non-academic areas was undertaken. In the opinion of many reviews, the Piers–Harris Children's Self-Concept Scale (Piers 1969) has received substantial reliability and validation support. For this study the scale was reduced to items in which the school might play a causal role; therefore, items dealing with physical attractiveness, for instance, have been excluded. The final measure consists of fifty-four items which reflect a possible transitory function of the school to broader dimensions of self-conception. Among the factors that remain in the scale were self-derogatory behavior, general anxiety, social competence, satisfaction with self, and family esteem.

The instruments were administered to the students in groups of three. Each item was read to the students, with possible confusing items explained by the investigator. A series of item-analysis procedures was conducted to test the appropriateness of the instruments for the age span under investigation, resulting in a number of scale revisions. Considering the cross-age comparisons that were planned, this was a crucial validating procedure.

In addition to the student measures, parents and teachers were asked to complete a behavior symptom report devised by Glidewell (1968) for screening of potential cases of maladjustment and inadequate self-esteem in elementary school children. The hope was to gain some concurrent validity from the significant others in the child's immediate environment. The symptoms centered on antisocial behavior, developmental problems, intrapersonal distress, and interpersonal ineptness. These ratings were supplemented by a series of teacher ratings of the student's mental health and resources (Stringer and Glidewell 1967).

THE RESULTS

The first issue addressed was the adequacy of the self-concept measures for the samples investigated in terms of their psychometric data, relationship to the ratings of other sources, and relationship to other kindred affective measures. In terms of internal consistency, the measures only approach the figures reported in the literature at the fifth and sixth grade levels (.77–.81). The item discrimination statistics aided in the elimination of certain questionable items. In general, it approaches a median of .45, which is quite adequate for discrimination purposes, and exhibited little change over the three age groups. The three tests were given to small samples of students on two occasions, four weeks apart, and the test–retest coefficients were exceptional ($r = .68–.78$) given the internal consistency estimates. Such psychometric evidence is critical given the developmental questions under investigation.

Another approach to verifying the dependability and accuracy of the student measures is to obtain parallel information from their significant others—parents and teachers. The resources inventory was completed by the teachers for each student, which focuses on positive affective qualities rather than the negative orientation of the symptom checklist, and had the highest cross-validity with the student measures. In general, the parent and teacher scales correlated with the self-concept scores with an $r = .25-.30$. It should also be noted that the three self-concept measures were strongly interdependent across the six grades with correlations ranging from $r = .25-.58$. There was no reason to exclude any of the self-concept measures due to poor convergent validity.

The next question addressed the inter-relationships among the three contextual variables. These results are presented on Table 21–2. It was predicted that the quality of instruction (Quality of Instruction = 1, 2, 3, depending on school membership) would be an increasingly strong predictor of standardized achievement over the early years of schooling while it would be a weak determinant of relative student achievement, that is, teacher's grades. The first column of Table 21–2 shows a strong correlation between school membership and standardized reading achievement at both the third and fourth grades ($r = .40$) and fifth and sixth grades ($r = .45$). The relationship of school and relative achievement is negligible at grades one and two and five and six, and is barely significant at grades three and four, which is expected given that it was measured by student rank within class.

The next inquiry concerning the inter-relationships among the three contextual variables was aimed at confirming the strong relationships noted in previous research between home environment and student achievement. As predicted, the home support variable was significantly linked to relative achievement; however, it is inconsistent, as shown on Table 21–2 [$r = .27$ (grades one and two), $r = .43$ (three and four), $r = .22$ (five and six)]. The results for standardized achievement, although incomplete due to lack of measures at the first and second grade levels, suggests that there exists a strong relationship between home concern and support and standardized achievement at both the third and fourth, and fifth and sixth grades ($r = .55$ and $.56$, respectively).

Somewhat surprising was the strong relationship between home concern and level of quality of instruction received by the students.

Table 21–2. Intercorrelations of School, Home, and Achievement Variables.

Contextual Variables	*Quality of Instruction (QI)*	*Home Concern and Support (HCS)*	*Relative Standing in Reading (RSR)*	*Standardized Achievement in Reading (SAR)*
Grades 1–2 (N = 117)				
Quality of instruction	1.0			
Home concern and support	.52[b]	1.0		
Relative standing in reading	.05	.27[a]	1.0	
Standardized achievement in reading	—	—	—	1.0
Grades 3–4 (N = 92)				
Quality of instruction	1.0			
Home concern and support	.44[c]	1.0		
Relative standing in reading	.26[b]	.43[c]	1.0	
Standardized achievement in reading	.40[c]	.55[c]	.65[c]	1.0
Grades 5–6 (N = 134)				
Quality of instruction	1.0			
Home concern and support	.36[c]	1.0		
Relative standing in reading	.15	.22[a]	1.0	
Standardized achievement in reading	.45[c]	.56[c]	.46[c]	1.0

a. $p < .05$.
b. $p < .01$.
c. $p < .001$.

Contrary to our expectation of a gradual sharpening of differences between the schools, the differences were already quite large at the first and second grades, quite likely the result of a strong parent program in the preschool years for the high quality of instruction group. The correlations on Table 21-2 suggest that home concern and support became slightly more similar [$r = .52$ (first and second grades), $r = .44$ (third and fourth), $r = .36$ (fifth and sixth)]. This intertwining of quality of instruction and home concern, a problem noted in many recent studies of home-school interactions, presents itself as a confounding factor in the analyses to follow.

The third major question involves the relationship of instructional quality to the affective network. It was believed that the quality of instruction (i.e., school membership) is an increasingly strong determinant of both academic and non-academic self-concept over the early years of schooling. A large portion of the impact of instruction is likely to be channeled through achievement, but it was thought that additional variation in affect would be accounted for by the instructional variable. The data for this question are presented in column one of Table 21-3. In addition, the plots of the three self-concept variables for each grade level and at the three levels of instructional quality are depicted in Figure 21-1. For academic self-concept reference-based, the exact opposite of the hypothesis would hold, that is, there would be a gradual convergence over the six grade levels. This result is understandable given its emphasis on self-comparison to the relative anchors of the student's class and friends. The use of this instrument should be questioned for any purpose other than within-class prediction. For academic self-concept behavior-based there exists both a strong grade level and school effect. This was exactly the pattern of development that was predicted, a gradual divergence between the instructional settings [$r = .13$ (1-2), $r = .20$ (3-4), $r = .42$ (5-6)]. For non-academic self-concept, the relationship with the quality of instruction is significant throughout [$r = .44$ (1-2), $r = .25$ (3-4), $r = .37$ (5-6)]. It is clear from these results that the quality of instruction is a strong determinant of the self-concept network. However, these analyses do not permit any inference as to the developmental patterns due to conflicting trends in the data.

The next issue concerns the relationship between home concern and support to the self-concept variables. To date, little evidence is available on this question with even less on developmental research.

Table 21–3. Correlation Between Explanatory Contexts and the Self-Concept Measures.

Affective Variables	*Quality of Instruction (QI)*	*Home Concern and Support (HCS)*	*Relative Standing in Reading (RSR)*	*Standardized Achievement in Reading (SAR)*
Grades 1–2 (N = 117)				
Academic self-concept-reference	.39[c]	.36[b]	.07	
Academic self-concept-behavior	.13	.14	.15	
Non-academic self-concept	.44[c]	.42[b]	.25[b]	
Grades 3–4 (N = 92)				
Academic self-concept-reference	.12	.15	.29[b]	.09
Academic self-concept-behavior	.20[a]	.25[a]	.49[c]	.35[b]
Non-academic self-concept	.25[a]	.36[b]	.25[a]	.21
Grades 5–6 (N = 134)				
Academic self-concept-reference	.09	.19	.31[b]	.42[c]
Academic self-concept-behavior	.42[c]	.13	-.03	.37[c]
Non-academic self-concept	.37[c]	.28[b]	.18	.40[c]

a. $p < .05$.
b. $p < .01$.
c. $p < .001$.

Figure 21–1. School by Grade Comparisons for the Three Self-Concept Measures.

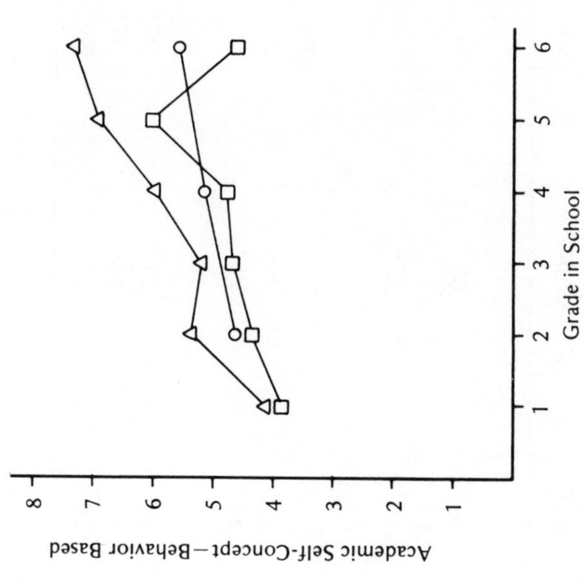

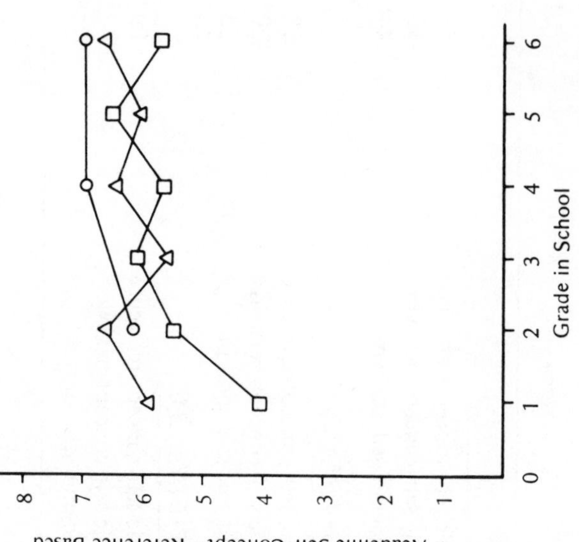

School, F = 12.6[a]
Grade, F = 4.5[a]
S X G, F = 3.5[b]

Figure 21–1. continued

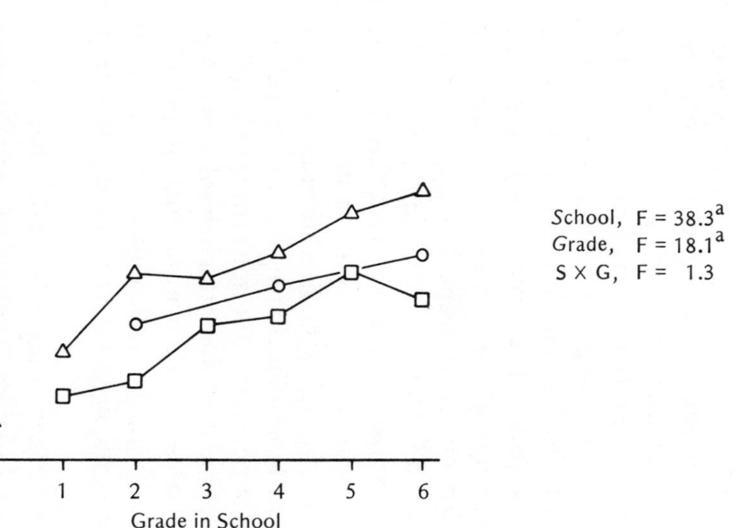

△ High Quality of Instruction
○ Contrast I
□ Contrast II

a. Significant at $p < .001$.
b. Significant at $p < .01$.
c. Significant at $p < .05$.

As can be seen in Table 21–3 it becomes clear that constant impact of home concern and support over the six grade levels on self-concept is not the rule. The general trend is for the impact of home to decline as time in school increases. For academic self-concept reference-based the relationship is strong at the early grades, but the effect diminishes at the fifth and sixth grade level. Academic self-concept behavior has little relationship to the home index at the first and second and fifth and sixth grade levels, but is significantly linked in the third and fourth grades. The decreasing effect of the home also is seen with non-academic self-concept. These results are the opposite of the previous hypothesis concerning the significance of the quality of instruction on self-concept development. One speculation at this point is the need for home support in the early school years to promote positive personal growth, but that this foundation of support must be supplemented by a positive instructional environment as a child progresses through school. Unfortunately, such a causal argument must await longitudinal analysis. It would also appear that the home might be a necessary but not sufficient condition for positive affective development in the latter school years. Again, there is no way of tracing back home environments of the older students who seem to benefit from the quality of instruction to see whether a supportive home is required for the instructional impact to take effect.

Now attention is shifted to the relationship between achievement and the self-concept variables. The achievement variables to be discussed include the student's relative and standardized achievement in reading. Given the past research on this topic, it was predicted that the relationship between achievement and self-concept would increase over the six years of schooling. As shown in Table 21–3, there is a slight trend for the relative achievement to be most powerful in the third and fourth grades, but decline at the fifth and sixth grade level. The exception to this is academic self-concept reference-based which is strongly linked to class rank at the fifth–sixth grade level. Standardized reading achievement was available only at the third through sixth grades, and shows an increasingly powerful relationship to the three self-concept measures. Although not reported in here, the entire set of nine affective variables points to a gradual trend for the affective variables to move from a base linked to the relative standards of the classroom to a base linked to more absolute standards early in their school career, particularly when the necessary standards of self-comparison are developed. But with increased time in school, this factor is not enough. Their conception of academic and non-academic self is increasingly related to more absolute achievement standards.

The final question of this study involves the power of the entire model. It was believed that mutual impact of the contextual variables will be of greater explanatory power than the analyses of separate contextual variables. It should be clear that the investigation of the effects of multiple contexts adds greatly to the external validity of the study, representing a more ecological framework that should enhance the construction of educational policy. The contextual variables will include quality of instruction, home concern, and relative achievement. Standardized achievement was not included in this model because of its overlap with the school variable and its availability at only the third through sixth grade levels. To begin to develop some evidence on this question, a stepwise multiple regression was performed at each of the three age categories, and the results are shown in Table 21-4.

A significant finding is the increasingly strong power of the instructional quality compared to the relative achievement and home concern. For academic self-concept-behavior based and nonacademic self-concept, the school is the major determining variable at the fifth-sixth grade level, taking over the earlier role of relative achievement and home concern. As with previous analyses, the academic self-concept-reference based continues to be primarily controlled by the relative achievement standing. Although not reported here, the general trend in testing all nine affective variables was that the school is able to take over the earlier positive impact of the home and relative achievement. This fact has major policy implications concerning the impact, timing, and type of intervention strategies appropriate for elementary school children.

IMPLICATIONS

The results of this study point to some conclusions about the nature and cause of self-concept development in the elementary school years. Given that the study was a local experiment focused on a relatively narrow range of students and parents, any conclusions must be dealt with cautiously in terms of generalization to other populations.

Table 21–4. Stepwise Regressions for Mutual Impact of Contextual Variables on the Self-Concept Measures.

	Grades 1–2 (N = 92)			
Affective Variables (Dependent)	*Independent Variables (IND. VAR.)*	*Standardized Beta (SB)*	*t-test (t)*	*Multiple Correlation (R)*
Academic self-concept-referenced based	1) School	.397	4.10[f]	.397
	2) School	.289	2.58[d]	
	HCS[a]	.205	1.83	.433
	3) School	.326	2.81[e]	
	HCS	.164	1.40	
	Reading[b]	.120	1.19	.448
Academic self-concept-behavior based	1) Reading	.225	2.19[d]	.225
	2) Reading	.232	2.26[d]	
	School	.141	1.38	.265
Non-academic self-concept	1) School	.441	4.66[f]	.441
	2) School	.453	4.94[f]	
	Reading	.246	2.69[e]	.505
	3) School	.355	3.25[e]	
	Reading	.193	1.99[d]	
	HCS	.182	1.60	.525

a. HCS = Home concern and support.

b. Reading = Relative standing within class in reading.

c. Math = Relative standing within class in math.

d. $p < .05$.

e. $p < .01$.

f. $p < .001$

Table 21–4. continued

Grades 3-4 (N = 76)				*Grades 5-6 (N = 106)*			
IND. VAR.	*S.B.*	*t*	*R*	*IND. VAR.*	*S.B.*	*t*	*R*
1) Reading	.354	3.26[e]	.354	1) Reading	.417	4.79[f]	.417
2) Reading	.536	2.72[e]		2) Reading	.485	5.47[f]	
Math[c]	-.218	-1.11	.374	School	.232	2.62[d]	.473
1) Reading	.534	5.44[e]	.534	1) School	.415	4.76[f]	.416
				2) School	.433	4.88[f]	
				Math	-.087	-.98	.425
1) HCS	.356	3.28[e]	.356	1) School	.369	4.15[e]	.369
2) HCS	.305	2.53[d]		2) School	.308	3.26[e]	
Reading	.120	.99	.372	HCS	.171	1.81	.402
3) HCS	.329	2.86[e]					
Reading	.569	2.97[e]					
Math	-.551	-2.93[e]	.480				

It was purposely a study of schooling extremes aimed at teasing out the possible range of effects on the self-concept profiles of students. It is likely that its main outcome will be more refined investigation of this rather broad research problem. The hope was to enhance past conceptualizations of the affective consequences of schooling experience. It centered more on increasing understanding, rather than developing a precise prediction model.

The implications of the study are aimed to counteract the recent discussions concerning the effects of schooling on students. If the results presented in this document are verified in future analyses, this might hopefully communicate something to policy-makers contemplating the relative costs and benefits of effective instructional strategies and home education efforts. In their arguments they must consider far more than the immediate cognitive benefits and must center more on the affective variables that are likely to be altered as well. Early school experience provides an unrivaled opportunity not only to establish a favorable attitude toward learning and the development of competence on the basic skills but also, where necessary, to improve the foundations for a child's development of mental health. Early school environments are alterable and can be changed to enhance such development.

It was shown that the history of the learner is a critical variable for understanding not only academic growth but also personal growth. Intervention programs must be supported over a wide span of early schooling to show significant impact on such growth. It is likely that individual teachers did not notice any change in the affective profiles of these students during a single year. It is only through a broader developmental perspective that divergence in self-concept development is noticed. Educators must be willing and able to invest in long-term efforts, otherwise the effects of limited interventions will not have time to emerge or fade away because they will not have time to stabilize. In areas where the school is the one outlet in an environment that lacks other societal supports, as is the case in many of our urban areas, long-term intervention can become a vital lever toward positive affective development if structured properly.

The study also points to a reconception of the home environment within a single level of social-economic status. A wide range of variation exists in home environments within levels of such static variables; the results point to individual differences there that are wide and adaptive. When we focus on alterable home process variables, we find impact within a low social class group on both achievement and affective outcomes. The notion of a "culture of poverty" that is unable to provide support for school performance is incorrect. This study suggests that parents can change specific aspects of their home environment. Specific techniques to engage parents to participate in home education efforts should be a major concern for future research. This research supports parent education programs that center on such alterable characteristics and suggests they can have important consequences for the child's early school career.

Finally, it seems unlikely that most teachers can be trained to become experts in mental health delivery, as is called for by many recent affective curriculum models. This is particularly the case since relatively little is known about the affective consequences of current school environments. It is far more likely that teachers will be able to gain the necessary skills to implement instructional techniques which will produce adequate achievement in their students. Such techniques are now available and have been proved effective in increasing academic competence in basic skills. It is strongly believed that the development of such academic competence can play a therapeutic role in students' lives. It was the hope that this research project could begin to document what the ramifications of such consistent positive instruction and home support over the early years of schooling are on the development of self-concept.

REFERENCES

Abelson, R. 1976. "Script Processing in Attitude Formation and Decision-Making." In *Cognitive and Social Behavior*, edited by J.S. Carroll and J.W. Payne. Hillsdale, N.J.: Lawrence Erlbaum Associates, pp. 33–45.

Adelson, J., and J.J. Doehrman. 1980. "The Psychodynamic Approach to Adolescence." In *Handbook of Adolescent Psychology*, edited by J. Adelson, pp. 99–116. New York: John Wiley and Sons.

Adkins, D.C., and B.L. Ballif. 1975. *Animal Crackers: A Test of Motivation to Achieve.* Monterey: CTB/McGraw-Hill.

____. 1972. "A New Approach to Response Sets in Analysis of a Test of Motivation to Achieve." *Educational and Psychological Measurement* edited by Frederic Kuder, 32: 559–577.

____. 1971. *Motivation Rating Scale.* Honolulu: University of Hawaii.

____. 1970. "Motivation to Achieve in School." Final report on contract OEO B 89-4576 and OEO 4121. Washington, D.C.: Office of Economic Opportunity.

Adkins, D.C.; F. Payne; and B.L. Ballif. 1972. "Motivation Factor Scores and Response Set Scores for Ten Ethnic-Cultural Groups of Preschool Children." *American Educational Research Journal* 9: 557–572.

Allen, V. ed. 1970. *Psychological Factors in Poverty.* Chicago: Markham.

Allport, G.W. 1961. *Pattern and Growth in Personality.* (2nd rev. ed.) New York: Holt.

____. 1961. *Becoming: Basic Considerations for a Psychology of Personality.* New Haven: Yale University Press.

Alschuler, A.; G. Weinstein; J. Evans; R. Tamashiro; and W. Smith. 1977. "Education for What? Self Knowledge and Levels of Consciousness Can Be Measured." *Journal of Simulations and Games.*

Ames, L.B. 1952. "The Sense of Self of Nursery School Children as Manifested by Their Verbal Behavior." *Journal of Genetic Psychology* 81(9): 193–232.

Amsterdam, B., and L.M. Greenberg. 1977. "Self-Conscious Behavior in Infants: A Videotape Study." *Developmental Psychobiology* 10: 1–6.

Amsterdam, B.K. 1968. "Mirror Behavior in Children Under 2 Years of Age." Unpublished doctoral dissertation, University of North Carolina.

Anderson, C. 1978. *Personal and Family Financial Education.* Presented at Staff Development Workshops, SUNY at Albany.

Anderson, R.B. 1977. *Education as Experimentation: A Planned Variation Model.* Cambridge, Mass.: Abt Associates.

Anderson, J.G., and F.B. Evans. 1974. "Causal Models in Educational Research: Recursive Models." *American Educational Research Journal* 11: 29–39.

Arbuckle, D.W. 1958. "Self Ratings and Test Scores on Two Standardized Personality Inventories." *Personnel and Guidance Journal* 37: 292–293.

Aronfreed, J. 1968. *Conduct and Conscience.* New York: Academic Press.

Asher, H.B. 1976. *Causal Modeling.* Beverly Hills: Sage Publications.

Asimov, I. 1973. *The Tragedy of the Moon.* New York: Dell Publishing Co.

Atkinson, J.W. 1964. *An Introduction to Motivation.* Princeton: Van Nostrand.

Atkinson, J.W., and J.O. Raynor. 1978. *Personality, Motivation and Achievement.* New York: John Wiley and Sons.

Auer, H.J.M. 1971. "Self-Concept of Academic Ability of West German Eighth Grade Students." Ph. D. dissertation, Michigan State University.

Back, K.W., and K.J. Gergen. 1968. "The Self Through the Latter Span of Life." In *The Self in Social Interaction*, vol. 1: *Classic and Contemporary Perspectives*, edited by C. Gordon and K.J. Gergen, pp. 241–250. New York: John Wiley and Sons.

Bagdikian, B.H. 1971. "How Much More Communication Can We Stand?" *The Futurist* 5: 180–183.

Baldwin, J.M. 1894. *Handbook of Psychology: Feeling and Will.* New York: Holt.

Ballif, B.L. 1977. *MOCOS: Motivation Components for Learning in School.* New York: Ballif Associates, Inc.

____. 1976. *AC-PIE: A Test of Motivation for Learning in School.* New York: Ballif Associates, Inc.

Ballif, B.L., and D.C. Adkins. 1968. *Gumpgookies: A Measure of Motivation to Achieve in School for Children.* Honolulu: University of Hawaii.

Ballif, B.L.; D.C. Adkins; and V. Crane. 1972. "Effects of Experiences Designed To Increase Confidence in Personal Ability To Achieve in Learning in School in Preschool Children." Final report on subcontract with University of Hawaii. New York: Fordham University.

Ballif, B.L., and D. Kramer. 1978. "Five Motivational Thought Patterns Among Junior-High School Students." Paper presented at the meeting of the American Psychological Association, Toronto, Ontario, Canada.

____. 1977. "Forty Curricular Activities Designed To Increase Motivation for Learning in School Among Eighth-Grade Students." Unpublished manuscript, Fordham University.

Baltes, P.B., and G. Reinert. 1969. "Cohort Effects in Cognitive Development of Children as Revealed by Cross-sectional Sequences." *Developmental Psychology* 1: 169-177.

Bandura, A. 1977. "Self-efficacy: Toward a Unifying Theory of Behavioral Change." *Psychological Review* 84: 191-215.

Bandura, A.; N.E. Adams; and J. Beyer. 1977. "Cognitive Processes Mediating Behavioral Change." *Journal of Personality and Social Psychology* 35(3): 125-139.

Bannister, D., and J. Agnew. 1976. "The Child's Construing of Self." In *Nebraska Symposium on Motivation*, vol. 24, edited by J.A. Cole. Lincoln: University of Nebraska Press.

Banks, J.H., and J.H. Wolfson. 1967. "Differential Cardiac Response of Infants to Mother and Stranger." Paper presented at the Eastern Psychological Association meeting, Boston.

Barclay, J.R. 1973. "Multiple Input Assessment and Prevention Intervention." *School Psychology Digest* 2: 13-18.

Barker, R.G.; T. Dembo; and K. Lewin. 1943. "Frustration and Regression in R.G. Barker." In *Child Behavior and Development*, edited by J.S. Kaunis and H.F. Wright, pp. 441-458. New York: McGraw-Hill.

Barron, A. 1953. "An Ego-strength Scale Which Predicts Response to Psychotherapy." *Journal of Consulting Psychology* 17: 327-333.

Baumeister, R.F., and E.E. Jones. 1978. "When Self-Presentation Is Constrained by the Target's Knowledge: Consistency and Compensation." *Journal of Personality and Social Psychology* 36(6): 608-618.

Becker, W. 1978. "Teaching Reading and Language to the Disadvantaged—What We Have Learned from Field Research." Unpublished paper, University of Oregon.

Beiser, M. 1965. "Poverty, Social Disintegration and Personality." *Journal of Social Issues* 21: 56-78.

Bem, D.J. 1972. "Self-Perception Theory." In *Advances in Experimental Social Psychology*, vol. 6, edited by L. Berkowitz, pp. 1-62. New York: Academic Press.

Bentler, P.M. 1978. "The Interdependence of Theory, Methodology and Empirical Data: Causal Modeling as an Approach To Construct Validation." In *Longitudinal Research on Drug Use: Empirical Findings and Methodological Issues*, edited by D.B. Kandel, New York: John Wiley & Sons.

Benton, J.A. 1969. "Perceptual Characteristics of Episcopal Pastors." In *Florida Studies in the Helping Professions*, University of Florida Monographs, Social Sciences No. 37, edited by A.W. Combs. Gainesville: University of Florida Press.

Bercheid, E., and E. Walster. 1974. "A Little Bit about Love." In *Foundations of Interpersonal Attraction*, edited by T. Huston, New York: Academic Press, pp. 355–381.

Berger, E. 1952. "The Relation Between Expressed Acceptance of Self and Expressed Acceptance of Others." *Journal of Abnormal Psychology* 47: 778–782.

Bertenthal, B.I., and H.W. Fischer. 1978. "Development of Self-recognition in the Infant." *Developmental Psychology* 14: 44–50.

Bertocci, P.A. 1945. "The Psychological Self, the Ego, and Personality." In *The Self in Growth, Teaching, and Learning: Selected Readings*, edited by D.E. Hamachek, pp. 14–26. Englewood Cliffs, N.J.: Prentice-Hall.

Bigelow, A. 1975. "A Longitudinal Study of Self-recognition in Young Children." Paper presented at the meeting of the Canadian Psychological Association, Quebec.

Bischof, L.J. 1969. *Adult Psychology*. New York: Harper and Row.

Bixler, P.A. 1965. "Changing Self-concept in Sixth-grade Class Groups. *Dissertation Abstracts* 26: 3750.

Blalock, H.M., Jr. 1964. *Causal Inferences in Nonexperimental Research*. New York: Norton & Co.

Bloom, B. 1976. *Human Characteristics and School Learning*. New York: McGraw-Hill.

Blos, P. 1979. *The Adolescent Passage: Developmental Issues*. New York: International Universities Press.

Blos, P. 1962. *On Adolescence: A Psychoanalytic Interpretation*. New York: Free Press.

Bobroff, A. 1956. "A Survey of Social and Civic Participation of Adults Formerly in Classes for the Mentally Retarded." *American Journal of Mental Deficiency* 61: 127–133.

Bogen, J.E. 1973. "The Other Side of the Brain: An Appositional Mind." In *The Nature of Human Consciousness*, edited by R.E. Ornstein. San Francisco: W.H. Freeman & Company, 101–125.

Bolea, A.S.; M.D. Barnes; and D.W. Felker. 1971. "A Pictoral Self-concept Scale for Children in K–4." *Journal of Educational Measurement* 8: 223–224.

Bolles, R.C. 1975. *Learning Theory*. New York: Holt, Rinehart & Winston.

Borg, W.R. 1966. *Ability Grouping in the Public Schools*. Madison, Wis.: Educational Research Services.

Brackbill, Y. 1958. "Extinction of the Smiling Response in Infants as a Function of Reinforcement Schedule." *Child Development* 29: 115–124.

Braine, M.D. 1963. "The Ontogony of English Phrase Structure: The First Phase." *Language* 39: 1-13.

Brehm, J.W., and A.R. Cohen. 1962. *Explorations in Cognitive Dissonance.* New York: John Wiley & Sons.

Brickman, P.; K. Ryan; and C. Wortman. 1975. "Causal Chains: Attribution of Responsibility as a Function of Immediate and Prior Causes." *Journal of Personality and Social Psychology* 32: 1060-1067.

Bridgeman, B., and V. Shipman. 1975. "Disadvantaged Children and Their First School Experience." Washington, D.C.: Project Head Start, Office for Child Development, U.S. Department of Health Education and Welfare.

____. 1970. "Preschool Measures of Self-esteem and Achievement Motivation as Predictors of Third-grade Achievement." *Journal of Educational Psychology* 70: 17-28.

Brim, O. 1976. *A National Policy for Children.* Washington, D.C.: National Research Council.

Brookover, W.B.; C. Beady; A. Flood; J. Schweitzer; and J. Wisenbaker. 1979. *School Social Systems and Student Achievement: Schools Can Make a Difference.* New York: J.F. Bergin.

Brookover, W.B.; E. Erickson; L. Joiner; and P. Paterson. 1962, 1965, 1967. "Self-concept of Ability and School Achievement, I, II, III, Report of Cooperative Research Project No. 1636, U.S. Office of Education, entitled, "Improving Academic Achievement Through Self-Concept Enhancement." East Lansing: Bureau of Educational Research Services, College of Education, Michigan State University.

Brookover, W.B.; A. Paterson; and S. Thomas. 1962. *Self-concept of Ability and School Achievement*, U.S.O.E. Cooperative Research Report, Project No. 845. East Lansing: Michigan State University.

Brookover, W.B.; T. Shailer; and A. Paterson. 1964. "Self-concept and School Achievement." *Sociology of Education* 37: 271-278.

Brooks, J., and M. Lewis. 1976. "Infants' Responses to Strangers: Midget, Adult & Child." *Child Development* 47: 323-332.

Brooks-Gunn, J., and M. Lewis. 1979. "The Effects of Age and Sex on Infants' Playroom Behavior." *Journal of Genetic Psychology* 134: 99-105.

____. 1978. "Early Social Knowledge: The Development of Knowledge About Others." In *Issues in Childhood Social Development*, edited by H. McGurk. London: Methuen, 79-106.

Bronfenbrenner, U. 1979. *The Ecology of Human Development.* Cambridge, Mass.: Harvard University Press.

____. 1977. "Toward an Experimental Ecology of Human Development." *American Psychologist* 32(7): 513-531.

Bronson, G.W. 1972. "Infants' Reactions to Unfamiliar Persons and Novel Objects." *Monographs of the Society for Research in Child Development* 47(148).

Brown, R.G. 1970. "A Study of the Perceptual Organization of Elementary and Secondary Outstanding Young Educators." Ph. D. dissertation, University of Florida.

Brown, W.F., and W.H. Holtzman. 1964. *SSHA Manual: Survey of Study Habits and Attitudes.* New York: The Psychological Corporation.

Bruner, J.S. 1973. *Beyond the Information Given.* Toronto: McLeod Limited.

Bruner, J.S., and H.J. Kenney. 1965. "Representation and Mathematics Learning." *Monographs of the Society for Research in Child Development* 30(1): 50–59.

Bruner, J.S., and R. Tagiuri. 1954. "The Perception of People." In *Handbook of Social Psychology*, vol. 2, edited by G. Lindzey, pp. 601–633. Cambridge, Mass.: Addison-Wesley.

Bugental, J.F.T. 1964. "Investigations into the Self-concept, III: Instructions for the W-A-Y Method." *Psychological Report* 15: 643–650.

____. 1949. "An Investigation of the Relationship of the Conceptual Matrix to the Self-concept." *Abstract Doctoral Dissertation* 57: 27–33.

Bugental, J.F.T., and S.L. Zelen. 1950. "Investigations into the "Self-concept." I: The W-A-Y Technique." *Journal of Personality* 18: 483–498.

Burke, P.J. 1980. "The Self: Measurement Requirements from an Interactional Perspective." *Social Psychology Quarterly* 43: 18–29.

Butler, R.N. 1975. *Why Survive? Being Old in America.* New York: Harper & Row.

Cady, H.L. 1967. "Toward a Definition of Music Education." In *A Conference on Research in Music Education, A Final Report*, edited by H.L. Cady. Columbus: Ohio State University.

Calsyn, R.J., and D.A. Kenny. 1977. "Self-concept of Ability and Perceived Evaluation of Others: Cause or Effect of Academic Achievement." *Journal of Educational Psychology* 69(2): 136–145.

Campbell, D.T., and D.W. Fiske. 1959. "Validation by the Multitrait-multimethod Matrix." *Psychological Bulletin* 56: 81–105.

Campbell, D.T., and J.C. Stanley. 1963. "Experimental and Quasi-experimental Designs for Research on Teaching." In *Handbook of Research on Teaching*, edited by N.L. Gage, pp. 171–246. Chicago: Rand McNally.

Capra, F. 1977. *The Tao of Physics.* New York: Bantam Books.

Carlson, R. 1965. "Stability and Change in the Adolescent's Self-image." *Child Development* 36: 659–666.

Carroll, L. 1968. *Alice's Adventures in Wonderland and Through the Looking-glass.* New York: Lancer Books, Inc.

Chandler, M.J. 1977. "Social Cognition: A Selective Review of Current Research." In *Knowledge and Development: Advances in Research and Theory*, vol. 1, edited by W.F. Overton and J.M. Gallagher. New York: Plenum, pp. 93–147.

Chang, T.S. 1976. "Self-concepts, Academic Achievement, and Teacher Ratings." *Psychology in the Schools* 13: 111–115.

Chiriboga, D., and M. Thurnher. 1975. "Concept of Self." In *Four Stages of Life: A Comparative Study of Women and Men Facing Transitions*, edited by M. Fiske-Lowenthal, M. Thurnher, and D. Chiriboga, pp. 62–83. San Francisco: Jossey-Bass.

Chomsky, N. 1967. "The Formal Nature of Language." In *Biological Foundations of Language*, edited by E. Lenneberg, pp. 397–442. New York: John Wiley and Sons.

Christie, R., and F.L. Geis. 1970. *Studies in Machiavellianism.* New York: Academic Press.

Cicourel, A. 1968. *The Social Organization of Juvenile Justice.* New York: John Wiley and Sons.

Cobb, H.V. 1970. "The Attitude of the Retarded Person Toward Himself." In *Social Work and Mental Retardation*, edited by Meyer Schribner, pp. 125–136. New York: The Job Day Co.

Coleman, J.C. 1977. "Current Contradictions in Adolescent Theory." *Journal of Youth and Adolescence* 7: 1–11.

Coller, A.R. 1971. *The Assessment of Self Concept in Early Childhood Education.* Urbana: ERIC Clearinghouse on Early Childhood Education, University of Illinois.

Combs, A.W.; C.S. Courson; and D.W. Soper. 1963. "The Measurement of Self Concept and Self Report. *Educational and Psychological Measurement* 23: 439–500.

Combs, A.W.; A.C. Richards; and F. Richards. 1976. *Perceptual Psychology: A Humanistic Approach to the Study of Persons.* New York: Harper & Row.

Combs, A.W., and D.W. Soper. 1969. "The Perceptual Organization of Effective Counselors." In *Florida Studies in the Helping Professions*, University of Florida Monographs, Social Sciences No. 37, edited by A.W. Combs. Gainesville, Fla.: University of Florida Press.

____. 1963. *The Relationship of Child Perceptions to Achievement and Behavior in the Early School Years*, Cooperative Research Project No. 814. Washington, D.C.: Office of Education.

____. 1963. "Perceptual Organization of Effective Counselors." *Journal of Counseling Psychology* 10: 222–226.

____. 1957. "The Self, its Derivative Terms, and Research." *Journal of Individual Psychology* 13: 134–145.

Combs, A.W., and D. Snygg. 1959. *Individual Behavior: A Perceptual Approach to Behavior*, 2nd rev. ed. New York: Harper.

Cooley, C.H. 1972 (originally published in 1909). *Social Organization: A Study of the Larger Mind.* New York: Schocken Books.

____. 1968 (originally published in 1902). "The Social Self: On the Meanings of "I." In *The Self in Social Interaction*, vol. I: *Classic and Contemporary Perspectives*, edited by C. Gordon and K.J. Gergen, pp. 87–91. New York: John Wiley and Sons.

____. 1922. *Human Nature and the Social Order* (revised). New York: Scribner's Sons.

Coopersmith, S. 1977. "Self Concept Development in Infancy," paper presented at the meeting of the American Psychological Association, San Francisco.

____. 1967. *The Antecedents of Self Esteem.* San Francisco: W.H. Freeman.

____. 1959. "A Method for Determining Types of Self-esteem." *Journal of Abnormal and Social Psychology* 59: 87–94.

Cornielson, I.S., and I. Arsenian. 1960. "A Study of the Responses of Psychotic Patients to Photographic Self Image Experience." *Psychiatric Quarterly* 34: 1–8.

Cornfield, J., and J. Tukey. 1956. "Average Values of Mean Squares in Factorials." *Annals of Mathematical Statistics* 27: 907–949.

Coser, R.L. 1960. "A Home Away from Home." In *Sociological Studies of Health and Sickness*, edited by D. Apple. New York: McGraw-Hill, pp. 154–172.

Costanzo, P.R. 1970. "Conformity Development as a Function of Self-blame." *Journal of Personality and Social Psychology* 14: 366–374.

Cottrell, L.S. 1969. "Interpersonal Interaction and the Development of the Self." In *Handbook of Socialization Theory and Research*, edited by D.Z. Goslin, , pp. 543–570. Chicago: Rand McNally.

Courson, C. 1968. "Personal Adequacy and Self Perception in High School Students: A Study of Behavior and Internal Perceptual Factors." *Journal of Humanistic Psychology* 8: 29–38.

____. 1963. "The Relationship of Certain Perceptual Factors to Adequacy." Ph. D. dissertation, University of Florida.

Cowen, E.L.; D. Don; et al. 1973. "The AML: A Quick-screening Device for Early Identification of School Maladjustments." *American Journal of Community Psychology* 1: 12–35.

Crandall, V.C., and V.J. Crandall. 1965. "A Children's Social Desirability Questionnaire." *Journal of Consulting Psychology* Feb.: 29, pp. 27–36.

Cronbach, L.J. August 1978. Personal communication.

____. 1975. "Beyond the Two Disciplines of Scientific Psychology." *American Psychologist* 29: 116–127.

____. 1971. "Test Validation." In *Educational Measurement*, edited by R.L. Thorndike, Washington, D.C.: American Council on Education, pp. 443–507.

Cronbach, L.J., and P.E. Meehl. 1955. "Construct Validity in Psychological Tests." *Psychological Bulletin* 52: 281–302.

Crosswhite, F.J. 1972. "Correlates of Attitudes Towards Mathematics." In *The National Longitudinal Study of Mathematics*, edited by E.G. Begle and J.W. Wilson. Palo Alto: School Mathematics Study Group. Report No. 20.

Crowne, D., and D. Marlowe. 1964. *The Approval Motive.* New York: John Wiley and Sons.

Crowne, D.P., and M.W. Stephens. 1961. "Self-acceptance and Self-evaluating Behavior: A Critique of Methodology." *Psychological Bulletin* 58: 104–121.

Damon, W. 1977. *The Social World of the Child.* San Francisco: Jossey-Bass.

Darwin, C. 1965 (originally published in 1895). *The Expression of Emotions in Man and Animals.* Chicago: University of Chicago Press.

Davies, E. 1968. "Needs, Wants, and Consistency." In *Theories of Cognitive Consistency: A Sourcebook*, edited by P. Abelson et al. Chicago: Rand McNally.

Dawkins, R. 1976. *The Selfish Gene.* New York: Oxford University Press.

Dedrick, C.V.L. 1972. "The Relationship Between Perceptual Characteristics and Effective Teaching at the Junior College Level." Ph. D. dissertation, University of Florida.

Deese, M.E. 1971. "Self-concept and Predictability of Behavior." Ph. D. dissertation, Auburn University.

Deikman, A.J. 1966. "De-automatization and the Mystic Experience." *Psychiatry* 29: 324–338.

Dellow, D.A. 1971. "A Study of the Perceptual Organization of Teachers and Conditions of Empathy, Congruence, and Positive Regard." Ph. D. dissertation, University of Florida.

Deutch, M., and R.M. Krauss. 1960. "The Effect of Threat on Interpersonal Bargaining." *Journal of Abnormal and Social Psychology* 61: 181–189.

Dewey, D., 3d. 1978. "Motivational Patterns of Retirement-aged Adults Participating in College." Ph. D. dissertation, Fordham University.

Dickman, J.F. 1969. "Perceptual Organization of Person-oriented and Task-oriented Student Nurses." In *Florida Studies in the Helping Professions*, University of Florida Monographs, Social Sciences No. 27, edited by A.W. Combs. Gainesville, Fla.: University of Flordia Press.

Dolan, L. 1978. "The Process of Cognitive and Affective Development in the Context of the Home and School Environment." Paper presented at the First Annual Meeting of the Eastern Educational Research Association, Williamsburg, Virginia, March 7–8.

Dollard, J.; L. Doob; W. Miller; O. Mowrer; and R. Sears. 1939. *Frustration and Aggression.* New Haven: Yale University Press.

Dooley, C.H. 1902. *Human Nature and the Social Order.* New York: Scribner.

Douvan, E., and J. Adelson. 1966. *The Adolescent Experience.* New York: John Wiley and Sons.

Doyle, E.J. 1969. "The Relationship Between College Teacher Effectiveness and Inferred Characteristics of the Adequate Personality." Ph. D. dissertation, University Northern Colorado.

Duncan, O.D. 1975. *Introduction to Structural Equation Models.* New York: Academic Press.

Durkheim, E. 1958. *Suicide.* New York: Free Press.

DuVal, S., and R. Wicklund. 1972. *A Theory of Objective Self-awareness.* New York: Academic Press.

Dweck, C.S.; W. Davidson; S. Nelson; and B. Enna. 1978. "Sex Differences in Learned Helplessness; II: The Contingencies of Evaluative Feedback in the Classroom, and III: An Experimental Analysis." *Developmental Psychology* 14(3): 268–276.

Dymond, R.F.; A.S. Hughes; and V.L. Raabe. 1952. "Measurable Changes in Empathy with Age." *Journal of Consulting Psychology* 16: 202–206.

Eklof, K.R.A. 1972. "Validation of a Component Theory of Motivation to Achieve in School Among Adolescents." Ph.D. dissertation, Fordham University.

Elder, G.H., Jr. 1974. *Children of the Great Depression.* Chicago: University of Chicago Press.

Engel, M. 1959. "The Stability of the Self-concept in Adolescence." *Journal of Abnormal and Social Psychology* 58: 211–215.

Epstein, S. 1980. "The Self-concept: A Review and the Proposal of an Integrated Theory of Personality." In *Personality: Basic Issues and Current Research*, edited by E. Staub. Englewood Cliffs, N.J.: Prentice Hall.

____. 1979. "Natural Healing Processes of the Mind: I. Acute Schizophrenic Disorganization." *Schizophrenia Bulletin* 5: 313–321.

____. 1976. "Anxiety, Arousal, and the Self-concept." In *Stress and Anxiety*, vol. 3, edited by I.G. Sarason and C.D. Spielberger. Washington, D.C.: Hemisphere.

____. 1973. "The Self-concept Revisited, *or* A Theory of a Theory." *American Psychologist* 28: 404–416.

Erikson, E.H. 1968. *Identity, Youth and Crisis.* New York: W.W. Norton.

____. 1963. *Childhood and Society* (2nd ed.). New York: Norton.

____. 1959. "The Growth and Crisis of the Healthy Personality." In *Psychological Issues: Identity and the Life Cycle*, vol. 1. No. 1 monograph 1. N.Y.: International Universities Press.

____. 1951. "A Healthy Personality for Every Child, A Fact Finding Report: A Digest." Mid Century White House Conference on Children and Youth. Raleigh, N.C.: Health Publications Institute.

Erickson, E.L.; L. Joiner; V. Stevenson; and L. Alonzo. 1967. *Scales and Procedures for Assessing Hearing-impaired and Visually Impaired Students*, U.S.O.E. Cooperative Research Project No. 6–8. Kalamazoo: Western Michigan University.

Ervin, S.M., and W.R. Miller. 1963. "Language Development." In *Child Psychology (62nd Yearbook, Nat. Soc. Stud. Educ.)*, edited by H. Stevenson, pp. 108–143. Chicago: University of Chicago Press.

Faris, E. 1940. "The Retrospective Act." *Journal of Educational Sociology* 14: 79–91.

Faris, R.E.L. 1952. *Social Psychology.* New York: Ronald Press.

Felsenthal, D.S. 1977. "Bargaining Behavior When Profits Are Unequal and Losses Are Equal." *Behavioral Science* 22: 234–240.

Fennema, E., and J. Sherman. 1977. "Sex-related Differences in Mathematics Achievement, Spatial Visualization and Affective Factors." *American Educational Research Journal* 14: 51–71.

Fernandez, C.; R.W. Espinosa; and S. Dornbush. 1975. "Factors Perpetuating the Low Academic Status of Chicano High School Students" R&D Memorandum #138. Stanford, Ca.: Stanford Center for Research and Development in Teaching.

Festinger, L. 1957. *A Theory of Cognitive Dissonance.* Evanston, Ill.: Row Peterson.

____. 1954. "A Theory of Social Comparison Processes." *Human Relations* 7: 117–140.

Filipp, V.S.H. 1979. *Selbstkonzept-Forschung: Probleme, Befunde, Perspektiven.* Stuttgart: Klett-Cotta.

Fisher, S., and S.E. Cleveland. 1968. *Body Image and Personality* (2nd rev. ed.). New York: Dover.

Fitts, W.H. 1972a. *The Self Concept and Psychopathology.* Nashville: Counselor Recordings and Tests.

____. 1972b. "The Self Concept and Psychopathology." *Dede Wallace Center Monograph*, No. 4. Nashville, Tennessee.

____. 1972c. "The Self Concept and Performance." *Dede Wallace Center Monograph*, No. 5. Nashville, Tennessee.

____. 1972d. *The Self Concept and Behavior: Overview and Supplement.* Nashville: Counselor Recordings and Tests.

____. 1970. "Interpersonal Competence: The Wheel Model." *Dede Wallace Center Monograph*, No. 2. Nashville, Tennessee.

____. 1965. *The Tennessee Self Concept Scale.* Nashville: Counselor Recordings and Tests.

Fitts, W.H.; J.L. Adama; G. Radford; W.C. Richard; M.M. Thomas; and W. Thompson. 1971. *The Self Concept and Self Actualization.* Nashville: Counselor Recordings and Tests.

Fitts, W.H., and W.T. Hammer. 1969. "The Self Concept and Delinquency." *Nashville Mental Health Center Monograph*, No. 1. Nashville, Tennessee.

Flapan, D. 1968. *Children's Understanding of Social Interaction.* New York: Teachers College.

Flavell, J. 1974. "The Development of Inferences About Others." In *Understanding Other Persons*, edited by T. Mischel. Oxford: Blackwell, pp. 66–116.

____. 1968. *The Development of Role-taking and Communication Skills in Children.* New York: John Wiley and Sons.

Frenkell-Brunswick, E. 1968. "Adjustments and Reorientations in the Course of Life Span." In *Middle Age and Aging*, edited by B. Neugarten, pp. 77–84. Chicago: University of Chicago Press.

Frenkel, R.E. 1964. "Psychotherapeutic Reconstruction of the Traumatic Amnesic Period by the Mirror Image Projective Technique." *Journal of Existentiation* 17: 77–96.

French, T. 1941. "Goal, Mechanisms and Integrative Field." *Psychosomatic Medicine* 3: Ann Arbor, Mich.: University Microfilms.

Freud, A. 1958. "Adolescence." In *Psychoanalytic Study of the Child*, vol. 13, edited by R.S. Eissler et al., New York: pp. 255–278. International Universities Press.

____. 1946. *The Ego and the Mechanisms of Defense.* New York: International Universities Press.

Freud, S. 1950. "Splitting of the Ego in the Defensive Process." In *Collected Papers.* London: Hogarth Press.

____. 1923. *The Ego and the Id.* Standard edition, 19.

Gallup, G.G., Jr. 1973. "Towards an Operational Definition of Self-awareness." Paper presented at the IXth International Congress of Anthropological and Ethnological Sciences, Chicago.

____. 1970. "Chimpanzees: Self Recognition." *Science* 167: 86–87.

Garfinkel, H. 1967. *Studies in Ethnomethodology.* Englewood Cliffs, N.J.: Prentice-Hall.

Gazzaniga, M.S. 1973. "The Split Brain in Man." In *The Nature of Human Consciousness*, edited by R.E. Ornstein. San Francisco: W.H. Freeman & Co. pp. 87–100.

Gergen, K.J. 1978. "Toward Generative Theory." *Journal of Personality and Social Psychology* 36: 1344–1360.

____. 1977. "Social Construction of Self-knowledge." In *The Self*, edited by T. Mischel. Oxford, Basil Blackwell. pp. 139–169.

____. 1976. "Experimentation in Social Psychology: A Reappraisal." Paper presented at the meeting of the American Psychological Association, Washington, D.C., September.

____. 1973. "Social Psychology as History." *Journal of Personality and Social Psychology* 26: 309–320.

____. 1971. *The Concept of Self.* New York: Holt.

____. 1965. "Interaction Goals and Personalistic Feedback as Factors Affecting the Presentation of Self." *Journal of Personality and Social Psychology* 1: 413–424.

____. "The Emerging Crisis in Life-span Developmental Theory." In *Life-span Development and Behavior*, vol. 3 pp. 31–63, edited by P.B. Baltes and O.G. Brim. New York: Academic Press.

Gergen, K.J., and M. Basseches. 1980. "The Potentiation of Social Psychological Knowledge." To appear in *Advances in Applied Social Psychology*, vol. 1, edited by R.F. Kidd and M. Saks. New York: L. Erlbaum.

Gergen, K.J., and M.G. Taylor. 1969. "Social Expectancy and Self-presentation in a Status Hierarchy." *Journal of Experimental Social Psychology* 5: 79–92.

Gergen, K.J. and B. Wishnov. 1965. "Others' Self Evaluations and Interaction Anticipation as Determinants of Self Presentation." *Journal of Personality and Social Psychology* 2: 348–358.

Giovannini, D., ed. 1979. *Identita Personale Teoria e Ricerca.* Bologna: Zanichelli.

Gesell, A. 1928. *Infancy and Human Growth.* New York: MacMillan.

Glidewell, J.C. 1968. "Studies of Mothers' Reports of Behavior Symptoms in Their Children." In *The Definition and Measurement of Mental Health*, edited by S.B. Sells, pp. 181–217. Washington, D.C.: Department of Health, Education and Welfare.

Goffman, E. 1959. *The Presentation of Self in Everyday Life.* New York: Doubleday.

Goldstein, D. 1939. *The Organism.* New York: American Book Company.

Goldberger, A.S. 1971. "Econometrics and Psychometrics: A Survey of Comunalities." *Psychometrika* 36: 83–107.

Goodenough, F. 1938. "The Use of Pronouns by Young Children: A Note on the Development of Self-awareness." *Journal of Genetic Psychology* 52: 333–346.

Gooding, C.T. 1969. "The Perceptual Organization of Effective Teachers." In *Florida Studies in the Helping Professions*, University of Florida Monographs, Social Sciences, No. 37, edited by A.W. Combs. Gainesville, Fla.: University of Florida Press.

Gordon, C. 1968. "Self Conceptions: Configurations of Content." In *The Self in Social Interaction*, vol. I: *Classic and Contemporary Perspectives*, edited by C. Gordon and K.J. Gergen, pp. 115–136. New York: John Wiley and Sons.

Gordon, I.J. 1968. *A Test Manual for the How I See Myself Scale.* Gainesville, Fla.: Educational Research and Development Council.

Gordon, I.J., and P.C. Wood. 1963. "Relationship Between Pupil Self Evaluation, Teacher Evaluation of the Pupil and Scholastic Achievement." *Journal of Educational Research* 56: 440–443.

Gordon, L. 1976. "Development of Evaluated Role Identities." *Annual Review of Sociology* 2: 405–433.

Gove, W.R., and T.R. Herb. 1974. "Stress and Mental Illness Among the Young: A Comparison of the Sexes." *Social Forces* 53: 256–265.

Greenberg, D.J.; D. Hillman; and D. Grice. 1973. "Infant and Stranger Variables Related to Stranger Anxiety in the First Year of Life." *Developmental Psychology* 9: 207–212.

Guardo, C.J. 1968. "Self Revisited: The Sense of Self Identity." *Journal of Humanistic Psychology* 8: 137–142.

Guardo, C.J., and J.B. Bohan. 1971. "Development of a Sense of Self Identity in Children." *Child Development* 42: 1909–1921.

Guilford, J.P. 1967. *The Nature of Human Intelligence.* New York: McGraw-Hill.

Haarer, D.L. 1964. "A Comparative Study of Self-concept of Ability Between Institutionalized Delinquent Boys and Nondelinquent Boys Enrolled in Public Schools." Ph. D. dissertation, Michigan State University.

Hall, C.S., and G. Lindzey. 1957. *Theories of Personality.* New York: John Wiley and Sons.

Hall, G.S. 1898. "Some Aspects of the Early Sense of Self." *American Journal of Psychology* 9: 351–395.

Hamachek, D.E., ed. 1965. *The Self in Growth, Teaching and Learning.* Englewood Cliffs, N.J.: Prentice-Hall.

Hamburg, B. 1974. "Early Adolescence: A Specific and Stressful Stage of the Cycle." In *Coping and Adaptation*, edited by G. Goelho, D.A. Hamburg, and J.E. Adams, pp. 101–122. New York: Basic Books.

Hamlyn, D.W. 1940. "Person-Perception and Our Understanding of Others." In *Understanding Other Persons*, edited by T. Mischel, pp. 1–36. Rowman & Littlefield.

Hara, T. 1972. "A Cross-cultural Comparison of Self Concepts and Value Orientations of Japanese and American Ninth Graders." Ph.D. dissertation, Michigan State University.

Harding, E.M. 1965. *The "I" and the "Not-I": A Study in the Development of Consciousness*, Bollingen Series LXXIX. New York: Pantheon.

Hardy, K.R. 1964. "An Appetitional Theory of Sexual Motivation." *Psychological Review* 71: 1–16.

Hartman, H. 1964. *Essays on Ego Psychology.* New York: International University Press.

Havinghurst, R., and D. Levine. 1977. "Instructional Improvement in Inner City Schools." Unpublished paper, University of Missouri, Kansas City.

Havinghurst, R.J., and D. Gottleib. 1975. "Youth and the Meaning of Work." In *Youth*, The *74th Yearbook of the National Society for the Study of Education*, edited by R.J. Havinghurst and P. Dreyer, pp. 145–160. Chicago: University of Chicago Press.

Hayakawa, S.I. 1963. *Symbol, Status, and Personality.* New York: Harcourt, Brace & World.

Heider, F. 1958. *The Psychology of Interpersonal Relations.* New York: John Wiley and Sons.

Henderson, G. 1973. "An Analysis of Self-concept of Academic Ability as Related to Social Psychological Variable Comprising School Climate in Black and White Elementary Children with Differential School Settings." Ph.D. dissertation, Michigan State University, East Lansing.

Henry, W. 1968. "Personality Change in Middle and Old Age." In *The Study of Personality an Interdisciplinary Appraisal*, edited by E. Norbeck, *et al.* pp. 209–217. New York: Holt.

Hilgard, E.R. 1949. "Human Motives and the Concept of the Self." *American Psychologist* 4: 374–382.

Hill, A. 1977. "Motivation Factors Affecting Achievement Among Black and White Low Socio-economic Level College Students." Ph.D. dissertation, Fordham University.

Hill, J.P., and W.J. Palmquist. 1978. "Social Cognition and Social Relations in Early Adolescence." *International Journal of Behavioral Development* 1: 1-36.

Hochman, J.S., and N.O. Brill. 1971. "Marijuana Intoxication: Pharmacological and Psychological Factors." *Diseases of the Nervous System* Oct.: 676-679, vol. 32 #10.

Hodge, R.W.; P.M. Siegel; and P.H. Rossi. 1964. "Occupational Prestige in the U.S., 1925-1963." *American Journal of Sociology* 70: 286-302.

Hoffman, M.L. 1975. "Developmental Synthesis of Affect and Cognition and its Implications for Altruistic Motivation." *Developmental Psychology* 11: 607-622.

Holmes, T.H., and R.H. Rahe. 1967. "The Social Readjustment Rating Scale." *Journal of Psychosomatic Research* 11: 213-217.

Howell, J. 1977. "Northern Community Center Summer Camp Evaluation." Paper presented at the Meeting of the New England Educational Research Organization, Manchester, N.H., May.

Hull, C. 1920. "Quantitative Aspects of the Evolution of Concepts: An Experimental Study." *Psychological Monographs* 28: 123.

Hunt, E.B. 1962. *Concept Learning: An Information Processing Problem.* New York: John Wiley and Sons.

Hurtig, A. 1980. "Cognitive Development, Ego Development and Sex Differences in Cognitive Performance." Paper presented at the annual meeting of the American Psychological Association in Montreal, September.

Inhelder, B., and J. Piaget. 1958. *The Growth of Logical Thinking: From Childhood to Adolescence.* New York: Basic Books.

James, W. 1890a. *The Principles of Psychology.* New York: Holt, Rinehart, & Winston.

James, W. 1890b. *Principles of Psychology.* London: Encyclopedia Britannica, 53, 1952.

Jennings, G.D. 1973. "The Relationship Between Perceptual Characteristics and Effective Advising of University Housing Para-professional Residence Assistants." Ph. D. dissertation, University of Florida.

Jarcho, H. 1980. "Cognitive Development and the Ability to Infer Others' Perceptions of Self." Paper presented at the annual meeting of the American Educational Research Association, Boston, April.

Jersild, A.T. 1952. *In Search of Self.* New York: Columbia University.

Jesness, C.F. 1970. *Behavior Checklist Self-appraisal Form Manual.* Palo Alto: Consulting Psychologists Press.

Jones, R.A. 1977. *Self-fulfilling Prophecies.* Hillsdale, N.J.: Lawrence Erlbaum.

Jordon, T.J. 1979. "Cognitive and Personality Factors Related to Academic Achievement of Innercity Junior High School Students." Ph. D. dissertation, New York University.

Kagan, J.; B.L. Rosman; D. Day; J. Alpert; and W. Phillips. 1964. "Information Processing in the Child." *Psychological Monographs* 78(1).

Kaplan, B., and W.H. Crockett. 1968. "Developmental Analysis of Modes of Resolution." In *Theories of Cognitive Consistency: A Sourcebook*, edited by P. Abelson et al. Chicago: Rand McNally, pp. 661–669.

Kardiner, A., and L. Ovesey. 1951. *The Mark of Oppression.* New York: World Publishing.

Katz, I. 1968. "Academic Motivation." *Harvard Educational Review* 38(1).

Katz, D. 1968. "Consistency for What? The Functional Approach." In *Theories of Cognitive Consistency: A Sourcebook*, edited by P. Abelson et al. Chicago: pp. 129–191. Rand McNally.

Keating, D.P. 1980. "Thinking Processes in Adolescence." In *Handbook of Adolescent Psychology*, edited by J. Adelson, pp. 211–246. New York: John Wiley and Sons.

Kelly, G.A. 1955. *The Psychology of Personal Constructs* (2 vols.). New York: Norton.

Kelly, H.H. 1973. "The Processes of Causal Attribution." *American Psychologist*, 28: 107–128.

Kelman, H.C., and R.M. Baron. 1968. "Determinants of Modes of Resolving Inconsistency Dilemmas: A Functional Analysis." In *Theories of Cognitive Consistency: A Sourcebook*, edited by P. Abelson et al. Chicago: Rand McNally, pp. 670–683.

Kerlinger, F.N. 1977. "The Influence of Research on Educational Practice." Paper presented at the meeting of the American Educational Research Association, New York, April.

Kessler, S.J., and W. McKenna. 1978. *Gender: An Ethnomethodological Approach.* New York: John Wiley and Sons.

Kikuchi, T. 1968. "Studies on the Development of the Self-concept: An Investigation on the Self-concept of Children and Adolescents by a Modified Method of Twenty Statements Tests." *Tohoku Psycholozia Folia* 27(1): 22–31.

Klein, M. 1932. *The Psychoanalysis of Children.* London: Hogarth.

Klinger, E. 1975. "Consequences of Commitment to and Disengagement from Incentives." *Psychological Review* 82: 1–25.

Koeske, G.F., and R.K. Koeske. 1975. "Deviance and a Generalized Disposition Toward Internality: An Attributional Approach." *Journal of Personality* 43: 634–646.

Koffman, R.G. 1975. "A Comparison of the Perceptual Organizations of Outstanding and Randomly Selected Teachers in Open and Traditional Classrooms." Ph. D. dissertation, University of Massachusetts.

Kohlberg, L. 1966. "A Cognitive Developmental Analysis of Children's Sex-role Concepts and Attitudes." In *The Development of Sex Differences*, edited by E.E. Maccoby, pp. 82–173. Stanford: Stanford University Press.

____. 1976. "Moral Stages and Moralization: The Cognitive Developmental Approach. The Study of Moral Development." In *Moral Development and Behavior*, edited by T. Lickona, pp. 31–53. New York: Holt, Rinehart & Winston.

____. 1969. "Stage and Sequence: The Cognitive-developmental Approach to Socialization." In *Handbook of Socialization Theory and Research*, edited by D.A. Goslin, pp. 347–472. Chicago: Rand McNally.

Komorita, S.S., and D.A. Kravitz. 1979. "The Effects of Alternatives in Bargaining." *Journal of Experimental Social Psychology* 15: 147–157.

Koocher, G.P. 1971. "Swimming, Competence, and Personality Change." *Journal of Personality and Social Psychology* 18(2): 275–278.

Kramer, D. 1979. "Increasing Motivation for Learning in School Among Eighth-grade Students." Ph. D. dissertation, Fordham University.

Kuhn, N.H. 1954. "Factors in Personality: Socio-cultural Determinants as Seen Through the Amish." In *Aspects of Culture and Personality*, edited by F.L.K. Hsu, pp. 43–60. New York: Abelard–Schuman, Inc.

Kuhn, M.H., and T.S. McPartland. 1954. "An Empirical Investigation of Self-attitudes." *American Sociological Review* 19: 68–76.

Ladner, J.S. 1977. *Mixed Families: Adopting Across Racial Boundaries.* New York: Anchor–Doubleday.

Laing, R.D. 1969. *Self and Others.* New York: Pantheon Books.

____. 1965. *The Divided Self.* Baltimore: Penguin.

Lazowick, L.M. 1955. "On the Nature of Identification." *Journal of Abnormal and Social Psychology* 51: 175–183.

Lecht, L.A. 1976. "Women at Work." *Conference Board Record* 13: 16–21.

Lecky, P. 1961. *Self Consistency: A Theory of Personality.* New York: Shoe String Press.

L'Ecuyer, R. 1978. *Le Concept de Soi.* Paris: Presses Universitaires de France.

____. 1979. "Lo Sviluppo del Concetto di Se Nelle Persone Dai 60 ai 100 Anni: Modificazioni Delle Loro Aspirazioni e Percezioni di Ruolo e di Status (Le Developpement du Concept de Soi Chez les Personnes Agees de 60 a 100 Ans: Modifications de Leurs Aspirations et de Leurs Perceptions de Leur Role et Statut)." In *Identita Personale: Teoria e Ricerca*, edited by D. Giovannini, pp. 92–106. Bologna: Zanichelli.

____. 1975a. *La Genese du Concept de Soi: Theorie et Recherches. Les Transformations des Perceptions de Soi Chez les Enfants Ages de Trois, Cing et Huit Ans.* Sherbrooke: Editions Naaman.

____. 1975b. "Self-concept Investigation: Demystification Process." *Journal of Phenomenological Psychology* 6(1): 17–30.

____. 1974a. "Les Perceptions de Soi Chez les Enfants de Trois Ans." *Psychologie Francaise* 19(3): 179–198.

____. 1974b. "The Self Concept of Five Year-old Children: Content Analysis." Unpublished manuscript, University of Sherbrooke.

Lennenberg, E.H. 1967. *Biological Foundations of Language.* New York: John Wiley and Sons.

Levin, J.; E. Karni; and Y. Frankel. 1978. "Analysis of the Tennessee Self Concept Scale as a Structured Instrument." *Psychological Reports* 43: 619–623.

Levinson, D. 1978. *The Seasons of a Man's Life.* New York. Alfred Knopf.

Levy-Agresti, J., and R.W. Sperry. 1968. "Differential Perceptual Capacities in Major and Minor Hemispheres." *Proceedings of the National Academy of Science* 61: 1151.

Lewis, M. 1977. "The Infant and its Caregiver: The Role of Contingency." Paper presented at a Conference on Infant Intervention Programs, University of Wisconsin, Milwaukee, June. Also, in *Allied Health and Behavioral Sciences* 1(4), in press.

Lewis, M., and J. Brooks-Gunn. 1979. *Social Cognition and the Acquisition of Self.* New York: Plenum Press.

____. 1974. "Self, Other, and Fear: Infants' Reactions to People." In *The Origins of Fear: The Origins of Behavior*, edited by M. Lewis and L. Rosenblum. New York: John Wiley and Sons.

____. 1975. "Infants' Social Perception: A Constructional View." In *Infant Perception: From Sensation to Cognition*, edited by L. Cohen and P. Salapatelc, vol. 2, pp. 102–143. New York: Academic Press.

____. Forthcoming. "Toward a Theory of Social Cognition: The Development of Self." In *New Directions in Child Development: Social Interaction and Communication During Infancy*, edited by I. Uzgiris. San Francisco: Jossey-Bass.

Lewis, M., and C. Feiring. 1978. "The Child's Social World." In *Child Influences on Marital and Family Interaction: A Life-span Perspective*, edited by R.M. Lerner, and G.D. Spanier. New York: Academic Press.

Lewis, M., and S. Goldberg. 1969. "The Acquisition and Violation of Expectancy: An Experimental Paradigm." *Journal of Experimental Child Psychology* 7: 70–80.

Lindesmith, A.R., and A.L. Straus. 1968. *Social Psychology* (3rd ed.). New York: Holt, Rinehart & Winston.

Lipsitz, J. 1977. *Growing Up Forgotten.* Lexington, Mass.: Lexington Books.

Livesley, W.J., and D.B. Bromley. 1973. *Person Perception in Childhood and Adolescence.* London: John Wiley and Sons.

Lock-Land, G.T. 1973. *Grow or Die: The Unifying Principle of Transformation.* New York: Delta.

Loevinger, J. 1976. *Ego Development.* San Francisco: Jossey-Bass.

Long, B.H.; R.C. Ziller; and E.H. Henderson. 1968. "Developmental Changes in the Self-concept During Adolescence." *School Review* 76: 210–230.

Luria, A.R. 1976. *Cognitive Development: Its Cultural and Social Foundations*, Cambridge, Mass.: Harvard University Press.

Lynch, M.D. 1978a. "Self Concept Development in Childhood." Paper presented at the National Symposium on Self Concept, Boston, Mass., September.

_____. 1978b. "Self Concept-related-frustration Tests as Measures of Situational Specificity." Paper presented at the American Psychological Association meeting, Toronto, August.

_____. 1970a. "Development and Validation of a Set of Semantic Differential Scales for Measuring Self Concepts of Elementary Grade Level Children." Paper presented at the American Educational Research Association Meeting, Chicago.

_____. 1970b. "Multidimensional Measurement with the D Statistic and the Semantic Differential." Paper presented at the American Educational Research Association Meeting, Chicago.

Lynch, M.D., and J.F. Chaves. Manuscript in preparation. "Structural Evolution of the Self Concept in Children."

Lynch, M.D., and K. Grew. 1972. "The Measurement of Dogmatism in Children." Paper presented at the American Psychological Association meeting, New Orleans, August.

Lykken, D.T., and C.G. Katzenmeyer. 1968. "Manual for the Activity Preference Questionnaire (APQ)." Reports from the Research Laboratories of the Department of Psychiatry, University of Minnesota, Report Number PR-68-3.

Lyle, J.R., and J.L. Ross. 1973. *Women in Industry.* Lexington, Mass.: D.C. Heath & Co.

Marcia, J.E. 1980. "Identity in Adolescence." In *Handbook of Adolescent Psychology*, edited by J. Adelson, pp. 159–187. New York: John Wiley and Sons.

_____. 1966. "Development and Validation of Ego Identity Status." *Journal of Personality and Social Psychology* 3: 551–558.

Markus, H. 1977. "Self-schemata and Processing Information About the Self." *Journal of Personality and Social Psychology* 35(2): 63–78.

Mandler, G. 1975. "Consciousness: Respectable, Useful and Probably Necessary." In *Information Processing and Cognition: The Loyola Symposium*, edited by R. Solso, pp. 229–354. Hillsdale, N.J.: Erlbaum.

Marshall, G. 1976. "The Affective Consequences of 'Inadequately Explained' Physiological Arousal." Ph. D. dissertation, Stanford University.

Maslach, C. 1979. "Negative Emotional Biasing of Unexplained Arousal." *Journal of Personality and Social Psychology* 37: 953–969.

Maslow, A.H. 1962. "Some Basic Propositions of a Growth and Self-actualization Psychology." In *Perceiving, Behaving, Becoming: Yearbook of the Association for Supervision and Curriculum Development*, edited by A.W. Combs. Washington, D.C.: Association for Supervision and Curriculum Development, NEA.

____. 1954. *Motivation and Personality.* New York: Harper.

McCall, G.J. 1977. "The Self: Conceptual Requirements from an Interactionist Perspective." Paper presented at the 72nd annual meeting of the American Sociological Association, Chicago, September.

McCall, G.J., and J.L. Simmons. 1966. *Identities and Interactions: An Examination of Human Association in Everyday Life.* New York: The Free Press.

McClelland, D.C.; J.W. Atkinson; R.W. Clark; and E.L. Lowell. 1953. *The Achievement Motive.* New York: Appleton-Century-Crofts.

McGuire, W.J.; C.V. McGuire; and W. Winton. 1979. "Effect of Household Sex Composition on the Salience of One's Gender in the Spontaneous Self-concept." *Journal of Experimental Social Psychology* 15: 77-90.

Mead, G.H. 1936. *Movements of Thought in the Nineteenth Century.* Chicago: University of Chicago Press.

____. 1934. *Mind, Self, and Society.* Chicago: University of Chicago Press.

____. 1895. "A Theory of Emotions from the Physiological Standpoint." Abstract of paper presented at the meeting of the American Psychological Association. *Psychological Review* 2: 162-164.

Meltzer, B.N. 1967. "Mead's Social Psychology." In *Symbolic Interaction: A Reader in Social Psychology*, edited by J.G. Manis and B.N. Meltzer, pp. 5-24. Boston: Allyn & Bacon.

Merleau-Ponty, M. 1964. *Primacy of Perception*, edited by J. Eddie and translated by W. Cobb. Evanston: Northwestern Universities Press.

Merrifield, P.R. 1978a. "Guilford and Piaget: An Attempt at Synthesis." In *Seventh Annual Piagetian Conference Proceedings.* Los Angeles: University of Southern California Press.

Merrifield, P.R. 1978b. "Sources of Variance in Self Concept Measures." Paper presented at the American Psychological Association Meeting, Toronto.

Miller, D.T. 1976. "Ego Involvement and Attributions for Success and Failure." *Journal of Personality and Social Psychology* 34(5): 901-906.

Miller, D.T.; S.Q. Norman; and E. Wright. 1978. "Distortion in Person Perception as a Consequence of the Need for Effective Control." *Journal of Personality and Social Psychology* 36(6): 598-607.

Miller, R.L.; P. Brickman; and D. Bolen. 1973. "Attribution Versus Persuasion as a Means for Modifying Attitudes and Behavior." Unpublished paper.

Michael, W.B; R.A. Smith; and J.J. Michael. 1975. "The Factorial Validity of the Piers-Harris Children's Self-concept Scale for Each of Three Samples of Elementary Junior High, and Senior High School Students in a Large Metropolitan School District." *Educational and Psychological Measurement* 35: 405-414.

Mintz, R., and D. Muller. 1977. "Academic Achievement as a Function of Specific and Global Measures of Self-concept." *The Journal of Psychology* 97: 53-57.

Miyamota, S.F. 1970. "Self, Motivation, and Symbolic Interactionist Theory." In *Human Behavior and Collective Behavior: Papers in Honor of Herbert Blumer*, edited by T. Shibutani, pp. 671–685. New York: Prentice Hall.

Miyamoto, S.F., and S. Dornbusch. 1956. "A Test of the Symbolic Interactionist Hypothesis of Self-conception." *American Journal of Sociology* 61: 399–403.

Monge, R.H. 1973. "Developmental Trends in Factors of Adolescent Self-concept." *Developmental Psychology* 8: 382–393.

Montemayor, R., and M. Eisen. 1977. "The Development of Self-conceptions from Childhood to Adolescence." *Developmental Psychology* 31(4): 314–319.

Morse, R.S. 1963. "Self-concept of Ability, Significant Others, and School Achievement of Eighth-grade Students: A Comparative Investigation of Negro and Caucasian Students." M.A. thesis, Michigan State University.

Morse, S.J., and K.J. Gergen. 1970. "Social Comparison, Self-consistency and the Concept of Self." *Journal of Personality and Social Psychology* 16: 149–156.

Moynihan, D.P. 1965. *The Negro Family: The Case for National Action.* Washington, D.C.: U.S. Department of Labor.

Mulford, H.A. 1955. "Toward an Instrument to Identify and Measure the Self, Significant Others, and Alcohol in the Symbolic Environment: An Empirical Study." Ph.D. dissertation, University of Iowa.

Murphy, G. 1968. "Psychological Views of Personality and Contribution to its Study." In *The Study of Personality, an Interdisciplinary Appraisal*, edited by E. Norbeck, D. Price-Williams, and W.M. McCord. pp. 15–38. New York: Holt.

____. 1947. *Personality a Biosocial Approach to Origin and Structure.* New York: Harper & Row.

Mussen, P.H.. J.J. Conger; and J. Kagen. 1969. *Child Development and Personality.* New York: Harper & Row.

Neisser, U. 1967. *Cognitive Psychology.* New York: Appleton-Century-Crofts.

Nenberg, H. 1960. *Practice and Theory of Psychoanalysis.* New York: International University Press.

Nesselroade, J.R., and P.B. Baltes. May 1974. *Adolescent Personality Development and Historical Change: 1970–72*, Monographs of the Society for Research in Child Development, serial No. 154, vol. 39.

Neugarten, B.L., and N. Datan. 1973. "Sociological Perspectives on the Life Cycle." In *Life-span Developmental Psychology, Personality and Socialization*, edited by P.B. Baltes and K.W. Schaie, Chapter 3, pp. 53–69. New York: Academic Press.

Nisbitt, R.E., and N. Bellows. 1977. "Verbal Reports about Causal Influences on Social Judgments: Private Access Versus Public Theories." *Journal of Personality and Social Psychology* 35: 613–624.

Nisbitt, R., and S. Schachter. 1966. "Cognitive Manipulation of Pain." *Journal of Experimental Social Psychology* 2: 227–236.

Nisbett, R.E. and T.D. Wilson. 1977. Telling more than we can know: Verbal Reports on Mental Processes. *Psychological Review* 84: 231–250.

Norem–Hebeisen, A. 1978. "Idiosyncratic Bases for Estimates of Real-Ideal Congruence." Paper presented at the meeting of the American Psychological Association, Toronto, August.

Nugent, J. 1970. "Some Correlates of Teacher Effectiveness." M.A. thesis, Northeastern University.

Offer, D., and K. Howard. 1977. "An Empirical Analysis of the Offer Self-image Questionnaire for Adolescents." *Archives of General Psychiatry* 27: 529–533.

Offer, D., and J.B. Offer. 1975. *From Teenage to Young Manhood.* New York: Basic Books.

Offer, D.; E. Ostrov; and K. Howard. 1977. *The Offer Self Image Questionnaire for Adolescents: A Manual.* Chicago: Author.

O'Roark, A. 1975. "A Comparison of Perceptual Characteristics of Elected Legislators and Public School Counselors Identified as Most and Least Effective." Ph. D. dissertation, University of Florida.

Osgood, C.; G. Suci; and P. Tannenbaum. 1957. *Measurement of Meaning.* Urbana: University of Illinois Press.

Papousek, H., and M. Papousek. 1974. "Mirror Image and Self-recognition in Young Human Infants: I, A New Method of Experimental Analysis." *Developmental Psychology* 7(3): 149–157.

Park, R.E. 1927. "Human Nature and Collective Behavior." *American Journal of Sociology* 32: 733–741.

Parker, J. 1964. "The Relationship of Self Report to Inferred Self Concept in Sixth Grade Children." Ph. D. dissertation, University of Florida.

Parsons, T. 1977. "The Changing Economy of the Family." Paper presented at an Interdisciplinary Seminar on Changing Economy of the Family, American Council of Life Insurance, Washington, D.C.: November.

Passalacqua, J. 1979. "Contextual Analysis of Self-concept of Academic Ability." M.A. thesis, Michigan State University, East Lansing.

Patterson, C.H. 1961. "The Self in Recent Rogerian Theory." *Psychologia Japanis* 4(3): 156–162.

Perron, R. 1971. *Modeles d'Enfants, Enfants Modeles.* Paris: Presses Universitaires de France.

Petersen, A.C.; H. Jarcho; and D. Offer. 1980, in preparation. *The Measurement of Self Image Among Early Adolescents.*

Petersen, A.C.; D. Offer; and E. Kaplan. 1979. "The Self-image of Rural Adolescent Girls." In *Female Adolescent Development*, edited by M. Sugar. New York: Brunner/Malzel.

Petersen, A.C., and D. Offer. 1979. "Adolescent Development: The Years 16 to 19." In *Basic Handbook of Child Psychiatry.* J.D. Noshpitz, Editor-in-Chief, pp. 213–232. New York: Basic Books.

Petersen, A.C., and B. Taylor. 1980. "The Biological Approach to Adolescence." In *Handbook of Adolescent Psychology,* edited by J. Adelson, pp. 117–155. New York: John Wiley and Sons.

Piaget, J. 1972. "Intellectual Evolution from Adolescence to Adulthood." *Human Development* 15: 1–12.

____. 1970. "Piaget's Theory." In *Carmichael's Manual of Child Psychology* edited by P. Mussen, pp. 703–732. New York: John Wiley and Sons.

____. 1952. *The Origins of Intelligence in Children.* New York: International University Press.

____. 1948. *The Moral Judgment of the Child.* Glencoe: The Free Press.

____. 1928. *Judgment and Reasoning in the Child.* London: Routledge & Kaegan Paul.

____. 1926. *The Language and Thought of the Child.* New York: Harcourt Brace.

Picht, L.P. 1969. "Self Concept in Relation to Effectiveness in Student Teaching." Ph. D. dissertation, University of Northern Colorado.

Piers, E.V. 1969. *Manual for the Piers-Harris, Children's Self-concept Scale.* Nashville: Counselor Recordings and Tests.

Piers, E.V., and D.B. Harris. 1964. "The Piers-Harris Children's Self-concept Scale." *Journal of Educational Psychology* 55: 91–95.

Pinneau, S.R., and A. Milton. 1958. "The Ecological Veracity of the Self Report." *Journal of Genetic Psychology* 93: 249–276.

Plutchik, R., and A.F. Ax. 1962. "A Critique of Determinants of Emotional State by Schachter and Singer." *Psychophysiology* 4: 79–82.

Posner, M.I., and C.R.R. Snyder. 1975. "Attention and Cognitive Control." In *Information Processing and Cognition: The Loyola Symposium,* edited by R.L. Solso, pp. 55–85. Hillsdale, N.J.: Lawrence Erlbaum Associates.

Preyer, W. 1893. *Mind of the Child, Vol. II: Development of the Intellect.* New York: Appleton.

Purkey, W.W. 1978. *Inviting School Success: A Self-concept Approach to Teaching and Learning.* Belmont, Ca.: Wadsworth Publishing Co.

____. 1970. *Self-concept and School Achievement.* Englewood Cliffs, N.J.: Prentice Hall.

Purkey, W.W.; B. Cage; and W. Graves. 1973. "The Florida Key: A Scale to Infer Learning Self Concept." *Educational and Psychological Measurement* 33: 979–984.

Quarentelli, E.L., and J. Cooper. 1966. "Self Conceptions and Others: A Further Test of Meadian Hypotheses." *Sociological Quarterly* 7: 281–297.

Raimy, V.C. 1943. "The Self Concept as a Factor in Counseling and Personality Organization." Ph. D. dissertation, Ohio State University, Columbus.

Rebelsky, F. 1971. "Infants' Communication Attempts with Mother and Stranger." Paper presented at the Eastern Psychological Association meetings, New York, April.

Reeder, L.; G. Donohue; and A. Biblarz. 1960. "Conceptions of Self and Others." *American Journal of Sociology* 66: 153–159.

Rescher, N. 1969. *Many-valued Logic.* New York: McGraw–Hill.

Rheingold, H.L. 1971. "Some Visual Determinants of Smiling Infants." Unpublished manuscript.

Rheingold, H.L.; J.L. Gerwirtz; and H.W. Ross. 1959. "Social Conditioning of Vocalizations in the Infant." *Journal of Comparative Physiological Psychology* 52: 68–72.

Riegel, K.F. 1973. "Dialectic Operations: The Final Period of Cognitive Development." *Human Development* 16: 346–370.

Robinson, W.S. 1950. "Ecological Correlations and the Behavior of Individuals." *American Sociological Review* No. 3, pp. 351–357, June 1950.

Rodriguez Tome, H. 1972. *Le Moi et l'Autre dans la Conscience de L'Adolescent.* Paris: Delachaux et Niestle.

Rogers, C.R. 1969. *Freedom to Learn: A View of What Education Might Become.* Columbus, Ohio: Charles E. Merrill Publishing Co.

____. 1963. "The Concept of the Fully Functioning Person." *Psychotherapy* 1: 17–26.

____. 1961. *On Becoming a Person.* Boston: Houghton Mifflin.

____. 1959. "A Theory of Therapy, Personality and Interpersonal Relationships, as Developed in the Client-centered Framework." In *Formulations of the Person and the Social Context*, vol. 3, *Psychology, the Study of a Science*, edited by S. Koch, pp. 184–256. New York: McGraw–Hill.

____. 1951. *Client-centered Therapy: Its Current Practice, Implications, and Theory.* Boston: Houghton Mifflin.

Rogers, C.R., and R.F. Dymond, Eds. 1954. *Psychotherapy and Personality Change; Coordinated Studies in the Client-centered Approach.* Chicago: University of Chicago Press.

Rogers, T.B., N.A. Kuiper; and W.S. Kierker. 1977. "Self-reference and the Encoding of Personal Information." *Journal of Personality and Social Psychology* 35(9): 677–688.

Rogosa, D. Forthcoming. "Causal Models in Longitudinal Research: Rationale, Formulation, and Interpretation." In *Longitudinal Research in Human Development: Design and Analysis*, edited by J.R. Nesselroade and P.B. Baltes. New York: Academic Press.

Rokeach, M. 1973. *The Nature of Human Values.* New York: Free Press.

Rose, A.M. 1962. "A Systematic Summary of Symbolic Interaction Theory." In *Social Processes: An Interactionist Approach*, edited by A.M. Rose, pp. 3–19. Boston: Houghton Mifflin.

Rosenberg, M.J. 1968. Discussion: The Concept of Self. In Abelson, et al (eds.), *Theories of Cognitive Consistency: A Sourcebook.* Chicago: Rand McNally.

____. 1979. *Conceiving the Self.* New York: Basic Books.

____. 1965. *Society and the Adolescent Self-image.* Princeton, N.J.: Princeton University Press.

Rosenberg, M., and R.G. Simmons. 1971. *Black and White Self-esteem: The Urban School Child*, Monograph Series, American Sociological Association. Wash.: American Sociological Association.

Rosenberg, S. 1978. *Implicit Beliefs in Person Perception: Idiographics and Nomothetics.* New Brunswick: Rutgers University, February. (Mimeo.)

Rosenberg, S., and A. Sedlak. 1972. "Structural Representation of Implicit Personality Theory." In L. Berkowitz (Ed.), *Advances in Experimental Social Psychology* 6: 235–297.

Rosenkrantz, P.; W. Vogel; H. Bee; I. Broverman; and D. Broverman. 1968. "Sex Role Stereotypes and Self-conceptions in College Students." *Journal of Consulting Psychology* 32: 287–295.

Rotter, J.B. 1966. "Generalized Expectancies for Internal vs. External Control of Reinforcement." *Psychological Monographs* 80: 2–28.

Sameroff, A.J. 1977. "Early Influences on Development, Fact or Fancy." In *Annual Progress in Child Psychiatry and Child Development*, edited by S. Chess, and A. Thomas, pp. 3–33. New York: Brunner/Mazel.

Sarbin, T.R. 1952. "A Preface to a Psychological Analysis of the Self." *Psychological Review* 59: 11–22.

Sarbin, T.R., and V.L. Allen. *Role Theory: The Handbook of Social Psychology*, vol. 1. Reading Mass.: Addison-Wesley Publishing Co.

Schaie, K.W. 1977–1978. "Toward a State Theory of Adult Cognitive Development." *Journal of Aging and Human Development* 8(2): 129–138.

Schachter, S. 1964. "The Interaction of Cognitive and Physiological Determinants of Emotional State." In *Advances in Experimental Social Psychology*, edited by L. Berkowitz, pp. 49–80. New York: Academic Press.

Schachter, S., and J.F. Singer. 1962. "Cognitive, Social and Physiological Determinants of Emotional State." *Psychological Review* 65: 121–128.

Schantz, C. 1975. "The Development of Social Cognition." In *Review of Child Development Theory and Research*, vol. 5, edited by M.E. Hetherington, Chicago: University of Chicago Press.

Scheff, T.J. 1968. "The Role of the Mentally Ill and the Dynamics of Mental Disorder: A Research Framework." In *The Mental Patient: Studies in the Sociology of Deviance*, edited by S.P. Spitzer and N.K. Denzin, pp. 8–22. New York: McGraw-Hill.

Scheirer, M., and E.R. Kraut. 1979. "Increasing Educational Achievement via Self-concept Change." *Review of Educational Research*, vol. 1. Ann Arbor, Mich.: University Microfilms.

Schilder, P. 1950. *The Image and Appearance of the Human Body.* New York: International Universities Press.

Schroder, H.M., M.J. Driver; and S. Streufert. 1967. *Human Information Processing.* New York: Holt, Rinehart, & Winston.

Schulman, A.H., and C. Kaplowitz. 1977. "Mirror-image Response During the First Two Years of Life." *Developmental Psychobiology* 10: 133–142. New York, Grosset & Dunlop.

Schultz, A. 1967. *Collected Papers I: The Problem of Social Reality.* The Hague.

Sears, P.S., and V. Sherman. 1964. *In Pursuit of Self-esteem.* Belmont, Ca.: Wadsworth.

Sears, R.R. 1958. "Personality Development in the Family." In *The Child: A Book of Readings*, edited by J.M. Seidman. New York: Holt, Rinehart & Winston.

Secord, P.F., and B.H. Peevers. 1974. "The Development and Attribution of Person Concepts. In *Understanding Other Persons*, edited by T. Mischel, pp. 117–142. Oxford: Blackwell.

Selman, R.L. 1976. "The Development of Social-cognitive Understanding." In *Morality: Theory, Research, and Social Issues*, edited by T. Lickona. New York: Holt, Rinehart, & Winston.

Shantz, C.U. 1975. "The Development of Social Cognition." In *Review of Child Development Research*, vol. 5, edited by M.E. Hetherington. Chicago: University of Chicago Press.

Shavelson, R.J.; J.J. Hubner; and G.C. Stanton. 1976. "Self-concept: Validation of Construct Interpretations." *Review of Educational Research* 46(Summer): 407–442.

Sheehy, G. 1977. *Passages: Predictable Crisis of Adult Life.* New York: E.F. Dutton.

Shepard, L.A. 1979. "Self-acceptance: The Evaluative Component of the Self-concept Construct." *American Educational Research Journal* 16(Spring): 139–160.

Sherif, M., ed. 1967. *Social Interaction Process and Products.* Chicago: Aldine Publishing Co.

Sherif, M., and H. Cantril. 1947. *The Psychology of Ego-involvements.* New York: John Wiley and Sons.

Sherwood, J. 1965. "Self Identity and Referent Others." *Sociometry* 28: 66–81.

Shibutani, T. 1961. *Society and Personality.* Englewood Cliffs, N.J.: Prentice Hall.

Shrauger, J.S., and S.E. Rosenberg. 1970. "Self-esteem and the Effects of Success and Failure Feedback on Performance." *Journal of Personality* 38: 404–417.

Sigall, H., and R. Gould. 1977. "The Effects of Self-esteem and Evaluator Demandingness on Effort Expenditure." *Journal of Personality and Social Psychology* 35(1): 12-30.

Simmons, R.G., D.A. Blyth; E.F. VanCleave; and D.M. Bush. 1979. "Entry into Adolescence: The Impact of School Structure, Puberty, and Early Dating on Self-esteem." *American Sociological Review* 44: 948-962.

Simmons, R.G., and F.R. Rosenberg. 1975. "Sex Differences in the Self-concept in Adolescence." *Sex Roles* 1: 147-159.

Simmons, R.G., and M. Rosenberg. 1971. "Functions of Children's Perceptions of the Stratification System." *American Sociological Review* 36: 235-249.

Simon, R.J., and H. Altstein. 1977. *Transracial Adoption.* New York: John Wiley and Sons.

Smith, E.R., and F.D. Miller. 1978. "Limits on Perception of Cognitive Processess: A Reply to Nisbett and Wilson." *Psychological Review* 85(4): 355-362.

Snider, J.G., and C.E. Osgood. 1969. *Semantic Differential Technique.* Chicago: Aldine.

Snygg, D., and A.W. Combs. 1965. "The Phenomenological Approach and the Problem of 'Unconscious' Behavior: A Reply to Dr. Smith." In *The Self in Growth, Teaching and Learning: Selected Readings*, edited by D.E. Hamachek, pp. 79-87. Englewood Cliffs, N.J.: Prentice Hall.

____. 1949. *Individual Behavior: A New Frame of Reference for Psychology.* New York: Harper & Row.

Solomon, B.; A. Boxer; D. Offer; and A.C. Petersen. 1980. "Parenting of Normal Adolescents." In *Parenting as an Adult Experience*, edited by R.S. Cohen, S. Weissman, and B.J. Cohler. New York: Guilford Press.

Spears, W.D., and M.E. Deese. 1973. "Self Concept as Cause." *Educational Theory* 23: 144-152.

Spitz, R.A., and K.M. Wolfe. 1946. "The Smiling Response: A Contribution to the Ontogenesis of Social Relations." *Genetic Psychology Monographs* 34: 57-125.

Spitzer, S.P. 1978. "Ontological Insecurity and Reflective Processes." *Journal of Phenomenological Psychology* 8: 203-217.

____. 1977. "Reflective Processes and Anxiety." *British Journal of Psychiatry* 130: 386-391.

Spitzer, S.P.; C. Couch; and J. Stratton. 1970. *The Assessment of the Self.* Davenport, Iowa: Bowdon Brothers.

Staines, J.W. 1954. "A Sociological and Psychological Study of the Self Picture and its Importance in Education." Ph. D. dissertation, University of London.

Stillwell, L.J.T. 1966. "An Investigation of the Interrelationships Among Global Self-concept, Role Self-concept and Achievement." *Dissertation Abstracts International* 27: 682A.

Stone, L.J., H.T. Smith and L.B. Murphy, (Eds.). 1973. *The Competent Infant.* New York: Basic Books.

Stoodley, B.H., ed. 1962. *Society and Self: A Reader in Social Psychology.* New York: The Free Press.

Streufert, S., and S.C. Streufert. 1969. "Effects of Failure and Success on Attribution of Causality and Interpersonal Attitudes." *Journal of Personality and Social Psychology* 11: 138–147.

Stringer, L., and J. Glidewell. 1967. *Final Report: Early Detection of Emotionality in School Children.* Clayton, Mo.: St. Louis County Health Dept.

Strole, L., and A.K. Fischer. 1980. "The Midtown Manhattan Longitudinal Study vs. the Mental Paradise Lost Doctrine." *Archives of General Psychiatry* 37: 209–221.

Stryker, S. 1968. "Identify Salience and Role Performance: The Relevance of Symbolic Interaction Theory for Family Research." *Journal of Marriage and the Family* 30: 558–564.

Sullivan, H.S. 1953. *The Interpersonal Theory of Psychiatry.* New York: Norton.

Swanson, J.L. 1975. "The Relationship Between Perceptual Characteristics and Counselor Effectiveness Ratings of Counselor Trainees." Ph. D. dissertation, University of Florida.

Symonds, P.M. 1951. *The Ego and the Self.* New York: Appleton–Century–Crofts.

Tagiuri, R. 1969. "Person Perception." In *The Handbook of Social Psychology*, edited by G. Lindzey and E. Aronson, pp. 395–449. Reading, Mass.: Addison–Wesley.

Tannenbaum, P.H. 1968. "Is Anything Special About Consistency?" In *Theories of Cognitive Consistency: A Sourcebook*, edited by Abelson et al. Chicago: pp. 343–346. Rand McNally.

Taylor, S.E., and S.T. Fiske. Forthcoming. "Salience, Attention and Attribution: Top of the Head Phenomena." In *Advances in Experimental Social Psychology*, vol. 11, edited by L. Berkowitz. New York: Academic Press.

Thomas, A., and S. Chess. 1980. *The Dynamics of Psychological Development.* New York: Brunner/Mazel.

Thomas, W.I., and F. Znaniecki. 1918. *The Polish Peasant in Europe and America.* Chicago: University of Chicago Press.

Thompson, W. 1972. "Correlates of the Self-concept." *Dede Wallace Center Monograph*, No. 6. Nashville, Tennessee.

Toffler, A. 1970. *Future Shock.* New York: Bantam.

Torshen, K.P. 1969. "The Relation of Classroom Evaluation to Students' Self-concepts and Mental Health." Ph. D. dissertation, University of Chicago.

Townsend, J.M. 1976. "Self-concept and the Institutionalization of Mental Patients: An Overview and Critique." *Journal of Health and Social Behavior* 17: 263–271.

Trickett, H. 1969. "Stability and Predictability of Children's Self-concept and Perceptions by Others: A Developmental Study." *Dissertation Abstracts International* 29: 2557A.

Troldahl, V.C., and F.A. Powell. 1965. "A Short-form Dogmatism Scale for Use in Field Studies." *Social Forces* 44: 211–214.

Trowbridge, N.T. 1972. "Self-concept and Socio-economic Status in Elementary School Children." *American Educational Research Journal* 9(4): 525–527.

Turner, R.H. 1977. *The Mutable Self: A Self-concept for Social Change.* Beverly Hills, Ca.: Sage Publications.

____. 1976. "The Real Self: From Institution to Impulse." *American Journal of Sociology* 81: 989–1016.

____. 1975. "Is There a Quest for Identity?" *Sociological Quarterly* 16: 148–161.

Turner, R.H., and G. Schutte. In Press. "The True-self Method for the Study of the Self Conception." *Symbolic Interaction.*

Turnure, C. 1971. "Response to Voice of Mother and Stranger by Babies in the First Year." *Developmental Psychology* 4: 182–190.

Usher, R.H. 1969. "Perceptual Characteristics of Effective College Teachers." In *Florida Studies in the Helping Professions*, University of Florida Monographs, Social Sciences No. 37, edited by A.W. Combs. Gainesville: University of Florida Press.

Valins, S. 1966. "Cognitive Effects of False Heart-rate Feedback." *Journal of Personality and Social Psychology* 4: 400–408.

Van den Daele, L. 1968. "A Developmental Study of the Ego Ideal." *Genetic Psychology Monographs* 78: 191–256.

Van Kaam, A.L. 1959. "Phenomenal Analysis: Exemplified by a Study of the Experience of Really Feeling Understood." *Journal of Individual Psychology* 15: 66–73.

Vaughn, E.D. 1977. *Teaching of Psychology*, vol. 4, No. 3. Washington, D.C.: American Psychological Association.

Vigotsky, L.S. 1962. *Thought and Language.* Cambridge, Mass.: Massachusetts Institute of Technology.

Vonk, H.G. 1970. "The Relationship of Teacher Effectiveness to Perception of Self and Teaching Purposes." Ph. D. dissertation, University of Florida.

Vortuba, J.C. 1970. "A Comparative Analysis of a Social-psychological Theory of School Achievement." M. A. thesis, Michigan State University.

Wahler, R. 1967. "Infant Social Attachments, a Reinforcement Theory: Interpretation and Investigation." *Child Development* 38: 1079–1088.

Wasicsko, M.M. 1977. "The Effect of Training and Perceptual Orientation on the Reliability of Perceptual Inference for Selecting Effective Teachers." Ph. D. dissertation, University of Florida.

Wass, H., and A.W. Combs. 1974. "Humanizing the Education of Teachers." *Theory Into Practice* 13: 123–129.

Wattenberg, W.W., and C. Clifford. 1962. "Relation of Self-concepts to Beginning Achievement in Reading." *Child Development* 35: 461–467.

Wergner, D.M., and R.R., Vallacher, eds. 1980. *The Self in Social Psychology.* New York: Oxford University Press.

White, R.W. 1959. "Motivation Reconsidered: The Concept of Competence." *Psychological Review* 66: 297–333.

White, S.H. 1972. *Federal Programs for Young Children: Review and Recommendations.* Washington, D.C.: U.S. Government Printing Office.

Wiener, B., and A. Kukla. 1970. "An Attributional Analysis of Achievement Motivation." *Journal of Social and Personality Psychology* 15: 1–20.

Wolff, P.H. 1963. "Observations on the Early Development of Smiling." In *Determinants of Infant Behavior*, vol. II, edited by B.M. Tass. New York: John Wiley and Sons.

Woodworth, R.S., and H. Schlosberg. 1954. *Experimental Psychology.* New York: Holt & Co.

Wylie, R.C. 1979. *The Self-concept.* (rev. ed., vol. I & II). Lincoln: University of Nebraska Press.

____. 1974. *The Self-concept, vol. I: A Review of Methodological Considerations and Measuring Instruments* (2nd rev. ed.). Lincoln: University of Nebraska Press.

____. 1968. "The Present Status of Self-theory." In *Handbook of Personality Theory and Research*, edited by E.F. Borgatta and W.W. Lambert. Chicago: Rand McNally.

Yamomotto, K., ed. 1972. *The Child and His Image.* Boston: Houghton Mifflin.

Youniss, J. 1975. "Another Perspective on Social Cognition." In *Minnesota Symposium on Child Psychology*, vol. 9, edited by A.D. Pick, pp. 173–193. Minneapolis: University of Minnesota Press.

Zajonc, R.B. 1980. "Feeling and Thinking: Preferences Need no Inferences." *American Psychologist* 35(2): 151–175.

Zazzo, B. 1972. *Psychologie Differentielle de l'Adolescence* (2nd rev. ed.). Paris: Presses Universitaires de France.

Zazzo, R. 1948. "Images du Corps et Conscience de Soi: Materiaux pour l'Etude Experimentale de la Conscience." *Enfance* 1: 29–43.

Ziller, R.C. 1973. *The Social Self.* New York: Pergamon Press.

Zurcher, L.A., Jr. 1977. *The Mutable Self: A Self-concept for Social Change.* Sage Library of Social Research, vol. 59. Beverly Hills: Sage Publications.

____. 1972. *The Mutable Self: An Adaptation to Accelerated Sociocultural Change*, et al. 3: 3–15.

NAME INDEX

Abelson, R., 134
Adelson, J., 191
Adkins, D.C., 251-53, 258
Agnew, J., 87-88
Allport, G.W., 5, 15, 203-205, 210
Alschuler, A., 138
Alstein, H., 171
Ames, L.B., 15, 112, 211
Amsterdam, B., 112, 114, 116
Anderson, J.G., 226
Anderson, L., 221, 226, 298
Anderson, R.B., 298
Arbuckle, D.W., 7
Aronfreed, J., 252
Asimov, I., 19
Atkinson, J.W., 252, 257
Auer, J.M., 285
Ax, A.F., 60

Back, K.W., 214
Bagdikian, B.H., 256
Baldwin, J.M., 103
Ballif, B., 221, 251-54, 258-59
Baltes, P.B., 100, 199
Bandura, A., 141, 145
Banks, J.H., 104
Bannister, D., 87-88
Barclay, J.R., 246
Barker, R.G., 128
Baron, R.M., 134, 137-38
Basseches, M., 219
Baumeister, R.F., 140
Bem, D.J., 63
Bentler, P.M., 225
Bercheid, E., 60
Berger, E., 49
Beiser, M., 220
Bertocci, P.A., 203
Bigelow, A., 110, 116
Bills, R.E., 2-3
Bischof, L.J., 214-15
Bixler, P.A., 230
Bloom, B., 273, 277, 285, 297
Blos, P., 191, 197
Bobroff, A., 126
Bogen, J.E., 68
Bonan, J.B., 106
Bolles, R.C., 252
Borg, W.R., 286
Brackbill, Y., 105
Braine, M.D., 120
Brehm, J.W., 32, 134
Brickman, P., 62
Bridgeman, B., 127, 253
Brill, W.O., 82
Brim, O., 296

Bromley, D.B., 173, 180
Bronfenbrenner, U., 146, 296
Bronson, G.W., 104
Brookover, W., 89, 92, 222, 230, 233, 237, 273, 283-85, 291, 300
Brooks-Gunn, J., 98, 103, 107-108, 110, 116
Brown, W.F., 254
Bruner, J.S., 102, 119-20, 123, 125
Bugental, J.F.T., 150, 204, 206, 209
Burke, P.J., 76
Butler, R.N., 218

Cady, H., 23-24
Cage, B.T., 237
Calsyn, R.J., 92, 145, 230
Campbell, D.T., 233
Cantril, H., 15, 41
Capra, F., 144
Carlson, R., 193
Chandler, M.J., 102
Chaves, J.F., 125
Cicourel, A., 64
Cleveland, S.E., 110, 209
Clifford, C., 145
Cobb, H.V., 126
Cohen, A.R., 32, 134
Coleman, J.C., 285
Coller, A.P., 7
Combs, Arthur W., 2, 5, 7-10, 11, 15, 22, 24, 29, 87, 89, 93, 174, 203-204
Cooley, C.H., 70, 75-76, 97, 102, 125, 203, 210
Cooper, J., 75
Coopersmith, S., 221, 237-38
Cornielson, I.S., 107
Coser, R.L., 79
Costanzo, P.R., 197
Cottrell, L.S., 257
Couch, C., 40, 150
Courson, C., 7-9
Cowen, E.L., 237
Crandell, V.C., and V.J. Crandell, 238
Crane, V., 258
Crockett, W.H., 137-38
Cronbach, L.J., 224, 226, 241
Crosswhite, F.J., 300
Crowne, D.P., 223

Damon, W., 173
Darwin, C., 102, 112
Datan, N., 100
Davison, 220
Davies, E., 134
de Charms, R., 251
Deese, M.E., 87, 92
Deikman, A.J., 82
Dewey, D., 254
Diggory-Farnham, 220
Doehrman, J.J., 191
Dolan, L., 222, 277
Dornbusch, S., 75, 292
Douvan, E., 192
Duncan, O.D., 232
Du Val, S., 89
Dweck, C.S., 141
Dymond, R.F., 180

Eisen, M., 138, 196
Elder, G.H., 100
Engel, M., 193
Epstein, S., 3, 31-32, 37
Erikson, E., 89-90, 98, 126, 191, 286
Ervin, S.M., 120
Espinosa, R.W., 292

Faris, E., 76-77
Faris, R.E.L., 76-77
Feiring, C., 107
Fennema, E., 197
Fernandez, C., 292
Festinger, L., 32, 72
Fischer, A.K., 199
Fisher, S., 110, 209
Fiske, D.W., 233
Fitts, W., 203, 221-22, 263, 268
Flapan, D., 180
Flavell, J., 173, 182
French, T., 121
Frenkel, R.E., 107
Freud, A., 191
Freud, S., 34-36, 97-98, 120-21

Gallup, G.C., 112, 114
Garfinkel, H., 64
Gazzaniga, M.S., 68
Gergen, K., 2-4, 62, 65-66, 72-73, 100, 146, 203, 214, 219
Gesell, A., 110, 112
Gewitz, J.L., 105
Gilberts, R., 221
Ginot, H., 17
Glidewell, J.C., 301
Goffman, E., 68, 79

Goldberger, A.S., 230
Goldstein, D., 27, 29
Goodenough, F., 211
Gordon, I.S., 203-205
Gordon, L., 220
Gordon, S., 2-4, 220
Gottlieb, D., 197
Gould, R., 140
Gove, W.R., 197
Greenberg, D.J., 110
Grube, 140
Guardo, C.J., 106
Guilford, J.P., 88

Haarer, D.L., 285
Hall, S., 210
Hamachek, D.E., 2, 220
Hamburg, B., 197
Hamlyn, D.W., 102
Hara, T., 286
Harding, E.M., 209
Hardy, K.R., 252
Harris, D.B., 193, 237
Hartman, H., 120-21
Havinghurst, R.J., 298
Hayakawa, S.I., 87
Heider, F., 102, 134
Henderson, G., 193, 285
Henry, W., 211, 214
Herb, T.R., 197
Hilgard, E.R., 204, 206
Hill, M.P., 254
Hochman, J.S., 82
Hodge, R.W., 177
Hoffman, M.L., 102
Holtzman, 254
Horney, K., 220
Howard, K., 193, 197
Howell, J., 124
Hull, C., 119
Hunt, E.G., 119
Hurtig, A., 192

Inhelder, B., 137, 192

James, W., 5, 20, 40, 93, 203-205
Jarcho, H., 192, 196
Jersild, A.T., 237
Joiner, L., 89
Jones, R.A., 140, 252, 257
Jordan, T., 4, 92
Jourad, S., 15

Kagan, J., 124
Kaplan, B., 137-38, 199, 202
Kaplowitz, C., 114
Kardiner, A., 220
Katz, D., 134, 285
Keating, D.P., 192
Kelley, H., 15, 102
Kelly, G.A., 31, 88-89
Kelman, H.C., 134, 137-38
Kenny, D.A., 92, 125, 145, 230
Kerlinger, F., 146
Kessler, S.J., 65
Kierkegaard-Laing model, 83
Kikuchi, T., 204
Klein, M., 120
Klinger, E., 251
Koeske, G.F., and Koeske, R.K., 60
Kohlberg, L., 137, 173, 188
Koocher, G.P., 145
Kramer, D., 253, 259
Kraut, E.R., 283
Kuhn, M., 40, 56, 150
Kukla, A., 62

Ladner, J.S., 171
Laing, R.D., 2, 83
Lazowick, L.M., 129
Lecky, P., 5, 15, 28, 31, 35, 87, 134, 203, 220
L'Ecuyer, R., 99-100, 203, 206, 209, 211-12, 214, 217
Lennenberg, E.H., 120-21
Levine, D., 298
Levy-Agresti, J., 68
Lewis, M., 98, 103, 105, 107-108, 110, 116-17
Lindesmith, A.R., 76, 286
Lipsitz, J., 197
Livesley, W.J., 173, 180
Loevinger, J., 137
Long, B.H., 193
Luria, A.R., 123-24
Lynch, M., 98-99, 125, 129

Mandler, G., 60
Marcia, J.E., 197
Marcus, H., 88, 135
Marshall, G., 60
Maslow, A.H., 5, 15, 124, 251, 286
McCall, G.J., 2, 76, 174
McClelland, D.C., 252
McGuire, C., 99

McGuire, W., 99, 150–52, 160, 162, 168
McKenna, W., 65
McNeil, D., 120
McPartland, T.S., 40
Mead, G.H., 5, 70, 75–77, 97, 102, 125, 136, 203, 205, 286
Meehl, P.E., 224, 226, 241
Meltzer, B.N., 136
Merrifield, P., 4, 88
Michael, W.B., 196
Miller, D.T., 135
Miller, E.R., 61–62, 135
Miller, R.L., 145
Miller, W.R., 120
Mintz, R., 92
Miyamoto, S.F., 75
Monge, R.H., 195–96
Montemayor, R., 138, 196
Morse, R.S., 285
Moynihan, D.P., 170
Mulford, H.A., 80
Muller, D., 92
Murphy, G., 5, 15, 103, 203
Mussen, P.H., 128

Neisser, U., 60
Nesselroade, J.R., 199
Neugarten, B.L., 100
Newcomb, T., 134
Nichols, K., 193
Nisbett, R.E., 60–61
Norem-Hebeisen, Ardyth A., 98, 127
Nugent, J., 129
Nunberg, H., 121

Offer, D., 191–93, 196–97, 199, 202
Osgood, C., 129
Ostrov, E., 197
Ovesy, L., 220

Padawer-Singer, A., 150–51, 152, 160, 162, 168
Palmquist, W.J., 192
Papousek, H., and M. Papousek, 116–17
Park, R.E., 40
Parker, J., 7
Passalacqua, J., 222, 292
Patterson, C., 203
Pavlov, I.P., 31–32
Perron, R., 204
Peterson, A., 99, 191, 196, 199, 202
Piaget, J., 90, 103–104, 119, 124, 180–82, 192
Piers, E.V., 122, 193, 237, 300
Pinneau, S.R., 7
Plutchik, R., 60
Ponty, M., 103
Posner, M.I., 252
Preyer, W., 112
Purkey, W.W., 227, 237–38, 283, 285

Quarentelli, E.L., 75

Raimy, V.C., 5, 15
Raynor, J.O., 257
Rebelsky, F., 104
Reeder, L., 75
Reinert, G., 100, 189
Rheingold, H.L., 105, 116
Richards, A., 15, 22
Richards, F., 15
Riegel, K.F., 137
Robinson, W.S., 284
Rogers, C., 15, 29, 87–89, 124, 135, 141, 174, 203, 220, 237, 251
Rogosa, D., 230
Rokeach, M., 32, 140
Rose, A.M., 76
Rosenberg, F., 99, 193, 197
Rosenberg, J., 134
Rosenberg, M., 2, 91, 177, 180, 202
Rosenberg, S., 145, 151
Rosenkrantz, P., 199
Ross, H.W., 105
Rossi, P.H., 177
Rotter, J.B., 252
Ryan, K., 62

St. John, N., 292
Sameroff, A.J., 192
Sarbin, T.R., 205, 220
Schachter, S., 60
Schaie, K.W., 137
Schantz, C., 173, 182
Scheff, T.J., 79
Scheirer, M., 283
Schilder, P., 209, 220
Schlossberg, H., 110
Schroder, H.M., 119
Schulman, A.H., 114
Schutte, G., 41
Sears, P.S., 128, 233, 237

Secord, P.F., 173
Selman, R.L., 192
Shane, C., 238
Shannon, D., 237
Shantz, C.U., 102, 192
Shavelson, R., 126, 220-23, 231, 233, 237, 273, 283, 297
Shepard, L.A., 274
Shepman, V., 127, 253
Sherif, M., 41, 286
Sherman, J., 197
Sherwood, J., 75
Shibutani, T., 76-77
Shrauger, J.S., 145
Shutz, W., 68
Sigau, H., 140
Simmons, R.F., 2, 174, 177, 193, 197, 220
Simon, P.J., 171
Smith, E.R., 61, 103
Smith, R.A., 196
Snider, J.G., 129
Snyder, C.R.R., 252
Snygg, D., 5, 15, 24, 28-29, 87, 89, 93, 174, 203-204
Solomon, B., 197
Soper, D., 7, 10
Spears, W.D., 87
Sperry, R.W., 68
Spitzer, S., 4, 40, 76, 80, 83, 150
Staines, J.W., 205
Stephens, M.W., 223
Stillwell, L.J., 92
Stone, P., 103
Stoodley, B.H., 2
Stratton, J., 40, 150
Strauss, A.L., 76, 286
Streufert, S., and Streufert, S.C., 62
Stringer, L., 301
Strobe, L., 199
Stryker, S., 174
Stuart, K., 220-22
Sullivan, H.S., 97, 220
Symonds, P.M., 205, 209
Tagiuri, R., 102
Tannenbaum, P.H., 134
Thomas, W.I., 40
Thompson, W., 214
Thurnher, M., 215
Toffler, A., 256
Tomé, R., 209, 211
Townsend, J.M., 79
Trickett, H., 230
Trowbridge, N.T., 286
Turner, R., 3-4, 41-44
Turnure, C., 104

Valiens, S., 60, 220
Van den Daele, L., 138
Vaughn, E.D., 31
Vigotsky, L.S., 123-24
Vortuba, J.C., 285

Walster, E., 60
Wasicsko, M.M., 8-9
Wass, H., 9
Wattenberg, W.W., 145
West, 80
White, S.H., 251, 298
Wicklund, R., 89
Wierner, B., 62
Wolff, P.H., 105
Wolfson, J.H., 104
Wortman, C., 62
Wylie, R.C., 2, 21, 87, 91, 126, 147-49, 219, 223, 237

Yamamotto, K., 87, 285
Youniss, J., 102

Zajonc, R.B., 252
Zazzo, B., 204
Zazzo, R., 110, 209
Zelen, S.C., 150, 206
Zeller, R.C., 193
Ziller, L., 193, 209, 211
Znamicki, 40
Zurcher, L.A., 2

SUBJECT INDEX

Academic achievement
and aggregated self-concept, 283–92
causal models of, 226–35
and self-concept, 220–22, 252–55
in self-concept and schooling study, 299–300
Academic self-concept, 273–74, 281–82
and academic achievement, 283–85
aggregated, 286–92
measures, 300
in schooling study, 304–309
Academic Self-Concept Scale (ASCS), 274–75
differences across grade levels, 279–81
technical quality of, 275–79
Achievement
vs. failure, 54
-insecurity, 54
-plastic, 54–55
and true self, 42–43, 45–46, 50, 57
Accommodation, 90
Activity Preference Questionnaire (APQ), 80
Adaptive self, 206, 210, 212
Adolescence, 98–99, 125–26, 136–38, 191, 193–97, 202, 208
and self-concept, 213–14, 254, 259–60
Adolescents
and academic self-concept, 254, 259–60
demographic factors associated with, 197–201
developmental theories of, 191–92
hypothetical model of, 192–93
and occupational aspirations, 175
qualitative changes in self-image, 195–96
quantitative changes in self-concept, 193–95
and self-confidence, 259–60
and SES, and ethnicity, 202
Adults
and academic self-concept, 254–55
and self-concept, 98, 136–38, 145, 208, 214–15
Age
as categorizing, 107–11, 118
and occupational status, 173, 174–89
and self-concept, 193–97, 205, 208, 209–17
and self-nonself differentiation, 210–11

Aggregated self-concept, 283–85
Aggressive, Moody and Learning Disability scale (AML), 237
Altruism, 42–43, 45–46
-insincerity, 55
-plastic, 55
-selfishness, 54
and true self, 42–43
Ambition, 42–43
Animals, unity principle and, 31, 32
Anxiety, 27, 29
and reflection, 77–78, 83–84
Applied settings, and self, 219–22
Ascriptions, 79
Australian National University (ANU), 44, 49
Authenticity, 3, 41–43, 44–45, 50–52, 55–57
and impulse-release function, 52–53
vs. institutions, 45
and intimacy-failure, 50–52

BASE (Behavioral Academic Self Esteem), 238–41, 246–49
Behavior, 30, 270–71
in new psychology, 14–16
perceptions affecting, 11–13
samples of, 8
and self-concept, 6–7, 11, 20–21, 62–66, 67, 69, 140
in self-concept research, 7–10
and self-esteem, 237–39
and self-recognition, 112–15, 117
and social reinforcement, 105
and unity principle, 30, 31–37
Behavior-based approach, 300, 304–308
Behavior change, 270–71
Behavior patterns, and maximization model, 133–34, 142–43, 144–45
Behavior Rating Form (BRF), 238–39
Beliefs, 47–48, 55, 274
Biology
influence on self-concept, 98, 120, 193
and maximization theory, 134, 137
Birthplace, effect on spontaneous self-concept, 158–59
Body-directed behavior, and self-recognition, 114
Body image, 121–22
and self-concept, 100, 209–16

Boys
and academic self-esteem, 241
and body image, 209–10
and change in academic self-concept, 222
and occupational aspirations, 177–83
self-concept of, 197–99, 202, 205, 208, 216

Categorical self, 106–107
Causal attribution, 61–62
Causal model, 220–24, 226–35
Causal role
of school, 300–301, 312–13
self-concept as, 92–93, 145
Change
in academic self-concept, 221–22, 261–62, 273
behavior, 270–71
group vs. individual, 264–65
in self-concept, 263–64
Change agent, and self-concept, 70–71, 72–73
Change strategies, 94
Childhood, early
and development of self-recognition, 107–17
and maximization model, 134–35
and mirror-image representation, 109, 112–15
and occupational aspirations, 175–84, 188–89
and ontogenetic sequence, 116–17
and pictoral representation, 108, 110–12
influence on self-concept, 98, 120–23, 209–12
and self-knowledge, 104–107
and social cognition, 101–104
and videotape representation, 109, 115–16
Childhood, middle
and academic self-esteem, 246
and change in academic self-concept, 221–22
and self-concept, 123–26, 208, 212–13
and self-concept and schooling, 300–309, 312–13
Children
and academic self-concept, 252–55

and academic self-esteem, 238–39, 241
and future occupational status, 173–88
in physical characteristics study, 154–60, 162
and self-concept, 136–38, 145
Children, preschool, 241, 248, 257–59
Children's Self-Concept Scale, 300
Clarity, of self-concept, 268
Classroom factors, 222. *See also* Educational settings
Cognitive development, 133, 135–39, 144, 192
and occupational aspirations, 173, 178, 182–84, 186, 188–89
Cognitive perspective, 2, 4, 59–61, 73, 87–88
and memory, 99
and self-concept, 98
Cognitive processes
and evaluation, 4, 88–89
and generation, 4, 88–90
and memory, 88
and new intervention directions, 93–95
as situation specific, 91–93
and transformation, 4, 88, 90
Cohort, 199
College students, 254–55
Communication skills, 73
Comprehensive Test of Basic Skills (CTBS), 243
Conceptual system, 3, 4
and unity principle, 27–31, 31–35
Consistency, 99, 133–36, 138–39, 143, 145–46, 214
Consistency theory, 133
and maximization theory, 134–36, 138–39, 143, 145–46
Construct-specific rules, 127
Construct validation theory, 80–84, 224–26, 241
Contingent feedback, 104–105
Contingent self, 115, 116–17
Criterion validation, 80
Customary self, 44, 50

Death instinct, 35
Defensiveness, 266–67
Depression, 37
Developmental patterns, 214–15, 215–18
Developmental processes, 174, 182–83
Developmental theories, 133, 135–39, 144, 192
of adolescent self-concept, 191–92
Differentiation, 99, 208, 209–11, 213–14
in early childhood, 121–23
in infancy, 104–106, 108–109, 110–17
in middle childhood, 125–26
Discriminant validation, 77–80
Distinctiveness postulate
and ethnic consciousness, 160–62
and gender, 165
and occupational aspirations, 181
and physical characteristics, 152, 154–60
and self-concept, 151–52, 168–71

"Ecological phenomenon," 284
Educational settings
and academic self-concept, 283–85
and self-concept, 220–22, 295–97, 312–13
Efficacy, 141–43
Ego psychology, 136–37
Elderly, and self-concept, 208, 215–17, 220
Eminence aspirations, 47–48
Empathy, 9, 125–26
Empirical test, definition, 75
Enhancement, 28, 29
Enigma of cross-category translation, 63–64
Environment
and contingent feedback, 105
and perception, 12
and self-concept, 140–41, 143–44, 257
Ethnicity
and academic self-concept, 255, 258–59
and self-concept in adolescence, 202
Ethnicity study, 160–64, 171
distinctiveness theory and, 160–62
methods used in, 162–63
results of, 163–64
and social relevance, 170–71

Evaluation, 4, 88–89, 91, 94–95
Exemplars, 181–83
Experience. *See also* Situation specific approach
 and maximization theory, 134–35, 138–39, 144
 and self-concept, 91–93, 137, 145
Experiential-perceptual psychology, 6, 13, 16
Existential self, 104–106, 107
External inputs
 and maximization model, 133, 135, 139
 and self-concept, 59, 65–66, 73, 97–98
 and self-knowledge, 106–107
Eyeglasses, effect on spontaneous self, 155, 159

Failure
 -achievement, 54
 -impulse release combination, 52–53
 -intimacy combination, 50–52
 and spurious self, 43, 45–46, 50–52
Faith in institutions, 47–48, 55
Faith in people, 47–48
Father absence, effect on spontaneous self, 168, 170–71
Feature recognition, 110–111, 116–17, 122
Florida Key, 238

Gender
 and academic self-concept, 259–60
 and academic self-esteem, 241
 and body image, 209–10
 as categorizing, 106–109, 111, 118
 and change in academic self-concept, 222
 and ethnicity, and self-concept, 161–63
 and intimacy-failure combination, 50–51
 and occupational aspirations, 177–83, 183–89
 and self-anchorages, 44, 47–48, 55
 and self-concept, 99, 205, 208, 216
 and self-concept in adolescence, 99, 193–95, 197–99, 202
Gender study, 152, 165–68, 169–71
Generalization, 205–206. *See also* Internal inputs
Generalized expectancy model, 105
General systems theory, 183–84
Generation, 4, 88–91, 95
Girls
 and academic self-esteem, 241
 and body image, 209–10
 and change in academic self-concept, 222
 occupational aspirations among, 183–88
 and self-concept, 205, 208, 216
 and self-concept in adolescence, 193, 197–99, 202
Grade level. *See also* Age
 and academic self-concept, 252–55
 and academic self-esteem, 243–47
 and ASCS differences, 279–81
 and self-concept and schooling, 301–304
 and self-confidence, 257–60
Groups, vs. individual, 284, 291–92
Gumpgookies, 252–53, 258

Hair/eye color, effect on spontaneous self, 157–58, 159
Height, effect on spontaneous self, 154–57, 159
Helplessness, 141–43
Hierarchical organization, 203, 212–14
Hierarchical sequencing, 137–38. *See also* Developmental psychology
Human being and becoming, 14–16
Human functioning, and self-concept, 133–44
Humanist approach, 98–99

Idealized self-judgments, 124, 126
Imitation, 114
Impulse anchorage
 -institution combination, 45, 54–55
 and self, 42–44, 44–49, 55–57
Impulse release
 -failure combination, 52–53
 and true self, 43, 45–46, 52–53
Index of Adjustment and Values, 21
Individual, vs. group, 284, 291–92
Individual anchorage, and self, 42–44, 45–49, 55
Infancy, and self-concept, 209–11. *See also* Childhood, early

Inference
  in self-concept research, 3, 7-10, 204
  vs. technique approach, 3, 22-23, 25
Information processing, 256-57
  and "distinctiveness postulate," 151-52, 170
  and self-concept, 140, 144-45
Information-processing model, 119-22, 127
  implications of, 126-27
  and research, 127-32
Information sources, in maximization theory, 134-35
Inner experience, of self, 59, 62, 62-66, 73
Insecurity
  -achievement, 54
  -altruism, 55
  -intimacy, 53
  and spurious self, 43, 45-46
Institution anchorage
  -impulse combination, 45, 54-55
  and self, 42-44, 44-45, 45-49, 52, 55-57
Institutions, and reflection, 79
Intelligence, and reflection, 80
Internal consistency, 268-69, 278-79, 301
Internal process, and self-concept, 97, 136-39, 205-206, 212, 214
Intervention, and cognitive processes, 91, 93-95
Intervention programs, 298-99, 308, 312
Intimacy, 43
  -failure combination, 50-52
  -insincerity, 53
  and true self, 45-46, 50-52

Kierkegaard-Laing model, 83
Knowledge
  acquisition of, 257-60
  expansion, 256-57

Language acquisition, 120-22, 211-12
La Trobe University (Australia), 44
Learning
  and self-concept, 251, 252-55
  and thought patterns, 255-56
Life span development, and self-concept, 100, 204-205, 208-17
  stage I (infancy), 209-11
  stage II (early childhood), 211-12
  stage III (middle childhood), 212-13
  stage IV (adolescence), 213-14
  stage V (adult), 214-15
  stage VI (longevous self), 215-17
Longevous self, and self-concept, 208, 215-17

Marital status, and institutional anchorage, 47-48, 55
Mark-directed behavior, 112-15, 117
Material self, 206, 212
Maturity, 208, 214-15
Maximization model, 133-46
  implications of, 144-46
  proposition 1, 133-34
  proposition 2, 134-35
  proposition 3, 135-39
  proposition 4, 139-43
  proposition 5, 143-44
Measures
  of self, 41-44
  of self-concept, 21-22, 25, 266, 300-301
  of self-concept-related frustrations, 129-32
  of self-esteem, 237-39
  vs. sequencing of definition, 22-23
  of spurious self, 41-44
  of true self, 41-44
Memory, 4, 88, 91, 94, 99
Michigan Objective Referenced Test, 284
Mirror-image representation, 109, 112-15
Morality, 42
Motivation
  patterns of thinking and, 251-52, 260
  and self-concept, 221, 251, 260
Motivation Components for Learning in School (MOCOS), 253, 255, 260
Motives, 30
Motor activity, 180
Multidimensional model, of self-concept, 204-205, 217-18
  experimental design, 206-208
  methods used, 206

Multiple changes hypothesis, 215

National Opinion Research Company, 177
Needs
  and perception, 12-13
  unity principle as, 27-29
Negative self-concept, 141-44, 162, 164
Noncontingent self, 115, 116-17

Occupational aspirations
  among,boys, 177-83
  and age of children, 174-88
  among girls, 183-88
Offer Self-Image Questionnaire (OSIQ), 193-95, 196
Ontologic acceptability, 68-71
Ontological insecurity, 83
Organismic well-being, 139-43, 145-46

Parents, 298-309, 312-13
Peak-like hypothesis, 214-16
Perception, and self-concept, 5-7, 10-13
  change in, 13
  and environment, 12
  and goals and values, 12
  and need, 12
  and physical organism, 11-12
  role in new psychology, 14-16
  in self-concept research, 7-10
Perceptual organization
  and self-concept, 2-3, 5-7, 11
  and self-recognition, 110, 115
Perceptual psychology, 14-16
Perceptual Psychology: A Humanistic Approach to the Study of Persons, 15
Performance, and evaluation, 89
Personal enhancement, 68-71
Personality, and conceptual system, 11, 28-29, 214-15
Personal pronoun usage, 108, 110, 112, 211
Personal self, 206, 210, 212
Phenomenal self, 28-29
Phenomenology, 2-4, 147-49, 169
Physical characteristics study, 152-60, 171
  methods used in, 153-54
  results of, 154-60
Pictorial representation, 108, 110-12
Plastic behavior
  -achievement combination, 54-55
  -altruism, 55
  and spurious self, 43, 45-46
Plateau hypothesis, 214, 215-16
Pleasure principle, 3, 30-31, 35, 37
Psychoanalysis, 34-37
Psychodynamic theory, vs. symbolic interaction, 97-98
Psychology
  behavioral, 13
  definition of, 6
  experiential-perceptual, 6, 13, 16
  humanistic-experiential, 6, 11, 13
  perceptual-humanistic, 7, 12-13
Psychology, new, 1
  need for, 13-14
  as perceptual psychology, 14-16
  and self-concept, 10--13
Psychologists, vs. phenomenologists, 29-30
Puberty, 193, 196-97, 202

Quality of instruction, in self-concept and schooling study, 298-309, 312-13

Race
  in aggregated data, 284-92
  and self-concept and academic achievement, 222
  and self-concept in adolescence, 202
  and self-concept as a learner, 254-55, 259
Reactive self-concept, 149-50, 169, 171
Reality principle, 3, 4, 17-20, 30-31, 37
Referenced-based approach, 302, 304-308
Reflection, 4, 84-85
  definition of, 76
  as sociological, 85
  types of, 77
Reflective processes, 77, 85
  construct validation, 80-84
  criterion validation, 80
  discriminant validation, 77-80

Reinforcement, 20–21
Repression, 36–37
Research
  and application of self theory, 2
  behavioral, 13
  on causal attribution, 61–62
  on cognition, 60–61
  and consistency-seeking process, 135
  on cortical hemispheres, 68
  on ethnicity, and spontaneous self-concept, 160–64
  on gender, and spontaneous self-concept, 165–68, 171
  use of inference for, 7–10
  on language development, 120
  on life-span development, 100
  on negative self-concept, 141–42
  and new psychology, 10–13
  on physical characteristics, and spontaneous self-concept, 152–60, 171
  on schooling, and self-concept, 295–97, 297–301
  on self-concept, 1–14, 5–7, 138, 145–52, 168–71, 285–86
  on self-concept in adolescence, 192
  on self-concept-related frustration, 130–32
  and self-concept rules, 126–27
  on self-concept through the life span, 203–204
  on situated self-concept, 65–66
Response, 20–21
Rural/urban, and self-concept, 99, 199–202, 255

Schooling experience, as factor in self-concept, 295–97, 312–13
Self
  definition of, 106
  as object or agent, 22, 93, 106–107
  and research on self-concept, 148, 169
  -social cognition relationship, 101–104
  as subject, 93, 104–106
  types of self, 45–49, 53–54
Self acceptance, 274, 278–79, 281
  and self anchorage, 48–49, 55, 57
Self-actualization, 29, 124
Self-anchorage, 42, 55–57
  and sex, 47–48, 55
  social structure and, 40–44
Self-awareness, 92
Self-Concept (Wylie), 147, 150
Self-concept, 22
  definition of, 6, 14
  definition of, as a problem, 17–24
  functions of, 68–73
  as groundless, 66–68
  as a set of rules, 120–29
Self-concept change, 221–22, 261–62, 263–64
  vs. behavior change, 270–71
  and clarity of self-concept, 268
  and defensiveness, 266–67
  internal consistency and, 268–69
  and need for synthesis, 271–72
  and patterns vs. levels, 269–70
Self-concept development, 2, 97–100, 119–20
  in early childhood, 120–23
  implications of, 126–27
  in middle childhood, 123–26
  and research applications, 127–29
Self-concepting, 88, 92–94
Self-concept of ability (SCA), 230–31
Self-Concept of Ability Scale, 300
Self-Concept of Academic Ability, 284–85
Self-concept-related frustration, 127–28
  definition of, 128
  measures of, 129–32
Self-concept theory, 286–92
Self-confidence, 257–60
Self control, 42, 50–51, 53, 54, 56
Self-enhancement, 92
Self-esteem, 92, 213–14, 216, 221, 237, 263, 267–69
  and academic achievement, 237–39
  and adolescence, 193–95, 197–99
  and behavior, 237–39
  and maximization model, 140
  and self-concept research, 149–50, 169, 171
Self-evaluation, 65–66, 122, 124, 127–29
Self-image, 191, 195–96, 210
Selfishness
  -altruism, 54
  and spurious self, 43, 45–46

Self-judgments, 128–29
Self-knowledge, 102
  categorical self, 106–107
  in early childhood, 104–107, 117–18
  existential self, 104–106
  and the social world, 117–18
Self-nonself, 206, 209, 212, 213–14
Self-perceptions, 274, 278–79, 281
Self-Perceptions Genesis (GPS), 206–208
Self-recognition, development in early childhood, 107–17
  and mirror-image representations, 109, 112–15
  and ontogenetic sequence, 116–17
  and pictorial representation, 108, 110–12
  and videotape representations, 109, 115–16
Self-report, 5–7, 11, 22
Self-satisfaction, 80
Self-search, 48–49
Self-transformation, 92
SES (Socioeconomic)
  and academic self-concept, 254–55, 258–61
  in aggregated data, 284–85, 287–89
  and self-concept in adolescence, 202
Sex-typing, 169–70, 174, 185–87, 189
Situation specific approach, 91–95, 127
Social anchorage, 42–44, 44–49
Social cognition, 101–104, 117–18, 192
Social construction, 4
Social environment, 136
Social group, 291–92
Social institutions, 98–99, 124–26, 212–13
Social interaction, 102–103
Social interchange, and self-concept, 59, 73
Socialization, early, 3, 56
Social learning, and occupational aspirations, 173, 178, 182–83, 187–89
Social negotiation, 3–4, 59, 65–66, 69, 73
Social psychology, 133–34, 136–37
Social reinforcement, 105
Social self, 84–85, 206, 210–12
Social structure, and self-anchorages, 39–44
Social world, and self-knowledge, 117–18
Societal rules, 122, 125
Sociology, and self-concept, 1–2, 40
Spontaneous self-concept, 149–52, 169–71
  and ethnicity, 152, 160–64
  and gender, 152, 165–68
  and physical characteristics, 152–60
Spurious self, 39, 55–57
  empirical evidence on, 44–49
  in impulse release-failure combination, 52–53
  and institution-impulse combination, 54–55
  in intimacy-failure combination, 50–52
  measures of, 41–44
  and pure types, 53–54
  vs. true self, 50–55
Survey of Study Habits and Attitudes (SSHA), 254
Symbolic interaction, 1, 4, 70, 75–76, 79, 84–85, 97

Teacher's ratings, of academic self-esteem, 241–48
  vs. student's ratings, 249
Technique, vs. inference approach, 22–23, 25
Tennessee Self-Concept Scale (TSCS), 214, 263, 266–68, 269, 271
Theory
  construction, 11
  definition of, 75
  and self-concept, 2–4, 219–22
  self, 2–4, 10–13
Therapeutic settings, 220
  and self-concept change, 262–63, 270–71
Thought patterns
  and ability to learn, 255–56
  and motivation, 251–52
Transformation process, 4, 88, 90–91, 95
True self, 39, 55–57
  empirical evidence on, 44–49
  in impulse-failure combination, 52–53

in intimacy-failure combination, 50–52
measures of, 41–44
and pure types, 53–54
vs. spurious, 50–55
Twenty Statements Test (TST), 40, 76–77, 79–80, 150–51

Undifferentiated rousing, 59–60
Unity principle, 3–4, 27–31
in animals, 31–32
beyond, 37
explanatory power of, 31–37
and normal behavior, 32–34
and psychoanalysis, 34–37
UCLA, 43, 49
University of Sherbrooke, 204
University of Surrey, 44, 49
Urban/rural, and self-concept, 99, 199–202, 255

Validation, of self-concept rules, 124, 127–28
Values, and perceptions, 12–13
Verbal behavior, and self-recognition, 108, 110–12, 115. *See also* Language acquisition
Videotape representation, 109, 115–16

Weight, effect on spontaneous self-concept, 155, 157, 159
"Who Are You? test (WAY), 150–51, 206

ABOUT THE EDITORS

Mervin D. Lynch earned a B.S. in Science Journalism from Iowa State University in 1956, and an M.S. and Ph.D. in Mass Communications Research from the University of Wisconsin in 1960 and 1963. He also was a Social Science Research Council Postdoctoral Fellow in the Department of Mathematical Statistics at Harvard University September 1967 to August 1968.

He has taught as both an associate and full professor in the College of Education at Northeastern University from 1968 to date, and taught in Journalism Schools as an assistant professor at the University of Missouri 1963 to 1967 and as a lecturer at the University of Indiana 1962–63. He also was a visiting professor at the Department of Psychology at University of California, Davis in 1976.

He has served as president of the Eastern Educational Research Association and vice president and president of the New England Education Research Organization and has participated as Newsletter Editor and member of the Executive Board of Division I of the American Psychological Association from 1976 to date. He has served on the editorial review boards of the *Journal of Reading Behavior* and the *Career Education Quarterly* and has reviewed manuscripts as an editorial consultant for the *Journal of Education Psychology* and the *American Psychologist.*

He has authored a book entitled *Elements of Statistical Inference for Education and Psychology*, several chapters in edited books, more than two dozen papers in scholarly journals, and has presented more than 200 conference papers.

A major focus of his research has been on self-concept. He has presented more than a dozen papers emanating from this research at meetings of the American Psychological Association, AERA, and EERA and has developed the Kiddicon and semantic differential measures of self-concept.

Ardyth Norem-Hebeisen earned a B.S. in English and Education from State Teachers College, Minot, North Dakota in 1955; an M.A. in Educational Psychology with specialization in Vocational Rehabilitation from the University of Minnesota in 1960; and a Ph.D. in Educational Psychology from the University of Minnesota in 1974. Her career roles have included teacher, vocational rehabilitation counselor, counseling psychologist, research assistant, program designer, and professor. In these roles she has worked among populations of mentally retarded, mentally ill, physically handicapped, parents, school age children ranging from elementary school through high school, and graduate students.

She has designed and evaluated several programs focused on self-esteem enhancement, and developed the Self Assessment Scales, a multidimensionsional measure of self-concept. In 1974 she was appointed to a faculty position in the College of Education, University of Minnesota, where she conducted research and taught courses directed toward increasing and communicating a knowledge base on adolescent alcohol and drug abuse. Her research was also focused in the area of self-concept with a further examination of the psychometric qualities of the Self Assessment Scales and delineation of the relation between self-concept and alcohol and drug use among adolescents.

Her research has been conducted in field settings, especially schools. Her primary theoretical works are the description of the Self Assessment Scales, "A Multidimensional Construct of Self-Esteem," and the chapter in this volume, "A Maximization Model of Self-Concept." Her most resent work has been development of a self-concept instrument appropriate for use in an industrial setting.

Kenneth J. Gergen earned a B.A. in Psychology from Yale University in 1957 and a Ph.D. in Psychology from Duke University in 1962. He has taught as an instructor and assistant professor in the

Department of Social Psychology at Harvard University from 1963 to 1967 and as an associate and full professor in the Department of Psychology at Swarthmore College from 1967 to date. He has held visiting professorships at Heidelberg University, Marburg University, Kyoto University, and the University of Copenhagen, and has served as a lecturer in summer programs at the University of Minnesota and University of Colorado. He has received Guggenheim and Fullbright–Hays research scholar awards for research study in Japan and France.

He has served on the editorial review boards of the *Journal of Personality*, the *Journal of Applied Psychology, Journal of the Theory of Social Behavior*, and *Blackwell Psychological Dictionary.* He has published more than seven dozen papers in journals, book chapters, or monographs and has been an author or editor of more than one dozen books.

A major focus of his research and writing effort has been devoted to the study of self-concept. He has published two books and more than a dozen journal articles on self-concept. His books were *The Self in Social Interaction, Vol. I: Classic and Current Perspectives*, and *The Concept of Self.*

ABOUT THE CONTRIBUTORS

Lorin W. Anderson, University of South Carolina, has published extensively in Affective Measurement with several papers focused on self-concept.

Bonnie Ballif, Fordham University, has authored several papers on motivation which have implications for self-concept.

Robert E. Bills Professor Emeritus, University of Alabama, has developed a measure of self-concept called the "Index of Achievement and Values," and has authored a book entitled *A System for Assessing Affectivity.*

Wilbur Brookover and **Joseph Passalacqua**, Michigan State University. Professor Brookover has developed a measure of self-concept of school achievement and has published a large number of bulletins and papers on this topic.

Arthur W. Combs, University of Northern Colorado, has authored a dozen papers and two books which are directly devoted to self-concept.

Stanley Coopersmith and **Ragner Gilberta**, Berkley, California. Professor Coopersmith is the author of *Antecedents of Self Esteem*, and has published one of the more widely used measures of self-concept, *The Coopersmith Self Esteem Inventory.*

Lawrence Dolan, University of Rochester, has authored several papers on self-concept.

Rene L'Ecoyer, University of Sherbrooke, Sherbrooke, Canada, has published *Le Concept De Soi*, Paris, University Press of France, 1978.

Seymor Epstein, University of Massachusetts at Amherst, has authored more than a half dozen papers on self-concept.

William Fitts, Nashville, Tennessee, is the developer of the *Tennessee Self-Concept Scale*, one of the more widely used measures of self-concept.

Theresa Jordan and **Philip Merrifeld**, New York University, have authored more than a half dozen conference papers on self-concept.

Michael Lewis and **Jeanne Brooks-Gunn**, Educational Testing Service, coauthored the book, *Infants: Perception of People.*

William J. McGuire, Yale University, has authored more than a half dozen papers on self-concept and currently has a book in press with Earlbaum and Associates, which focuses on various aspects of self-concept.

Anne C. Peterson, University of Chicago, has authored a half dozen papers on self-concept.

Morris Rosenberg, University of Maryland and **Florence Rosenberg**, C.A.R.A. in Washington, D.C., are authors of more than one dozen papers on self-concept. In particular, Morris Rosenberg authored, *Society and the Adolescent Self-image.*

Richard Shavelson and **Kenneth Stuart**, U.C.L.A. Professor Shavelson has a major paper in *The Review of Educational Research* entitled, "Self-Concept: Validation of Construction Interpretations."

Stephen Spitzer, University of Minnesota has published a book, *The Assessment of the Self*, Iowa: Effective Communications, 1970.

Ralph H. Turner and **Steven Gordon**, U.C.L.A. Professor Turner has published more than a half dozen papers on self-concept including "The Real Self: From Institution to Impulse." *The American Journal of Sociology*, 1976.